Investigating White Collar Crime

Investigating White Collar Crime

Tom Bazley, Ph.D.

Upper Saddle River, New Jersey 07458

Library of Congress Cataloging-in-Publication Data

Bazley, Tom.
    Investigating white collar crime / Tom Bazley.—1st ed.
        p. cm.
    Includes bibliographical references and index.
    ISBN-10: 0-13-158954-7 (alk. paper)
    ISBN-13: 978-0-13-158954-4 (alk. paper)
    1. White collar crime investigation—United States.   2. White collar crimes—United States.   I. Title.
    HV8079.W47B39 2008
    363.25'9680973—dc22

                                                                2007024286

Editor-in-Chief: Vernon R. Anthony
Senior Acquisitions Editor: Tim Peyton
Editorial Assistant: Alicia Kelly
Marketing Manager: Adam Kloza
Production Liaison: Joanne Riker
Cover Design Director: Jayne Conte
Cover Design: Bruce Kenselaar
Cover Illustration/Photo: Comstock Images Royalty Free
Full-Service Project Management/Composition: Integra Software Services, Ltd.

Credits and acknowledgments borrowed from other sources and reproduced, with permission, in this textbook appear on appropriate page within text.

Pearson Education LTD.
Pearson Education Singapore, Pte. Ltd
Pearson Education, Canada, Ltd
Pearson Education–Japan

Pearson Education Australia PTY, Limited
Pearson Education North Asia Ltd
Pearson Educación de Mexico, S.A. de C.V.
Pearson Education Malaysia, Pte. Ltd

ISBN-13: 978-0-13-158954-4
ISBN-10:   0-13-158954-7

Contents

Chapter 3 *The Paper Chase: Documentary Evidence*   *41*

Chapter 4 *Interviews: Gathering Testimonial Evidence* 63

Chapter 5   *Search Warrants*   *92*

Chapter 6   *Injunctions and Forfeitures: Halting The Crime and Taking Away The Profits*   *123*

Chapter 7   *Evidence Analysis: Using The Experts*   *147*

Chapter 8   *The Grand Jury and Criminal Charges*   *168*

Chapter 10   *Reaching a Disposition*   *209*

Boxes, Tables, and Figures

Preface

The goal of this book is to present a general, comprehensive approach to investigating white collar crime. While other volumes focus on the basics of criminal investigation and, to a lesser extent, the investigation of specific crime types (including white collar crime), what makes this undertaking unique is the broad approach it presents and advocates. As is discussed in Chapter 1, this volume adopts an all-inclusive definition for white collar crime, ranging from the more "street-level" varieties such identity theft, check forgery, and credit card fraud to the more classic "crimes in the suites" committed by upper-echelon individuals. This approach is being taken because it tends to mirror how the law enforcement community labels these types of offenses and then structures itself to address them. Additionally, this volume also views white collar offending to be both criminal and noncriminal (i.e., civil/administrative) in nature. A great of deal of misconduct that rightfully belongs under the white collar crime umbrella is addressed within the civil/administrative enforcement arenas, and taking such actions requires investigation before doing so. Thus, any comprehensive approach to investigating white collar crime cannot focus solely on criminal investigation techniques and powers. Moreover, a blend of criminal and civil/administrative powers is often available to address white collar offending, thus requiring familiarity with a broader range of tools than is necessary when cases are pursued in only one forum.

While it is believed that pursuing such a broad approach to white collar crime investigation is necessary, it must be recognized that what is being presented here is, in fact, an approach or general guide, and not necessarily specific, step-by-step instructions for every type of white collar crime case. The varieties of white collar crime are too numerous, as are the jurisdictions and agencies that address them, to permit more than general guidance in one volume. However, the general guidance being offered here is indeed comprehensive, in that it brings together the whole range of approaches that can be used to address this misconduct that is so varied in nature. Having said that, readers should also understand that this volume is *not* a basic investigative text and does not go into detail when referencing procedures that are universal to the investigative profession. Rather readers are encouraged to review general investigative texts and/or agency training and policy materials when further information is needed in these areas.

The material in this book reflects a combination of academic research and professional training/personal experience spanning more than a quarter century in the investigation and management of white collar crime cases. Having served as a U.S. Postal Inspector over this period of time, I had the advantage of learning white collar crime investigation in an organization with an institutional history in this area that dates back to enactment of the federal mail fraud statute in 1872.

I also had the good fortune over these years of working side by side with outstanding investigators from numerous other agencies, as well as many highly talented prosecutors. Aside from being enjoyable associations on both professional and personal levels, they were also tremendous learning experiences. Thus, the "personal experience" being offered here is really an amalgamation of knowledge and experiences that were collected over the course of a career. Most importantly, this amalgamation of knowledge and experiences does not represent memoirs, war stories, or theorizing; rather, it represents effective and successful steps and approaches that were applied time and again in actual white collar crime investigations.

The organization of this book follows a somewhat developmental chronology. Chapter 1 takes an academic look at white collar crime, a foundation necessary if an investigator is to fully understand and appreciate the environment in which he/she is working. Chapter 2 discusses the development of information about white collar offending and its initial evaluation. Chapters 3 and 4 address documentary and testimonial evidence respectively. Important investigative tools such as search warrants, civil injunctions, and forfeiture are covered in Chapters 5 and 6. Chapter 7 presents perhaps overlooked applications of forensic science in white collar crime investigations. Chapter 8 is devoted to the criminal charging process, most notably the use of the grand jury. Chapter 9 addresses investigative considerations in civil/administrative forums. Chapter 10 concludes with a discussion on reporting and investigator roles in bringing cases to a final disposition.

The book contains features that facilitate learning and understanding. Each chapter begins with a set of "Keywords and Concepts" that should assist readers in identifying important terms as they come across them in the text. Each chapter concludes with a "Chapter Highlights" section that brings together the major points in the chapter. Finally, in many chapters, selected, *specific* investigative steps are identified and labeled as *best practices*, in an effort to ensure that their importance is impressed upon the reader. In chapters where *best practices* are identified, they are reiterated after the "Chapter Highlights" section.

Additionally, various boxes, tables, and figures are included throughout the text, as well as a set of appendices that follows Chapter 10. The material contained in the boxes, tables, figures, and appendices supplements the chapter narratives. In particular, examples of actual case affidavits, an indictment, and other routinely required written documents are provided as examples, the development of which are discussed in detail.

Acknowledgments

The journey a book and its author take from the concept stage to publication is often a long one, if not uncertain and circuitous, as well. The fact that this book has completed its journey can be attributed to the unwavering help, assistance, and support I received from the staff at Pearson Prentice Hall. One of the truly pleasant highlights of this journey was the opportunity I had to work with Margaret Lannamann of O'Donnell and Associates, who was assigned to shepherd me through the development of this manuscript, from the first draft, through the review process, and on to its final submission. Soon thereafter, Kavitha Kuttikan of Integra Software Services took over as Project Manager and in a highly competent, punctual fashion turned a stack of papers into an attractive bound volume.

I also had the distinct advantage of receiving excellent feedback and input from a group of reviewers who examined both my initial proposal and the draft manuscript. This group included Bruce Delphia, ECPI Technical College; John Hill, Salt Lake Community College; David LaRose, Remington College; A. L. Marstellar, Drury University; Robert E. Moore, Delta State University; Mark Noe, Florida Metropolitan University; and Kip Schlegel, Indiana University. I wish to thank these individuals for their knowledgeable and insightful comments, all of which were carefully evaluated and considered.

Finally, in addition to thanking my family for their support and encouragement throughout this endeavor, I must acknowledge their substantive contributions, as well. My wife Lyn was my primary proofreader/"in-house editor" as the manuscript was being written, while my daughter, Kristen E. Bazley, Ed.D., was my co-author on the Instructor materials.

Tom Bazley, Ph.D.
Tampa, FL

Introduction: Why Bother?

Key Terms and Concepts

- Criminal Offense versus Civil/Admini-
  stration Violation
- Federal Jurisdiction versus State
  Jurisdiction
- Law Enforcement Agency versus
  Regulatory Agency

- Loss Estimates
- Offender versus Offense
- White Collar Crime

INVESTIGATE WHITE COLLAR CRIME? WHY BOTHER?

Consider the following:

Item—On August 28, 2001, the Securities and Exchange Commission in Fort Worth, TX, opened an investigation into possible accounting and related-party irregularities following a *Wall Street Journal* story that reported that Enron Corporation had transferred billions of dollars of assets and millions of shares of stock into complex partnership transactions in which its own Chief Financial Officer, Andrew Fastow, was involved. On October 2, 2002, Fastow was arrested for securities and wire fraud, money laundering, and conspiracy for netting a reported $60 million in connection with Enron's implosion, an event that one observer likened to "shorthand for corporate wrongdoing."[1] Later, the other principals in Enron, Ken Lay and Jeff Skilling, were convicted for their roles in Enron's demise following a lengthy jury trial.

Item—In 1984 Charles H. Keating, Jr., bought the Lincoln Savings & Loan. He, like many other savings and loan executives of that era, looted money from his institution and diverted it to personal investments and other financial transactions. After years of fighting off regulatory intervention, in 1989 the federal government seized Lincoln Savings & Loan, an action a federal judge subsequently upheld in finding Lincoln unsafe and unsound to conduct business. The collapse of this institution eventually cost the U.S.

taxpayers over $3 billion. Keating ironically, after being convicted in both state and federal courts on criminal charges arising in part from the debacle at Lincoln, managed to have both convictions overturned on appeal (although not before serving four and one-half years in federal prison).[2]

Okay, maybe these are exceptional cases, those that reached levels of national notoriety. Who could argue against the untold investigative hours and other resources expended on these crimes that not only reflected excessive greed and extravagance, but more importantly caused victims huge losses, if not financial ruination? By now, some readers might be breathing a sigh of relief, thinking they will never work on such cases as an investigator or prosecutor or be confronted by unimaginable corporate wrongdoing on "their watch" as an auditor/accountant, business executive, or corporate security official. But to the contrary, for those of us who do take on investigative/prosecutive duties or have responsibility for corporate operations such experiences may very well come our way. The good news is that like criminal justice counterparts who investigate and prosecute other forms of crime such as homicide, kidnapping, rape, and drug trafficking, high profile cases tend to be the exception while most day-to-day work involves "garden variety" white collar crimes. Note, however, that I did not use words such as *simple, easy, unsophisticated*, or similar labels that might suggest *de minimus* effort is in any way associated with the term *garden variety*. For instance, consider one final case example.

Item—After a year and one-half of investigation, a joint federal agency task force known as *Operation Take Back* began to unravel corrupt practices in the health care industry throughout the state of Florida. The agents identified a network of mobile diagnostic services and clinical laboratories that paid kickbacks as a means to entice health care providers to utilize their services, a practice which is a felony under the Medicare program whether one offers or receives such payments. Thus, not only were the payers of these kickbacks targeted, but also those who accepted them, including physicians. Numerous indictments and convictions soon followed. While the individual amounts of the kickbacks tended to total a few thousand dollars each, $2 million in false claims to the Medicare program were linked to one of the diagnostic service operators.[3]

This last example is simply to illustrate what might be described as a "garden variety" white collar crime: a case without huge losses, prominent individuals as defendants, and/or widespread publicity. And yet, as you would correctly infer from the brief description, this "garden variety" case was very time consuming, involved multiple defendants (some of whom went to trial), and the offenses took place in a complex environment, that is, the health care industry—characteristics that seem to have that "big case" ring to them. But perhaps the most important point to be made by this "garden variety" case is that it ultimately employed the full spectrum of investigative techniques and prosecutive resources available, a commonality it shared with the likes of the Enron, Keating, and any number of other prominent white collar cases. With this in mind, it is the goal of this volume to introduce the full range of investigative tools and prosecutive resources that are available to address white collar crime, "garden variety" or otherwise. While it will be frequently echoed throughout the following pages that a "one size fits all" approach is not being advocated here, readers will be exposed to general strategies and the integration of a variety of investigative/prosecutive techniques that can be applied in a wide array of white collar crime scenarios. But you're still wondering, "Why bother?" Let's answer that question by first getting into defining what it is that we are talking about.

WHAT IS WHITE COLLAR CRIME?

A cursory study of American history will reveal that the conduct we commonly refer to as white collar crime is not a product of our modern society, but rather examples can be found even during the American colonial era. For example, Christianson cited such American patriots as George Washington, Alexander Hamilton, and John Jay as being involved in "shady" land deals.[4] The passage of legislation to curb business-related abuses in the 1800s provides further evidence that white collar crime is not a new phenomenon. The federal mail fraud statute was enacted in 1872 in response to interstate frauds that were conducted through mails.[5] In 1890 the Sherman Anti-Trust Act was passed to address the problem of antimonopolistic practices that evolved incident to the rise of American corporate giants, while the early 1900s saw the enactment of the Pure Food and Drug Act and the Meat Inspection Act in response to unhealthful conditions in meat-packing plants.[6]

Introducing White Collar Crime

However, it was not until Edwin Sutherland, the noted U.S. criminologist, published an article entitled "White-Collar Criminality" in 1940 (*American Sociological Review*, 5(1), pp. 1–12) that crimes committed by the business community were viewed within academic and government circles as a unified category of offenses, that is, white collar crime. In addition to calling attention to these offenses by categorizing them under one banner, Sutherland also argued that the upper classes committed crimes in connection with their business activities, but these crimes were not looked upon as such and therefore upper-class criminality was excluded from criminological consideration and theory. Moreover, he felt that crime statistics were skewed because they focused only on crimes committed by the lower classes and therefore forced theorists to work only within the framework of lower-class offenders.

Conceptually, Sutherland's article was important in at least four respects. First, it argued for the recognition of white collar crime as a serious problem. Second, it advocated a reorientation of criminology/sociology and societal institutions concerned with criminal behavior to consider the illegal activities of both the upper and lower social classes. Third, the effect of such a reorientation would be that the study and control of this type of crime would need to consider not only the offense characteristics but also the offender's social and class characteristics as well. As he was concerned about crimes committed by the upper classes in the course of their business activities, class and social characteristics provided upper-class individuals offending opportunities not available to lower-class individuals. Heretofore, crime was viewed as solely a lower-class phenomenon and thus, all criminal offenders were believed to share common lower-class social characteristics.

The fourth conceptual issue raised by Sutherland (1940) was the inclusion of illegal but not necessarily criminal activities as conduct worthy of attention by both criminologists/sociologists and criminal justice policy makers. He acknowledged that much of the conduct he considered white collar crime was neither investigated by traditional law enforcement agencies nor adjudicated in the criminal courts. Rather, these offenses were usually handled civilly or administratively, often by regulatory-type agencies. However, he felt that most of these types of actions arose because the offenders did engage in the type of conduct that would also constitute a criminal violation, usually in the form of criminal fraud. He also noted in this article that juvenile delinquency is not adjudicated in the criminal courts, but there is little public debate over whether this type of conduct is, in actuality, a criminal concern.

Sutherland expanded on his argument to bring noncriminal offenses under the white collar crime umbrella in his 1949 book *White Collar Crime* (New York: Holt, Rinehart and Winston). Here he reported his study of the offending activities of the 70 largest American corporations. Among the points he made in support of his position was that since the antitrust statutes have both civil and criminal provisions, even when handled civilly, an antitrust matter could be looked upon as a criminal offense as well. Likewise, he contended that misrepresentation cases handled by the Federal Trade Commission or Food and Drug Administration as administrative matters were essentially criminal fraud violations.

Sutherland's views on including technically noncriminal conduct under the banner of white collar crime, however, did not go unchallenged. A particularly argumentative response from the academic community came from P. W. Tappan in a 1947 article entitled "Who is the Criminal?" that appeared in the *American Sociological Review*, 12(1), pp. 96–102. Tappan did not take issue with the notion that individuals of the upper classes committed crimes, but he was critical of Sutherland's concept that the definition of white collar crime should include conduct that violates any law, civil or criminal. Tappan felt this type of definition allowed for too much discretion in terms of who is considered "criminal" for the purposes of criminological study. He was an advocate of criminology focusing its attention on those who are labeled as criminal by the criminal code. He believed that the criminal code was established (at least in democracies) by representatives of the citizenry and that, although imperfect, it reflects the generally accepted norms of the society. Those who violate the code conducted themselves in a specifically proscribed manner. Moreover, by focusing on those who violated the criminal code, he argued that criminology could also focus on the control mechanisms that the society has established in response to those it labels as criminal. He disputed the notion that by not taking a wider approach, criminologists are ignoring a large population of criminals and simply focusing on those who become enmeshed in legal difficulties because they are poor and ignorant. He said that unless a person being called a white collar criminal violates a criminal statute, his/her offensive behavior should only be considered a conduct norm violation or a result of antisocial behavior, neither of which is relevant for study by criminologists. On the other hand, he felt that law becomes a peculiarly important pressure toward conformity and, therefore, criminals are a sociologically distinct group because they are violators of these norms and are subjected to official government sanction as a result.

Although the purpose here is not to fully delve into a debate which has raged on in academia, the fact is that this controversy has not been resolved and, in turn, has had an adverse impact on our ability to assess the frequency and cost of white collar crime (remember the *Why Bother* question?). Support for Sutherland's all-inclusive definition of white collar crime has come largely from the academic community.[7] But how do policy makers and law enforcement personnel view white collar crime and how do they go about assessing the frequency of this type of crime and its cost? One quick way to answer this question is to consider our most widely watched national crime statistical database, the Uniform Crime Report (UCR), and even its planned, eventual successor, the National Incident Based Reporting System (NIBRS). These databases reflect crimes reported to the *police*. Reflected in Table 1–1 are the crimes tracked by these databases that could be considered white collar offenses (and we will get more into that issue in a later section).

The offenses listed in this table support the contention made by Sutherland over a half century ago that our crime databases do not capture a great many white collar violations because these databases rely on input from general police agencies as opposed to specialized white collar crime investigative organizations. In fact, even though federal agencies play the leading role in white collar crime enforcement, no data from federal criminal investigations of any type are reported in the UCR. Thus, it goes without saying that noncriminal enforcement actions that Sutherland was so concerned about are not

Table 1–1   White collar crime offenses reported in the UCR and NIBRS

UCR:
1. Fraud
2. Embezzlement
3. Forgery/Counterfeiting

(Note: These are all Part II Offenses as opposed to Part I or Index Crimes, which are crimes considered to be the most serious offenses)

NIBRS:
1. False Pretenses
2. Swindles
3. Confidence Games
4. Credit Card and ATM Fraud
5. Wire and Welfare Fraud
6. Impersonation
7. Bribery
8. Embezzlement
9. Counterfeiting and Forgery
10. Bad Checks

included here in any fashion. And for those of you wondering about NIBRS, while it offers some definite advantages over the UCR in terms of types of data provided (including expanded white collar crime categories) it is and has been for years a "work in progress." Currently agencies submitting data to NIBRS cover only a fraction of the U.S. population and this data is still of the "crimes reported to the *police*" variety. Assuming NIBRS will eventually fully replace the UCR, in its current form it appears uncertain whether it will ever truly report the amount of white- collar crime committed in this country. Certainly, there is no reason to believe that it will incorporate noncriminal enforcement actions. Thus, a statement made by Rosoff, Pontell, and Tillman seems to having an enduring ring to it: "There are virtually no systematic counts, for instance, of the numbers of white collar offenses that occur in a given year or of the number of individuals arrested for these offenses."[8] Burns expanded on this sentiment by stating that there is nothing equivalent to the *Sourcebook of Criminal Justice Statistics* for white collar crime offenses (making reference to the widely used and detailed compendium of criminal justice data that is compiled by Pastore and Maguire; available online at http://www.albany.edu/sourcebook/index.html).[9]

Considering the continuing uncertainty whether the white collar crime umbrella should include noncriminal offenses, it should come as no surprise then that there is no definitive list of white collar crimes, even among criminal enforcement agencies. Contrast this situation to conventional crimes such as homicide, rape, robbery, burglary, and so on. Although we never totally avoid definitional differences between agencies and/or jurisdictions, there tends to be enough agreement about what constitutes these types of offenses to permit comparisons as well as broad compilations of data. For instance, we can compare homicide rates from one jurisdiction to another and we can compile a homicide rate for a state or the entire nation with a great degree of confidence that we are talking about the same conduct. Likewise, we can lump together homicide with rape, robbery, and aggravated assault and call this group of crimes *violent crimes*. Because of generally agreed-upon definitions and because these are offenses that are universally addressed by the law enforcement community at some level, we are able to come up with an evaluation of the amount of violent crime for our locality, an entire state, or the country as a whole. Try doing the same thing for white collar crime as an umbrella category in the same vein as violent crime. We have already talked about the fact that we have conduct that could fall under the white collar crime umbrella, but is not pursued in the criminal prosecutive forum. We will be talking later about the nature of these types of enforcement actions, but in brief these proceedings do not result in the criminal justice system measures we commonly look at, such as arrests, indictments, and convictions. So to make matters simple, what if we just consider those offenses that are, in fact, handled in the criminal forum only? Even here we start to encounter obstacles.

Offense or Offender?

If we go back to the beginning, so to speak, Sutherland's concept of white collar crimes took into consideration the social class of the offender, that is, upper-class businessmen (*sic*). Thus, it is not surprising that the white collar offenses on which he based his 1949 study

Table 1–2 White collar offense categories: Sutherland (1949)

1. Restraint of Trade (e.g., anti-trust violations)
2. Rebates (i.e., kickbacks)
3. Patents, Trademarks, and Copyrights Violations
4. Misrepresentation in Advertising
5. Unfair Labor Practices
6. Financial Manipulations (e.g., embezzlements, stock fraud, false financial statements)
7. War Crimes (violations of emergency war time regulations affecting corporations)
8. Miscellaneous (includes Food and Drug Act violations)

were activities that were clearly in the domain of the business *executive*. These offenses are displayed in Table 1–2.

Again, Sutherland's purpose in taking this focus was to bring attention to crimes that had been previously ignored by academics, policy makers, and enforcement agencies. Not surprisingly, the business community scorned his study and in fact the study that was published in 1949 did not identify the corporate offenders by name for fear of litigation. It was not until 1983 that an "uncut" version of this study was available that "named names."[10]

One point that should not be overlooked when considering the offense or offender criterion is that Sutherland's study focused on corporations as offenders, with the implication that the illegal actions they engaged in were the responsibility of the upper-class individuals who inevitably held executive power in these organizations. Nevertheless, in many instances in his study, enforcement actions were taken against the corporate entities and not individuals. The practice of targeting corporate entities as opposed to individuals for enforcement action is unique to white collar crime.[11] Although such an approach is more frequently taken to address regulatory violations, criminal prosecutions at times have also targeted corporate entities, either in addition to or to the exclusion of individual defendants. Thus, regardless of whether white collar crime is defined by offender characteristics or the nature of the misconduct, both individuals and corporate entities can be subject to enforcement action.

On the other hand, Sutherland's upper-class approach has had its supporters, especially within the academic community, although even within these ranks there has evolved widespread acknowledgment of the need for a broadened concept of white collar crime that does not rely on upper-class social status as a prerequisite. Much of this support stems from the fact that the approach taken by policy makers and law enforcement agencies to address Sutherland's concerns goes beyond considering only upper-class offenders. For instance, Friedrichs expressed the sentiment that limiting the definition of white collar crime to the "elites" is probably not realistic because its use as a crime category and descriptor has broadened beyond what Sutherland had intended. He stated that as a result of government bureaucracy, the term *white collar crime* has been applied to many crimes committed by the middle and lower classes.[12]

This broadened focus, however, is not simply some Byzantine function of "government bureaucracy," but rather has a sound basis in our present-day reality. Weisburd, Wheeler, Waring, and Bode found in their study of white collar offenders that ordinary people were committing white collar crimes because these types of people now had greater access to the white collar crime world of paper fraud. When they culled out from their study sample of white collar offenders those individuals who would be considered upper class, only 319 out of 1,090 remained. However, when they defined white collar crime as "use of occupation to commit the crime," they retained 95% of the sample. From this finding they concluded:

> It is also understandable that Sutherland may have failed to give attention to this category, given the structure of society and the labor force during the time his ideas were being formed. During the 1920s and 1930s, the white-collar class as a category of labor was smaller than it is today, and it is possible that not much was lost by concentrating on the crimes at the bottom and top of the social order, and leaving out the white-collar middle. But by the latter part of the twentieth century, the postindustrial world generated vast numbers of white-collar jobs and white-collar families. By now, if not so clearly half a century ago, the image of only two classes of offenders is misplaced, for it leaves out a large part of what may be the heart of the American population.[13]

Attempts to Define White Collar Crime

Nevertheless, even with widespread acceptance of the idea that white collar crime applies to the nature of the offense and not the social class of the offender, coming up with a universal definition that in turn permits the development of an inclusive typology has remained elusive. Friedrichs has called a single, all-encompassing definition an illusion.[14] He also noted that because so many different agencies are involved in white collar crime enforcement, there is not a standard set of labels or definitions for these offenses.[15] To be sure, there have been ample efforts in this direction, however. For instance, from the academic world Coleman defines white collar crime as a violation of the law committed by a person or group of persons in the course of an otherwise respected and legitimate occupation or financial activity.[16] Others including Friedrichs have simply offered laundry lists of categories covering a wide spectrum of frauds, abuses of trust, and occupational/business offenses as a means toward defining white collar crime.[17]

Needless to say, however, a laissez-faire approach to defining enforcement activities would seldom meet with approval in government bureaucracies. Being guided by a definition for white collar crime will direct agency resources to certain types of cases and away from others. Agencies that have wide jurisdiction in white collar crime enforcement are more likely to be guided by a broader definition for white collar crime. For example, Coleman points out that the Federal Bureau of Investigation (FBI) has the broadest investigative jurisdiction over white collar crime.[18] Displayed in Box 1–1 is the definition developed by the FBI for white collar crime, a comprehensive statement reflective of its broad jurisdiction in this area.

> **Box 1–1**   Federal Bureau of Investigation: definition for white collar crime
>
> White collar crimes are categorized by deceit, concealment, or violation of trust and are not dependent upon the application or threat of physical force or violence. Individuals and organizations commit these acts to obtain money, property or services; to avoid payment or loss of money or services; or to secure personal or business advantage. (http://www.fbi.gov/libref/factsfigure/wcc.htm)

On the other hand, many agencies with investigative authority in the white collar arena have limited jurisdiction due to the nature of their agency mandates, and they are guided by narrow definitions that direct their efforts to very specific white collar crime activity (e.g., Internal Revenue Service, Inspector General agencies).

Notwithstanding the FBI's broad definition of white collar crime, as we have seen, its own statistical databases report very little of this type of activity. So, you may ask, if the agency with the broadest jurisdiction in this area does not compile data consistent with its own definition, just how do we assess the frequency and victimization impacts of white collar crime? One answer would be, "with difficulty and educated guess work." In support of such an assessment is Friedrichs' observation that a multitude of agencies investigate white collar crime and these agencies maintain their unique records of this activity. This data is not compiled at any central location and, thus, the total number of incidents is unknown as is the total number of victims.[19] So to help answer the *Why Bother* question, let's look at some of the educated guesses.

LOSS ESTIMATES

Both the government and the academic community have put forth estimates of white collar crime victimization. One of the most frequently cited white collar crime loss estimates came from a Senate Judiciary Committee report, a figure calculated to be $250 billion annually.[20] Curiously, however, this estimate would seem now to be quite dated as the report was issued in 1986. Nevertheless, what might put this figure in some perspective is to compare it to losses attributable to conventional crimes. Based on data reported in the *2003 Sourcebook of Criminal Justice Statistics* for robberies, burglaries, larcenies, and motor vehicle theft, the total losses attributable to these crimes (based on an average loss figure per incident) was less than $15 billion for 2002.[21] Then consider that Friedrichs, at one point, estimated white collar crime losses to be ten times greater than losses from traditional crimes on a yearly basis.[22] Using this multiplier, the loss figure for white collar crime would be around $150 billion. So who knows—a $250 billion estimate from 1986 or an estimate based on multiples of the yearly conventional crime losses? The point is that while we may not have a precise dollar loss figure attributable to white collar crime, the estimates we do have clearly dwarf the costs of conventional crimes.

A further consideration with regard to these dollar losses is just who are the victims, that is, the losers of all this money? Many would be quick (and correct) to answer, individuals in their capacities as consumers, investors, employees, and so on. To make matters worse, many individuals who are victimized by white collar crime come from vulnerable segments of society where a lack of marketplace acumen, diminished mental capacity, ability to speak English, and so on are preyed upon. Not surprisingly, individuals falling into these categories can often ill afford to be fleeced by the unscrupulous. Even when examining securities fraud victimization, a province where many would expect the rich and sophisticated, one study described victims as most likely to be simply gullible and middle class.[23] Now, if you are not moved by gullible, middle-class people losing their investments through criminal acts, consider the type of person that another study found to be the favored target of fraudulent telemarketers: elderly victims who are isolated and possibly have diminished capacity.[24]

Suffice it to say that abysmal stories of the financial harm endured by individual victims of white collar crime are legion. However, it is also important to recognize that while we might have a tendency to look upon businesses and corporations as the white collar culprits in our society, they too are frequently victimized by white collar crimes. For instance, antitrust activity not only denies consumers the advantages of a competitive marketplace, but it can also drive out of business those competing entities that are not part of the collusive practices. In other instances, some corporations/businesses have engaged in bribery to influence the purchase of their products by other corporations/businesses even though their products are higher in price and/or inferior in quality. Individuals, themselves, have proven to be white collar culprits at the expense of corporations/businesses. Insurance companies are all too frequently victimized by false and inflated claims submitted by their insured's. Credit card, loan, and check fraud committed by individual offenders are similarly prevalent and cause large losses to the credit card and banking industries.

It is also important to recognize that governmental entities are victimized as well by white collar crime. Tax fraud deprives both the federal and state/local governments the income needed to provide vital services/benefits. Both individuals and corporations/businesses have committed such frauds. Moreover, many of these tax-supported services and benefits have been targeted by white collar criminals, of both the corporate/business variety and individuals. Healthcare providers ranging from individual practitioners to corporate entities such as hospital and diagnostic laboratory chains have engaged in false billing and kickback schemes to the detriment of both the federal Medicare and Medicaid programs. In terms of individuals who target government programs, those who falsely obtain welfare and Social Security benefits come readily to mind.

Injury and Death

The *Why Bother* issue doesn't stop with financial losses. Some white collar crimes have caused illness, injuries, and deaths as well. This aspect of white collar crime victimization has been most frequently found among manufacturers who have produced and sold unsafe products and those who have ignored proper disposal of toxic materials. Employers who have failed to provide a safe working environment for employees have also added to the white collar crime injury and death toll as well. Unfortunately, arriving at illness, injury, and death figures arising from white collar offenses is even more elusive than establishing a reliable dollar loss estimate. For instance, the Consumer Product Safety Commission reports injuries and deaths associated with (but not necessarily caused by) product use by-product category. Thus, establishing the numbers of injuries and deaths from defective or dangerous products from this data would be problematic.

Nevertheless, some consumers have suffered direct injury from defective products they purchased. For example, consider the case outlined in Box 1–2, which features a press release issued by the U.S. Attorney's Office in Miami, FL. This case involved four individuals who suffered severe botulism poisoning as a result of being administered a fake form of the cosmetic drug Botox®.

Box 1–2   Press release: Fake Botox investigation

Press Release: U.S. Department of Justice

Marcos Daniel Jiménez
United States Attorney for the
Southern District of Florida

FOR IMMEDIATE RELEASE: February 02, 2005

THREE INDIVIDUALS AND FOUR CORPORATIONS
CHARGED IN FAKE BOTOX SCHEME

Marcos Daniel Jiménez, United States Attorney for the Southern District of Florida; and David Bourne, Special Agent in Charge, Food and Drug Administration, Office of Criminal Investigation, Miami Field Office, announced today that a 48-count Indictment has been unsealed charging three (3) doctors and four (4) corporations in connection with a scheme to distribute fake Botox for use on humans, even though the product was never approved by the Food and Drug Administration (FDA) for such use. The Indictment charges defendants, Chad Livdahl, N. D., Zarah Karim, N. D., Bach McComb, D. O., Toxin Research International, Inc. ("TRI"), Powderz, Inc., Z-Spa, Inc., and The Cosmetic Pharmacy, Inc., with conspiracy to defraud the United States, engage in mail and wire fraud, and misbrand a drug, in violation of Title 18, United States Code, Section 371. Additionally, all of the defendants are charged with substantive counts of mail fraud, in violation of Title 18, United States Code, Sections 1341 and 1346, and Livdahl, Karim, McComb, TRI, and Powderz, Inc. are charged with wire fraud, in violation of Title 18, United States Code, Sections 1346 and 1343, and misbranding of a drug, in violation of Title 21, United States Code, Sections 331(c) and 333(a) (2). Livdahl also is charged with perjury, in violation of Title 18, United States Code, Section 1623(a). The Indictment seeks forfeiture of the ill-gotten gains, including $1,500,000.

According to the Indictment, the defendants purchased 3,081 vials, each containing five (5) nanograms of Botulinum Toxin Type A and other ingredients, in a formulation

Continued

designed to imitate Allergan's Botox® Cosmetic, the only product made with Botulinum Toxin Type A that is approved by the FDA for use in human beings. The defendants then engaged in a scheme to defraud by marketing and selling to health care providers for use in human patients the fake Botox as a cheap alternative to Allergan's Botox® Cosmetic, without the administering health care providers advising their human patients that the fake Botox was not Allergan's Botox® Cosmetic and was not approved by the FDA for use in human beings.

Additionally, McComb is charged with one (1) count of misbranding a drug in relation to his obtaining 10,000 nanograms of full-strength, raw Botulinum Toxin Type A from List Biological Laboratories, Inc., and administering this product to individuals as though it were Allergan's Botox® Cosmetic, when, in fact, it was not. Based on prior court filings by the United States, this incident led to the development of severe botulism in four (4) individuals in the South Florida area, including McComb. The conspiracy count carries a maximum statutory penalty of five (5) years' imprisonment and a $250,000 fine. The maximum statutory penalty for each of the mail and wire fraud counts is twenty (20) years' imprisonment and a $250,000 fine. The maximum statutory penalty for each misbranding violation is three (3) years imprisonment and a $250,000 fine. As for the maximum statutory penalty on the perjury count, Livdahl faces a maximum of five (5) years imprisonment and a $250,000 fine on that count.

Prior to filing criminal charges, the United States sought civil relief against Livdahl, Karim, Powderz, Inc., TRI, The Cosmetic Pharmacy, and Z-Spa, Inc. to stop these defendants from distributing the fake Botox. On January 11, 2005, in response to the United States's motion for a preliminary injunction, United States District Judge James I. Cohn issued a civil injunction prohibiting these defendants from further distributing the fake Botox and requiring the defendants to initiate a recall of all previously distributed product and submit to inspections by the FDA, after a day-long hearing that included testimony from Livdahl and Karim. The criminal indictment includes one (1) count of perjury against Livdahl arising from his testimony at the preliminary injunction hearing on January 10, 2005.

"This deadly toxin packaged in harmless looking vials, wrapped in the guise of medicine, and used on unsuspecting members of our community represents a grave threat," said Mr. Jiménez. "Upon hearing of this threat, our prosecutors, along with the FDA, worked tirelessly to stop the vials from being sent out to anyone else and to hold those who seek to profit from them accountable."

"FDA applauds this indictment by the U.S. Attorney's office against these companies and individuals who were marketing potentially dangerous unapproved drugs as a less expensive alternative to Botox Cosmetic—the botulinum toxin type A product approved by FDA," said Dr. Lester M. Crawford, Acting FDA Commissioner. "Once again we have learned how people can be harmed when they are given products that are not approved for use in human beings. FDA recommends that consumers go to licensed, reputable health providers and get assurances that they are getting the FDA approved product."

Mr. Jiménez commended the investigative efforts of the Food and Drug Administration, Office of Criminal Investigation. The criminal case is being prosecuted by Assistant United States Attorneys Robin S. Rosenbaum and George Karavetsos. The civil case is being handled by Assistant United States Attorney Russell Koonin.

While the linkage between a harmful product and injury or illness is clear in this case, we hear all too frequently disturbing stories about groups of individuals living in the same neighborhoods or working for the same employer who develop life-threatening illnesses and/or whose children are born with rare disorders, with exposure to toxic materials resulting from violations of environmental laws and/or worker safety regulations being the suspected culprit. In these situations, not only is there the usual argument about cause and effect, but harm in terms of illness and death can sometimes take years to develop, thus prolonging the deleterious impact and delaying appropriate enforcement action.

SO AGAIN, WHY BOTHER?

Hopefully by now the answer to this question is quite clear: white collar crime costs us huge amounts of money annually, far more than is lost through conventional crimes; but even more importantly and tragically, in some forms it causes illness, injury, and even death. Thus, the real question that needs to be asked is, "What are we doing about it?" The goal of this book is to do something about it by providing a comprehensive approach to investigating these crimes. And a first step in this direction is to revisit the issue of "what is white collar crime?" Just as government agencies need to define what they will address as white collar crime, the comprehensive investigative approach presented here must do likewise.

WHAT IS WHITE COLLAR CRIME?

An All-Inclusive Concept

This volume will follow in the Sutherland tradition by viewing white collar crime as offenses that are addressed in both criminal and civil/administrative enforcement forums. This position is being taken not just because of philosophical agreement on this issue, but also because (and more importantly for the goal of this book) investigation is normally a prerequisite to pursuing enforcement action in any type of government forum. Accordingly, the white collar crime addressed by this book will include conduct that violates criminal statutes as well as conduct that constitutes civil or administrative offenses. As may be noted through a quick perusal of the Table of Contents or by thumbing through the chapters, this volume discusses issues and limitations encountered when investigating civil or administrative violations. In brief, many white collar crime enforcers have criminal investigative authority, but the powers associated with this authority are often limited to developing evidence of criminal violations. Conversely, many other white collar crime enforcers possess only authority to investigate civil or administrative offenses and the investigative tools available under such authority are generally more limited than those in criminal cases. A point that will be emphasized throughout this volume, however, is that both types of investigations do share steps in common. Thus, the comprehensive approach presented here is intended to apply to both criminal and noncriminal investigations, with distinctions drawn between the two as warranted.

The inclusiveness of the approach taken here toward white collar crime also extends to the offender characteristics. As will become apparent in the next section, the white collar crime addressed in this volume will be based on the nature of the offense and not on the social class of the offender, a distinct departure from Sutherland's concept. Additionally, white collar offenders can be either individuals or corporate entities.

A Definition or A Typology?

As discussed above, there is no universally accepted definition for white collar crime. Many government agencies have developed or adopted their own definitions in an effort to guide their investigative efforts, and many writers/academics have done likewise to provide parameters to their research. This volume will not pursue what Friedrichs termed the illusory goal of developing an all-encompassing definition for white collar crime.[25] Instead, this volume will adopt a typological approach to defining white collar crime, that is, by categories of offenses that have been commonly designated as white collar crime by both government agencies and within the research community. Further, rather than reinventing the wheel so to speak, representative typologies appear in Table 1–3 that will serve to identify the broad categories of misconduct considered white collar crime within this volume. Additionally, Appendix A describes in more detail commonly encountered white collar crime cases.

The one defining or typological concept that *will* be adopted here is Croall's observation that "However defined, white collar crime encompasses an enormous range of activities …"[26] Interestingly, the adoption of this observation along with Croall's *catch-all* fraud category provides rationale for the inclusion of those relatively few offenses that are captured by our national crime databases that could be considered white collar crimes (see Table 1–1; e.g., forgery and counterfeiting, check fraud, and credit card fraud). As may be recalled, the crimes in these databases are largely reported by state and local law enforcement agencies and the statistical data gathered on these offenses reflect important contributions made by these agencies in white collar crime enforcement. Then who investigates the many other offenses specifically identified in the typologies presented in Table 1–3? To a large extent, this burden falls on federal agencies for reasons that will be discussed next.

FEDERAL VERSUS STATE JURISDICTION

The characteristics of many white collar crimes mandate that they be addressed at the federal level rather than by state or local law enforcement agencies. One very common characteristic of white collar crime is that it tends to be interstate in nature, that is, an offender who is located in one governmental jurisdiction/geographic area causes victimization in other jurisdictions and geographic areas. Statutory authority possessed by state and local agencies is generally limited to the state in which they are located. Thus, success in interstate white collar crime investigations by state/local agencies would be largely dependent upon cooperation between jurisdictions (and no doubt there has been excellent cooperation in many instances), and not because of reciprocal law enforcement powers between these jurisdictions. One good example of an important limitation would be obtaining business records in one state using the legal powers or process (e.g., subpoena) from another state. To be sure, under these circumstances many legitimate business entities may honor the out-of-state process out of a willingness to

Table 1-3   Representative white collar crime typologies

FBI[1]	Friedriches[2]	Coleman[3]	Rosoff et al.[4]	Croall[5]
Antitrust violations	Crimes by corporations	Employee theft	Crimes against consumers	Employee theft
Bankruptcy fraud	Crimes within occupations	Embezzlement	Unsafe products	Computer crimes
Environmental crimes	Crimes by governments	Computer crimes	Environmental crimes	Tax fraud
Government program fraud	Crimes arising from "state/corpo-rate relationships" and "globalization"	False advertising	Institutional corruption, e.g., media, religion	Crimes against consumers
Health care fraud		Consumer fraud		Employee and public safety violations
Internet crime		Fraud in professions	Securities fraud	Pollution violations fraud
Insurance fraud	Crimes within the financial industry	Financial fraud	Corporate fraud	
Securities/ Commodities fraud	Crimes arising from technology, e.g., computers	Tax evasion	Fiduciary fraud, e.g., banking, insurance, pension funds	
Telemarketing fraud	Corrupt/illegal business practices	Bribery/Corruption		
		Conflicts of interest		
		Manipulating the marketplace	Crimes by governments	
	Illegal individual practices, e.g., insurance fraud, tax fraud	Civil liberties violations	Public corruption	
		Political violence	Medical crime	
		Unsafe products	Computer crime	
		Unsafe workign conditions		
		Environmental crimes		

Notes:

[1] From http://www.fbi.gov

[2] D. O. Friedrichs, *Trusted Criminals: White Collar Crime in Contemporary Society*, 3rd ed. (Belmont, CA: Wadsworth, 2007), p. 7.

[3] J. W. Coleman, *The Criminal Elite: Understanding White Collar Crime*, 5th ed. (New York: Worth Publishers, 2002), 16–88.

[4] Stephen M. Rosoff, Henry N. Pontell, and Robert H. Tillman, *Profit Without Honor: White-Collar Crime and the Looting of America*, 3rd ed. (Upper Saddle River, NJ: Pearson Prentice Hall, 2004); as generally outlined by chapter headings in the Table of Contents.

[5] H. Croall, *White Collar Crime* (Buckingham, UK: Open University Press, 1992), pp. 27–42.

cooperate with an official investigation being conducted by a bona fide authority. However, note the conditions of "legitimate business entities" and "willingness to cooperate." When these conditions are not present, obtaining basic records necessary to pursue an investigation of an out-of-state offender could become very difficult.

Conversely, federal agencies possess nationwide authority to investigate offenses, and the legal processes available to them must be honored throughout the United States. Federal investigators in one part of the country can travel to another part of the country to conduct an investigation, although in practice they usually will coordinate with their agency's local office when doing so, as a matter of courtesy and/or policy. This highlights another important asset federal agencies possess incident to investigating multijurisdictional offending: these agencies typically have investigative personnel assigned to various parts of the country. State/local agencies might undertake an investigation of an out-of-state offender because of many victims within their jurisdiction. In federal investigations, this same offender would most likely be targeted by the appropriate federal agency office in closest proximity to the offender, thus eliminating the travel time and expense that would have to be incurred at the state/local level. Moreover, in federal cases that require investigative work to be completed at a distant location, these investigators can often be assisted by their agency counterparts in this area, unlike their state/local counterparts who might have to travel to this jurisdiction even to complete the simplest investigative tasks.

Another distinction between the state/local and federal levels lies in the traditional areas of enforcement responsibility. Under our federal system of government, state and local governments have responsibility for investigating conventional crimes, for example homicide, rape, robbery, assault, burglary, larceny, and drug enforcement. Unfortunately, these crimes are all too abundant in our society and there tends to be a very clear public mandate that they be addressed. This burden falls on our state and local agencies and a good deal of their investigative resources is directed in these areas.

In addition to being better able to address crimes committed on an interstate basis, many white collar crimes have an inherent federal connection. For instance, federal law plays a large role in regulating the banking and securities industries. Moreover, the federal government underwrites the lawful operation of these industries by providing the public insurance against bank failures and malfeasance in the securities industry. These are complex industries that have spawned bodies of specialized knowledge, both for those who work in these areas and for those who oversee these operations. Thus, the federal government has established highly specialized and trained enforcement agencies to investigate both criminal and civil violations in these industries. This same scenario plays out when one considers the oversight required of our Medicare program and the proper administration of many other government spending programs.

Thus, the federal government not only has the investigative authority and powers necessary to address white collar crime, but in many instances it has an inherent mandate to do so. Accordingly, the federal government has established many specialized agencies to address a vast array of white collar offending, the majority of which falls outside the purview and resource limitations of state and local agencies.

Again, however, it must be *emphasized* that state and local agencies play an important role in white collar crime enforcement. Not only do they address the white collar crimes that are captured in the UCR and NIBRS (see Table 1–1), but also most states do take on regulatory functions that mirror federal activities, although again their focus is usually limited to within state borders. For instance, many states have very active consumer protection agencies that have enforcement powers. In addition, most states have environmental protection agencies that aggressively take on polluters. The banking and insurance industries in most states come under the oversight of state regulatory agencies, and the health care program for the poor is monitored by Medicaid fraud units. The position being taken here is to encourage even greater involvement by state and local agencies in white collar crime enforcement through increased funding and authority as means to better addressing the enormity of this national problem.

Nevertheless, the comprehensive investigative approach presented here will have a federal orientation for two reasons. First, the myriad of statutory and procedural variations across the 50 states prevents a common state-level approach to white collar crime investigation. Second, white collar crime enforcement responsibility in this country lies predominantly within the federal domain. Again, however, just as there are common steps in both criminal and noncriminal investigations, there are more similarities than differences between investigations conducted at the federal and state/local levels. Accordingly, most of what is presented will apply to investigators of white collar crime within any forum, state or federal, criminal agency, or regulatory agency.

CHAPTER HIGHLIGHTS

- Popularizing, if not originating, the term *white collar crime* can be credited to American criminologist Edwin Sutherland.
- Sutherland's concept of white collar crime focused on upper-class offending, but did include offenses litigated in both the criminal and civil/administrative forums.
- There is no universal definition for white collar crime in either the law enforcement/public policy community or the academic/research community.
- White collar offending is not tracked in any single database (e.g., UCR); thus, the prevalence and harms (both financial and physical) attributable to these violations can only be roughly estimated.
- The estimated losses and harms, however, far exceed those arising from conventional "street" crimes.
- This volume adopts an all-inclusive view of white collar crime—that is, both criminal and civil/administrative offending and offenders from all socio-economic levels—and offers investigative approaches and strategies that can apply to a broad spectrum of offending.

Notes

1. A very brief overview of events contained in *Conspiracy of Fools: A True Story* by Kurt Eichenwald (New York: Broadway Books, 2005).
2. Stephen M. Rosoff, Henry N. Pontell, and Robert H. Tillman, *Profit Without Honor: White-Collar Crime and the Looting of America*, 3rd ed. (Upper Saddle River, NJ: Pearson Prentice Hall, 2004), pp. 338–343.
3. G. H. Montilla, T. D. Bazley, and P. Roberts, "Kickback prosecutions in the Middle District of Florida: A blue collar approach to a white collar crime," *Health Care Fraud 1999* (Chicago: American Bar Association, 1999), pp. C-1–29.
4. S. Christianson, *With Liberty for Some: 500 years of Imprisonment in America* (Boston: Northeastern University Press, 1998), p. 101.
5. L. E. Norrgard and J. M. Norrgard, *Consumer Fraud: A Reference Handbook* (Santa Barbara, CA: ABC-CLIO, 1998), p. 12.

6. J. W. Coleman, *The Criminal Elite: Understanding White Collar Crime*, 5th ed. (New York: Worth Publishers, 2002), pp. 104, 113.

7. For example, see A. J. Reiss and A. D. Biderman, *Data Sources on White-Collar Law Breaking* (Washington, DC: U.S. Department of Justice, National Institute of Justice, 1980), p. xxvii.

8. Rosoff, Pontell, and Tillman, *op. cit.*, p. 23.

9. R. Burns, "Toward a Sourcebook of White Collar Crime Statistics: A Collection of Environmental Crime Data," a paper presented at the annual meeting of the Academy of Criminal Justice Sciences, Anaheim, CA, March 2002, p. 2.

10. E. H. Sutherland, *White Collar Crime: The Uncut Version* (New Haven, CT: Yale University Press), 1983; in Introduction by Gilbert Geis and Colin Goff.

11. G. Geis and J. Dimento, "Should we prosecute corporations and/or individuals?" in F. Pearce and L. Snider, eds, *Corporate Crime: Contemporary Debates* (Toronto: University of Toronto Press, 1995), pp. 72–86.

12. D. O. Friedrichs, "White crime and the class-race-gender construct," in M. D. Schwartz and D. Milovanic, eds, *Race, Gender, and Class* (New York: Garland Publishing, 1996), pp. 141–158.

13. D. Weisburd, S. Wheeler, E. Waring, and N. Bode, *Crimes of the Middle Classes: White Collar Offenders in the Federal Courts* (New Haven, CT: Yale University Press, 1991), p. 182.

14. D. O. Friedrichs, *Trusted Criminals: White Collar Crime in Contemporary Society*, 3rd ed. (Belmont, CA: Wadsworth, 2007), p. 8.

15. Ibid., p. 41.

16. J. W. Coleman, *The Criminal Elite: The Sociology of White Collar Crime* (New York: St. Martin's Press, 1985), p. 5.

17. Friedrichs, *op. cit.*, 2007, p. 8.

18. J. W. Coleman, *The Criminal Elite: Understanding White Collar Crime*, 5th ed. (New York: Worth Publishers, 2002), pp. 16–88.

19. Friedrichs, *op. cit.*, 2007, pp. 40–43, 45.

20. Rosoff, Pontell, and Tillman, *op. cit.*, p. 27.

21. Ann L. Pastore and Kathleen Maguire, eds, *2003 Sourcebook of Criminal Justice Statistics*, http://www.albany.edu/sourcebook/, p. 297, Table 3.111.

22. D. O. Friedrichs, *Trusted Criminals: White Collar Crime in Contemporary Society* (Belmont, CA: Wadsworth, 1996), p. 55.

23. S. P. Shapiro, *Wayward Capitalists: Target of the Securities and Exchange Commission* (New Haven, CT: Yale University Press, 1984).

24. G. S. Coffey, "The Criminal Exploitation of Ambiguity: A Multi-Level Analysis of Fraudulent Telemarketers," unpublished doctoral dissertation. University of Tennessee, Knoxville, TN, 2003, p. 103.

25. Friedrichs, *op. cit.*, 2007, p. 8.

26. H. Croall, *White Collar Crime* (Buckingham, UK: Open University Press, 1992), p. 10.

CHAPTER 2

Getting Started

Key Terms and Concepts

- Informant
- Information Analysis
- Initial Inquiries
- Inside Information
- Intent
- Pattern of Misconduct
- Prosecutor

Hopefully, Chapter 1 has established a foundation of motivation and enthusiasm to take on white collar crime. Frankly, these are important prerequisites for success given the ambiguities, frustrations, uncertainties, and lengthy involvements frequently associated with these investigations. For many investigators, white collar crime is just not their "thing." These cases can be ambiguous because unlike many conventional crime scenarios, whether a violation of law occurred might not be readily apparent. Again, unlike many conventional crime investigations, suspects in white collar crime cases are often inaccessible for interview due to the presence of legal representation, which, along with the need to acquire and analyze large volumes of records, can lead to frustration. Compounding these feelings is a sense of uncertainty that can arise about whether the investigation will lead to any type of enforcement action. The suspects are often known at the outset of the case (or soon thereafter); they either refuse to cooperate or are only accessible for interview in the presence of their attorneys, so information developed through such interviews can be quite limited and/or the alleged wrongdoing is explained away in an arguably defensible manner; and it is not clear that other available evidence will sustain the sought-after enforcement action. And of course, this scenario can be playing out over a period of months, if not longer.

Fortunately, these same case characteristics that encourage many investigators to seek positions in "street crime" squads are looked upon as interesting challenges by others in the profession. While interest, enthusiasm, motivation, and/or a sense of challenge may be necessary prerequisites for the white collar crime investigator, these attributes alone do not spell success. Would-be white collar crime investigators need to acquire a skill set that is uniquely applicable to these types of cases, and ideally the opportunity to work along with experienced white collar crime investigators. While the process of evolving into a skilled white collar crime investigator takes time, it is a necessary learning curve to overcome. Without establishing this type of foundation, even those most enthusiastic and motivated to conquer white collar crime are likely to find themselves "spinning their wheels."

Obviously, investigative agencies with white collar crime responsibilities must play an institutional role in providing training and mentorship to develop investigators who can handle these types of cases. What might not be readily apparent, however, is the need for other structural components within an agency that help to foster success in these investigations. Among the necessary structures are programs to gather complaints, intelligence, and other information about offending that lie within an agency's investigative jurisdiction. Both investigators and agency managers need to recognize the fundamental roles that these types of structures and programs play in the eventual success of their white collar crime enforcement efforts.

INFORMATION GATHERING: INQUIRIES, COMPLAINTS, AND INTELLIGENCE

While not true in all instances, many white collar crime investigations begin as a result of information received from outside the investigative arena, such as members of the public and whistleblowers. One exception to this general rule can arise in agencies that have authority to conduct routine compliance audits and inspections on activities within their oversight jurisdiction. Such inspections or audits can provide a proactive means to identify misconduct. Another proactive approach includes undercover investigations, although such efforts are commonly predicated upon the receipt of information that alleges wrongdoing.

Thus, given the importance of receiving and/or identifying information about white collar crime violations, the need to establish the means to acquire this information is essential to investigative success. While the frequency of many types of crime is somewhat in question due to nonreporting, this problem is especially true for white collar crime. In fact, Rosoff, Pontell, and Tillman claim that most white collar crimes are not reported.[1] They further claim that many victims of white collar crime do not even know they have been victimized,[2] an assessment also put forth by Friedrichs.[3] Thus, collecting information about white collar offending presents special challenges that must be overcome if an agency and its investigative personnel are to successfully address this problem.

Agency Approaches

In general, if information about white-collar offending is to be reported, victims and potential victims need to understand what risks and harms are lurking about and what to do or where to go if they become aware of such activity. Thus, for agencies with white collar crime investigative responsibility, it makes little sense to maintain a low profile about who they are and what they do. It can be argued, in fact, that marketing and public relations do have a role in this type of law enforcement. Consumer protection agencies play a well-established role in white collar crime prevention by publicizing the latest consumer frauds and frequently acting as intermediaries in attempting to resolve consumer disputes. While their crime prevention efforts are laudable and should be pursued by all white collar crime agencies, to what extent victimization is prevented through these programs is difficult to measure. To be sure, it is likely that many would-be victims have avoided becoming loss statistics, but one very valuable by-product of these crime prevention programs is that the agency that can provide consumer help is identified and such agencies are often the recipients of a good deal of information about this type of offending. Particularly when consumer protection agencies have only civil/administrative authority, it is not uncommon for criminal investigators to rely on these agencies for complaints when criminal violations are believed to be present.

Thus, the lessons that can be learned from the consumer protection agency scenario are as follows:

- White collar enforcement agencies need to be visible to either the general public or the specialized constituency they serve. This means they need to inform the general public or their special constituency who they are, where they are located and how they can be contacted, and what they are responsible for in terms of investigation/enforcement.

- The above efforts will be of little value unless they are preceded by information as to why this agency is important to the general public or special constituency, which usually means the identification of risks and dangers within the jurisdictional environment of the agency that can cause harm and victimization. If the general public or select members thereof are first alerted to the potential for being harmed or victimized in an environment they frequent, they are more likely to pay attention to the organization that is bringing this message. All of which means an effective crime prevention campaign is essential for agency visibility. Such campaigns should include information about types of prevalent offending, how to prevent becoming victimized, and how to report violations when encountered. If feasible and applicable to the agency context, offering a dispute resolution service in appropriate circumstances may motivate victims to submit reports even if response/compliance on the part of the offending party is voluntary. Many customer/business-type complaints arise through mistakes or misunderstandings and can be resolved by bringing the two parties together. The typical practice in this regard is to refer the customer's complaint to the offending party and request a response back through the agency.

- Making use of the mass media and the Internet are probably two of the most cost-effective strategies for increasing agency visibility and engaging in a victimization prevention campaign. However, preparing informative and attractive printed material will also be necessary for public dissemination. Needless to say, these types of responsibilities would seem to fall outside the normal range of the knowledge and skills possessed by the typical investigator, and many investigative organizations, taking a cue from the corporate sector, have employed public relations or media professionals to provide these services. This would certainly be a *best practice* to adopt.

Information Submission

Again, a primary reason for increasing agency visibility is to enhance its access to information about offending within its jurisdiction. It follows then that the agency must also establish a structure or program that will facilitate the flow of this information. The Internet comes readily to mind as a convenient way (for some) to communicate this type of information. The same website that is developed to enhance agency visibility and provide prevention advice, can be designed to afford opportunities for submitting inquiries, complaints, and/or information on offending. Of course, this means that responses to the website must be monitored by "live" people who have the training and experience to evaluate the information being submitted.

Obviously, not everyone (at least as of this writing) has or will use computer/Internet technology. Therefore, agencies must establish systems to receive inquiries, complaints, and information by mail and telephone as well. Submissions via mail can be evaluated by the same personnel who monitor website submissions. Procedures for receiving information submitted by telephone will vary depending upon the size and scope (i.e., geographic) of the agency. National agencies might find it advantageous to establish toll-free numbers that are received at a call center. Alternatively, each office location of an agency might wish to receive inquiry, complaint, and/or information calls directly, a procedure that is obviously applicable to local and small state-level agencies. In any event, personnel who take telephone calls of this nature require special training in dealing directly with individuals who in all likelihood will present a wide range of emotions and abilities to communicate. Needless to say, having agency personnel on hand who can converse in languages other than English, as necessary, is essential. Regardless of the language, however, being able to elicit necessary information from the angry, the distraught, the reluctant, and/or those who are simply verbally challenged, and then making an appropriate evaluation of how to handle the information received are underappreciated and all too rare skills. The point is that telephone staffing is a very important function within any organization not only because of the information that is received in this manner, but also because the employees performing these duties can place the organization in a positive or negative light, depending upon their telephone finesse. And aside from etiquette, whether at a centralized call center or in a local office, one absolutely essential skill for these personnel to master is to know when a call needs some type of immediate attention, such as referral to an investigator. For example, a telephone call from a disgruntled employee at a company allegedly engaged in fraud reporting that records are being removed or destroyed needs immediate referral to an investigator, not a written report that might reach an investigator's desk days later.

Keep in mind as well that individuals might want to simply walk into an agency office to file a complaint or provide information. Depending upon the nature and location of the agency or office, this may or may not be a common practice, but in all instances arrangements to receive information in this manner should be established, consistent with the need to do so.

What Information Should Be Collected?

Whether by mail, over the phone or Internet, or on a "walk-in" basis, agencies should formulate a standard set of questions that will furnish a basis to properly evaluate the information provided and facilitate follow-up as necessary. That said, while it is very important to collect the right information, there is a balance between asking what is needed and asking for too much. Completing lengthy forms for mail-in or Internet submission can discourage would-be providers of information. Thus, it is recommended that complaint/inquiry forms be designed for ease of completion, keeping in mind that details can be ascertained in follow-up interviews, if necessary.

The three primary elements to capture are the (1) identity of the provider of the information; (2) the identity of the person/firm that the information bears on; and (3) the substance of the information. Provider identity should include name, address, telephone number (work/home), and e-mail address. Along with this information, some agencies have begun requesting respondents to provide their year of birth because of enhanced penalties for victimizing the elderly. Aside from the enhanced penalties themselves, white collar offending that appears to be targeting elderly people would likely have prosecutive appeal due to the vulnerability of these victims. Thus, requesting this data along with contact information does not seem overly burdensome and could also be highly relevant in evaluating the merits of any case that might evolve from this referral.

Identifying the person or firm that is the subject of the information being provided should follow the usual format of name, address, telephone number, and e-mail/website address. Here, however, if information concerns a business entity or other type of organization as opposed to an individual, inquiry should be made about the names and titles of the persons who were dealt with.

Requesting the substantive information perhaps requires the greatest judgment and consideration. Whether the provider is self-completing/submitting the information or agency personnel are taking it over the telephone or in person, this initial process should focus on acquiring the salient points only. Just as removing impediments to the acquisition of information from the public is a consideration, so too is the reduction of burden and inefficiency on agency personnel who receive and analyze this data. In this regard, a determination should be made whether to simply solicit a brief narrative of the complaint/information or have it furnished through a series of appropriate prompts or categories. Arguments can be made one way or another and the decision as to which way to proceed might vary from agency to agency depending upon unique needs and circumstances. The "free-form" brief narrative option does allow for flexibility in the response that is sometimes valuable, especially in complex scenarios that do not fit into limited choice answer selections. Whether the information acquired in this manner, however, is sufficient and/or intelligible might vary considerably and it also might prove to be a more time consuming option for agency evaluation and analysis. In addition, it is often important for agency evaluation to fully understand the scope of any alleged victimization, including the amount of money lost and the dates of the events being reported. Most agencies will also have concerns about geographic and/or statutory jurisdiction and the specifics in these respects must be requested. For instance, federal agencies may need to know about interstate involvement and/or the means of communication that were employed. (See Box 2–1.) Accordingly, this type of information must be specifically requested when applicable. For many agencies, a combination of necessary specific questions and a "free-form" brief narrative option might be the best design for their information-gathering instruments.

Box 2–1   The "workhorses" in white collar crime enforcement: mail fraud and wire fraud

Throughout this volume frequent mention is made about charging mail and/or wire fraud in federal white collar crime prosecutions. As discussed in Chapter 1, the federal mail fraud statute (18 USC 1341) was enacted in response to interstate frauds that were conducted through the mails. As technology advanced and brought forth electronic forms of communication, the federal wire fraud statute (18 USC 1343) was enacted to combat frauds conducted via the telephone, radio, television, and now computers/Internet. These two statutes have proven invaluable in federal white collar crime enforcement efforts as they have been successfully applied to a wide array of schemes to defraud. Accordingly, the collection and analysis of information alleging white collar crime should identify any uses of the mails, telephones, radio, television, and/or Internet communications that *further* a scheme to defraud, in addition to any agency or crime-specific violations. The text of these two statutes follows:

18 USC 1341: Mail Fraud

Whoever, having devised or intending to devise any scheme or artifice to defraud, or for obtaining money or property by means of false or fraudulent pretenses, representations, or promises, or to sell, dispose of, loan, exchange, alter, give away, distribute, supply, or furnish or procure for unlawful use any counterfeit or spurious coin, obligation, security, or other article, or anything represented to be or intimated or held out to be such counterfeit or spurious article, for the purpose of executing such scheme or artifice or attempting so to do, places in any post office or authorized depository for mail matter, any matter or thing whatever to be sent or delivered by the Postal Service, or deposits or causes to be deposited any matter or thing whatever to be sent or delivered by any private or commercial interstate carrier, or takes or receives therefrom, any such matter or thing, or knowingly causes to be delivered by mail or such carrier according to the direction thereon, or at the place at which it is directed to be delivered by the person to whom it is addressed, any such matter or thing, shall be fined under this title or imprisoned not more than 20 years, or both. If the violation affects a financial institution, such person shall be fined not more than $1,000,000 or imprisoned not more than 30 years, or both.

18 USC 1343: Wire Fraud

Whoever, having devised or intending to devise any scheme or artifice to defraud, or for obtaining money or property by means of false or fraudulent pretenses, representations, or promises, transmits or causes to be transmitted by means of wire, radio, or television communication in interstate or foreign commerce, any writings, signs, signals, pictures, or sounds for the purpose of executing such scheme or artifice, shall be fined under this title or imprisoned not more than 20 years, or both. If the violation affects a financial institution, such person shall be fined not more than $1,000,000 or imprisoned not more than 30 years, or both.

Seeking Out Information

One of the basic premises of this chapter is that unlike many types of offending, white collar crime is believed to be heavily underreported. While establishing agency structures to better elicit offending information can be an essential component of successful investigations, investigators must recognize that this source alone may not be adequate to develop sufficient evidence and other information needed to pursue an investigation. Now the burden shifts to them to develop additional and alternative sources.

Depending upon the agency and its mission, there may or may not be other organizations that share similar jurisdiction or have a mutual interest in a particular type of offending. However, in most instances there will likely be such other organizations, whether in the public or private sectors, or perhaps both. Effectively addressing white collar offending is best accomplished when all parties sharing a common interest cooperate and place whatever information they have in the hands of the agency that can best address a particular case. Again using the example of consumer fraud, in most jurisdictions several different organizations might receive information and complaints on this type of activity. Private organizations such as the Better Business Bureau have no investigative authority but are usually willing to provide information to agencies that do have such authority, especially when their efforts to resolve consumer complaints on a voluntary basis are not meeting with success. Likewise, in some jurisdictions, state and local consumer protection agencies are more compliance/resolution oriented than enforcement oriented, and these organizations are usually excellent sources of complaints and information when an investigation needs to be pursued. Needless to say, investigators in enforcement agencies that handle consumer frauds would be wise to develop close working relationships with personnel in these types of organizations. In fact, the ideal relationship for investigators to strive for with these organizations is one where they are contacted whenever suspicions arise about the volume of complaints being received and/or nature of the complaints.

An alternative scenario involving multiple agencies with shared interest and/or jurisdiction is one where these agencies have actual investigative/enforcement authority. Two "best case" results can evolve out of this type of scenario. First, there is some decision on the part of one or more of these agencies that while they have received complaints and/or information alleging a particular offense, another agency is viewed as better suited to pursue the matter and all relevant material will be turned over to that agency. This type of decision can evolve from jurisdictional considerations, the availability or absence of appropriate statutes, resource limitations including the lack of expertise, and/or perhaps other issues. The second "best case" result is an agreement to pursue a joint investigation among those agencies with shared jurisdiction. Not only does taking this approach sometimes satisfy the often-competitive nature of investigators and their agencies, but it is also a means to provide additional resources to the investigation that might not be available when only a single agency is involved.

However, a twofold caveat needs to be issued in order for this approach to be truly a "best case" result. First, specific interagency authority and responsibility should be established at the outset. While this sometimes means that a "lead" agency is designated and essentially that agency will have ultimate decision-making authority in the case, successful joint investigations have proceeded with decision-making authority shared by supervisors of the participating organizations. Another successful approach to organizing and managing a multiagency effort is for the investigation to be managed by the prosecutor's office. As will be discussed at the conclusion of this chapter, typically the role of the prosecutor in white collar crime cases is by nature collaborative with the investigators. Thus, a well-respected and experienced prosecutor can sometimes be an excellent consensus selection to lead a multiagency investigation.

The second caveat involves personal relationships among the investigators. Multiagency investigations work best when there is harmony among the investigators working on the case. Obviously in the "real world" it will not always be possible to achieve this goal, but it is also in the "real world" that friction and animosity within an investigative team can become so disruptive as to impede progress on the case. In situations where an agency is requested to participate and contribute personnel to a multiagency investigative team, it is wise to consider the "human" element when selecting investigators for such assignments. Those who have previously established effective working relationships with one or more of other agency representatives and/or who possess good interpersonal skills are most likely to make a positive contribution to the case.

Among the many reasons to establish liaison with investigative counterparts in other agencies is to lay a foundation for an effective working relationship in the event of a multiagency investigation. An ideal scenario is one in which the investigators who share jurisdictional interests in a given geographic area are in routine contact with one another and join forces on cases where there is a mutual benefit to do so.

Informant/Inside Information

The term *informant* tends to take on a "cloak and dagger" connotation that is sometimes accurate and sometimes not. The cultivation and use of informants in law enforcement, including white collar crime investigations, is well established. However, just as the parameters for white collar crime that are being applied here are broad, so too is the definition of an informant. Certainly some white collar crime investigators have responsibility for cases where the traditional "cloak and dagger" concept of informant applies, that is, a person whose personal affiliations afford knowledge of criminal wrongdoing, perhaps on an ongoing basis. Cases involving credit card and check fraud, insurance fraud, and telemarketing fraud, to name a few examples, would seem to fall into the category of white collar crime cases where this type of informant could be encountered. However, an informant does not have to be a "wanna be" underworld type. Nor does an informant have to be a person who provides information on an ongoing basis. A respectable and honest employee or coworker who furnishes information about wrongdoing in their occupational setting can also be considered an informant, even on a one-case basis. Likewise, a nonvictimized customer or vendor who has dealings with a company might become aware of wrongdoing and wish to pass this information along to the appropriate authorities. Aside from illustrating that informants do not have to fit the "cloak and dagger" stereotype, these examples should also point out that even for white collar crime investigators, whose responsibilities do not include the more traditional "informant-type" cases, opportunities to develop information in this manner are sometimes available and should be pursued accordingly.

It must be recognized, however, that informant development and management in the more traditional sense, that is, a person closely aligned with criminal activity, perhaps on an ongoing basis, requires training, experience, and oversight that may lie beyond the scope of many white collar crime agencies, especially those with only civil/administrative authority. Conversely, those agencies with broad criminal enforcement jurisdiction will most likely have developed management and training programs for applying this investigative approach to the full range of case types they address. As the focus of this volume lies beyond general investigative techniques, only limited guidance on this topic will be offered here:

1. use of informants can prove valuable in white collar crime cases;
2. investigators must follow their agency policies and practices in developing and managing informants; and
3. investigators in agencies that do not permit the use of this technique or where training and oversight programs are not established should not pursue information in this manner.

However, the guidance offered above is with regard to dealing with informants in the more traditional sense, and not members of the law-abiding public who wish to voluntarily (although perhaps confidentially) provide information on a one-time basis about offending they have become aware of. While such individuals can be looked upon as informants, they could also simply be considered witnesses or sources (if this is a more palatable agency designation). Since such individuals could provide valuable information about offending that might be difficult to detect otherwise, another agency-level initiative could be the establishment of a confidential "tip" line to solicit telephone calls from people who wish to report violations. Again, the agency website, literature, and media announcements could be used to publicize this means of providing information to the agency.

On the individual level, investigators may find it advantageous to align themselves with organizations whose purpose is to bring together individuals who share a concern with regard to a particular type of offending, often from both public and private sectors. In many locations industry groups such as insurers, credit card issuers, and bankers, as well as consumer protection advocates such as the Better Business Bureau, have undertaken initiatives that bring together security and law enforcement officials for educational and information-sharing purposes. Such opportunities provide a basis not only for establishing effective interagency working relationships but also for the referral of information, including the identities of individuals who can be of assistance relative to a case.

Finally, agencies with regulatory/investigative oversight of particular industries, especially when this oversight includes authority to conduct compliance audits and inspections, should recognize that they could be in an excellent position to receive "insider" information from individuals who work within the area of their jurisdiction. Compliance audits and inspections often place regulatory officials "on-site" in circumstances that might be of a more routine nature, which might, in turn, provide opportunities to develop friendly professional relationships with some employees. Such relationships might at some point pay off with the referral of "insider" information about offending within the company. Agency personnel who have frequent contact with industry employees, while maintaining a necessary professional distance, might find that avoiding an overly officious demeanor will make them more approachable for such overtures.

Information from Records

Again, keeping in mind that white collar offending is underreported and individuals might not even be aware of their victimization, in most cases voluntarily submitted complaints represent only a fraction of the victims. Thus, it can be very advantageous to the investigation to make inquiries with people or organizations who have had contact with the subject of the case but who have not complained. Identifying potential victims from records obtained from the alleged wrongdoer and/or third party organizations can be very necessary to the investigation. Without making such inquiries, the full scope of the case might not be determined. Frankly, the more victims, the more likely an enforcement action will be undertaken and be successful. Moreover, ascertaining the experiences of noncomplainants might very enlightening with regard to the alleged misconduct. Experiences that are in stark contrast to the voluntarily submitted complaints can provide a warning sign that a consistent pattern of misconduct is not present, a topic that will be discussed further below. The point to be made for now is that an affirmative attempt to identify and contact noncomplaining potential victims should be undertaken, and identifying such potential victims is often accomplished through the analysis of documents and records.

INFORMATION ANALYSIS

Once sources of information and intelligence are established, the next step in identifying white collar offending is to ensure proper analysis of the data being collected. An initial review should determine whether the information being reported is within the jurisdiction of the agency to which it has been submitted. For instance, the Federal Bureau of Investigation would normally refer information about federal income tax violations to the Internal Revenue Service. Likewise, local agencies that receive consumer fraud complaints about a company in another state will frequently refer this information to that state's consumer protection agency and/or the Federal Trade Commission or other federal agency. Alternatively, a local law enforcement agency that receives a consumer fraud complaint about a local firm will likely refer this matter to the appropriate local or state consumer protection agency.

Once jurisdictional issues are settled, whether the information constitutes evidence of some type of law violation should be evaluated. Perhaps, the better way to address this question in the white collar crime context is to determine whether the information provides potential evidence of some type of offending. The reason for having to take this cautious approach is that on an isolated basis, information that suggests wrongdoing might simply reflect a mistake or oversight. It is in these types of situations that agencies can often be successful in acting as an intermediary to facilitate a resolution. Alternatively, the receipt of multiple complaints or inquiries on the same firm or individual should be a basis for further examination.

Patterns of Misconduct

Again, white collar offending tends to be underreported and many victims don't even know of their victimization. However, the emphasis placed here on establishing aggressive programs to solicit information about white collar offending has less to do with fully identifying the scope of this problem generally, and much more to do with being able to develop a pattern of misconduct by those who are white collar crime violators. Isolated complaints about a person or firm, especially in the case of well-known business entities are often easily explained away as a mistake, oversight, customer misunderstanding, and so on. In these situations, they are often satisfactorily resolved once the parties are "brought together." However, multiple complaints or inquiries can begin to establish a pattern of misconduct that should be viewed as a "red flag" in terms of evidence of offending. Most individuals or firms who conduct transactions with the public do so legitimately, both because it's a "good business/customer relations" practice and out of a sense of fairness and decency. Yes, mistakes and oversights do occur and sometimes with more than just an isolated impact. Most individuals and firms that operate in good faith do not hide from such problems, but rather acknowledge them and make amends. Thus, information that establishes a pattern of misconduct can possibly constitute evidence of wrongdoing, whether criminal or civil/administrative in nature. Certainly, a strong pattern of misconduct provides a compelling basis to pursue civil/administrative enforcement where appropriate, but such a pattern can also be powerful evidence in a criminal case as well. In white collar crime prosecutions juries must often make inferences from the evidence presented as to the intent of the defendant(s). When presented with multiple tales of victimization from witnesses, many defendants find themselves hard-pressed to provide a viable explanation about why these events occurred if they were not, in fact, intended. Voluntarily submitted complaints and inquiries tend to be the "tip of the iceberg" in terms of victimization, and relying solely on this method of establishing a pattern of misconduct for purposes of a criminal prosecution is often insufficient. However, an agency program that aggressively solicits complaints, inquiries, and other information which in turn is properly evaluated (as will be further discussed below) is likely to identify those situations that warrant further investigative attention as possible violations.

INITIAL INQUIRIES

To be clear, at the initial complaint/information analysis stage a pattern of misconduct is only one factor (although an important one) in determining whether to investigate further. Other factors that might be a sound basis for doing so include a large financial loss and the nature of the circumstances being reported. A single complaint alleging credit card fraud and/or identity theft once in the hands of the appropriate agency will normally trigger an investigation. However, other frauds are more subtle and again, often underreported; thus, an obvious pattern of misconduct may not present itself. For example, consider a relatively common fraud known as an advance fee scheme. In this scheme a purported loan broker represents that he/she can obtain needed financing for a would-be borrower, but an up-front payment usually consisting of a percentage of the loan proceeds is required. Of course, after the payment is made the loan never material-izes and if the broker just doesn't disappear altogether, he/she will put forth a string of stalling tactics and eventual false excuses why the deal could not be consummated. These types of schemes often do not generate many voluntarily submitted complaints because the borrowers tend to be embarrassed; they simply write off the up-front fee as a business expense; and/or are sometimes reluctant to deal with law enforcement (e.g., people who seek out exotic forms of financing instead of dealing with traditional lenders often have poor credit histories, have something to hide, and/or are involved in ill-conceived or risky business ventures). This would be the type of situation where just one complaint should provide a basis for further inquiry. Most agencies can probably point to types of allegations that are unique to their jurisdictions that are almost always indicators of wrongdoing, even based on only one complaint.

Of course, other factors also come into play when evaluating complaints, inquiries, and information that might suggest the need for further investigation. For example, names or aliases of known offenders and/or business names or addresses that have previously been associated with complaints might be spotted. Whatever the basis for deciding to look into complaints, inquiries, or information further, there are several routine investigative steps that can be taken to determine the likelihood of illegalities. If the information being evaluated provides the name of an individual(s), a criminal history check can be performed using all available agency (federal and local) databases. Some commercially available databases that compile public information can also be queried by name of individual, and might be able to provide personal identifiers, addresses, driver's license and vehicle registration information, and so on. In fact, this latter information might be necessary in order to conduct the aforementioned criminal history check. Keep in mind that the names furnished in complaints, and so on, might be aliases. Again, with regard to databases, government agency and otherwise, keeping apprised as to what is available is a character-istic of the successful investigator. As agencies have advanced technologically many have computerized records of their investigations, thus facilitating interagency inquiries. The key issue then is to become aware of what agencies might have helpful information on hand that they can share. The bottom line relative to all of these types of inquiries, however, is that if the individuals in question have prior criminal records, especially for the same type of activity currently being examined, and/or were subjects of prior investigations by other agencies, another "red flag" has been raised.

Searching public records such as business, occupational, and corporate records is another relatively easy inquiry that can affect the evaluation of complaints, inquiries, or other information alleging wrongdoing. Depending upon the jurisdiction, most organizations, if they are conducting some type of business transactions with the public or providing some service to the public, often have to register with a governmental authority, usually at the state and/or municipal level. Certainly, when these requirements are avoided altogether, concern about the bona fides of the subject organization is justified. However, another important benefit to be derived from these types of inquiries is identification of the principal(s) in the organization and in turn, they can then be run through the above-described criminal history and agency indices. Also, taking an enforcement action against a business (as opposed to individuals) normally requires the identification of responsible individuals within the organization so that service of process can be effected, thus providing another reason to conduct these inquiries. Of course, information on these types of filings, too, can be falsified, a finding which would also be another "red flag."

Finally, these types of inquiries might help to establish true individual identities in an organization as opposed to assumed names/aliases. The use of an assumed names/alias in some types of business scenarios such as sales to the public is sometimes done for allegedly benign reasons (e.g., to protect the privacy of one who has dealings with the public). In other instances, the rationale is simply to escape identification/association with wrongdoing. While the former scenario should not be dismissed without any level of suspicion, obviously the use of an assumed name for the latter reason raises another "red flag."

Verifying the address of the subject of the complaint, inquiry, or information can provide two benefits. First, if there is need to make contact by mail or in person, verifying the address (through an inquiry with the Postal Inspection Service, real estate records, utility company inquiries, etc.) might be a time-saving step in the event the subject has moved (which in that case, a forwarding address might be provided incident to an inquiry with the Postal Service). Conversely, if the subject in question is not known to reside or do business at the location provided in the complaint, inquiry, or other information, or perhaps left without leaving any forwarding order, further investigation might be in order. Such steps could include determining the identities of the current occupants at the address using the same sources discussed above. An inquiry through the Postal Inspection Service of the letter carrier who serves the address *might* result in useful information about the current and former occupants. However, before making this type of inquiry it should be understood that letter carriers are under no obligation to cooperate in this manner (and may not if they feel it might jeopardize their safety) and if they do so, they can only furnish information from their memory (as opposed to referring to particular pieces of mail they might have on hand for delivery). Also, no guarantees can be made that the inquiry will be kept confidential.

Finally, a visit to the location can be made whether simply for "ride-by" purposes, a covert surveillance in an attempt to identify individuals who are present at the location, or to interview current occupants about the previous occupants. Visiting the location in person offers several opportunities. First, it can be determined if the address really exists and what type of structure (or lack thereof) is in place. As will be discussed in a later chapter on search warrants, the premises to be searched must be fully described in an application for a search warrant and these details should be obtained through on-site observation. Second, when the identities of the subjects are not known or if it is necessary to identify other individuals who frequent the premises in question (e.g., employees, customers), a covert surveillance might afford opportunities to address these needs by taking note of vehicle tags and/or photographing people and activities of interest. Third, if the party in question has departed the premises, interviews of current occupants (when appropriate) might develop useful information about the departed party's activities and whereabouts. Also, this type of visit might offer the opportunity to take possession of any relevant abandoned property (e.g., business records and other evidence relating to matter being investigated) left behind by subjects of the inquiry. However, seizing abandoned property should only be undertaken if it can be established that (1) the items of interest have, in fact, been abandoned; and (2) the person currently controlling/occupying the property where they are located consents to their seizure.

A final initial investigative step to consider is to interview one or more persons who filed a complaint, inquiry, or other information in an effort to obtain further details. Especially in complex transactions, this interview might very well be the first of several, but at the very least this first personal interview should verify facts that could be construed as violations of law and establish the extent of any victimization. These initial interviews can be used to help establish probable cause, the basis for many investigative and enforcement actions that will be discussed in later chapters.

Initial Investigative Results

The results from the initial investigative steps described above should answer some important questions about any further course of action. First and foremost would be to determine what violation(s) is alleged and at least preliminarily assess the likelihood of proving that this violation(s), in fact, occurred. While identifying the type of alleged violation in a complaint might not be problematic, assessing the probability of a successful enforcement action at this point can be fraught with uncertainties. For instance, complaints of failure to receive merchandise or receipt of misrepresented merchandise incident to telemarketing sales can be correctly viewed as potential mail and/or wire fraud violations, but in the early stages of an investigation it might be difficult to predict the likelihood of a successful prosecution. Conversely, it would be easier to look upon complaints of credit card fraud and/or identity theft as viable (meaning prosecutable) violations of law. Likewise, complaints alleging the receipt of fictitious invoices (i.e., documents that are actually solicitations for the purchase of goods/services, but resemble invoices with a "payment due" amount prominently displayed) are an easier scenario to assess. The mailing of solicitations in the guise of billings is defined as illegal by statute with a prescribed remedy [39 USC 3001(d); and 39 USC 3005(a) which authorizes the issuance of an administrative False Representation Order in these cases]. The distinctions being drawn here revolve around the critical issue of being able to prove intent to violate the law when that element is required. In the telemarketing scenario described above, the nonreceipt of merchandise could be blamed on shipping and manufacturing delays, situations that would not establish intent to defraud. Allegations of merchandise misrepresentation could be defended by arguing the promotional material was accurate, but misinterpreted by the buyers; or if it was misleading, this outcome was not intended. Whether such arguments forestall a prosecution or persuade a jury not to convict will vary from case to case, but in these types of cases as well as others, uncertainties in proving intent will be encountered time and time again.

The good news is that even in some criminal prosecutions, the intent issue is less problematic. Again referring to the examples provided above, why else would someone take over another person's identity and use it to obtain credit cards, cash advances, loans, and the like, if there was no intent to defraud? On the civil/administrative side, some regulations can be violated without the necessity of having (or least proving) intent to cause a violation. A sanction can be levied simply by establishing a preponderance of the evidence that the violation occurred and was caused by the respondent. Of course, these sanctions involve civil penalties and various types of compliance orders and not criminal penalties such as imprisonment.

Beyond the Intent Issue

Make no mistake: when intent to commit the offense is an issue, it will loom large throughout the investigation and probably into the prosecution stage as well. Nevertheless, in further evaluating the preliminary investigative results, developing evidence of intent, while crucial when necessary, is not the only type of evidence that will be necessary. Anticipate establishing the standard "Who," "What," "Where," "When," "Why," and "How." All the allegations of the illegal act(s) as outlined in a charging document (e.g., indictment, civil complaint) must be proven through the presentation of evidence, both testimonial and documentary (which is normally introduced through testimony). Thus, an inventory, so to speak, must be undertaken to survey what evidence is already on hand and what needs to be acquired and/or developed.

This inventory can start with assessing what the initial provider(s) of the information that caused the investigation to be undertaken has on hand. In most instances, evidence from this source would at least be testimonial in nature (i.e., what happened), although it is wise to inquire about the existence of any types of relevant documents in their possession as well, such as promotional literature, correspondence, contracts/work agreements, payment records, and so on. If the source is a business or government agency (as opposed to an individual complainant), it may be necessary to identify the individuals in the organization who have personal knowledge of the alleged violation and the existence/whereabouts of the relevant records. Although infrequent, even when organizational entities are victims, they still might request a subpoena for the release of any needed documents; so don't be surprised if this request occurs. In fact, it might be prudent to inquire up front about whether they will voluntarily surrender any needed documents and make available employees who can provide testimony for interviews.

The need for other witness interviews should also be anticipated. Individuals aside from victims often have information about the offending conduct. Such witnesses can be of the "innocent bystander" variety or perhaps employees, associates, neighbors, friends, and relatives of the alleged offenders. Of course, consideration can also be given to interviewing the investigative subjects themselves. Later chapters will discuss in detail interviewing and obtaining testimonial evidence. For now, it is simply important to start thinking about who needs to be interviewed, and establish any appropriate strategy and/or the level of priority in each case. In addition, the level of cooperativeness of each person so identified should also be assessed. In those instances where a person is anticipated to be reluctant or hostile, an appropriate plan to address such an encounter should be established, which might include obtaining this person's testimony before a grand jury.

Next, consider what types of documentary evidence might be needed and assess the availability of this evidence. Aside from public records, documentary evidence under the control of third parties will likely require subpoenas for their release. The need for records from banks, telephone companies, insurance companies, mortgage and title companies, real estate agencies, and investment firms frequently arise in white collar crime investigations and normally will be released only incident to the receipt of a subpoena.

As suggested above, accessing public records incident to making an initial evaluation of allegations is routine, but if the investigation is to move forward, consider the need or availability of any other records that either fall into this category or are maintained by government agencies that can be released for official uses.

Gaining access to records of the alleged offender is often a necessary component of a white collar crime investigation. The more pertinent question then is, how best to go about doing this? Some regulatory agencies might have access to the types of records needed by simply exercising inspection authority or utilizing their own administrative subpoenas. Agencies with criminal investigative authority normally must determine whether to obtain the needed records through a grand jury subpoena or search warrant. These techniques will be discussed at length in later chapters, but for now some preliminary considerations will be put forth in order to formulate an investigative strategy. Obtaining records through the execution of a search warrant is highly effective since investigators go on site to personally seize what they have identified as necessary and relevant to their case. Needless to say, this is a very intrusive action that must be approved by a judge and the investigator seeking such approval must provide probable cause that a particular crime was committed and that particular evidence of this crime is present at the location to be searched.

Obtaining offender records through a grand jury subpoena does not require probable cause and is much less intrusive. However, the alleged offender, not an investigator, accomplishes the gathering and production of records sought by a subpoena. Although subpoenas are demands and not requests for the production of the requested items, in some cases there can be concerns about full and truthful compliance. In determining the appropriate route to take in obtaining the alleged offender's records, such issues as knowing where the needed records are located and the nature of the alleged offender are often considerations. Don't be surprised that absent information about impending destruction of records or other acts of obstruction of justice, subpoenas will typically (but not always) be issued when well-known, established firms are the subjects of the inquiry. This standard might also apply to individuals who are well known in the community, as well. However, this generalization is far from being "hard and fast." At the other end of spectrum is ongoing activity that is clearly criminal in nature and is being committed by either unknown individuals or those with a known offending history. When and if the location of records can be established in these situations, obtaining them via search warrant is the obvious choice.

And finally, we come full circle and get back to where we started off in this chapter. A very relevant question is what is known about the scope of the alleged misconduct. When the fact scenario at hand suggests possible widespread victimization, as indicated above, experience teaches that voluntarily submitted complaints represent only the "tip of the iceberg." However, even in cases that might seem to be more limited in scope, it is worthwhile to look beyond the complaints on hand. A complaint of credit card or identity theft might be related to others. An alleged insurance fraud might be one of many by the same offender. A history of regulatory violations might be found by looking beyond the reported incident. All of which argue for both agencies and their investigators to aggressively seek out information about offending.

As suggested earlier, the search for additional victims is especially important in the initial evaluation of complaints where the issue of an actual violation is in question. However, if there is evidence to justify moving forward, the identification of victims needs to become more probing to include reviewing bank records and telephone records of the alleged offender, as well as the alleged offender's own business records for their identities and subsequent follow-up. Developing additional victimization can only help to establish a pattern of misconduct, which can be critical in proving intent. Additionally, these records are also likely to divulge the monetary loss attributed to the misconduct, a feature that is likely to be of concern to prosecutors.

While the question of whether an actual violation occurred or the need to prove intent might not be present in all white collar crimes, the case can only be strengthened and more "sellable" to a prosecuting attorney with additional victims and/or incidents of misconduct. Covering this base might be somewhat easier when a government agency is victimized or a regulatory violation is being investigated because the records needed for review would be consolidated and more readily available for examination by investigators and/or other government officials. The issue of intent is usually not of paramount concern in cases such as insurance fraud, credit card fraud, loan fraud, and the like, but identifying the full scope of these types of offenses is sometimes more difficult because of private sector involvement. For example, while one lender or credit card issuer might find that they have been victimized, whether other victims of the same scheme will make a similar discovery and/or report it to the same agency can be uncertain. Investigators with these types of cases should become acquainted with security personnel in the credit card, banking, and insurance industries to facilitate inquiries about possible victimization. In many locales, security personnel in these industries have formed organizations for the express purpose of sharing investigative information and intelligence, and law enforcement representatives are usually welcome to participate. When these organizations are available, it would behoove investigators to become actively involved as a way to enhance liaison with companies that can be both sources of information and potential victims.

When this "inventory" process is complete, an investigator should be able to (1) make an informed judgment about whether a viable case (meaning actionable in a prosecutive forum) is at hand and if so, (2) identify the steps necessary to complete the investigation. If the answer is "yes" to the first issue, the next step is usually for the investigator to introduce a prosecuting attorney to the case.

THE INVESTIGATOR–PROSECUTOR RELATIONSHIP

This volume focuses only on investigating white collar crime. Prosecuting white collar crime lies in another domain and is addressed elsewhere in the literature. Nevertheless, perhaps unique to white collar crime enforcement generally is the frequent early involvement of prosecutors in these investigations. For our purposes in this volume, the term *prosecutor* is applied generically to the entire realm of government enforcement attorneys, recognizing that in some instances these individuals may bear other titles.

Investigators of other types of crimes often find themselves discussing a case with the prosecutor when charges are ready to be brought or even after an arrest has been made. Not only is this typically not the situation in white collar crime investigations, but also more frequently the prosecutor plays an active role in putting these cases together. Moreover, the reality is that in most prosecutive forums the attorney assigned to handle a case (or their supervisors) ultimately makes the decision whether or not to proceed against the alleged offender. Thus, the picture that is being painted here of how a white collar crime investigation evolves into a white collar crime prosecution is that of a team effort consisting of one or more investigators and one or more prosecutors working together, and hopefully in harmony. Frankly, there is no more important professional relationship a white collar crime investigator can establish than with the prosecutors that handle these types of investigations. Government attorneys rely heavily on the facts and analyses about a case put forth by the investigating agents. This information will be the basis for making a decision whether to go forward with a prosecution and it will very possibly be put forth in judicial proceedings. Needless to say, prosecutors will want to have the utmost confidence in the trustworthiness and reliability of information the investigator provides. Thus, the position being taken here is that the burden for establishing a sound investigator–prosecutor working relationship falls on the investigator. It is critical for investigators to furnish only accurate, reliable, and properly obtained information about offending to prosecutors. Prosecutive decisions can have a profound impact on all parties involved, especially the defendants, and these decisions cannot be based on faulty information. Therefore, it should come as no surprise that an effective investigator–prosecutor relationship is first and foremost based on a high level of confidence and trustworthiness a prosecutor has in an investigator. And be mindful that such a level of confidence is earned, perhaps over time. An investigator's agency affiliation and/or title alone will not "do the trick." Also be mindful that reputations can be fleeting, meaning that investigators must continually put forth the effort that earns their confidence and trustworthiness.

Whether just starting out or a seasoned veteran, an important time to earn a prosecutor's respect and confidence is when making an initial presentation of a case. As indicated, in white collar crime cases this is usually done relatively early in the investigation, frequently just after the assessment of the initial information gathered as described above provides evidence of a prosecutable offense.

Introducing the Case: A Key Meeting

Just to be clear: Early contact with a prosecutor is no reflection on an investigator's capabilities to pursue these types of cases. Rather, the investigator and the case can only benefit from bringing a prosecutor on board in the initial phases. First, prosecutors usually have a great deal of discretion in terms of whether or not to move forward with a case. Cases that do not meet prevailing priorities, are relatively inconsequential or *de minimus* in nature, and/or possess a fact situation that does not bode well for a successful prosecution are likely to be declined. It is far better for an investigator to have the merits of his/her case assessed by a prosecutor in the early stages of an investigation before spending countless additional hours only to find the case will not be prosecuted. Having said that, a careful decision must be made by the investigator as to just how soon this contact should be made. When complaints, inquiries, and/or information warrant follow-up evaluation and investigation as outlined above, the facts gathered through this process often provide a sufficient basis for scheduling the initial meeting with the prosecutor. In any event, the investigator must have enough information on hand to be able to present facts indicating a likely violation of law and at least an estimate of the known harm (e.g., victim loss) that has occurred. Any additional information that has been gathered should also be disclosed. Although this initial presentation is a "sales" job, in the interest of establishing that all-important investigator/prosecutor relationship discussed above, *do not* fail to disclose any known weaknesses, problems, or mitigating features that might be encountered in the case.

If the prosecutor agrees to go forward with the case, this initial meeting also affords an opportunity to discuss a proposed course of action including the issuance of subpoenas and assistance in pursuing a search warrant and/or other actions that require court approval, such as forfeitures or injunctions (all of which will be discussed in later chapters). With regard to subpoenas, it would be wise to come prepared with the necessary information (i.e., names and addresses of the intended recipients; records being sought, etc.) in order to facilitate this process.

Again, it is emphasized that this meeting is likely the first introduction a prosecutor has to the case and there is an old adage about the need to make a favorable first impression. The impression involved here is twofold in nature. First, the facts of the case itself must be attractive and persuasive enough to demand what might become an extensive prosecutive undertaking. Although the "facts are the facts," a case presentation can be enhanced and be persuasive by undertaking the initial investigative steps discussed earlier in this chapter with special attention to developing a pattern of misconduct.

Second, the investigator making the initial presentation is an important part of this equation. Do not treat this meeting casually! Come fully prepared to present and discuss all that is known about the case at this point in a clear and coherent manner. Also, think ahead about questions that might be asked, including potential problems and weaknesses that might be encountered, and be prepared on how to respond to these questions. While the answers to some questions as well as the existence of potential problems might be presently unknown, an investigator who has anticipated these issues is sure to make a better impression than one who responds with a "blank stare." And finally, never underestimate the value of a professional appearance and demeanor in making a favorable impression.

GETTING STARTED: A FINAL THOUGHT

Already references have been made to computer searches and the Internet. The roles that computers and the Internet play in daily activities, business and personal, legal and illegal, are pervasive. Within the investigative profession, white collar crime investigators are perhaps more impacted by this technology than others. Thus, white collar crime investigators should be computer literate and have computers and Internet access at their personal disposal as basic investigative tools. While computer knowledge and technology will not eliminate the need for traditional field investigation approaches, these assets will enable investigators to function within the prevailing technological environment and will greatly enhance their efficiency and effectiveness.

CHAPTER HIGHLIGHTS

- As white collar offending tends to be underreported, white collar crime enforcement agencies should have programs and structures in place to solicit and accept complaints and information from the public. It makes little sense for these agencies to maintain a low profile about who they are and what they do. The identification of as many complaints and as much victimization related to a complaint as possible plays an important role in any subsequent investigation, and the development of this type of information should be aggressively pursued.

- The primary data to capture in the complaint-gathering process includes the identity (and related contact information) of the complainant/inquirer; identity (and contact information) of the person/entity on which the complaint or inquiry is being made; and the substance of the complaint or inquiry.

- When multiple agencies share interest in a given case, either responsibility for pursuing the case should be ceded to the agency that is best able to handle it or an effective working relationship to pursue the case jointly should be established.

- Information from informants and those who otherwise have "inside" information can play an important role in the investigation of white collar crime.

- Investigators should align themselves with, and participate in applicable consumer protection and/or corporate security organizations as a means to developing information on offending and helpful contacts.

- An initial analysis of complaints should look for "red flags" that are often associated with offending. A red flag should be raised when there is a pattern of misconduct (i.e., multiple complaints alleging a similar set of circumstances); the subjects of the complaint (individuals or business entities) have a prior complaint and/or offending history; and initial inquiries detect falsified information and/or use of aliases.

- White collar crime cases are commonly introduced to prosecutors early in the investigation, usually because of the need for prosecutive support (e.g., subpoenas, search warrants, etc.) and legal advice (especially when complex offending is involved).

- An effective, professional working relationship between investigator and prosecutor is particularly important in white collar crime cases and it is incumbent upon investigators to establish the necessary trust and respect that such a relationship will be built upon.

- Having computer equipment and Internet access available for use along with the requisite skills, especially ability to access information on the Internet, are important assets for white collar crime investigators.

CHAPTER BEST PRACTICE

- Making use of the mass media and the Internet are probably two of the most cost-effective strategies for increasing agency visibility and engaging in a victimization prevention campaign. However, preparing informative and attractive printed material will also be necessary for public dissemination. Needless to say, these types of responsibilities would seem to fall outside the normal range of the knowledge and skills possessed by the typical investigator, and many investigative organizations, taking a cue from the corporate sector, have employed public relations or media professionals to provide these services. This would certainly be a *best practice* to adopt. (See page 21.)

Notes

1. S. M. Rosoff, H. N. Pontell, and R. H. Tillman, *Profit Without Honor: White-Collar Crime and the Looting of America* (Upper Saddle River, NJ: Pearson Prentice Hall, 2004), p. 23.
2. Ibid., p. 23.
3. D. O. Friedrichs, *Trusted Criminals: White Collar Crime in Contemporary Society* (Belmont, CA: Wadsworth, 1996), p. 53.

CHAPTER 3

The Paper Chase: Documentary Evidence

Key Terms and Concepts

- Business Records
- Communication, Utilities, and Travel Records
- Documentary Evidence
- Financial Records
- Proactive Evidence Gathering
- Public and Government Agency Records
- Search Warrants
- Subpoenas
- Victim Records

The monikers *paper cases* and *paper chases*, whether attached lovingly or derisively, nevertheless aptly describe most white collar crime investigations. Normally, the resolution of these cases hinges on the collection and analysis of evidence in documentary format. This particular characteristic is perhaps definitive when comparing white collar crime investigations to other types of investigations. As will become apparent throughout the following chapters, white collar crime investigators must conduct interviews and often utilize other tools and approaches common to a wide range of cases, for example physical and electronic surveillance, undercover and informant operations, forensic examinations, and so on. However, unlike their counterparts responsible for conventional or street crime cases (e.g., homicides, rapes, bombings, robberies, etc.), white collar crime investigators use these standard investigative tools and approaches to help in understanding and/or corroborating evidence derived from the review and analysis of volumes of documents, correspondence, records, and so on. Likewise, their focus tends to be less on the "scene of the crime" per se, and more on documentary material they retrieve from there or elsewhere. So, it is not uncommon for a white collar crime investigator's office to be ringed with file cabinets and boxes (and perhaps having access to other storage facilities as well), notwithstanding the pervasiveness of electronic document storage in today's business offices and homes. In fact, while computer technology solves document storage and management problems in the home and office, it only complicates the retrieval and review of documentary materials for the investigator, a topic that will be further addressed in later chapters.

This chapter will identify and discuss categories of documentary evidence frequently encountered and/or necessary in white collar crime cases. These categories include documents normally available from victims or witnesses, publicly available records, financial and business records, both in the possession of third parties and investigative subjects, and communication, utility, and travel records. In discussing the acquisition of these records, frequent references will be made to the use of subpoenas and search warrants. Although these investigative tools are discussed in greater detail in later chapters, brief introductions are warranted here before proceeding further.

Subpoenas

First, subpoenas are legally enforceable demands for the production of evidentiary information. Such information can include documentary evidence as well as testimonial evidence, although the latter is limited to grand jury authority and in connection with some civil/regulatory proceedings. In the federal system, the courts, grand juries, and many investigative and regulatory agencies have the legal authority to issue subpoenas (*note*: agency subpoenas are sometimes referred to as *civil investigative demands*). For the purposes of this chapter, references to subpoenas indicate that the records in question are not publicly available and require some type of legal mandate for their release. The type of subpoena that is issued in a given situation can vary with the circumstances of the case and the agency(s) involved, matters that will be discussed further in Chapters 8 and 9. In any event, this method of obtaining documentary evidence involves the presentation of the subpoena to the intended recipient (or sometimes to a designated representative), and the recipient within a specified timeframe then produces items identified therein. It is a method of obtaining documentary evidence in both criminal and civil investigations.

Search Warrants

Search warrants are the topic of discussion in Chapter 5. In brief, a search warrant is a court order that permits investigators to search and seize evidentiary items relative to a criminal offense in areas where there is otherwise an expectation of privacy. In order to obtain a search warrant, an investigator must present probable cause to a judge that a crime occurred and that specified evidence relating to this crime is located at a particular place. Unlike subpoenas, a search warrant permits an investigator to intrude into the private area and physically search and seize the items identified in the warrant. Thus, investigators are not reliant on the possessor of the desired evidentiary material to surrender it (as is the case with subpoenas), but rather search for and seize the material themselves. This tool is limited to criminal investigations although information obtained in this manner can be used in civil proceedings. Moreover, some regulatory agencies possess authority to conduct on-site compliance inspections, including the review of business operations and records that must be maintained in connection with these activities. The exercise of this type of regulatory authority is somewhat akin to a search warrant since it permits governmental intrusion onto private property (although statutes clearly put on notice the exercise of this authority to those who operate in affected regulated industries) and any evidence of violations gathered can be used in subsequent enforcement proceedings.

VICTIM RECORDS

The collection of documentary evidence in white collar crime cases often begins incident to contact with victims or other witnesses to the activity under investigation. While interviewing these individuals is crucial and will be addressed in detail in the next chapter, these individuals are also important sources of documentary evidence. Moreover, at least with regard to victims, documentary evidence from such individuals is normally available to investigators by way of voluntary surrender. Having said that, it is not uncommon for business/corporate victims to nevertheless request a subpoena for records relating to their victimization, especially when there are privacy concerns about the release of proprietary, customer, and/or employee information they contain. Thus, unless there are other indicators present suggesting that the business/corporate victim is not interested in cooperating in the investigation, a request for a subpoena should not be looked upon with surprise or suspicion.

Types of Victim Records

Promotional, advertising, and/or sales material.   While this type of material might also be available elsewhere, obtaining it from a victim provides the important opportunity to develop witness testimony relative to its receipt and impact. The manner in which promotional material was received often determines what statutes will apply and the appropriate investigative jurisdiction. For instance, when the mails are used to convey promotional material (including advertisements in newspapers/magazines since copies of these publications are routinely mailed), the federal mail fraud statute would apply. Conversely, suspect promotions that distribute advertising materials in personal visits and/or at meetings *might* avoid (and this is by no means a certainty) federal jurisdiction.

With regard to the impact of promotional/advertising materials, victims should be asked to explain what role these materials played in their decision making to conduct a transaction. In obtaining their explanation, attempt to distinguish between the overall effect of the advertisement and specific statements/representations contained therein. It is not uncommon for victims to voice the sentiments that they simply trusted the publication that carried the advertisement or since it was being sold through the mails, they assumed some government agency had "okayed" the promotion. Likewise, investigators must carefully review advertising and promotional material from perspectives that might vary from case to case. In some types of cases (e.g., sale of merchandise or service) a word-by-word analysis is required to identify possible differences between the overall effect of the advertising and what the "fine print" says. A common defense to charges that a promotion was misrepresented is to disregard the overall impact of the material (e.g., glossy photos, suggestive headlines) and instead to demonstrate through a word-by-word analysis that victims did not understand the true terms of promotion. However, such defenses can sometimes be overcome through witness testimony that illustrates the overall impact of the advertising along with alternative interpretations to any "clinical" word-by-word analysis that is offered. It is also not uncommon for promotional material to contain false information, statements, and/or photographs regarding the promotion to falsely enhance credibility and trustworthiness. Addresses and the structures located there on, experience, qualifications, and reference information including supporting studies and research should all be subject to verification. The identification of falsehoods and misrepresentations of this nature strengthens arguments about deceptive and fraudulent intent of the promotional material.

Payment(s)/financial records. —These records can be in the form of cancelled checks, money order or cashier check receipts, credit card receipts, and so on. Cash payments can sometimes be documented by a receipt provided incident to the transaction or perhaps by a withdrawal receipt from a bank, if this was the source of the funds. Payment records document the amount of loss and when payments were made. Obtaining these records directly from the victim again provides an opportunity to elicit necessary testimony to introduce them into evidence and often helps to refresh recollection about the events in question. Moreover, for the investigator the negotiated checks and money orders and credit card merchant account information can provide valuable leads as to the parties involved and further financial records, for example bank accounts, credit card merchant accounts. Therefore, careful examination of these records is in order and in some instances forensic examination might be as well (see Chapter 7).

In identity theft, embezzlements, credit card, and loan frauds, victim financial records are also necessary to document the unlawful events and losses incurred. Acquiring and examining bank account statements, credit card statements, and in the case of businesses, in-house financial records are necessary both to further the investigation and to have on hand the necessary evidence for prosecution.

Other records, documents, and correspondence. One of the challenges in attempting to address white collar crime investigation is to account for all the possible scenarios that can fall under this umbrella. This multitude of scenarios, in turn, can produce a wide variety of documentary material that might be in the possession of victims. As a general proposition, victims should be asked to produce all records, documents, and correspondence that they possess incident to the transaction in question. Investigators should recognize they might experience a "learning curve" in the early phases of an investigation in terms of what items to look for, especially when tackling a new type of offense. Additionally, when dealing with business entity or government agency victims, unique forms and documents can be involved in fraudulent transactions, scenarios that often require investigators to gain a detailed understanding of the industry or government program they are dealing with. As will be encouraged in the next chapter, a detailed interview with the victim helps to prompt the identification of documents that might otherwise be forgotten or viewed as inconsequential, and if the existence of any documents are later identified nothing precludes follow-up with victims to ensure that complete documentation is acquired. Whatever other documentary items are obtained, investigators should thoroughly examine the contents and obtain an explanation from the victim regarding his/her understanding of this item/contents. Again, this examination should also be geared to identifying false statements and information as well. In some fraud scenarios, correspondence is generated to falsely explain delays in providing the promised goods or services when the real intent is to simply "buy time" and continue to operate and/or flee before complaints are filed with authorities. This type of correspondence is known as a "lulling" letter and could be charged as a substantive violation or an overt act in a conspiracy.

As with negotiable instruments, forensic examination might be appropriate in some instances where handwriting identification and/or possession of the document would be useful. Credit card and loan applications and insurance claim forms are types of documents possessed by victimized companies where forensic examination can play a useful role.

Tangible items.   In the event the case involves a product for sale or other acquisition of a tangible item (e.g., equipment that was part of a purported business opportunity investment), victims should be requested to furnish such items and explain their dissatisfaction. Again, this category of victim evidence could be quite expansive in terms of possibilities involved, and alternatives to taking physical possession might be necessary. For instance, in home repair scams it might be necessary to photograph the shoddy or incomplete work since taking physical possession in most cases may be impractical.

PROACTIVE EVIDENCE GATHERING

Although many, if not most, cases begin through complaints or inquiries lodged by the public, again recognize that voluntarily submitted complaints and inquiries usually represent the tip of the iceberg. This reality often provides investigators motivation to proactively identify suspect white collar crime operations. Taking such an approach is nothing new for many regulatory agencies that exercise monitoring and inspection authority over the industry or activity under their jurisdiction. However, many other potential white collar crime activities are not under any such oversight or are marketed outside of the customary industry environment. For example, mail order promotions, investment and business opportunities, health-related products, lending services, travel offerings, and a host of other products and services are routinely advertised through the print and broadcast media, the mails, and increasingly over the Internet. Rather than waiting for voluntary complaints or inquiries to surface before taking any action, investigators should view these marketing efforts as opportunities to proactively identify and assess suspect promotions. As material being made available to the general public, investigators may acquire advertising and promotional literature for review and analysis and then make contact/conduct transactions, if further investigation appears necessary. Obviously, in undertaking these steps, investigators will seldom want to disclose their official status and thus it will be necessary to employ rudimentary undercover tools (a topic that will be touched upon in later chapters) such as fictitious identities, mailing addresses, and perhaps a telephone number in order to correspond and conduct transactions with suspect promotions.

This proactive approach begins with monitoring publications, broadcasts, and Internet sites that routinely advertise suspect activities/promotions. Evaluating activities and promotions carried in these sources may require training or the development of experience/expertise, which of course will vary with agency jurisdiction. As a general proposition, however, the well-worn adage "If it sounds too good to be true, it usually is" is a basic guide in assessing the truthfulness of representations that are being made. For example, statements promising huge earnings and/or returns on investment, miracle cures, easy work and big pay, and so on typically warrant follow-up attention, especially when specific results are represented (e.g., *25% APY*; *Double your money!*; *lose 50 pounds without trying*; *make over $100,000 from the comfort of your easy chair*).

If a decision is made to investigate further and engage in a transaction or make contact, begin to treat the advertising material as evidence. Date and initial the original material and store in a container that fully identifies it and its source. Material on the Internet should be printed in hard copy form and downloaded in electronic format on a portable storage device, with the URL and date retrieved identified on the storage container, and these items should be treated as evidence.

Copies of any order forms, correspondence, and payment instruments (the purchase of money orders is recommended absent the availability of more elaborate undercover checking accounts or credit cards) should be made, as well as the exterior of any mailing envelope. All these items again should be dated and initialed to identify the date of mailing. Copies of orders submitted over the Internet should be printed off/downloaded, with date submitted and URL noted.

Any material/items received in return should also be dated and initialed to indicate date of receipt and evaluated in terms of appropriate follow-up attention. The point to remember is that anything acquired through this process should be treated as evidence.

Taking this type of proactive approach can identify unlawful activities at their inception, which in turn could permit early intervention, thus minimizing victimization. Also, the acquisition of important evidence directly by an investigator (as opposed to through a victim witness) can sometimes be advantageous in the preparation of search warrants or injunctive actions and possibly in providing testimony in enforcement proceedings. In these circumstances, the use of hearsay testimony and/or issues involving witness cooperation is eliminated since the investigator acquiring the evidence can introduce this material.

Abandoned Records

Another form of proactive evidence gathering is to seek out and take possession of abandoned records. The term *abandoned records* applies to items that have clearly been discarded or those on which the rightful owner has otherwise relinquished custody and control. A standard technique used in many types of criminal investigations is to search through trash that either has been placed in a trash receptacle at curbside before pick-up by collectors or perhaps after collection. No doubt, this technique would be useful in some white collar crime scenarios, although when pursuing noncriminal investigations, it may be wise to consult with legal counsel to ensure that any evidence acquired in this manner will be admissible.

While the intent to abandon is arguably clear when items are in the trash, other scenarios might also afford an opportunity to seize abandoned evidence as well, albeit with caution. For instance, evidence that was left behind by departed occupants of rented office space or a leased residence may very well constitute abandoned evidence. However, in taking possession of such material investigators would want to ensure that they are lawfully obtaining access to the premises/material and that the lease has expired. Normally, this could be accomplished by working through the landlord, although it is conceivable that the landlord might request a subpoena for the release of the items in question. If the lease is still in effect, but the occupants have seemingly departed the premises, then seizing any items as abandoned property *might* be subsequently challenged if used as evidence. Investigators wishing to take possession of evidence found under these (and other "murky") abandonment circumstances would be wise to discuss an appropriate and defendable course of action with the prosecutor assigned before taking further action.

PUBLIC AND GOVERNMENT AGENCY RECORDS

As suggested in Chapter 2, an analysis of public records can play an important role in the initial evaluation of complaints. However, this category of records can continue to play an important role as a case proceeds, not only in the sense of being an information source but in many instances by being of evidentiary value as well. Records maintained by governmental organizations are often useful in identifying and/or obtaining information about individuals or businesses (and the principals therein); they can be reviewed to determine compliance with mandated licensing and registration requirements; and the information provided on these records can be investigated for accuracy (as furnishing false information can be an indicator of illegal activity and/or a violation in itself).

The term *public records* generally implies information that is not private, but rather is available to the public upon request. For the most part, these are records collected and maintained by governmental organizations at all levels, municipal, county, state, and federal. While at the federal level the designation of information as "public" is consistent nationwide, variations do exist at other levels of government that are often mandated by prevailing state law.

The distinction being drawn here between public and government agency records is that at all levels of government, agencies collect and maintain information that they do not routinely make available for public inspection. Again, federal disclosure practices are uniform nationwide, but state laws vary in terms of the types of government records that can be withheld from public disclosure. However, investigators acting within the scope of their agency authority, whether criminal or civil/administrative, can often (although not always) gain access to many, if not most, forms of nonpublic government records upon request. Note, however, this statement largely applies to information an agency collects and maintains as part of its normal "business activity." Not surprisingly, obtaining closely held law enforcement or intelligence information is sometimes more problematic. In any event, requests for nonpublic government agency records might need to be made in writing on agency letterhead (and perhaps even from an agency head) or through the submission of a special request form. However, in many instances verbal requests will suffice. Thus, regardless of a public versus nonpublic designation, the challenge that white collar crime investigators must take on to be effective is to (1) identify information of interest that is collected and maintained by government agencies and then (2) learn how to access it, that is, whether it is public information, where it is available, who the appropriate contact person is, and what to request and how to go about it, and so on. Especially with regard to publicly available records, one good place to start is the Internet. Many agencies at all governmental levels maintain websites that, in turn, provide access to public records they maintain. For instance, whether on the county or municipal level, a great deal of property ownership and tax evaluation/collection data is available online. At the very least, agency websites usually provide contact information, and through the description of their responsibilities and activities, the types of records they might have on hand could be identified.

The following are government agencies that have proven to be routine "stops" in the course of many white collar crime investigations:

- Municipal and county police agencies—aside from any pertinent investigative data that might be on file and made available, traffic citations, accident reports, and information arising from name index queries are sometimes of interest. Establishing personal contacts with local law enforcement officials is always helpful in gaining access to these types of records.

- Municipal governments—for business, occupational, marriage, and pet licenses, and birth certificates/death certificates. Municipal health departments maintain licensure and inspection reports on types of businesses where health and sanitation issues are present. Depending upon the prevailing practice within a given state, municipalities can also be responsible for tax assessment and collection. Thus, real property ownership, assessed value data, and property tax payments would be available and this type of data is normally public information. In fact, many jurisdictions make this data available online. Municipal governments also maintain employee personnel files and records relative to contracting and vendor relationships (including school district operations in many locales). However, the conditions under which this latter type of information would be released could vary with the nature of the investigation and agency involved. Be mindful that local, county, or state investigative agency involvement is often helpful in these situations. As suggested earlier, even when the municipality is a victim or otherwise cooperative, a subpoena might be requested for this type of material.

- Court records—Whether at the municipal, county, state, or federal levels (including bankruptcy courts), court clerks' offices are responsible for filing and managing a vast array of legal actions that are filed with and/or adjudicated by judges within the particular jurisdiction. Unless a document is filed under seal, it is publicly available. Not only are records of criminal actions available (including indictments, conviction and sentencing records, and if not under seal, arrest and search warrants with the accompanying affidavits), but also the whole range of civil actions. Such actions include civil suits, divorce and other family law proceedings (although the latter may frequently be sealed due to involvement of children), liens and mortgage filings, real estate transfers, bankruptcy proceedings, and so on. Keep in mind that an increasing number of court jurisdictions permit online access to some of their records.

- County governments—The roles of county governments vary somewhat from state to state and it is incumbent upon an investigator to distinguish the records that are available at the county level as opposed to the municipal level. Many county jurisdictions, however, are charged with real estate tax assessment and collection. As indicated above, this type of data can be helpful in establishing property ownership, value, and tax payments, and as with court records more and more of this data can be accessed through an agency website. Again, depending upon the state, county clerks' offices maintain marriage license applications and birth/death certificates. Likewise, in many states public schools are county operations; counties maintain files on their employees; and they engage in various procurement and contracting activities, all of which could be of potential interest in white collar crime cases. However, as cautioned above, the degree to which any of these types of data are publicly available or turned over to investigators upon request will vary depending upon the nature of the investigation and agency(s) involved. Again, in this scenario the involvement of a county or state investigative agency in the case can often be helpful.

- State governments—Most investigators quickly recognize the value of information maintained by the state motor vehicle departments: vehicle registration and driver's license data (often accompanied by a photo of the licensee). These databases are usually accessible through a computer linkage available to law enforcement agencies. Additionally, most investigators also quickly become familiar with computerized state criminal history indices and state departments of corrections can provide information on current or former prison inmates. Another state-maintained set of records that tends to be of particular interest to white collar crime investigators includes corporation filings/corporate officers and registered-agent databases. Again, these databases are increasingly available through Internet access. As indicated earlier many, if not most, state governments take on enforcement and regulatory responsibilities similar to those found at the federal level. Thus, it would be common to find state agencies involved in consumer protection; environmental protection; health care, welfare, and insurance fraud; food and drug violations; banking, securities and insurance industries oversight; and professional licensing. Depending upon the nature of a given white collar crime case or the normal investigative jurisdiction of a white collar crime investigator, contact with one or more of these kinds of state agencies might prove very helpful. In fact, as encouraged earlier, establishing liaison with personnel in shared areas of jurisdiction facilitates the acquisition of information and often expedites case resolutions. Finally, like municipal and county governments, state governments also maintain personnel, procurement, and contracting records.

- Federal government—While the vast number of municipal, county, and state entities presents one set of problems in comprehending the availability of governmental records, accessing information maintained by the federal government may be no less complicated if only because of the size of this bureaucracy. In fact, identifying and accessing records maintained by the federal government could be a book topic in itself. Again, perhaps the wisest approach with regard to federal records is to become familiar with the federal agencies with shared jurisdictions and interests and establish channels of communication to facilitate access to records and information. That said, the following are among the information/record sources that have proven to be of frequent value to white collar crime investigators:

  - National Crime Information Center (NCIC), the computerized system operated by the FBI that contains outstanding warrants, criminal histories, and stolen item reports including securities;[1]

  - Address verification, mail forwarding and postal box information, mail cover requests, consumer complaints, and negotiated postal money orders are available through the Postal Inspection Service;

  - Currency transaction reports (CTRs)—reports from banks of financial transactions valued over $10,000 that are maintained by the federal Financial Crimes Enforcement Network (FinCen);

  - Currency monetary instrument reports (CMIRs)—reports of transporting over $10,000 into or out of the United States)—and foreign travel records of individuals are available through U.S. Customs;

  - Passport records/applications on file with the U.S. State Department;

  - Consumer complaints filed with the Federal Trade Commission;

  - Corporate filings with the Securities and Exchange Commission;

  - Many federal agencies, particularly those with regulatory authority such as the Federal Trade Commission and the Securities and Exchange Commission, post records of enforcement actions on their websites. Also, the website FedStats (http://www.fedstats.gov/?) provides links to a vast amount of public data maintained by federal agencies.

FINANCIAL RECORDS

The goal of white collar crime is money or something of value, even if it is intangible in nature such as power or control (which often, in turn, translates to money or something of value). Hence the old saying "Follow the money." An analysis of financial records can disclose whether the monies collected were used in a legitimate manner or diverted to other purposes, and who benefited from the monies obtained and to what extent (including the identification of lavish lifestyles through ill-gotten gains). Thus, it should come as no surprise that the acquisition and analysis of financial records is a routine step in most white collar crime investigations.

Financial records encompass a wide range of possibilities, the applicability of which can vary with individual(s)/entities under investigation and the nature of the case. For the purposes of this chapter, financial records will be considered as those held by third party custodians such as banks, credit card companies, and so on, while business records will include those of a financial nature in the custody of the business entity (e.g., canceled checks, bank statements, bookkeeping, and accounting records). Note that in most instances, the acquisition of financial records maintained by third parties will require the issuance of a subpoena, although in rare instances search warrants have been executed upon custodians of third party financial records in order to gain this type of data.

Banking Records

Among the most commonly sought and analyzed financial records in white collar crime cases are those maintained by banks. These records can include account information (the type of account, name and address of account holder(s) when it was opened [and closed], and the names and signatures of those who have authorized access to it); periodic statements of account that reflect account activity and balances; copies of canceled checks (fronts and backs); copies of deposited and withdrawal items, including wire transfer records, cashier's checks, and money orders; and certificates of deposit. Be aware that many banks offer other types of products and services such as loans (car loans, personal loans, commercial loans, and home equity loans) and real estate mortgages, and most recently investment accounts. Thus, it is wise to craft language on a subpoena to a bank to cover all possible types of business transactions that the investigative subject could have engaged in with the institution. In doing so, provide on the subpoena all known individual and/or business names along with personal identifiers such as social security numbers and/or tax identification numbers for the subject(s) of interest. Normally, the bank records being requested need to be defined by inclusive dates. These dates should span the broadest period possible, keeping in mind the scope of activities under investigation and possibly statute of limitation criteria. On this issue, from a practical perspective banks charge for their records search and copying, and obtaining a large volume of records can be costly. Also there can be lengthy delays in obtaining these documents depending upon the volume of records sought and how busy a bank is handling other subpoena requests. Neither of these realities is a reason not to request all the records needed in any given case. However, they do speak to the issue of the need for careful assessment of what is necessary in an effort to avoid wasteful costs and unnecessary delays.

In any event, when reviewing bank records the types of data that can be collected, tracked, and analyzed include (but are not limited to)

- dates on items;
- payee and signature names;

- amounts;

- account numbers;

- identity of the bank the item was drawn upon;

- final deposit bank;

- first endorsement, second endorsement, and so on;

- sources of deposited items; and

- any notes on the items.[2]

Credit Card Records

A review and analysis of credit card transactions can identify the types of purchases the card-holder makes; a travel history that places a person in a certain geographic area on a certain date; and a payment history/indebtedness status. Information to capture when reviewing credit card records includes date of transaction, vendor, credit card number, amount, signer, and anything unusual or of interest concerning the transaction.[3] Additionally, credit card merchant account agreements can be obtained from credit card issuers, which will help to identify the party(s) responsible for establishing this relationship along with other required information. Verifying the truthfulness of this type of information is often important.

Real Estate Transactions

Some documents relative to real estate transactions, such as deeds and mortgages, are publicly available through court filings. Property tax data is also publicly available from the local taxing authority. Moreover, both of these publicly available categories of real estate information are increasingly available online. However, real estate agents, mortgage lenders, title insurance companies, and closing agents maintain files of real estate transactions which contain details of the transaction, including the identity of the purchaser(s) and seller(s), social security/tax identification numbers, sales price, sales contract, payment and financing arrangements, value of mortgage, income sources, and employment. Aside from whatever other ramifications that fictitious information might have in a given case, keep in mind that falsifying information on a mortgage application can be a federal violation in itself.

Investment Accounts

As employers have shifted the burden of funding pensions onto workers through individual retirement accounts (IRA) and 401(k) programs, it would now be almost unusual not to find individuals without some type of business affiliation with brokerage and/or mutual fund firms. Thus, if "following the money" is an issue in white collar crime cases, investigators would be wise to affirmatively search for investment accounts. Absent other sources, such accounts can often be identified from bank records (e.g., checks deposited into an investment account; redemption checks from an investment firm deposited into a bank account) and occasionally from return addresses that are reported on mail covers. Information that can be acquired includes the identity of the account holder(s) and any associated personal identifying information; the nature of the investment account; its value; dates of deposit and source of deposited funds; and dates of withdrawal and disposition of these proceeds and the identities of beneficiaries.

Insurance Records

Records maintained by insurance companies include both policy information (i.e., policy-holder, type of policy, policy applications, beneficiaries, and records of payments) and claims information (e.g., claim forms and related correspondence and documentation, litigation proceedings, and claim payments). Information that can be gleaned from such files includes personal history and identifiers, types and amounts of coverage, sources of premium payments, types of reported losses, the amounts received incident to claims including the disposition of these proceeds, and any litigation history. As insurance fraud is a white collar crime category unto itself, these types of records would be central to any investigations of this nature.

Loan Records

Nonbank business entities that are engaged in lending money (e.g., loan companies, finance companies, pay-day advance businesses) maintain loan applications, loan disbursement records, and loan repayment information. Personal information concerning the borrowers typically available include address history, personal identifiers, occupation and employment history, the identification of collateral, disposition of the loan proceeds, and loan repayment information, including sources of funds for repayment.

Credit Reporting Agencies

Data available can include borrowing and repayment histories; and the identification of bank accounts, addresses; insurance coverages, and collection/litigation information.[4]

Tax Filings

This category applies to records of both federal and state tax authorities and includes income tax, personal property tax, and sales tax filings. Obviously, this type of information can provide a comprehensive view of the financial status of an individual or business entity, including sources and amounts of income/revenue and assets. Equally obvious is the fact that falsification of information submitted to tax authorities can result in both civil and criminal action. Be aware that the Internal Revenue Service (IRS) closely guards federal income tax information by law. It can be released to investigators incident to a nontax, federal criminal investigation, but a court order issued by a federal judge must first be obtained. Moreover, agencies must establish security procedures consistent with IRS requirements for storing these documents once they are released.

Financial records might also be of forensic interest, a topic that will be discussed more thoroughly in Chapter 7. When possession of certain documents and/or knowledge or involvement in illegal activities is in question, handwriting and fingerprint analyses might prove useful. In addition, obtaining known, normal course of business handwriting samples of investigative subjects might also be necessary. If forensic examination is anticipated, acquiring original, as opposed to copies, of documents is usually imperative. Also preserving them from any further contamination and/or damage is essential. Any such items that are immediately recognized to be of forensic value should be handled with care (i.e., by the edges and/or with rubber gloves) and placed in envelopes or other appropriate forensic document holders such as glassine sleeves.

BUSINESS RECORDS

For purposes here, this category of records refers to both financial and operating/business activity records maintained by a business entity that is the subject of an investigation. While the voluntary surrender of such records can be requested (and sometimes obtained in this manner when investigative subjects desire to cooperate), in the majority of cases acquisition of this material will be accomplished through the issuance of a subpoena or execution of a search warrant. Whatever route is taken, the following documents are among those commonly sought:

- Corporate documents including filings, articles of incorporation, minutes of corporate meetings, and so on—These records can be useful in establishing individual responsibility for a business operation. Changes in ownership and when these changes occurred should be noted. The use of fictitious individual identities to incorporate or falsely referring to a business entity as a corporation could be important evidence of unlawful intent.

- Business correspondence, policies, and instructions/directives—Reviewing these documents could identify intent, motive, and/or operating procedures that are contrary to legitimate business operations. The lack of any policies, instructions, and directives might be of value in demonstrating lack of intent to operate lawfully.

- Personnel records—these records can be useful in identifying (including background information) and locating employees who could be witnesses or targets in the investigation. Also, they might be helpful in establishing the use of aliases in the course of illegal activities since presumably these records would contain the true identities of the employees.

- Payroll records—While not providing complete information as personnel files might, these records could at least identify individuals who were on the payroll and thus might be witnesses or targets in the case. Again, these records might help establish the use of aliases based on the presumption that compensation would be made in true names. Finally, payroll records might be useful in determining the existence of "ghost employees," that is, compensation payments to individuals who are not actually employed or totally fictitious individuals. When names on payroll records have no corresponding personnel file, further investigation into this possibility is warranted. A case in point encountered by this author involved payroll checks bearing the name of the son of a healthcare provider, who was known to be a full-time law student in another state. The father cashed these checks and used the proceeds to fund an illegal kickback scheme that was essential to his business success.

- Bookkeeping and accounting records, including all journals, ledgers, accounts receivable and payable, and so on, that reflect the financial activities and condition of the business entity—Establishing the amount of loss in a case is usually an important factor in determining whether any prosecutive action is taken. Moreover, penalties and restitution are often based on the financial harm incurred. For instance, under federal sentencing guidelines, the loss attributed to a white collar crime offender is a primary factor in calculating a sentence, including the amount of incarceration time. Another consideration is to determine whether revenues reflected on bookkeeping and accounting documents are consistent with amounts identified elsewhere such as in bank records, sales records, and complaint data.

- Tax filings and supporting records (federal, state, and local)—Another possible approach to obtaining tax filings is directly from the tax payer and in this scenario it might be possible to obtain the documents that were used in preparing these filings. Looking for discrepancies between these filings and other financial data might prove helpful.

- Banking records, including statements, deposit slips, withdrawal slips, and all documents relating to banking activities—While these records are usually available and more complete when obtained from the banking institution, it is possible that not all banking relationships are known. Thus, seeking this type of information directly from the investigative subject is one way to avoid such an oversight.

- Credit card merchant account information—Like banking records, this type of information can be obtained directly from the credit card company, but there may be credit card relationships that are unknown. Thus, seeking such information directly from the investigative subject will sometimes reveal unknown merchant accounts. Moreover, some illegitimate operations have been known to use credit card merchant accounts that have been established at other business entities, either because they could not obtain a merchant account on their own or because they wanted to conceal their identity. These arrangements usually involve tendering a fee to the merchant account holder, who may or may not be in complicity with any wrongdoing. In fact, in some cases the cooperating merchant account holder can be victimized by charge-backs due to customer dissatisfaction or nonreceipt of merchandise/service, that is, the credit card company deducts monies payable to the account to honor customer requests for refunds. Needless to say, these types of scenarios warrant full investigation.

- Sales records—These records would identify the volume of sales and revenues generated for specified periods that can be compared to other records that contain revenue data. These records could also include names and addresses of customers, along with nature and amount of each transaction. Thus, these records could be a way to identify unknown victims.

- Customer lists including names, addresses, nature of transaction, and amount of transaction, and all other customer account information—Again, this type of information could help to identify victims. Customer lists can be a valuable commodity for legitimate marketing but can also be a means to target victims by the unscrupulous. Lists of individuals who have a propensity to be victimized are the "lifeblood" of many fraudulent promoters. Determining whether customer lists were sold and to whom might afford an opportunity to identify other unlawful operations.

- Customer complaints and records relating to the disposition of these complaints— Customer complaints not only provide another source of victim identification, but also provide evidence that the operator was put on notice about customer dissatisfaction. Determining whether the receipt of these complaints resulted in any operational changes and/or how they were responded to or resolved can provide evidence of the promoter's intent. When complaints are ignored and the offending activity continues unabated, evidence of intent to violate the law is strengthened. Conversely, businesses that recognize problems and attempt to correct them and who are responsive to customer complaints are less likely to be viewed in this manner. However, sophisticated offenders have found that relatively few customers complain and that satisfying these complainants is often a means of diminishing suspicion and keeping the authorities away. In these situations, it is often important to show through other victimization that while a few complaints were satisfied, the offending conduct continued unchanged and unabated. More-over, depending upon agency authority, even in situations where there is evidence that changes were implemented to alter offending behavior, a civil/administrative action to ensure compliance with the law may be appropriate.

- Sales, advertising, and promotional material—While much advertising and promotional material might be available in the public domain, there could be variations geared to different geographic and/or socioeconomic groups, thus potentially making it difficult to be aware of all versions of this material. Some sales material might only be available "in-house," that is, it is used only in a negotiation/transaction with a customer. This would be especially true with regard to sales instructions and procedures. In any event, these materials must be carefully examined for misrepresentations and intent to deceive. Keeping in mind the above admonition, a common defense is to dismiss all advertising representations except those (often literally) in the "small print." To reiterate, a counter to this approach can be to (1) identify falsehoods in the "large print," (2) highlight the overall effect of the advertising piece on the reader (e.g., bold colors and print, slick glossy photos, testimonials), and (3) demonstrate the impact of the advertising piece through victim testimony; all as means to prove that the "small print" is nothing but a disingenuous attempt at providing the truth.

- Sales presentation scripts—Whether in face-to-face or telemarketing sales, scripts are often devised to artfully (if not deceptively) entice a person to enter into a transaction. Not only should these scripts, themselves, be carefully analyzed, but importantly compare them to what victims were actually told. Often prepared sales scripts are "sanitized" to be nonoffending, but in practice the use of deceptive tactics is condoned, if not encouraged. The question then becomes whether the sales people departed from the script on their own or whether company management was complicit in this practice.

- Sales training material—This material must be examined not only to possibly identify illegal company practices, but perhaps more realistically to determine whether the actual sales practices were consistent with company policy, and if not, were any departures condoned and/or encouraged by the management. In this regard, inquiries with employees who were trained through this material should probe whether there was a "wink and nod" attitude on the part of company trainers, that is, the formal sales material was presented, followed by the "real way we do business."

- Audio and video recordings of sales transactions—Many telephone sales are recorded to ensure that the customer knowingly engaged in the transaction, and in some instances, face-to-face transactions might be videotaped for the same reason. Since such recordings might very well be used in any defense of alleged misconduct, it is wise to acquire them to review the disclosures made to the customers, the manner in which this was done (often hastily via a prepared script), and how any questions were answered. If anything, these recordings are probably more effective in persuading a customer who develops "buyer's remorse" following a transaction not to renege on the sale because their knowing consent is played back to them. From a prosecutive point of view in a fraudulent transaction, however, any "knowing consent" would have been inappropriately provided due to earlier false representations.

- Records relating to customer testimonials and product testing/research—Many promotions present satisfied customer testimonials and/or results from testing or research to enhance the credibility of a product or service. In some instances, access to satisfied customers is granted to prospective customers in the form of telephone calls or opportunities to inspect services rendered or work performed. Likewise, references are often made in advertising and sales presentations to product/service testing or research to substantiate reliability and value. In legitimate offerings, this type of information can be helpful in making an informed decision about entering into a transaction, but both testimonials and testing and research results can also be fabricated and/or manipulated by those who wish to deceive. While testimonials that appear in advertising will seldom fully identify the provider, they should reflect the sentiments of an actual satisfied customer and there should be a record on hand accordingly. When false testimonials are provided, an illicit promoter will not be able to provide any documentation, or perhaps attempt to offer fabricated documentation. Also along these lines is the practice of referring prospective customers to purported satisfied customers who are really working with an illicit promoter. Obviously, these purported satisfied customers, or "shills," provide glowing but untruthful recommendations in an effort to encourage the prospective customer to participate. Finally, references to testing or research results can be (1) totally fictitious (and thus no records would be available); (2) can be misrepresented and misinterpreted; (3) or can be of dubious reliability and trustworthiness (i.e., studies that are not conducted in accord with rigorous scientific standards and/or conducted by biased researchers). While documentation might be provided in scenarios (2) and (3), in many instances this material will need to be evaluated by experts to determine if it is accurately represented or if the research was properly conducted.

- Product inventory records—In cases involving the sale of a product where there are complaints of nonreceipt, determining whether the product was, in fact, available for distribution would be essential. Alternatively, in cases where products are faulty or misrepresented, follow-up inquiries with manufacturers with regard to product specifications or changes in manufacturers would be appropriate.

- List of vendors and service providers and records relating to transactions with them—These records might be useful in identifying subcontractors or providers of services that are pertinent to the business entity and/or activity under investigation. In cases where there is common ownership between the investigative subject(s) and a vendor or service provider, the possibility of excessive fees charged and/or no service/product rendered should be examined.

- Loan, real estate, and insurance documents—Loan documents provide evidence of indebtedness that might be indicative of a motive to engage in illegal activity. Additionally, the identity of the lender should be established and if the lender is a private party, his/her relationship to the investigative subject should be fully explored. Loans obtained through established lending institutions should be examined to determine if representations made on the loan application including collateral are accurate. Examination of insurance documents might be useful in verifying coverage that is represented and/or normally in force in a particular type of business operation. In fact, if this were the goal of seeking such documents, the failure to obtain them would actually be of greater significance. Insurance documents might also provide evidence of overinsuring the value of assets or perhaps insuring nonexistent assets. While insurance coverage could be established through the carrier, all policies might not be known. Thus, seeking insurance documents directly from the insured might identify previously unknown policies.

- Records relating to any previous or pending investigations or litigation—Highly relevant in most investigations is a history of similar or even other illegal behavior. There may be little record of prior investigations and while records of any prior litigation would be available elsewhere, knowing where to look can be problematic. Thus, there are advantages, if possible, to obtain this type of information directly from the investigative subject.

- Records of all corporate assets, including real estate, transportation conveyances, and investment accounts—Real estate holdings generally add to net worth, a factor that might be relevant in terms of forfeiture and restitution considerations. Also relevant to examining real estate holdings is how it was acquired and/or the impact of its acquisition on the financial condition of a business entity (or individual) (e.g., a diversion of company revenues). Records relating to other assets such as cars, boats, aircraft, and investment accounts might be useful in determining how they were obtained, what their roles were (if any) in the scheme (e.g., used as a facilitating conveyance or to launder funds), and what their values are. Again, this information might be helpful in exploring improper diversions of company funds and identifying assets for forfeiture and restitution.

- Business travel records—Examining these records also might be valuable when there is a concern about diverting company funds to personal or illegal activities. Referring again to the healthcare kickback scheme discussed earlier, travel expenses were falsified as another way to divert company monies to fund illegal kickbacks. Of course, in some instances, purported business travel isn't really company business, but rather personal in nature and travel records would be needed to pursue such cases.

COMMUNICATIONS, UTILITIES, AND TRAVEL RECORDS

The documents in this category of records are normally in the custody of third parties, that is, the providers of communication facilities, utility services, and companies that provide travel-related services. Thus, the issuance of a subpoena is usually required to obtain them, although in some instances the execution of a search warrant will be necessary. These records are often helpful in providing leads to and/or establishing communication links between individuals and/or business entities under investigation, the identity of individuals at a location and the travel itineraries of subjects of interest, respectively.

Communication Records

There was a time not long ago when the term *communication records* was a fancy way of referring to telephone toll records. To be sure, telephone toll records are still useful in identifying telephone calls between individuals of interest or possibly in the identification of victims. When requesting telephone toll records be sure to request subscriber information as well, which discloses the name and address of the holder of the telephone service, along with toll records for a specified time period.

Possibly complicating the task of obtaining telephone subscriber information and toll records, however, is the wide variety of service choices that are available, including cell phone service and service plans that do not charge for long distance calls, thus making the availability of toll records uncertain in some instances.

As e-mail now seems to rival voice communication via telephone in terms of popularity and volume, the acquisition of e-mail account information and stored e-mail messages has become a frequently encountered task. The controlling procedures for obtaining these types of records are statutorily defined in federal law under the Electronic Communications Privacy Act (ECPA), 18 U.S.C. Sections 2701–2712. This legislation was enacted to address the perceived imbalance that while a search warrant must be issued to search a home, subpoenas had previously been used to obtain the contents of e-mail accounts. Under the ECPA, subscriber information can be released incident to a request via a subpoena. However, the ECPA provides for the release of the contents of e-mail communications in storage up to 180 days with an information service provider (ISP) upon service of a search warrant. Moreover, obtaining this information in this manner does not provide for any notice to the account holder.[5] This matter will be revisited in Chapter 5, but suffice it now to say that when the contents of e-mail communications are pertinent to a case, it's time to start preparing to take this approach.

Although lacking the "glitz" of high tech and perhaps diminishing in its role, hard copy delivery is still widely utilized (for now any way) and will be routinely encountered as means of conducting business and communicating. While records of mailings and shipments can usually be obtained from hard copy delivery services with a subpoena, be prepared to execute a search warrant to take possession of any package or envelope while in their custody. In fact, the U.S. Postal Service will honor only federal search warrants to search and seize U.S. Mail. Coordinating with the Postal Inspection Service on such undertakings will facilitate the process.

Utility Services

Agencies/companies that provide utility services, including electricity, water, sewer, gas, and trash pick-up, maintain records that identify the party responsible for payment at service locations. This party may be the occupant of the premises or if not, utility records will identify another party that is likely to have some type of relationship with and knowledge of those occupying the location of interest. In the event this "other" party is a landlord, rental/lease records should be available that might provide helpful information. In instances where the "other" payer is not a landlord, exploring the relationship between this party and the occupants might be quite pertinent to the case. In any event, applications for utilities sometimes inquire whether the applicant has been a utility customer elsewhere, prior addresses, and employment, all of which may be of investigative interest. Moreover, payments submitted to utility companies might also identify banking relationships and accounts. Expect a subpoena to be necessary to obtain documents from utility providers although verbal information is sometimes provided upon request.

Travel Records

Investigators are sometimes faced with the task of placing an individual at a certain geographic location at a certain time or desire to track an individual's travels, generally. Travel tickets such as those for air, rail, or bus transportation, hotel records, and rental car records can be sought to accomplish these ends. Examining the names and addresses of individuals listed on these records might identify any falsifications and/or travel companions. Finally, obtaining payment records might also be of interest since such records might reveal unknown credit card and/or bank accounts. Once again, expect a subpoena to be necessary to obtain these documents.

DOCUMENTARY EVIDENCE: CONCLUDING COMMENTS

Given the wide range of investigative scenarios that can fall under the white collar crime umbrella, the above listings should be modified as necessary to acquire pertinent documentation as applicable. Having said that, one interesting observation has been that business entities created for the purpose of engaging in illegal activities often forego customary business protocols with regard to record keeping and documentation. Thus, the failure to maintain customary business records could certainly raise suspicion as to the bona fides and intent of a business operation.

A final, and perhaps ironic, comment with regard to documentary evidence is an admonition against adopting a literal *paper chase* perspective, that is, a mindset that emphasizes only the identification and acquisition of this type of material. Equally important is the understanding that this material must be reviewed, analyzed, and integrated into the case with witness testimony, the topic that follows in the next chapter. This can be a tedious process, but cases do not go forward without first taking this step. In fact, when a white collar crime case seems to be lagging in terms of progress toward a prosecution, it is not uncommon to find volumes, boxes, or even rooms full of documentary evidence that have never been touched.

CHAPTER HIGHLIGHTS

- The need to identify, acquire, and analyze documentary evidence is a defining characteristic of white collar crime cases.

- Records may be obtained through voluntary surrender/request, abandonment, public access channels, and the use of legal processes including subpoenas and search warrants.

- Documentary evidence that is often important in white collar crime cases includes:

  - Promotional and transaction-related material in the custody of victims (although such materials can sometimes be obtained using proactive investigative approaches);

  - Public records and nonpublic records in the custody of government agencies;

  - Financial records (for purposes here—in the custody of third parties);

  - Business records (for purposes here—in the custody of investigative subjects); and

  - Communication, utility, and travel records (for purposes here—in the custody of third parties).

- While identifying and gathering of documentary evidence is a necessary step in white collar crime investigation, the review and analysis of this material, along with integration with testimony, will be crucial in resolving a white collar crime case.

Notes

1. W. W. Bennett and K. A. Hess, *Criminal Investigation*, 8th ed. (Belmont, CA: Wadsworth, 2007), p. 161.

2. G. A. Manning, *Financial Investigation and Forensic Accounting* (Boca Raton, FL: CRC Press, 1999), pp. 196–199.

3. Ibid., pp. 199–200.

4. Ibid., p. 214.

5. Computer Crime and Intellectual Property Section, Criminal Division, U.S. Department of Justice (2002, July), *Searching and Seizing Computers and Obtaining Electronic Evidence in Criminal Investigations.* Retrieved from U.S. Department of Justice website, http://www.usdoj.gov/criminal/cybercrime/searching.html#A (accessed March 7, 2005).

CHAPTER 4

Interviews: Gathering Testimonial Evidence

Key Terms and Concepts	
■ Complainants	■ Noncomplainants
■ Cooperative versus Noncooperative Victims	■ Target
	■ Testimonial Evidence
■ Electronic Surveillance	■ Undercover Operations
■ Investigative Questionnaire	■ Written Statements
■ Memorandum of Interview	
■ Miranda Warnings	

The fact that the previous chapter addressed the gathering of documentary evidence should not be interpreted to mean that gathering testimonial evidence can only be accomplished after records, and so on are identified and collected. In the normal course of an investigation, these two processes are likely to coincide. If there is any justification for the ordering of these discussions, two considerations come to mind. The first consideration does have a sequencing aspect. While victim interviews are likely to be conducted early on in these cases, as will be discussed below, approaching the alleged offenders (if at all) and individuals close to them (employees/business associates, friends, relatives, etc.) might very well be a later investigative step that is taken once a good understanding of the facts are obtained.

The second consideration involves the overall importance of testimonial evidence in these cases and the necessity for it not to be overlooked. Although white collar crime cases are widely referred to as "paper" cases, their successful resolution through an enforcement proceeding will still rely heavily on testimonial evidence. Even the "paper" in these cases, to be useful in most enforcement proceedings, must be introduced through witness testimony. Thus, without disputing the "paper case" moniker that is almost universally applied to white collar crimes, the importance of gathering testimonial evidence can not be over emphasized. For the investigator this means conducting interviews of those who have been affected and/or have knowledge of the alleged wrongdoing and providing prosecutors with the information so obtained. It can also mean employing other avenues to obtain testimonial evidence, such as use of undercover techniques and electronic surveillance. These latter topics will be touched upon at the conclusion of this chapter, while victim interviews will be our initial focus.

INTERVIEWING VICTIMS OF WHITE COLLAR CRIME

Complainants

As discussed earlier, some victims of white collar crime do submit voluntary complaints. When such complaints indicate a basis to go forward with an investigation, not surprisingly these individuals are often among the first to be interviewed for a number of reasons. They have identified themselves as victims and, thus, are known to possess information of probable interest to the investigation and perhaps relevant documents/records as well. Normally, their complaint report provides contact information, thus facilitating follow-up attention. In a typical scenario, not only would an investigator have a telephone number (or perhaps e-mail address) at hand, but most importantly the complaining party is probably waiting to hear from the authorities. The point is that a high degree of cooperation can be expected from voluntary complainants and they will be familiar with (at least in general terms) what the investigator wishes to discuss. Moreover, such individuals are usually motivated to assist in the investigation, which usually means meeting with the investigator.

In Chapter 2, the need to establish liaison with other agencies that might receive complaints and information of mutual interest was emphasized. Obviously, whenever voluntarily submitted complaints are received from such sources, these victims should normally be viewed in the same manner as those who voluntarily submit complaints directly to the agency conducting the investigation, that is, cooperative and conversant with the problem at hand. In the initial contact with such victims it is usually helpful to explain that their complaint was referred by the organization they originally submitted it to, for follow-up investigation.

Personal, face-to-face interviews with victims is a *best practice* and such face-to-face contact should be made prior to identifying any victim as a trial witness, that is, the first time an investigator should meet face to face with a victim witness should not be during trial preparations. Having said that, when time is of the essence and face to face victim interviews would prove too cumbersome to pursue, telephone interviews of voluntary complainants can be considered. Notwithstanding the common perception of white collar crime investigations being slow moving and nonemergent in nature, there are times when expedience counts. Later chapters will discuss arrest and search warrants, injunctive actions, and forfeitures, enforcement actions that sometimes must be accomplished on a timely basis to prevent targets and records from disappearing, further victimization, and/or seizing illegally obtained assets. Although basing these actions, in part, on victim information obtained during face-to-face interviews would be preferable, the fact that voluntary complainants have usually submitted some type of record of their victimization for review and their cooperation would normally be anticipated, telephone interviews could often suffice.

Other Victims

As suggested in Chapter 2, voluntary complaints about white collar offending typically are the tip of the iceberg in terms of overall victimization. Consequently, it is usually necessary to identify and make contact with individuals who are potential victims but for a variety of reasons have chosen not to make any report to authorities. These reasons can include *inter alia*, they don't know they have been victimized; they don't care if they have been victimized; they don't know who to make a report to; they don't want to become involved in an investigation; or they don't want to deal with any type of law enforcement agency. Not surprisingly, these possible reasons for nonreporting can affect the reception any investigative inquiry will receive. The issue here is that while those who voluntarily submit complaints can be viewed as cooperative and sophisticated enough to report their victimization, a similar level of cooperation and/or sophistication might not be found among those who do not self-report their victimization. Among these categories, the group that professes not to know of their victimization might pose the least problem in this respect, especially if the scheme is particularly complex and/or has not fully played out to the point that they would know something has gone awry. There is an old saying "The best scheme is the one where people don't know they've been had."

On the other hand, be on the lookout for individuals falling into this category who simply lack the capacity to understand what has occurred. Witness evaluation will be summarized in the next section, but keep in mind that victims are potential witnesses, and for witnesses to be effective, they must be articulate enough to verbally communicate their experience and withstand cross-examination on their testimony in this respect.

Another variation in this regard is the person who does not believe they have been victimized and might even feel satisfied with their dealings with the subject of the investigation. Identifying such individuals can actually be valuable for at least a couple of reasons. First, information supplied by such individuals might warrant a reconsideration of whether an actionable violation occurred. It is far better to uncover this type of information early in the investigation and evaluate it than after a complaint or charges have been filed. Second, even if there is still reason to go forward with the case, knowledge of the existence of individuals who had satisfactory dealings with the subject should be used to help strengthen the investigation. Possible explanations for the variance in dealings with the subject can be explored and as testimony from any satisfied customers is likely to be offered by the defense, the prosecution can be prepared to deal with it.

Individuals who fail to voluntarily report their victimization because they did not know who to turn to might possibly be very cooperative once contact is made. The caveat to consider when dealing with this group, however, is again the sophistication issue as it applies to being a potential witness. In a highly specialized type of white collar crime where reporting venues are not local and not well advertised, this lack of knowledge might be very plausible. When the case involves a matter that is routinely reported to the local police or the local consumer protection agency, the ability to be a witness would need to be carefully assessed.

Finally, what about those victims who don't care, don't want to become involved in an investigation, and/or don't want to deal with an investigative agency? The question that arises when dealing with victims in these categories is what level of cooperation (possibly over a long period) can be expected from individuals who were victimized but, nevertheless possess such attitudes. It would be unwise to eliminate from further consideration any of these types of individuals during the investigative phase. However, in the event charges are brought, the last type of uncooperative witness a prosecutor will want to deal with (and this should hold true for the investigator as well) is a victim witness. Accordingly, it would be wise to make note of the anticipated level of cooperation from any potential witness. And one final thought with regard to those who display a reluctance not to become involved or who seem ill at ease when dealing with law enforcement personnel: run a criminal history check in these instances. It is best to learn about a potential victim witness' past sooner rather than later.

Identifying Noncomplainants

As discussed earlier, investigators should always attempt to identify the greatest amount of victimization as possible, which in many cases means identifying actual individuals who could become victim witnesses. However, once voluntarily submitted complaints from both inside and outside the agency are identified and compiled, developing additional victims might very well be possible, but will require focused investigative effort. These efforts include (but are not limited to) the following:

- Review of subpoenaed records—records from bank accounts that hold customer deposits are particularly useful. Be sure, however, to request actual copies of deposited items in order to identify these individuals. Depending upon the case, other third party records might also be helpful in a similar manner, most notably telephone and Internet records. Finally, if the decision is made to subpoena records from the alleged offender, include among the requested items customer lists, customer orders, customer fulfillment records, any tape recordings of customer transactions, and any customer correspondence and complaints.

- Review of records seized via search warrant—The real issue here is to insure that customer records including customer lists, customer orders, customer fulfillment records, tape recordings of customer transactions, customer correspondence and complaints, and the like are included in the search warrant so that they can be seized. As will be discussed more at length in the next chapter, utilizing a search warrant in a white collar crime case is a two-pronged undertaking: (1) obtaining and executing the warrant and (2) carefully examining and evaluating the materials seized. Obviously, the activity we are discussing here falls into the latter category and represents a very viable method to identify others who have been victimized by the crime under investigation.

- Mail covers can be obtained through application to the Postal Inspection Service. Mail covers record only information that appears on the exterior of envelopes (name/address of sender and name/address of recipient; postmark information) and do not involve opening or examining contents of any mail. The issuance of mail cover is not dependent upon establishing probable cause, but an investigator must be able to articulate a basis for believing a crime is being committed and how information from a mail cover will assist in the investigation. In cases that rely on customers' mailing correspondence/remittances to the alleged offender, mail covers will provide the names and addresses of these potential victims. It should also be noted that mail covers can be useful in identifying banks and other financial institutions utilized by an alleged offender, as well as other individuals/business entities that the alleged offender might be in contact with.

- Do not forget to inquire of those who submitted complaints voluntarily whether they know of any others who dealt with the alleged offender. Occasionally, this type of inquiry can pay off.

These are but four established methods of identifying and developing victims who do not voluntarily complain. Depending upon the skillfulness of the investigator, agency authority, and unique aspects of a case, other methods might certainly be available. Keep in mind, however, the reasons discussed above about why some potential victims do not voluntarily complain. Approaching such individuals in an effort to solicit their cooperation should be done with tact. At the very least, some noncomplaining victims might be offended simply by perceived government intrusion, no mater how well intentioned. Accordingly, it is usually safer to avoid statements such as, "I obtained your name and address from a mail cover," or "I found your check in reviewing subpoenaed bank records" (which if obtained via a federal grand jury subpoena would be best to avoid for other reasons as well; see Chapter 8). Conversely, it is often sufficient to simply explain that inquiries are being made incident to complaints or concerns about the subject and that their name was discovered while reviewing records acquired through the investigation as possibly having dealings/ contact with this individual/company.

Contacting/Interviewing Victims

To reemphasize a point made earlier, it is always preferable to interview *any* potential witness in person. However, for practical and logistical reasons, face-to-face interviews may not be possible in the early stages of an investigation, often because of exigency or volume considerations. As discussed earlier, victims who submit complaints voluntarily are often good candidates for telephone interviews when time is of essence because of investigative considerations. These individuals have demonstrated their concern and motivation to cooperate and their complaint usually exists in hard copy format, which might include pertinent documents as well. Nevertheless, at some point a face-to-face interview should be conducted in these instances and certainly before these individuals appear as witnesses in any type of judicial proceeding.

However, what about other scenarios involving victim contact? General concerns about contacting noncomplaining victims who have been identified through investigative techniques have been touched upon in the previous section. In addition, two other scenarios warrant consideration and they are somewhat intertwined: volume of victims and investigative urgency. First, in keeping with the general proviso that all witnesses should be personally interviewed, when this number is relatively small, personal interviews can usually be accomplished in a timely fashion. However, even with a small number of victims, conducting face-to-face interviews in a timely manner can become complicated when they are located over a wide geographic expanse. Most federal agencies have established processes to assist investigations being conducted in other parts of the country to include conducting requested interviews in their assigned areas. As discussed at the outset of this volume, this is one of the assets that enable federal agencies to investigate white collar crime more effectively and efficiently than state and local agencies. Nevertheless, the reality is that there are limitations to this system as well. Whether the local office can conduct the interview within a necessary timeframe and whether an investigator not familiar with the complexities of a case can adequately conduct an interview are questions that need to be considered. Fortunately, federal investigators have nationwide jurisdiction and can travel outside their duty station, if necessary (travel budgets and policies permitting), to deal with any such limitations.

Then, of course, there is the scenario where time is of the essence. Investigators can be faced with the need to execute a search warrant or acquire an injunction on an urgent basis. To reiterate once again, voluntary complainants are most suitable for telephone interviews, if and when an investigative urgency makes such interviews necessary. If information is needed in these circumstances from noncomplaining victims, seek out individuals nearest in proximity and approach them on a face-to-face basis. Although later chapters will address the details of taking various types of enforcement actions, these actions all require investigators to submit sworn affidavits containing information about the facts of their investigation. It is imperative that this information be accurate and truthful. Although not ideal, taking information supplied by voluntary complainants and then following up with a telephone interview in urgent situations will usually provide an adequate comfort level in this respect. Conversely, for reasons already discussed, interviewing noncomplaining victims via telephone could be fraught with problems including unintentionally providing faulty information. Thus, it would be wise in these situations to contact individuals via telephone and set up an appointment for a face-to-face interview, if they are willing to cooperate. This practice permits a better opportunity for the victim to recollect facts and gather thoughts together, than engaging in a "cold call" interview with an investigator on a subject that for any number of reasons they did not report. The investigator, in turn, can expect to engage in a more probing interview and will be better able to assess the information provided.

A final scenario to consider is how to deal with a large volume of potential, noncomplaining victims. This scenario can arise as a result of reviewing alleged offender bank deposit records or business records acquired via subpoena or search warrant. One answer would be to send questionnaires to these potential victims along with a cover letter that explains the nature of the inquiry being made and soliciting their assistance in completing the questionnaire. The completion and return of the questionnaire can be viewed as an indication of cooperation and interest in the investigation, and the information provided can be evaluated prior to any follow-up contact. The questionnaire can also ask for copies of any relevant documents to be included as well. A pattern of victimization established in this manner can be quite compelling to a prosecutor, even without any follow-up contact. These questionnaires can also provide a basis for investigators to choose victims for follow-up interviews. Those respondents who provided a detailed account of their experience, especially when their experience falls into a consistent pattern would be likely candidates for follow-up interviews. Of course, again, these interviews should be conducted on face-to-face basis and the completion and submission of the questionnaire will facilitate investigator contact in making these arrangements. Moreover, in the absolutely necessary situation where urgency demands a telephone interview, those respondents who appear most cooperative and whose information appears most detailed might be suitable for this type of approach and it will not be a "cold call."

Finally, it should be noted that questionnaire results could identify variations in the scheme or victimization or even raise questions about the viability of the case due to a pattern of *satisfied* respondents. Inquiries should be pursued into this latter scenario, nevertheless, to determine if a crime occurred only during a particular period of the operation under investigation. For instance, a company under investigation for selling a defective product might have been operating legitimately at one point, but purposely began to substitute the defective product for a period of time.

The Investigative Questionnaire

While an investigative questionnaire seeks out information similar in scope to a general agency complaint form, to be most useful it must also focus on the specifics of the case at hand and should be tailored accordingly. A *best practice* is to ask for the respondent's name, address, telephone numbers, and e-mail address at the outset. When this information is sought at the end of a questionnaire, it is sometimes omitted. As discussed with general agency complaint forms, keep the questionnaire as brief and simple as possible so as not to discourage completion. Finally, enclose a post-paid return envelope that is large enough to accommodate copies of pertinent documents.

Fair Warning: As an affirmative solicitation that targets a particular subject that in many instances has not been charged with any offense, care must be taken to avoid criticisms and challenges that have occasionally been leveled against investigators who have used this technique. First, the cover letter should contain a disclaimer that states that the inquiry at hand should not be construed as a claim or charge that the subject has violated any law. Second, avoid leading questions in the questionnaire.

Appendix B contains a sample cover letter and questionnaire for guidance in developing these documents.

Victim Witness Interviews and Evaluation

Out of necessity, there has already been a good deal of discussion about dealing with victim witnesses. Thus, the following will break little new ground and serve to summarize points already made. The one exception in this respect will be witness evaluation considerations.

A primary concern for investigators vis-à-vis victim witnesses frankly is to keep them happy and cooperative, possibly over a long period of time. Of the various types of witnesses that might be needed to take an enforcement action, victim witnesses are especially important because a good deal of the evidence against the offenders will come from them. Thus, uncooperative, reluctant victim witnesses are troublesome to both investigators and prosecutors; hence the emphasis above on the value of voluntary complainants (and providing a means for voluntary complaints to be submitted) and conversely, the possible uncertainties surrounding those victims who did not complain. Nevertheless, the eagerness of even the most cooperative of victim witnesses can fade over the months (and hopefully not years) that it can sometimes take to bring an enforcement action. The "sting" of the financial loss and/or deception will have long passed and undoubtedly for some, the need to personally appear at a trial or other proceeding will be a hardship or otherwise in conflict with prevailing priorities. And this lack of interest potential applies not only to individuals, but to victimized business entities, as well.

What can investigators do to offset victim witnesses' lack of interest that, in turn, could manifest itself in noncooperation? Obviously, the bottom line is that in most types of enforcement proceedings witnesses can be compelled to appear through subpoena power. However, investigators can endeavor to complete the case as quickly as possible, identify victim witnesses for testimony who have displayed the most enthusiasm and cooperation, and extend as much courtesy to these individuals as possible. While it is important to develop the full scope of victimization, when a case has numerous victims it is often not necessary to present testimony from all of them, thus affording an opportunity to be selective. And to be clear, those individuals who were identified as victims through some type of affirmative efforts as opposed to voluntary complainants should not be discounted if they are found to be cooperative and eager to assist.

Interviewing victim witnesses can normally be approached in a friendly, if not sympathetic manner. For best results, both in the short run and the long term, these interviews should normally be held at the convenience (meaning both location and time/date, within reason) of the victim. In many cases, by the time these interviews are undertaken, investigators have had an opportunity to review voluntarily submitted complaints and thus should have an understanding of the events surrounding victimization. With this knowledge in hand, investigators should develop a general outline for the initial interview (i.e., the major areas/points that need to be covered), but otherwise allow the victim to explain what happened. Unlike a highly structured interview that might appear officious, this type of format allows the victim to "vent" and fosters a better atmosphere for developing a rapport between the victim and the investigator. Through a freer-flowing interview format, new information might surface (i.e., material that was not sought and not mentioned by others) and it might permit a better evaluation of the witness.

However, an investigator would be wise to at least structure the interview chronologically, for example, "Tell me how and when this all began." The standard investigative questions need to be covered: who, what, when, where, how and why? Basically, it is necessary to fully understand the victim's story, but in doing so make sure these standard investigative points are covered, but in a way that captures information unique to the investigation at hand:

- While many crimes are "whodunits," white collar offenses frequently do not (but not always!) fall into this genre. Therefore, the "who" is often known although when dealing with a business, it is important to establish the name(s) of the person(s) the victim dealt with.

- The "what" involves a general explanation of the facts surrounding the case. Was this a consumer fraud, a stock swindle, a business embezzlement, agency program fraud, identity theft, and so on? This aspect of the interview will probably consume most of the discussion. Establish during this phase the outcome of the alleged wrongdoing and the nature and scope of any loss/harm.

- The "when" is important for statute of limitations reasons and this "when" issue not only involves the date of first contact, but also dates that tie in certain statutory violations. For example, under the federal mail fraud statute (18 USC 1341) the five-year statute of limitations is based on the dates the mails were used. Thus, dates items were received in the mail or deposited in the mail need to be identified (fortunately, postmarks can often help in this regard).

- The "where" issue establishes venue, that is, in what judicial district may the case be brought. For practical purposes, prosecutions are normally brought in the district where the alleged offender engaged in the wrongdoing; however, some federal offenses permit venue in districts where the victims are located, as well. For example, if an alleged offender operating from New York City used the mails to defraud individuals in Iowa and Nebraska only, the mail fraud statute allows for venue in these victim locations based on the fact that items that furthered the scheme to defraud were delivered into these states and mailings back to New York may have originated from them. Whether this scenario would be compelling enough to bring the prosecution in Nebraska or Iowa rather than New York City would probably be resolved through discussions between government attorneys at these locations.

- The "how" means understanding the mechanics of the offense, for example, what sequence of events took place and what events enabled the offense to occur. Again, if it hasn't already been established, this would be the time to determine often required statutory connections such as use of the mails, wires, affect on interstate commerce, federal programs, and so on. Exploring the "how" also involves gaining a detailed understanding of any misrepresentations made to the victim that resulted in their decision to engage in a transaction in which they suffered a loss.

Such an understanding can often involve having the victim witness recount the details of verbal communications that they had with the alleged offender either in person or over the telephone, as well as what they understood from any written materials provided to them. While it is important to identify any specific misrepresented verbal or written statements, it is equally important to determine any "macro" effect that the overall scheme methodology had on victim witnesses. The reasons to look in this direction are twofold:

1. Defense arguments can be made about the *materiality* of a given misrepresentation, that is, how important or how much weight should be attributed to a particular falsehood in causing an individual to a make a decision to enter into a transaction with the defendant. Obviously, statements promising a 30% return on investment in a case where victims received nothing at all including return of their principal would constitute a material misrepresentation. Likewise, false representations of multiple, nationwide locations or even a photograph of a large office building in an opulent setting purporting to be corporate headquarters of the investment firm would be more material (especially if it was determined that the real address was simply a box at a commercial mail receiving agency!). On the other hand, misinformation about how long the company has been in business or at a particular location, the experience of its owners, and the number of satisfied customers, *by themselves*, might be explained away as inconsequential, misunderstood, and/or oversights. However, investigators should attempt to have victims articulate the impact of the entire methodology that they encountered in terms of how it affected them in making decisions that led to their victimization. In fact, having the victims recall voice inflections, gestures, facial expressions, and paperwork procedures they encountered when dealing with the alleged offender(s) is an important exercise in evaluating the overall impact of a scheme's methodology. This author recalls a case involving the sale of whole life insurance policies that were misrepresented as "portable retirement plans" to nurses. An important part of the fraudulent sales methodology was for the insurance agent, upon completing a successful transaction, to insert the policy in an envelope, seal it, and hand it to the victim/purchaser with instructions to "put it away in a safe place until you are ready to retire." This paper work methodology was purposely designed to reduce the likelihood a victim/purchaser would examine the documents and discover she had not purchased a retirement plan, but rather a whole life insurance policy.

2. The second reason to evaluate the "macro" effect is to bring into question the supposed good faith that might be offered by "fine print" disclaimers presented in the literature provided to victims. The inclusion of disclaimers can be an obstacle for undertaking an enforcement action, especially a criminal prosecution, because it will be argued that the alleged offender really did set forth the true set of facts surrounding the transaction and there is no intent

to defraud. However, a sordid practice associated with disclaimers is to not prominently display them, present them in complicated "legalese" language, and print them in tiny font with faint color. These circumstances should not dissuade investigators from pursuing a case, when the "macro" effect of the scheme's methodology is to defraud. Very often if the presence of disclaimers forms a basis for not proceeding criminally, a civil enforcement action can nevertheless be applied.

- Inquiring about the "why" question can take on two directions. First, the witness can be quizzed about why they were told to take certain actions or provide certain information. This type of information would dovetail into a further exploration of the "how" of a case since it would expose the victim witnesses' thought processes based on representations made by the target. The other direction here is one for the investigator to ponder. Based on information being gathered from victim witnesses, investigators should consider why the target took certain actions or provided certain information to the victim witness. Especially early in an investigation, this type of critical analysis might help the investigator formulate future strategies.

Attempt to obtain a voluntary surrender of any pertinent documents they may have on hand, including advertising literature, correspondence and notes of conversations, contracts, invoices, copies of payments, and any other documents or records of their contact and/or transaction with the subject of the investigation. Review these documents with the victim witness and obtain an explanation for each of them. Ideally, take possession of the original documents at this time and make copies of them for the victim witness, if requested. Otherwise, retain copies and inform the victim witness to securely maintain the originals because they might be needed for introduction as evidence in the future. As *best practice*, have the victim witness date and initial each documentary item so that the source of the document can be identified and the date it was turned over to the government is recorded (even if only a copy).

Just as testimony can be compelled through a subpoena, production of documents can be as well. For individual victim witnesses, the need to compel the production of records of their victimization would certainly raise questions about their willingness to cooperate in the investigation. However, do not be surprised if business victims will request a subpoena for needed records relating to their victimization. Often they will justify such a request on grounds that they need to protect themselves against concerns that the records contain privileged customer, employee, and/or vendor information.

The issue of witness evaluation has been raised on several occasions already and evaluation criteria have been suggested or implied. Again to be clear, *the case is the case*; meaning if a violation occurred, it is necessary to work with the evidence at hand to prove it. In the context of victim witnesses this could mean few if any of them possess ideal characteristics. This does not mean that the case cannot go forward. The bottom line is that that witnesses are simply asked to provide truthful testimony under oath; that's all.

Nevertheless, when choices can be made, in addition to displaying cooperation an articulate person certainly offers advantages for the purposes of providing oral testimony. Witnesses whose testimony contains aggravating features would obviously be beneficial. Aggravating features could include particularly large financial losses, financial losses that have a particularly devastating impact, a particularly offensive scheme, and the like. Conversely, witnesses who feel they have not been victimized or who feel they have contributed to their victimization should be avoided, when possible. However, under *Brady* v. *Maryland* (373 US 83 [1963]), exculpatory evidence may be requested by defendants, so it is quite likely that the identities of victims who would present testimony that might mitigate the offense would be made known to defense counsel. Nevertheless, it would still be preferable for the government to be aware of these individuals and their testimony, rather than being surprised by it.

Finally, victim age, gender, race/ethnicity, and health factors should be noted. Age is important since under federal law and the law in some states, defendants who target the elderly can be eligible for enhanced sentencing provisions. For instance, in the U.S Code under section 2326 of Title 18, if 10 or more individuals over age 55 are victimized in a telemarketing scheme or if a telemarketing scheme is designed to specifically victimize individuals over age 55, a judge can impose a term of up to 10 years in addition to that imposed for the substantive offenses.

Likewise, although it might be apparent by the nature of the scheme and/or an obvious victim pattern, some schemes also target victims by gender or race/ethnicity. This type of selected targeting because of a particular vulnerability could be cast as an aggravating feature of the case, both for "selling" the case to a prosecutor and for enhancing chances of success in any subsequent enforcement action. Unfortunately, not withstanding subpoena power, health issues can limit the availability of witnesses. When these issues are evident, they should be tactfully explored early in the investigation.

"OTHER" WITNESS INTERVIEWS

This category includes sources of witness testimony that are either necessary to introduce documentary evidence; provide some type of technical or expert explanation of how a particular industry or program operates; or furnish direct information about the offense as a result of some type of nonvictim relationship with the subjects of the investigation. Each of these groups presents different investigator considerations. Typically, the least problematic are those individuals whose testimony is needed to introduce documents into the evidence. In most instances, these individuals will be employees of businesses that maintain the records in question and they are designated to provide testimony when necessary. Normally, these individuals and their employers will be cooperative in terms of interviews and testimonial appearances. Hopefully, they will be well versed with regard to the records in question so that they can assist investigators in understanding and analyzing them, as well as providing informative testimony. When such a witness has testified previously, this type of experience should help to add to the effectiveness and professionalism of their presentation.

A technical expert witness is sometimes necessary to explain how a particular type of business or industry operates to provide a needed foundation or understanding of the alleged misconduct in a case. For example, in a securities fraud case it might be necessary to have an industry representative testify as to the normal and proper procedures that are followed with regard to certain types of transactions. Likewise, it is sometimes necessary for government officials to explain department procedures in cases involving agency program fraud. For instance, in a Medicare fraud case it might be necessary to have testimony from a government official who can explain the inner-workings of this program and perhaps any specialized terminology.

As with the first group discussed, expert or technical witnesses should pose little problem in terms of cooperation. However, there are considerations that investigators must recognize if they need to identify and interview individuals as prospective technical or expert witnesses. First, to be most effective, these witnesses should be articulate and present an appropriate professional image. Along these lines, they should be able to explain their area of expertise, as simply and as straightforward as possible, and ideally in a manner that will maintain interest despite a possibly dry or complicated subject. Second, as the term clearly indicates, these witnesses should be technical or subject matter experts in their field and investigators should be satisfied that the individual being considered to fulfill this role does, in fact, possess the required knowledge, training, and/or experience. Moreover, it would be best to avoid any controversial experts, for example, those who have advocated a position that is at odds with the mainstream in their field or whose personal background could raise credibility questions. Third, it is wise to inquire of the selected expert whether his/her testimony could be challenged on the basis of differing interpretations or theories within the field. If so, the appropriate follow-up would include querying this expert about how these challenges can be dealt with. It might very well be necessary for investigators to undertake research on their own as well as to interview other experts to obtain a consensus opinion. In the process, however, the case will benefit from becoming informed on any possible variations in relevant technical testimony. As an aside, with these kinds of opportunities it is not uncommon for white collar crime investigators to become well versed in a variety of industries and professions. In fact, as a young investigator this author took it as a great compliment when a mortgage broker he was interviewing incident to an advance fee loan case inquired why he knew so much about the mortgage business.

A final type of individual who falls into the "Other Witness" category are those who have knowledge of the events under investigation but are not victims, records custodians, experts, or the alleged offenders themselves. These individuals can have simply been in the right or wrong place (depending upon how that is viewed) at the right time or they can be individuals who are in some way associated with the alleged offender(s), but are not being targeted for enforcement action. Both types of individuals pose potential problems as witnesses that need to be considered. The person who has valuable testimony to offer but is otherwise unconnected with the case as a victim or in some way related to the subject(s) of the investigation might see little advantage to becoming involved. Accordingly, it would behoove investigators to approach such individuals in as accommodating a manner as possible. However, it would certainly be advantageous to be as prepared as possible in terms of the type of information this person could provide and why. Again, these types of potential witnesses might simply not want to get involved, but when confronted with information that shows that "you know what they know," they might be persuaded to extend their cooperation. Granted, these individuals, too, can be subpoenaed to acquire their testimony. However, as has been evident, the emphasis being put forth here is that establishing and maintaining cooperative relationships with witnesses will make resolving the case an easier task.

Individuals who have or had some type of personal or professional relationship with the investigative subject(s), not surprisingly, can be problematic for interviews and testimonial purposes. Of course, there are exceptions. Disgruntled employees, coworkers, and business associates are sometimes only too eager to exact their revenge. Likewise, on the personal side, soured romantic/domestic relationships and fallouts with friends and relatives can provide motives for individuals close to the target(s) to cooperate. When these types of situations present themselves, investigators should not hesitate to explore them, keeping in mind the necessity to corroborate information that comes from highly biased sources.

However, a likely scenario that will confront investigators will be the need to interview and evaluate for witness potential those individuals who have or had business, employment, and/or social relationships with the investigative subject(s) who at the very least are reluctant to cooperate, if not protective and loyal. Again, as has been suggested above and as will be discussed in later chapters, investigators will often have subpoena authority at their disposal that can compel testimony from even reluctant and hostile witnesses. The powers provided by grand juries in criminal cases are particularly useful in this regard and uncooperative witnesses can also be subpoenaed to testify at criminal trials. Civil and administrative proceedings do not have access to tools of equal power, but subpoena and deposition authority are frequently available and can be applied in recalcitrant witness situations.

Of course, the first step in addressing this type of scenario is to assess what type of information might be available from the individual and then evaluate the likelihood for cooperation and/or truthfulness. In instances where little would be gained from making contact with a close associate, the time and effort to do so might not be warranted (unless there is a tactical advantage to letting the subject know inquiries are being made about him/her). On the other hand, an assessment of uncooperativeness, hostility, and/or untruthfulness should not be a reason to avoid a person who is believed to possess helpful information.

In preparing for such an interview, do not discount the possibility that individuals thought to be uncooperative will attempt to avoid being located. Updated information on their whereabouts should be acquired before venturing out and knocking on doors, only to find they are no longer there. As information, strategies for locating reluctant/hostile individuals incident to serving grand jury subpoenas are discussed in more detail in Chapter 8. Another consideration is where would it be best to approach and interview this type of witness. Usually, confronting uncooperative or hostile witnesses in situations where they are alone and without any support group will prove most fruitful, especially when this is accomplished without forewarning and two investigators are present. It is not unusual that these tactics will result in at least some discussion and perhaps some useful information, as opposed to a refusal to talk at all. One approach that might be considered (and is a 180 degree departure from the surprise visit) is to simply contact the person of interest by telephone and invite them to the office for an interview. Although judgment must be exercised in employing this tactic (it is obviously not appropriate in all instances), the advantage is that interview can be done under more ideal circumstances and if they agree to appear, they might actually be more cooperative and truthful than if approached on their own turf. For those who decline or fail to appear, their intentions with regard to cooperation will be clearly established and can be subpoenaed, if necessary.

Success in dealing with uncooperative or hostile witnesses is also dependent upon the investigator being fully prepared to interview the person. Time should be taken before attempting any interview to establish what the desired objectives are and what information needs to be solicited to get there. However, when the interview subject is expected to be uncooperative, hostile, and/or untruthful, this preparation is especially important. Being familiar with the facts of the case (gathered till that point) and assessing what the witness should know and why they should know it are essential. If these types of individuals agree to be interviewed, they may feign lack of knowledge and/or attempt to provide untruthful information. These tactics can often be countered by good preparation. A well-prepared interviewer might obtain information that would otherwise not be volunteered through challenging, knowledgeable questions, and pointing out inconsistencies and inaccuracies in the interview subject's responses. Moreover, the interview subject might be less likely to be untruthful when he/she senses the interviewer is very conversant with the matter under investigation, especially when the alleged wrongdoing took place in a highly technical, complex environment.

Although the interview scenario being painted here is not one of a friendly meeting, investigators would be wise to extend courtesy and avoid inciting animosity among individuals who fall into this witness category. First, a tactful investigator might actually "win over" an uncooperative or hostile witness with a more friendly approach. Second, be mindful that it might be necessary to maintain a relationship with this unfriendly witness over an extended period of time and it would be to the investigator's advantage not to heighten any hostility or worse yet, have any ill will arise over personal as opposed to official duty issues. The point being made here is to keep the relationship professional and courteous as opposed to engaging in any type of remarks or dialog that would give rise to personal animosity. In fact, over time the hostile relationship might improve to at least a working relationship with the exercise of good human relations skills on the part of the investigator.

INTERVIEWING THE TARGET

Generally speaking, the term *target*, as used here, refers to the alleged offender. As will be introduced in Chapter 8, this is a term of art, so to speak, in Grand Jury proceedings to denote a person who is an imputed defendant in a case. In any event, whether this person is referred to as a suspect, alleged offender, or target, in most types of criminal investigations interviewing this person would be considered a priority, if not a crucial step, in the case. This is not necessarily the case in white collar crime investigations. To be clear, this does not suggest that there exists any prohibition against doing so, or that it is unnecessary or of little value to do so in these cases. In fact, especially in those white collar crime cases where the target's identity is unknown (e.g., identity theft, credit card fraud, check fraud), interviewing the person believed to be responsible might be essential to bringing charges in the case.

However, a larger proportion of white collar crime cases involve situations where the identity of the alleged offender(s) is known and the issue in need of resolution is whether a violation of law occurred and whether this person(s) can be held responsible for it. This type of scenario gives rise to two considerations relative to interviewing targets. Given the nature of many white collar crimes, it is not uncommon for individuals who become of interest to investigators as possible targets to obtain legal counsel not after being charged, but upon the first hint of an investigation. Not surprisingly, defense attorneys will typically put clients "off limits" to any investigative inquiries, thus shutting off any possibility for investigators to conduct an interview. Another approach along these lines is where defense attorneys make their clients available for interview but under very controlled circumstances. These circumstances will invariably include the attorney being present, but can also include making certain topics nondiscussable. Of course with a defense attorney present, expect interruptions and interjections (e.g., "don't answer that question") as well as a favorable "spin" to the events in question presented by the client, attorney, or both. The entire purpose of offering this "controlled" interview is to convince investigators no violation has occurred or at least the subject of the interview is not responsible for any violation. Certainly in some instances this can be the case while in others this tactic, whether devised by the client or the defense counsel, could be employed in an attempt to simply deflect responsibility for the misconduct. In any event, it would be foolish not to take advantage of this type of interview opportunity because it affords a view of a possible defense in the event charges are brought. It goes without saying, however, that any information gleaned from an interview under these circumstances needs to be carefully evaluated and corroborated.

A second consideration for interviewing a target flows from this notion of a "favorable spin." Even without the benefit of the presence of legal counsel, many targets in white collar crime investigations have a knack for being able to "explain away" their conduct in a manner that at the very least places no liability on them, and can perhaps be quite convincing in doing so, as well. The terms *Con*, *Glib*, *Scam Artist*, and the like have well-earned origins in the history of white collar crime. Individuals who commit white collar crime can be personally engaging if not sophisticated and intelligent as well—characteristics that sometimes enable such individuals to handle themselves quite well in an interview with investigators. Thus, when interviewing targets be prepared for three possible outcomes: (1) a total denial of wrongdoing by way of an explanation that admits no liability; (2) statements that are untruthful; (3) and in perhaps the best-case scenario, a partial, but not full admission or acknowledgment of responsibility. With certain exceptions (e.g., identity theft, credit card fraud, check fraud), it was this author's experience that there was little likelihood of obtaining anything but denials and self-serving or untruthful statements from individuals believed to be responsible for white collar offending during the investigative phase of the case. Thus, in most cases a decision to interview a white collar crime target should not be based on the misperception that it would result in admissions of guilt, if not a complete confession. However, there may be strategic or tactical advantages to be gained, such as learning about possible defenses; obtaining partial admissions or incriminating statements; and other information that may be helpful in pursuing the investigation. When an investigator is permitted to enter the premises where the offending conduct is believed to have taken place for the purpose of conducting an interview, this visit can serve as an opportunity to survey the premises for the presence of evidence of a crime. These observations may prove helpful in developing probable cause for a search warrant (as will be discussed in the next chapter). Of course, absent a likelihood of obtaining a confession, there may be a distinct disadvantage to approaching a target prior to taking an action such as a search warrant because of the possibility of destruction of evidence and/or flight. On the other hand, approaching a person believed to be responsible for white collar misconduct and asking to speak with him/her incident to being a target of an investigation certainly sends a strong message about the government's intentions. Sometimes taking that approach forces this person to "table," so to speak, that is, it brings about a negotiated plea or settlement.

The point to this whole discussion, however, is that seeking to interview the target in a white collar crime case is not an "automatic" step in these investigations. There are times when such opportunities will not be available. There are times when it might be attempted for a tactical or strategic advantage, and times when it might not be done to preserve a tactical or strategic advantage. And frankly, there are times when a decision is made not to interview the target (at least during the investigative phase) because it is believed that little if anything would be gained and the case can proceed with evidence gathered through other means. Again, even when the interview is attempted or the opportunity is provided through counsel, approach it with limited goals and expectations.

If the decision is made to attempt to interview the target or if this opportunity is afforded through the target's counsel, thorough preparation is a must if the maximum benefit is to be derived. First, unlike the unstructured approach recommended when dealing with victim witnesses, here a more structured format will likely yield better results. At the very least, the topics of conversation will be dictated by the investigator and not vice versa, which could be the case if the target were given a freer rein. Preparation should begin with an outline of the topics to be covered, followed by the development of specific questions in each topical area. Be mindful that these specific questions can focus on pertinent documents to include interpretations of language contained therein, the identification of signatures on these documents, and authorship responsibility, among others. Also, inquire whether the target will voluntarily surrender records of interest.

Investigators might be limited to the extent they can determine the time and place of a target interview. Ideally, an investigator would prefer interviewing a target on "home turf," for example, the agency office or prosecutor's office. Occasionally, this opportunity will present itself, although it is probably more likely to occur when accompanied by defense counsel. More frequently, investigators will find themselves approaching targets elsewhere to include home, work, public places, or in attorney's offices when defense counsel is retained. Interviewing a target on his/her "turf" at home or work can possibly be a limiting factor. However, this factor can be offset by the impact of an unannounced visit. Although it is necessary to take advantage of the opportunities that present themselves in this regard, a home interview might be less desirable than the work location in terms of investigator control of the interview and perhaps in potentially hostile situations, investigator safety as well. The latter concern arises in interview scenarios that could be contentious in nature, and especially when friends or relatives are present at the residence. Conversely, approaching a target unannounced, when alone, in a public place might shift the "turf" advantage to the investigators and reduce this type of potential. Of course, a question to be answered with this tactic is whether an interview can be effectively conducted in a public environment.

The bottom line is that if a decision is made to interview the target because it would be in the best interest of the investigation, pursue what opportunities are available and make the best of them. However, two basic ground rules apply:

1. a second investigator should always be present in these types of interviews for witness purposes and occasionally to ensure investigator safety;
2. absent the presence of legal counsel, the interview should be conducted with only the target and investigator in attendance (i.e., no relatives, spouses, friend, coworkers) and plans to approach the target for this purpose should be made accordingly.

In criminal investigations, the question of whether a target must be advised of his/her *Miranda* rights incident to an interview with investigators should be addressed. Most criminal investigators are well schooled in the governing case law in this area and their agency policies that have risen in response to it. Thus, an in-depth discussion will not be pursued here, especially in light of the sometimes-limited importance of, and/or access to, target statements. In any event, generally speaking, *Miranda* warnings need to be administered in a custodial interrogation of a target of criminal investigation. Obviously, a person who has been arrested is in custody and questioning this person about the case incident to the arrest would constitute a custodial interrogation. However, an arrest, in and of itself, need not trigger the *Miranda* litany, if the investigators involved do not plan to question the accused.[1] Nevertheless, a *best practice* might be to administer these warnings whenever a suspect is taken into custody even though no questioning is planned. Largely due to the widespread media exposure given to the use of *Miranda* warnings, when they are recited to a person who has been taken into custody it sends a very clear message: "they're in trouble!; this is not a civil matter." Moreover, even when the intent is not to question the target incident to arrest, some people have a propensity to talk. As suggested above it would be unusual in these types of cases to ever hear a full confession except perhaps incident to a plea agreement that calls for complete cooperation. However, incriminating statements, even if snippets of remarks, can be made in times of stress and/or surprise, for example, incident to arrest. Thus, it would be prudent to protect the potential usefulness of any such statements by always making it a practice to *Mirandize* white collar crime targets being taken into custody, even when there are no plans for questioning. Yes, case law has sided with the government on the use of unsolicited, incriminating statements obtained in these types of situations.[2] However, why raise the possibility of getting bogged down in extraneous litigation in this regard when it can be avoided?

A clearer mandate exists with regard to administering *Miranda* warnings when a person is interviewed as a target in an investigation and is incarcerated, either pretrial or in prison. As long as the topic of the interview focuses on the incarcerated person as a target, this would be considered a custodial interrogation. It follows then that *Miranda* warnings would be needed even if the reason for a person's incarceration is unrelated to the subject of the interview.

Perhaps a bit more perplexing are circumstances where a target is to be interviewed, but is not in physical custody. These circumstances could typically arise when a decision is made to interview a target in a criminal investigation during the investigative phase (i.e., prior to any charges being brought). While a quick (and arguably correct) answer to this type of scenario is that *Miranda* warnings are not required since the interview would not be custodial in nature, investigators do need to be mindful that the notion of not being in custody or in a coercive environment might not be shared by a target interview subject. An investigator can have no plans to take the target into custody during or immediately after the interview, but what does the person of the interview think, especially if the nature of the questioning implicates them in criminal activity? Does this person understand that he/she is not in custody, and that their freedom is not being significantly deprived as a result of the interview with the investigator?[3] If this person can successfully convince a judge that he/she believed they were in custody or otherwise could not leave the interview with the investigator, any statements made *could* be excluded from evidence. Some agency policies might simplify this dilemma by mandating that *Miranda* warnings be issued whenever a target is to be interviewed, thus negating further deliberation on this subject.

Hopefully, however, most agency policies are not so restrictive and permit investigators to be guided by the concept of custodial interrogation when deciding whether or not to provide *Miranda* warnings. To reiterate again, thanks to their widespread recitation in the movies and on television, *Miranda* warnings have become the widely known indicator of "Oh, Oh, I'm in trouble." Consequently, issuing *Miranda* warnings when not necessary is not advantageous to the investigator. When targets are automatically presented *Miranda* warnings in noncustodial situations, many will decline to be interviewed, thereby eliminating the opportunity to engage him/her in any conversation. Even interviews that do not result in incriminating statements can still provide valuable information about possible defenses and/or alibis, and help in identifying other involved individuals and understanding the operation of the scheme, and so on. Thus, it is to the investigator's advantage not to "scare off" a target from talking by reciting *Miranda* at the outset of the interview whenever taking this approach is lawful.

Nevertheless, investigators might still wish to be sensitive to the perceptions of the target to preclude litigation over the admissibility of statements by targets in noncustodial interview situations. For instance, when a target interview takes place in an investigator's or prosecutor's office on a *voluntary* basis, this type of environment could be perceived as custodial and coercive in nature. Thus, while providing *Miranda* warnings is arguably not necessary (and might actually convey an erroneous notion of custody, in doing so), depending on the savvy, sophistication, and/or English-speaking skills of the target interview subject (i.e., lack thereof) it would not be unwise in some instances to remind this person that their appearance is voluntary, they are not in custody, and they can leave whenever they choose. On the other hand, it might be more difficult for a target to raise a custodial and/or coercive environment argument when attempting to suppress incriminating statements that are elicited from an interview that took place on the target's "turf" (e.g., their residence, place of business, or perhaps a public place). Thus, such circumstances would seem to provide a less compelling basis to be concerned about the voluntary nature of any incriminating statements obtained. Finally, providing *Miranda* warnings when interviewing a target in the presence of a defense attorney generally can be approached in two ways. If the warnings are provided and the target does make incriminating statements, there *might* be a greater likelihood of their eventual admissibility (although a successful claim of ineffective counsel could offset any advantage in this regard). On the other hand, if a defense attorney plans to be present during a target interview, most likely he/she will discuss with the investigator and/or prosecutor the nature of investigation and status of the client (i.e., as a target), establish ground rules that he or she feels is in the best interest of the client, and referee the interview. Under these circumstances, an investigator could feel that the target's rights are sufficiently protected and, thus, forego the formality and foreboding nature of *Miranda* warnings. Taking this approach *might* even result in a more cooperative atmosphere for the interview.

Target Interviews: In Summary

They are not an automatic step in white collar crime investigations. Don't expect to gain much from target interviews in terms of cooperation or truthfulness. Nevertheless, learning of possible defenses and alibis through such efforts can be helpful and some other strategic advantages might be achieved. Confessions are rare, but incriminating statements can be obtained in some instances. Thus, when the decision is made to approach a target for the purposes of an interview, be thoroughly prepared.

INTERVIEW WORK PRODUCTS

Notes

Investigators should always prepare notes incident to interviews with victims, targets, and all other types of witnesses. Moreover, notes should always reflect the date, place, and time of the interview (starting and ending) of the interview and the identities of those present.

Whether notes can or should be written contemporaneously with the interview will vary with the circumstances at hand. Generally, this can be done in cooperative witness situations, and perhaps even expected. However, sometimes with less cooperative witnesses, it can be a source of distraction and in fact, the investigator might want to focus on maintaining a flowing conversation, to the extent possible, rather than writing. Of course, in any type of interview scenario it is ideal to have one investigator conduct the interview with a second investigator on hand to take notes. However, when this is not possible and taking notes contemporaneously is not in the best interest of conducting the interview, the investigator should make notes immediately after concluding the discussion. In fact, one alternative to handwritten notes in these circumstances would be to dictate notes into a handheld recorder immediately following the discussion. Keep in mind, though, that handwritten notes made contemporaneously with or immediately after an interview have sometimes played a crucial role in corroborating investigator testimony. For notes transcribed from dictation to be similarly credible, they should reflect the date and time (starting and ending times) of the interview as well as the date and time of the dictation, which should be immediately upon the conclusion of the interview. Retaining the actual dictation tape should be considered in consequential situations.

Memorandum of Interview

Notes, in turn, should then become the source document for the formulation of a narrative report of the interview. Agency practices might dictate the title and format of this document, but for purposes here it will be referred to as a Memorandum of Interview. The Memorandum of Interview should reflect the date, place, and time (ending and starting) of the interview and the persons present. In clear narrative style, the contents of the Memorandum of Interview should identify the basis for interview, that is, the nature of the investigation, and relate what the interview subject stated in a *detailed manner* consistent with notes taken during the interview. Interview notes should reflect major points of information from the interview and provide a basis for the recall of the minor points A Memorandum of Interview is not a summary of the interview. Rather it is a detailed reconstruction of the entire discussion with the interview subject.

Appendix C contains a sample Memorandum of Interview that was prepared incident to a telephone interview. This was a short telephone interview with an out-of-state victim witness who had previously complained that was undertaken to expedite the filing of an injunctive action. Take note that (1) a detailed description of the conversation is provided and (2) statements made by the interview subject were always attributed to that person (i.e., sentences started with "She stated"; "She said").

Written Statements

Written statements authored and penned by a witness can be of great value in terms of memorializing information furnished incident to an interview. However, there are also important limitations that need to be considered which will frequently bring into question this practice, especially in white collar crime investigations. First, recognize that asking a person to provide a written statement can be a burdensome request and in many instances, one that is not necessary. In the case of victim witnesses, these individuals may have already provided some form of written complaint. And even in those instances where they did not, the question to consider is would taking a written statement further or support the investigation? Perhaps in cases with a limited number of victims and there is some concern they will be pressured to change important details of their story, there might be some value to taking the precaution of obtaining a written statement. Conversely, as will be discussed in a later chapter, such situations might be better handled through a grand jury appearance. Moreover, another problem with taking a written statement, especially early in an investigation, is whether it will be truly comprehensive and complete. Keep in mind that white collar crime scenarios can be complex and drawn out over a period of time. Victim witnesses can forget information and until an investigator fully understands the nature and scope of the case, he/she might not be able to ask appropriate questions that could assist in arriving at a comprehensive, accurate written statement. As witness statements can be subject to discovery by the defense, an inaccurate written statement might be used to place a victim witness's credibility in doubt in an enforcement proceeding.

Of course, an argument in favor of taking a written statement from a victim witness might be in those situations where the continued availability of this person is in question, perhaps due to illness or travel. In fact, when these types of scenarios present themselves it would be wise to discuss with a prosecutor the most viable means to preserve their testimony. Affidavits, depositions, grand jury appearances, and/or tape-recorded statements (as will be discussed later) might be possibilities to consider.

Obtaining a written statement from witnesses that fall into the "Other Witnesses" category might be a more frequent practice, again depending upon the circumstances. Also, obviously providing a written statement is voluntary on the part of the interview subject. It would probably not be necessary to take this step for business or government representatives who would be called to provide and discuss records and/or procedures. However, members of the public who can provide valuable testimony due to encountering certain events or people might be candidates to consider for a written statement. Whether such individuals will continue to be available, cooperative, and able to recollect pertinent facts/details after a possibly long period of time would be important facts to consider. In a worst-case scenario where a valuable witness becomes uncooperative (often because of the inconvenience providing testimony can impose), being presented with a statement in one's own handwriting often provides an excellent basis for recollection, if not further encouragement to cooperate.

Much the same rationale applies when interviewing witnesses who have some type of close relationship with the targets of the investigation. As discussed above, whether such individuals will submit to an interview at all is certainly questionable. However, especially in those instances where there is an initial cooperation and valuable information is imparted (perhaps due to a "falling-out"), memorializing these statements in writing might be wise. It would not be uncommon for this type of witness to change his/her allegiance once formal charges are brought, and a written statement might prove useful in compelling testimony that would rather not be uttered.

Finally, what about written statements from the investigative targets? As discussed above, unlike investigating conventional crimes, seeking an incriminating statement or complete confession from a suspected white collar offender is frequently (although not always) a fruitless endeavor. Conceivably in cases such as identity theft, check fraud, credit card fraud and perhaps insurance fraud, it is worth a try and in turn, attempting to obtain a written statement. While the full scope of the illegal activity might still be denied, a written statement acknowledging responsibility for the offense is a big step toward a conviction. Unfortunately, such situations tend to be the exception rather than the rule when considering the savvy and sophistication of many of the offenders who fall under the white collar umbrella. Many targets of white collar crime investigations avoid investigative interviews altogether or if they do agree, it will be a self-serving conversation full of denials and/or half-truths. In these instances obtaining a written statement would seem an unlikely (although not impossible) outcome. For the written statement to be of value to the investigation, it must provide incriminating statements that are made on a voluntary basis. It would do an investigation little good to walk away from a target interview with a handwritten statement full of exculpatory information (unless a handwriting sample was being sought!). Whatever alibis or defense strategies the target might want to divulge can simply be recorded in note form and reduced to a Memorandum of Interview.

Recording Interviews

An increasingly common practice in many types of criminal investigations is to electronically record (both audio and video) interviews of targets. Such recordings can provide powerful evidence of admissions of wrongdoing while at the same time protecting investigators from allegations of misconduct or illegalities. While this technique might have applications in white collar crime investigations (and might even be required by policy in some agencies), the downside to consider is the "glib tongue" of some savvy white collar offenders. In a nonrecorded interview of a target, notes and Memoranda of Interview must reflect denials, alibis, and other exculpatory information. This information is discoverable in the event of an enforcement action and can be used in the target's defense. The impact of this same information in the voice of the target, however, could be even more damaging to the prosecution's case. In fact, an articulate, sophisticated target could attempt to control the interview and/or seize this platform as an opportunity to plead his/her case. Thus, absent an agency mandate, it would seem that the risks of recording a target interview would need to be carefully weighed against the possible benefits. Again, in some of the more clear-cut, less complex white collar crimes, there might be some anticipation of obtaining a confession on tape. However, the more complex the offense and/or the more sophisticated the offender, the less likely this outcome will occur. As indicated earlier, often in these interviews, the best hope is to obtain limited admissions and possible defense strategies. A worst-case recording would be one replete with denials, alibis, and inaccurate if not irrelevant information.

USE OF UNDERCOVER AND ELECTRONIC SURVEILLANCE TECHNIQUES

Valuable and powerful testimonial evidence in white collar crime cases can be obtained through engaging in undercover initiatives and electronic surveillance. The value and power of these techniques lies in their surreptitious nature that permits an "insiders view" of the suspected illegal activity and those who are responsible for it. In fact, often it is only through these approaches that rare glimpses of a white collar offender's intent can be gained. To be clear throughout this discussion, it must be remembered that these techniques are not necessarily two separate approaches. Rather they are tools that are frequently used in tandem as circumstances permit. Also, the use of these techniques often involves informants, a topic discussed in Chapter 2, since such individuals can be used in an undercover capacity. The point is that whenever either informants or investigators take on undercover roles, it is common to equip them with transmitting/recording devices to monitor and/or record conversations they have with investigative targets.

Nevertheless, other than to emphasize the value and encourage the application of these tools in white collar crime cases, it will be left to other volumes (and agency training) to *fully* detail these topics. As suggested earlier when discussing informants, undercover techniques and electronic surveillance are applicable in most types of criminal investigations and as stated at the outset here, this volume is not intended to be a general investigative guide. Moreover, effectively and safely engaging in undercover operations and the proper use of electronic surveillance equipment/techniques, while having widespread application, are normally viewed as "advanced" investigative subjects due to legalities and complexities associated with their use.

Undercover operations require planning, skill, and careful oversight whether the undercover operative is an informant or investigator. The value of using informants in these roles is that such individuals might have easy entrée into the activities under investigation, but controlling and monitoring their behavior in such circumstances can sometimes be problematic. While such problems would not be anticipated when using investigators in undercover roles, their access to, and the credibility they might have among offenders (even when introduced through an undercover informant) can be uncertain. Just as in the theater and the movies, an investigator must be the "right fit" for the role she or he is to assume. Most importantly, investigators should be trained in undercover techniques. Equally important, regardless of who the undercover operative may be, is the need for agency oversight and support. Of special concern here is the safety of the undercover operative. Planning undercover operations must include "brainstorming" the full range of possibilities that could pose a risk to the operation generally and to the safety of the operatives, and the development of viable responses.

The use of electronic surveillance in investigations is highly regulated by federal and state statutes. In addition, electronic surveillance equipment often requires instruction in order for it to be effectively deployed, and tape recordings incident to electronic surveillance must be handled in a manner that ensures their preservation and integrity. Thus, once again most investigative agencies have detailed policies and instructions to ensure that their investigators comply with applicable laws and have developed training programs that teach not only these laws and agency policies relative to them, but also how to use the equipment and handle the tape-recorded evidence.

All of which is to say that while the use of undercover techniques and electronic surveillance can be extremely valuable in white collar crime investigations, strict conformance to agency policies, experienced oversight, and undergoing agency training are prerequisites to employing these tools. Be mindful, however, that many agencies with responsibility in this area might not consider or permit the use of undercover approaches and/or electronic surveillance because their investigative authority is limited to civil/administrative cases. Admittedly, these techniques are normally associated with criminal investigations. Nevertheless, the possible adoption and application of these techniques in the noncriminal investigative environment (absent statutory prohibitions) is more fully discussed in Chapter 9.

Again, while the intent here is to leave a detailed discussion of these tools to other writers and agency training programs, there are a couple of "white collar crime" points to be made before moving on.

Undercover Techniques

Undercover approaches in white collar crime cases can vary from the classic "cloak and dagger" scenarios to simply posing as a private citizen/potential victim to acquire information or conduct a transaction in a suspected fraudulent promotion. In white collar crime cases, the "cloak and dagger" scenarios can entail informants and/or undercover investigators meeting with suspected offenders to discuss and/or conduct an illicit transaction, or gain employment or other affiliation in a fraudulent operation. Obviously, these types of operations require agency training, support, and oversight to ensure success and safety for those involved.

However, in white collar crime cases it is perhaps more common, at least in the initial phases, for an investigator to assume a fictitious private citizen identity for the purpose of acquiring information that is being made available to members of the public whether by hard copy mail, electronic mail, over the telephone, or in person. While such undertakings nevertheless require rudimentary undercover planning, many white collar crime investigators will find they will routinely utilize such tools as fictitious identities accompanied by addresses (physical, postal, and e-mail) and telephone numbers they control. These very basic undercover tools facilitate the receipt of information about suspect promotions that are being publicly advertised and any desired follow-up transactions. Thus, investigators can personally acquire/evaluate (and testify there to, when necessary) evidentiary material that can be used in subsequent proceedings.

Likewise, some suspect promotions might be offered at public gatherings, through personal telephone contact, or one-on-one meetings. Attending a public-gathering–type meeting might require a fictitious name and address for registration purposes. Recording presentations at such meetings through the use of electronic surveillance equipment should certainly be considered although background noises emanating from large group gatherings can interfere with the quality of recordings made in this type of environment. Making mental notes of the proceedings (along with acquiring any available pertinent literature) and then reducing these notes to writing immediately after the meeting would be the alternative to recording the proceedings.

Another variation that could arise is the opportunity to meet one-on-one in an undercover capacity with the subject of an investigation in the context of a "sales" presentation.

While the purpose of this undertaking is again to acquire first hand information that is normally made available to the public, this scenario should nevertheless be considered a more advanced undercover initiative. Logistical issues such as the location of the meeting and the safety of the undercover operative need to be considered.

A final thought on this purposely limited discussion on undercover operations in white collar crime cases involves the placement of undercover operatives in employment positions where out of necessity they might be committing offenses such as defrauding customers, and so on. If taking this step were a consideration, a *best practice* would be to consult with agency counsel and the appropriate prosecutors' office prior to doing so. It should not be assumed that an undercover operative acting under the "color" of legal authority can actively participate in offending conduct. It has been this author's experience that depending upon the specific circumstances of the case and the nature of the employment gained in an undercover capacity, these types of operations have sometimes been approved, at other times disapproved, and sometimes approved with the proviso that the government reimburse any victimization directly related to the undercover operative's involvement. For instance, if it would be sufficient for the purposes of developing the case for the undercover operative to go through a hiring and training process without actually engaging in "live" fraudulent transactions there might be little objection. On the other hand, a longer-term and fuller involvement with the alleged offender might be met with resistance both "in-house" and with the prosecuting attorney if the operative would have to engage in law violations to preserve his/her cover. Of course, this evaluation would be based on the nature of the position gained by the undercover operative and the likelihood that he/she would have to be involved in any illegal conduct. As suggested, however, a "fall-back" position *might* be to determine the feasibility of identifying and tracking victimizations directly attributable to government involvement and then reimburse these individuals through agency funds.

Electronic Surveillance

Without delving into the domain of electronic surveillance investigative techniques, legalities, and technicalities, it is nevertheless important to lay a foundation for this brief discussion. Keep in mind that this brief discussion, however, is from a federal perspective and that state laws governing electronic surveillance might vary from federal law.

Investigators are confronted with two types of electronic surveillance approaches, consensual and nonconsensual. The term *consensual* means that one of the parties to a conversation consents to its monitoring/recording. Thus, an undercover investigator or informant operating under agency control could be a consenting party and, thus, covertly record conversations with suspects. The term *nonconsensual* means that neither party to conversation agrees to its monitoring/recording. Nonconsensual electronic surveillance techniques include wire taps and covertly placed transmitting devices in areas where there is an expectation of privacy (e.g., a residence, private office, etc.).

Both types of electronic surveillance are used in all varieties of criminal investigations, including white collar crime cases, although consensual electronic surveillance is the more common approach due to less-burdensome approval and oversight requirements. While a very powerful, and in the right circumstances a very necessary tool, nonconsensual electronic surveillance requires court approval and oversight. As a general assessment, courts have shown a reluctance to approve requests for nonconsensual electronic surveillance except when there are no other evidence-gathering avenues available and there is probable cause that the crime in question is ongoing. Moreover, courts can place limitations on the length of the nonconsensual surveillance and/or the nature of the conversations that can be recorded. The bottom line is that many investigators consider this a burdensome and last resort effort, when no other alternatives are available. However, when necessary and when the facts are available to support an application for court approval, this last resort should be pursued.

On the other hand, by federal statute (Section 2511 in Title 18 of the United States Code) it is not unlawful for a person acting under color of law to intercept a wire, oral, or electronic communication, where such person is a party to the communication or one of the parties to the communication has given prior consent to such interception (Paragraph 2c). Thus, investigators or individuals cooperating under agency supervision can lawfully intercept, monitor, and record conversations incident to carrying out official enforcement responsibilities. Generally, agencies do have policies and guidelines that regulate the use of consensual electronic surveillance, but no court order and court oversight are necessary.

As with undercover techniques, "a little bit of electronic surveillance can go a long way." For instance, as discussed above, establishing a telephone number for covertly making and receiving telephone calls can be a very useful undercover tool. This tool can become even more valuable when provisions are made to record the conversation, with an investigator or cooperating individual as the consenting party. The equipment necessary to make such recordings is inexpensive and readily available.

The value of verbal statements/conversations made by suspects to undercover investigators, informants, or cooperating individuals acting as potential customers can be greatly increased if they are recorded. In white collar crime investigations this is a frequently applied technique, although one that requires undercover planning and, for best results, the use of specialized electronic surveillance equipment (as opposed to a tape recorder hidden in a shirt pocket).

Whenever electronic surveillance techniques are employed it is important to treat the recordings obtained as evidentiary material. A duplicate of the tape recording should be made for "working" purposes, which includes the preparation of a transcript. The original tape recording should be stored consistent with agency evidence procedures so that its authenticity can be attested to at any type of litigation proceeding. Written notes should be made regarding the time, place, location, identities of persons involved, and recording equipment used.

Two final words of caution about electronic surveillance or the fruits thereof:

First, paragraph 2(d) in Section 2511 of Title 18 also permits private citizens to record conversations with others, either with all parties consenting or just one party consenting (i.e., the party recording conversation, unbeknownst to the other party). Unlike federal law, many states prohibit private citizens from recording conversations without both parties consenting. An enterprising citizen who takes it upon himself or herself to record a conversation with someone suspected of wrongdoing (or so they believe) without their knowledge and then turns it over to authorities could be creating two types of problems: (1) depending upon the state where this act occurred, he or she *might* have committed a crime; and (2) government use of such evidence thereafter *might* be challenged.

Second, an investigator could request a cooperating private citizen to record a telephone conversation without the investigator being present, a scenario that might be attractive if a call is anticipated, but at an unknown time; and it also protects the citizen from any allegation of illegal conduct since he/she would be acting on behalf of the government. However, the investigator must ensure the cooperating citizen can properly operate the recording equipment and does not use the equipment for any other purpose. Also, it should be impressed on the cooperating citizen to make written notes of the time and date of the call.

Again, the point to the preceding discussion about undercover techniques and electronic surveillance is more to emphasize their value in white collar crime cases than to provide the details of utilizing these investigative tools. Look elsewhere for such guidance, especially to agency policy and training, due to the associated complexities and risks involved. Having said this, keep in mind that relatively simple undercover and electronic surveillance approaches will have frequent applications in white collar crime investigations and can potentially play important roles in their successful dispositions.

CHAPTER HIGHLIGHTS

- White collar crime investigations often begin with interviewing those that have submitted voluntary complaints of victimization. Not all victims voluntarily complain and investigative efforts must be undertaken to identify victims who do not complain.

- One approach to interviewing victim witnesses is to have them recount the events of their victimization in a chronological fashion, but be sure to gather the standard who, what, when, where, how, and why data.

- Some important, nontarget witnesses may be reluctant to cooperate, if not hostile. Tact and professionalism on the part of the investigator are essential when dealing with such individuals in an attempt to avoid animosities that can hinder a necessary working relationship.

- While often necessary in some varieties of white collar crime (e.g., check fraud, insurance fraud, identity theft), interviewing the investigative target(s) is not always of paramount concern, especially in highly complex offenses and/or those involving sophisticated, articulate individuals. In these latter instances, although there may be other strategic, investigative reasons to do so, do not expect confessions or significant admissions of guilt. More commonly, such interviews will result in denials and self-serving, if not untruthful statements, although possible defenses/alibis may surface as a result of such discussions.

- Handwritten statements authored by witnesses can memorialize important information, but at the same time investigators must evaluate the likelihood of obtaining a truthful, complete statement versus one that is incomplete/inaccurate (even if unintentionally) or contains self-serving denials. Little is gained from obtaining a written statement that reflects these latter outcomes.

- Undercover and electronic surveillance techniques can have widespread application in white collar crime cases. Even when undertaken in a rudimentary fashion these approaches can provide valuable evidence. These techniques, however, must be used in accordance with prevailing legal requirements and agency policies, and preferably only employed by investigators who have undergone specialized training.

CHAPTER BEST PRACTICES

- Personal, face-to-face interviews with victims is a *best practice* and such face-to-face contacts should be made prior to identifying any victim as a trial witness, that is, the first time an investigator should meet face to face with a victim witness should not be during trial preparations. (See page 64.)
- While an investigative questionnaire seeks out information similar in scope to a general agency complaint form, to be most useful it must also focus on the specifics of the case at hand and should be tailored accordingly. A *best practice* is to ask for the respondent's name, address, telephone numbers, and e-mail address at the outset. When this information is sought at the end of a questionnaire, it is sometimes omitted. (See page 69.)
- As *best practice*, have the victim witness date and initial each documentary item so that the source of the document can be identified and the date it was turned over to the government is recorded (even if only a copy). (See page 73.)
- In any event, generally speaking, *Miranda* warnings need to be administered in a custodial interrogation of a target of criminal investigation. Obviously, a person who has been arrested is in custody and questioning this person about the case incident to the arrest would constitute a custodial interrogation. However, an arrest, in and of itself, need not trigger the *Miranda* litany, if the investigators involved do not plan to question the accused. Nevertheless, a *best practice* might be to administer these warnings whenever a suspect is taken into custody even though no questioning is planned. (See page 80.)
- A final thought on this purposely limited discussion on undercover operations in white collar crime cases involves the placement of undercover operatives in employment positions where out of necessity they might be committing offenses such defrauding customers, and so on. If taking this step were a consideration, a *best practice* would be to consult with agency counsel and the appropriate prosecutors' office prior to doing so. (See page 88.)

Notes

1. L. K. Gaines and R. L. Miller, *Criminal Justice in Action: The Core*, 3rd ed. (Belmont, CA: Thomson/Wadsworth, 2006), p. 178, 180.
2. Ibid., p. 180.
3. Ibid., p. 178.

CHAPTER 5

Search Warrants

THE VALUE OF SEARCH WARRANTS IN WHITE COLLAR CRIME INVESTIGATIONS

Search warrants are a powerful investigative tool for securing evidence that might not become available through other means. Certainly in conventional crimes such as robbery or drug trafficking, suspected offenders are not likely to voluntarily surrender any evidence of their involvement or the fruits of their efforts/contraband. Thus, the use of search warrants in these types of crimes is well established. Conversely, evidence in white collar crime investigations can often be collected using other methods such as voluntary surrender or through subpoena authority. However, search warrants do play a vital role in these investigations and their utilization can make the difference between bringing a case to a successful conclusion and failing to develop sufficient evidence to bring any charges at all.

There are at least five reasons for this potentially wide variation in outcomes:

1. Under *Andresen v. Maryland* (427 U.S. 463, 1976) the Fifth Amendment may protect an individual from complying with a subpoena for the production of his personal records in his possession because the very act of production may constitute a compulsory authentication of incriminating information (this limitation has the application only to documents held by a sole proprietor or private individual; it has long been recognized that collective entities such as corporations and some partnerships cannot assert the Fifth Amendment, even if the subpoenaed documents would incriminate one of the organization's officers).[1] Thus, in some instances suspects who are believed to have in their possession incriminating

evidence might not be compelled to produce them incident to the issuance of a subpoena. Seizure via a search warrant eliminates this problem. Investigators may seize any evidence which they have cause to believe will be incriminating. This includes documentary evidence.

2. While the records of collective entities such as corporations or some partnerships are subject to production pursuant to a subpoena, investigators cannot always be certain that the records sought will, in fact, be turned over. Documents can be produced on a selective basis (usually in favor of the suspect); they can be altered; and they can be destroyed. While search warrants must identify items sought with some particularity (as will be discussed in more detail later), the fact that investigators are given the power to seize these items themselves greatly increases the likelihood that they will be in government hands.

3. Unknown incriminating evidence might be discovered on the search premises.

4. The execution of a search warrant can sometimes result in individuals with useful information coming forward and cooperating with the investigation.

5. Although the purpose of a search warrant is to gather evidence and is *not* an injunction against a business entity from operating, the impact of executing the warrant might result in a cessation of the alleged unlawful activities due to the disruption caused by the search and seizure of records, and any negative publicity that arises. Thus, the investigation can proceed without concern for additional public loss (unless, of course, the operators reopen under a different name and at a different location, a scenario that is not without precedent). It should be noted, however, that under the Federal Rules of Criminal Procedure, 41(e), the owners of seized property can move for its return if they can convince a court of improprieties in its seizure or demonstrate harm from being deprived of its use. One way to remedy a deprivation claim when the property in question consists of business records is to permit, under supervision, copying any needed items.

Thus, it cannot be emphasized too strongly that white collar crime investigators should consider employing search warrants whenever possible. Although a comprehensive discussion of the Fourth Amendment is beyond the scope of this volume, a brief discussion of search and seizure case law peculiar to white collar crime investigations is offered in the following section to ensure a common understanding of the legalities upon which these actions are based.

THE FOURTH AMENDMENT: WHITE COLLAR CRIME CONSIDERATIONS

The Fourth Amendment to the Constitution states, "The right of the people to be secure in their persons, houses, papers, and effects, against unreasonable searches and seizures, shall not be violated, no Warrants shall issue, but upon probable cause, supported by Oath or affirmation, and particularly describing the place to be searched, and the persons or things to be seized." Accordingly, the Fourth Amendment establishes that the government can undertake reasonable searches and it lays out the methodology for obtaining such a warrant, including the requirement that the warrant be specific in terms of what is to be seized as opposed to a general warrant.[2] While this governmental power was established in the nation's infancy, the unique circumstances present in many white collar crime cases have been examined by the courts only in relatively recent times. For instance, in *Gouled v. United States* (1921) the Supreme Court ruled that the government did need a search warrant to search a business premises. In this case, a government agent searched the office of Gouled without a warrant incident to a fraud against the government investigation. In a more recent case, *Mancusi v. DeForte* (1968), the Court reaffirmed the position that business premises such as private offices provide an expectation of privacy to those who do business in such premises, thus making a warrant essential if they are to be searched.[3] Conversely, the Court ruled in *Maryland v. Macon* (1985) that if commercial property is open to the public, such as a retail store, the privacy expectation is different. In this case a police agent entered a retail store premises and observed and purchased suspected items for evidentiary purposes. The Court did not view the agent's entry and purchase as a search and seizure.[4]

In perhaps an even more fundamental ruling for white collar crime investigations, the Supreme Court actually changed legal doctrine in *Warden v. Hayden* (1967). Before this decision, police could only seize fruits of the crime, weapons used to commit a crime, and contraband. Evidence of a crime was viewed as the lawful property of the owner and police could not take the private property of citizens. This change came about as the Supreme Court moved away from legal doctrine based on technical property rights to an analysis of expectation of privacy. Thus, protection of individual rights is based on probable cause and not solely on the nature of the property to be seized.[5] As will be detailed below, much of what is typically sought via search warrants in white collar crime cases falls into the "evidence of a crime" category, the acquisition of which prior to *Warden v. Hayden* would have been impermissible.

Particularity

Nevertheless, the concluding phrase of the Fourth Amendment, "particularly describing the place to be searched, and the persons or things to be seized," can be troublesome for white collar crime investigators seeking evidence of a crime. In fact, some would suggest that the highest standard of particularity applies to documents because by their nature they require an analysis to see whether they do or do not fit within the classes of items that are seizeable under the warrant.[6] Describing documentary evidence (especially when large quantities are involved) with particularity can be difficult, if not impossible. Fortunately, the courts have considered these circumstances and have provided guidance on how investigators can comply with the particularity requirement in such cases. A number of courts have adopted a philosophy that where a search is for business records generally, as opposed to a specific record, a general description is often all that is possible due to the general nature of the documentary evidence sought (e.g., *State v. Tidyman* (568 P., 2nd 666, 671 [Or. App, 1977]); *James v. U.S.* (416 F 2nd, 467, 473 [5th Cir., 1969] cert. denied 397 U.S. 907 (1970))).[7]

In some instances, generic descriptions (descriptions by class or group) alone may be sufficient. Some courts have approved broad generic descriptions when the evidence sought is very similar to other innocuous items, and for all practical purposes the collection cannot be precisely described for the purpose of limiting the scope of the seizure (*U.S. v. Cortellesso*, 601 F. 2nd, 28, 32 (1st Cir., 1979)). In those cases the supporting affidavit must show that a large collection of similar items are present and explain how the officers will distinguish the suspected items from the innocent items. A standard must be set to enable the executing officers to separate the papers to be seized from the general class of documents described. This standard is referred to as a limiting phrase. There are many possibilities for drafting limiting phrases. One is to limit the generic descriptions by referring to a smaller identifiable category within the class. In *U.S. v. Scharfman* (448 F. 2nd 1352 [2nd Cir. 1971] cert. denied, 405 U.S. 919 [1971]) the court ruled that the language, "as are being used as means and instrumentalities of the theft of fur articles," was a sufficient limiting phrase for the seizure of books and records. However, several courts have been critical of limiting phrases that limit the search merely by reference to a broad criminal statute. For example in *U.S. v. Roche* (448 F. 2nd 1352 [2nd Cir. 1971] cert. denied, 405 U.S. 919 [1972]), the court ruled that the limiting phrase, "evidence of violation of 18 USC 1341" was too broad.[8]

In addition to the likelihood of not being able to identify with particularity the evidence being sought, investigators in white collar crime cases must also recognize that they might not even know the existence of certain evidentiary items that are present at the search premises. Again, legal precedent has been established to provide guidance for investigators in this eventuality. In *Andresen v. Maryland* (427 U.S. 463 [1976]), a warrant contained the limiting language, "together with other fruits, instrumentalities and evidence of crime at this time unknown." In this case, the court ruled that this language was not overly broad because it acknowledged that officers will not always know the precise nature of all the documents needed to prove their case. While probable cause may exist to believe that relevant documents are present, a particular description may be impossible and a catch-all description might be the best that can be provided.[9]

Regulatory Enforcement

As has been noted earlier, this book will consider both criminal and regulatory enforcement actions. It is important to remember that the Fourth Amendment cannot be ignored when an enforcement action is regulatory in nature. In both *See v. City of Seattle* (1967) and *Camara v. Municipal Court* (1967), the Supreme Court ruled that the Fourth Amendment protects people from any invasion of government officials, not just the police. Thus, when regulatory officials (in these cases fire inspectors and health inspectors, respectively) want access to certain premises, they must have a warrant if they are not permitted voluntary access.[10] The remainder of this discussion will focus on search warrants in a criminal enforcement context. However, many of the steps discussed with regard to developing and presenting probable cause are likely to apply in the regulatory environment. Nevertheless, regulatory investigators are urged to consult and work closely with their counsel to ensure that they are complying with any requirements unique to their jurisdiction and authority.

DEVELOPING PROBABLE CAUSE AND PREPARING THE AFFIDAVIT

Probable cause can be defined as facts that could lead a reasonably prudent person to draw conclusions about unknown facts.[11] This standard of probable cause is one of fair probability and not certainty or near certainty.[12] Nevertheless, it is the standard of evidence that triggers several types of official governmental actions, including search warrants, arrest warrants, and indictments. Evidence is any kind of proof offered to establish the existence of a fact. In white collar crime cases, evidence can include statements by witnesses as to what was heard or seen, as well as information from physical items such as documents.[13] Some of the specific types of evidence commonly presented to establish probable cause include:

1. Details from a physical surveillance.
2. Observations by the affiant or other agents.
3. Corroborative information provided by governmental or private business sources, such as vehicle registration information, fair market value, proof of purchase from car dealers, or title companies.
4. Information about a subject's bank accounts and the source of the information.
5. What was seen in plain view.
6. Information from telephone toll records and the source of the information.
7. Information from an authorized pen register.
8. Information concerning the subject's travel and the source of the information.
9. Federal income tax returns contain extremely valuable financial information. (Note: Title 26 of the United States Code permits access to them only in connection with federal criminal investigations. Another avenue to obtain this information is from the preparer, who might be identified from state returns).
10. Results from trash searches.[14]

Before a judge or magistrate will issue a search warrant, he or she must be satisfied that probable cause exists (and has been presented in affidavit form) (1) that a crime has been committed; (2) that specific items constitute evidence of that crime; and (3) that such evidence is at the place specified in the affidavit.[15] Developing probable cause and presenting it in an affidavit are two distinct steps. The development of probable cause is essentially investigative in nature while developing an affidavit is an exercise in writing. As distinct as these steps may seem, however, there is a great advantage to be realized when a coordinated strategy is adopted that considers both of them. A *best practice* is for investigators to identify as early as possible in the case whether the execution of a search warrant would be appropriate, and if so, the initial investigative steps should be geared toward the development of probable cause for the acquisition of the warrant. Moreover, the affiant can begin writing the affidavit even if only in outline or "skeleton" form at this early stage. This initial effort in developing the affidavit will help to highlight information/evidence that is not on hand, which in turn will help to guide further investigative efforts.

White collar crime cases can be bewildering undertakings that lead investigators in many directions, and all too often wandering aimlessly. The execution of a search warrant might not be appropriate or possible in all white collar crime cases. Moreover, even when employed, a search warrant still might not be the key to a successful resolution. Nevertheless, the experience of many investigators has been that search warrants often offer the best opportunity to obtain the necessary evidence to reach this goal. Therefore, determining whether a search warrant is appropriate at the early stages of a case and then focusing the initial investigative efforts in this direction is the strategy being recommended here as both efficient and ultimately effective.

Box 5–1 contains a search warrant affidavit that was developed incident to a business opportunity fraud investigation. Names, addresses, and other identifying information have been changed or deleted. On the one hand, this case is a relatively simple scenario in that the facts are not complex, the number of victims/loss is small, as is the number of potential defendants, thus making it a good case for illustrating the development and presentation of probable cause.

Box 5–1   Search warrant affidavit

Affidavit

State of Florida

County of Smith

I, S.L Lincoln, first being duly sworn, depose and say:

I have knowledge of the facts hereinafter set forth, with the exception of those matters specifically designated as based on information derived from others.

1. I am a United States Investigator assigned to the Florida Division of the U.S. Investigation Service. I have been an Investigator for over eighteen years. As an Investigator, it is part of my duties to investigate violations of the mail fraud statute, Title 18, United States Code, Section 1341 and money laundering, Title 18, United States Code, Section 1956.

2. I am submitting this affidavit to support an application for a search warrant for the premises located at 123 Main St., ___ (*city will remain unidentified*), Florida. Located on these premises are believed to be business records of Vendor's World, Inc. These records are believed to be evidence and instrumentalities of violations of federal law, specifically 18 USC 1341, mail fraud, and 18 USC 1956, money laundering.

3. Investigator Wood of the New Jersey Division of the United States Investigation Service advised your affiant he conducted an investigation of Joseph Mitchell that

Continued

subsequently led to his indictment and conviction in federal court in New Jersey. Wood advised that Mitchell along with his wife and brother-in-law conducted a scheme to defraud in which they sold pay telephones, vending machines and cigarette machines, to persons who responded to advertisements which these defendants placed in newspapers (*the original affidavit contained a sample advertisement as an exhibit*). These advertisements invited those interested in purchasing these machines to call a toll free number for further information. Mitchell and his co-defendants would then correspond and/or meet personally with prospective buyers, and made numerous fraudulent representations concerning the physical condition of the machines that were available for sale, and the services that Mitchell and his co-defendants would provide in establishing these purchasers in a vending machine business. Wood has told me that his investigation disclosed that Mitchell and his co-defendants either failed to deliver any equipment, delivered equipment that was faulty or inoperable, and/or failed to install equipment at locations which would generate income. Wood told me that the indictment charged Mitchell and his co-defendants with conspiracy to commit mail fraud, mail fraud, interstate transportation of property obtained by fraud and interstate threatening communications. (*A copy of this indictment was attached as an exhibit to the original affidavit*). He further advised that Mitchell was sentenced on July 28, ___ (*year purposely omitted here*) to two years imprisonment and is scheduled to begin his incarceration on August 17, ___ (*year purposely omitted here*).

4. Wood has advised me that he has received information suggesting Mitchell has conducted a similar scheme to defraud while his case was pending resolution in New Jersey. He told me he bases this belief on the fact that he has been contacted by several Florida residents claiming that they have had unsatisfactory dealings with Mitchell. Wood told me that these dealings involve the sale of vending machines, and the experiences these purchasers have had are similar to the problems experienced by the victims in the case which resulted in Mitchell's conviction in New Jersey. He suggested that I contact one of these Florida residents, Complainant #1 (*the complainant's real name was included in the original affidavit*), for further details.

5. Complainant #1 was contacted on August 3, ___ (*year purposely omitted here*). She provided me the following information:

She stated she saw a classified advertisement in the local newspaper (*which was fully identified in the original affidavit*) under the Business Opportunity Section. She said the advertisement read as follows: "Vending routes operate your own machines—snack, soda, etc., location and service provided, 1-800-xxx-xxxx" (*actual number was provided in the original affidavit*). Complainant #1 stated she saw this ad in April ___ (*year purposely omitted here*) and called the number to obtain further information. In response to her telephone call, she said Robert Anderson representing Vendor's World visited her at her residence. Complainant #1 told me Anderson showed her a brochure depicting a video game machine known as Bar Brain and told her Vendor's World would sell her two of these machines for $5000, and provide her locations for these machines. She told me she was also guaranteed $400-$450 net profit per month per machine. She said Anderson showed her a brochure that had photographs of the machines she would be purchasing and she was assured these were, in fact, the machines she would be acquiring. Complainant #1 said that based on these representations, she provided Anderson $1000 and signed a contract for the purchase of the machines and services to be provided by Vendor's World. Complainant #1 told me she had subsequent telephone conversations with Joseph Mitchell concerning possible locations for her machines. She said that Mitchell told her she could place her machines in one of four establishments he had made arrangements with and she selected the City Lounge (*not the actual name*). Complainant #1 said that Mitchell came to her residence on April 29 to receive an additional $2000 payment due as a result of identifying the location for her machines. She said that Mitchell arrived at her residence driving a white Jaguar automobile. She said she wrote the check out for $2000, but refused to give it to Mitchell because he failed to produce a contract with the establishment that would house her machines, City Lounge. Complainant #1 stated that Mitchell told her he did not have the contract with him to which she replied that she would not give him a check without it. Complainant #1 claims that Mitchell nevertheless absconded with her $2000 check without her knowledge, upon leaving her residence on this occasion.

6.   Complainant #1 further advised that David Robinson, another representative of Vendor's World called on May 20 to tell her that her machines were now available and the final $2000 was due. Complainant #1 said she gave Robinson a cashier's check for $2000 and he delivered the two machines to her home. She said instead of finding the machines to be similar to those depicted in the brochure, she found them to be older models. She also found them to be in disrepair. She stated one machine would not accept quarters and the picture screen appeared to be fading. She said the picture on the other machine was blurry. She also stated that upon examining one of the machines, she noted it was manufactured in 1983. She said Anderson advised her during their April meeting that these machines would not be over four months old. Complainant #1 then contacted the manager of the City Lounge and found that Vendor's World had not made arrangements for the placement of her machines at this location. Complainant #1 then contacted other establishments mentioned to her by Mitchell as locations he had identified for her machines. Of these four establishments, she found only one that had any contact whatsoever with Vendor's World. On May 26 Complainant #1 said she telephoned Mitchell and told him she wanted the machines she had ordered as identified in the brochure shown to her at her initial meeting with Vendor's World. The next day she said she received a call from Robinson who advised that her machines had been ordered and should be in by May 29. However, Complainant #1 said her machines, in fact, never arrived on this date. On June 4 she said she demanded from Robinson the return of her $5000 and he responded that he would only give her back 60% of her investment since it would cost her 40% to break the contract. She said she had additional settlement discussions with both Robinson and Mitchell but none of their offers involved a total refund of her $5000. In summary, Complainant #1 feels she was promised two nearly

Continued

new video vending machines, in good operating order, to be placed in an agreed upon location which would generate $900 per month in income. Instead, she said she received two inoperable, old machines, and the location promised to her had not been procured.

7. Complainant #1 told me Robinson gave her a telephone number where he could be reached. This number is XXX-YYY-ZZZZ (*the actual number was provided in the original affidavit*). According to telephone company records, this number is assigned to Credit Counselors/Finance Leasing Group, which is located at 123 Main St. Complainant #1 told me she has called this number several times and on occasion has spoken with a female who has identified herself as Robinson's stepdaughter.

8. Complainant #1 told me that on June 10 she traveled to 123 Main St. and found Robinson to be at this location. She told me that Robinson invited her and a companion into his office and he displayed to them corporate records of Vendor's World and a fax from Mitchell. Complaint #1 told me she visited Robinson again at 123 Main St. on June 24 during which time Robinson faxed a proposed settlement agreement to Mitchell. During this second meeting she said that Robinson showed her brochures on other vending machines. She said he had these brochures in a file cabinet in his office. Complainant #1 said that both of these meetings were held in connection with her efforts to obtain a refund of her money.

9. On August 5 I interviewed Complainant #2, an individual identified by Complainant #1 as having had a transaction with Vendor's World. Complainant #2 confirmed that he had such a transaction. He stated he responded to an advertisement in the local newspaper in mid-February concerning a vending machine route. He said that upon telephoning the number provided in the advertisement he was advised he was dealing with Vendor's World. He stated that he asked for information concerning their vending machine opportunity be mailed to him and literature arrived via U.S. Mail shortly thereafter. Complainant #2 said his initial dealings with Vendor's World were with Alex Marx, who met with him on March 6. He said during this meeting he was provided, in writing, that he would receive reconditioned vending machines in good operating condition; was guaranteed $350 per month in income; and locations for these machines would be arranged. Complainant #2 said he then began dealing with Joseph Mitchell and then with David Robinson. He said he made subsequent payments of $4500, $800, and $4,421 to Vendor's World between March 25 and April 11. He said it was not until the end of July that his machines, two soda machines and a snack machine, finally arrived at the prearranged location. However, unlike the machines described in the initial literature he received from Vendor's World, the machines provided to him were old and the snack machine did not function properly.

10. On August 5, I interviewed Complainant #3, another individual identified by Complainant #1 as having had transactions with Vendor's Word. Complainant #3 stated she responded to an advertisement in a local newspaper in January. This advertisement offered a vending route opportunity. She said she telephoned the number contained in the advertisement and spoke to Joseph Mitchell. She said Mitchell advised her she could purchase new or used vending machines which would provide her an income of $300-$350 per month, per machine. He also said he would procure

the locations for these machines. She said these representations were also subsequently made to her in writing, on a contract Mitchell provided her. She said that Mitchell and Robert Anderson visited her following her telephone call to further describe this opportunity. On January 21 Complainant #3 gave Mitchell a check for $4500 to participate in this program. She said she and her husband agreed to purchase five machines. She stated that Mitchell next visited her in early March at which time she provided another check for $2500 for his service in identifying locations for the machines. A final payment of $5,500 was made to Mitchell on May 21. Shortly after this payment four of the ordered machines were placed in business establishments. However, these were not the establishments agreed upon at the outset and only one of these locations agreed to keep a machine. Complainant #3 said that another Vendor's World representative, David Robinson, was responsible for removing three machines that were unwanted at the locations where they were placed. She said she received no refunds for the machines that were removed and furthermore her fifth machine was never placed at all. Complainant #3 concluded that instead of receiving $300-$350 per month from the one machine that was in operation, she has earned only about $60 in six weeks.

11. Two other individuals filed complaints directly with the U.S. Investigation Service concerning their dealings with Vendor's World. Complainant #4 was interviewed on August 5 and he stated he responded to an advertisement in the local newspaper that appeared in late May or early June. He said he called the telephone number in the advertisement and received a return call back from Joseph Mitchell, who subsequently met with him personally. He said that Mitchell guaranteed him that he would realize income of $350 per month, service and support, and locations for placing the machines. Complainant #4 said these representations were also reflected on the contract he signed on June 10. At this time he gave Mitchell $4000 in cash for the purchase of two machines. Thereafter, he received only one machine and it was not the machine he contracted to purchase. He described this machine as a cold drink machine that does not operate properly. He said the machine is dented and leaks and has no dollar bill changer as was initially promised.

12. Complainant #5 was also interviewed on August 5 and he too responded to an advertisement in a local newspaper, which appeared in late June. He said this advertisement invited those interested in a vending machine business to call a telephone number for further information. He said on July 1 he called this number and spoke to an individual who identified himself as Robinson. He said Robinson told him he would make $350 per month through this program and that he subsequently received in the mail brochures and information about this vending machine opportunity. Complainant #5 stated that on July 15 Mitchell came to his residence and told him he would provide him with vending machines in pre-arranged locations. He was again guaranteed an income of $350 per month, both verbally and in a contract. On July 17 Complainant #5 gave Mitchell a check for $7000. He said that Mitchell was driving a white Jaguar when he arrived to pick up this check. Complainant #5 said

Continued

his purchase was for six re-conditioned machines, three snack machines and three soda machines. However, he said that Mitchell asked him to change his order to two snack machines, two game machines, and two soda machines because he had found a "hot bar" where the game machines would do well. When these machines became available, Mitchell asked for a final payment of $3500 that Complainant #5 sent to him via U.S. Mail. However, shortly after mailing the check, Complainant #5 stopped payment on this check because he became aware of a television news story that reported Mitchell's prior involvement in a fraudulent vending machine operation in New Jersey.

13. Complainant #5 advised me that he decided to seek a refund of his initial $7000. He told me he contacted Robinson to arrange a meeting with him and was told by Robinson that offices of Vendor's World were located at 123 Main St. Complainant #5 arranged to meet with Robinson on August 6. He agreed to be accompanied by an undercover agent, Investigator L.W. Harris, who would be introduced as Complainant #5's sister. During this meeting Robinson advised that he was now the owner and operator of Vendor's World pending Mitchell's resolution of his legal problems in New Jersey. Robinson also advised that ". . . we're going to be closing our other office and we're going to move everything here." Robinson further stated, ". . . we got to be honest with you, we got three customers having some problems and I got all their files right here . . ." Robinson indicated that he had two warehouses for storing vending machines, one of which was local near the airport. During the meeting Complainant #5 made his request for a refund and Robinson told him that he would contact him on August 10 with an answer for him concerning his refund. However, Complainant #5 has never heard from anyone from Vendor's World about his refund request.

14. Complainant #5 told me on August 11 that the $3500 check he placed a stop payment on was cashed by a restaurant owner named Bruno, who called him with this information at his residence. He said that Bruno would not name his restaurant nor provide a phone number.

15. On August 4, I spoke with Evelyn Jones, the classified customer service manager at the newspaper (*which was fully identified in the original affidavit*) that ran Vendor's World advertising. Jones confirmed that Vendor's World did place classified advertising with the newspaper on several occasions and she provided me a copy of recent advertisement (*which was attached as an exhibit in the original affidavit*). Jones advised that the newspaper has thousands of mail subscription customers, and thousands of copies of each edition are mailed daily.

16. Contact with the post office (*fully identified in the original affidavit*) on August 12 disclosed that 123 Main St. had been vacant for some time, but mail is now being delivered to Credit Counselors/Finance Leasing Group at that address. Postal personnel believe that a Mr. Ronald is associated with this firm. Contact with the local electric utility company (*fully identified in the original affidavit*) on August 12 disclosed that electric service to 123 Main St. is held in the name of Mr. Ronald. No occupational licenses could be found in the municipal records for Credit Counselors/Finance Leasing Group or Vendor's World. A search of state corporate records found a listing for Vendor's World on Ocean Blvd., ___ (*city fully identified in the original affidavit*). It

was determined that this address was a shipping and mail box rental business. No listing for Credit Counselors/Finance Leasing Group could be found in state corporate records.

17. Investigator Harris described the interior of 123 Main St. as consisting of a reception area; a combination common area and hallway and two offices (*see attached sketch made by Harris*). She advised that the meeting between Robinson and Complainant #5 was held in the rear office and that the rear office contained two desks and file cabinet. Complainant #1, however, told me that in her two meetings with Robinson, she met with him in the first office rather than the rear office. She said the first office contained a desk and file cabinet.

18. It has been your affiant's experience that records and documents relating to business activities are normally maintained on business premises and are normally stored in and on desks and file cabinets. Your affiant believes that documents and records relating to Vendor's World would be found on the premises located at 123 Main St. This premises is the last unit on the west end of a single story, white stucco building. There is no business sign on this unit, but the number, 123, clearly appears on the exterior door.

19. Your affiant submits there is probable cause to believe that Mitchell, Robinson, and possibly other individuals affiliated with Vendor's World have been and are currently conducting a scheme to defraud individuals interested in entering into the vending machine business. Mitchell, Robinson and other Vendor's World representatives have misrepresented the condition and operating ability of the machines they are selling; they have misrepresented the amount of income potential from these machines and have misrepresented their services in providing acceptable locations for these machines. These misrepresentations are identical to those which Mitchell was responsible for in the investigation that resulted in his indictment and conviction in New Jersey. He continued the same course of conduct while he was awaiting the resolution of these other charges and the commencement of his prison term.

20. Wherefore, your affiant submits there is probable cause to believe that located on the premises of 123 Main St. are books, records, brochures, customer information, complaints, correspondence, and other documents relating to the business activities of Vendor's World, all of which constitute evidence and instrumentalities of crimes, to wit: 18 USC 1341, Mail Fraud and 18 USC 1956, Money Laundering. Accordingly, your affiant requests that a warrant be issued to search and seize all documents relating to Vendor's World located at 123 Main St.

S.L. Lincoln

U.S. Investigator

Sworn and Subscribed to before me on this ___ day of August, ___

_____

United States Magistrate

Attachment to Affidavit: Sketch of Premises

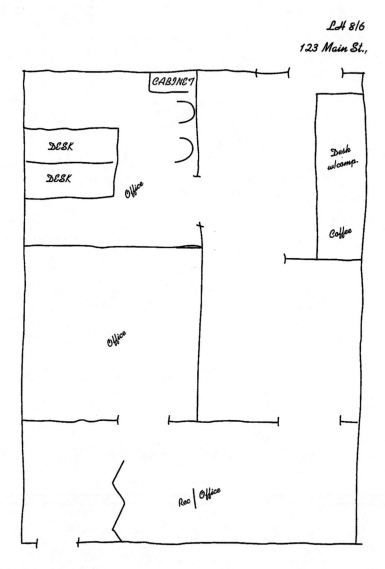

On the other hand, the case possesses some of the subtleties, if not difficulties, often encountered in white collar crime investigations. For instance, it is all too easy to dismiss a single
unsatisfactory business transaction as appropriate for a private party civil action. It is not until
investigators make an attempt to develop a pattern of unsatisfactory transactions that the
potential for public agency action becomes apparent. Additionally, this case relied heavily on
victim testimony of oral misrepresentations made to them by the defendants. Unlike
cases where misrepresentations are made in writing, cases of this nature can falter on poor

recollection by witnesses and defenses that contend that customers simply didn't understand the terms of the transaction. However, victim interviews that delve into the details and minutiae of the entire transaction can often successfully overcome these pitfalls. Thus, the basic approach and format taken in the development of this affidavit can be adopted for many types of white collar crime cases, keeping in mind that each investigation has its own unique circumstances. The purpose of presenting this affidavit is to highlight the investigative steps taken to obtain sufficient probable cause and how this information was then presented in written form.

The introductory paragraph identifies the affiant and what his professional qualifications are. Although not reflected here, if the affiant possesses highly specialized training that is pertinent to the investigation at hand, this information should be included as well. The second paragraph identifies the premises to be searched and items believed to be present on these premises, and the crimes believed to have occurred. The allegations received suggest this case essentially involves a scheme to defraud. As discussed earlier, the mail fraud statute, 18 U.S.C. 1341, has been utilized in the federal system to address a wide array of fraudulent conduct. Under this statute, the mails do not have to play some type of prominent role in the fraud. Rather, they only have to *further* the scheme to defraud. Moreover, the statute does not require the mails to cross state lines in order for a violation to occur. Sufficient use of the mails did occur in this case (as was demonstrated through victim interviews) and thus was an appropriate violation to consider charging. Investigating any money laundering activities, 18 U.S.C. 1956, associated with this scheme not only had the potential to provide additional charges, but such activity would have established a basis to pursue asset forfeiture, a matter that is the topic of the next chapter.

Beginning with paragraph 3 and continuing through paragraph 17, a chronological presentation of the investigation that had been conducted thus far is provided, an effort that had a primary focus of developing probable cause for a search warrant at the suspect place of business. How the affiant initially became involved in the investigation is detailed in paragraphs 3 and 4. In this case, another investigator relayed information about a possible ongoing fraud scheme. This investigator reported he received a complaint from an individual outside his jurisdiction that the subject of a case he investigated might be conducting a similar scheme while awaiting sentencing on that case. Paragraph 3 provides an overview of the fraud perpetrated in this investigator's case so that this case can be compared to the experiences of those possibly victimized in the newly alleged scheme. The indictment used to charge this subject was attached to the affidavit to provide even more details about this earlier scheme, but in the interest of space is not included here. The fact that Mitchell had pled guilty to charges in the indictment furnished evidence of his knowledge to conduct such a scheme and presented an aggravated circumstance that he might have done so while on bail and awaiting sentencing in this earlier case.

Paragraphs 5–8 review in a detailed manner the experiences of a possible victim in this new fraud. This person reported on August 3 that in April she responded to a classified advertisement for a vending machine business that would include both the machines and locations to place the machines. Anderson, a sales representative from Vendor's World, subsequently visited her. He promised an income or $400–$450 per month and provided her with brochures which depicted the machines available. The total cost for two machines was $5,000. Based on the representations made to her, she agreed to make this purchase and gave Anderson $1,000, with additional monies due upon being provided the locations where her machines would be placed. Shortly thereafter, Mitchell, the purported company owner and individual involved in the earlier investigation, visited her. He took her check for $2,000 even though he failed to provide any documentation that he, in fact, had any arrangements with the location promised. Within a month, she was contacted by another individual, Robinson, who advised that her vending machines were available. She gave Robinson another $2,000 upon the machines' arrival at her home, but found them to be nothing like the models promised to her nor were they in working order. Moreover, when she contacted the location promised to her, she found no arrangements had been made for placement of her machines there. Further contacts with the individuals she dealt with in this transaction met with denials and delaying tactics, but no resolutions. This victim's experience closely resembled the scheme outlined in the earlier indictment of the subject: (a) classified ads were used to attract customers; (b) promises were made that operable equipment would be placed in locations that would produce good income, representations which caused customers to give money to the defendants; (c) but in reality the equipment that was furnished did not function properly and no prime income producing locations were provided.

Paragraph 7 presents the first information linking the premises to be searched to the investigation. An inquiry with the local telephone company revealed the phone number provided by the person who delivered the defective machines to the victim was located at 123 Main St., but this number was not held in the name of the suspect company or individuals. However, the victim had spoken to her delivery person, Robinson, at this number several times and on occasion to an individual who identified herself as his stepdaughter. Thereafter, as discussed in paragraph 9, the victim personally visited this location twice (June 10 and June 24) and met with Robinson, events that should be noted were not prompted by any law enforcement personnel. However, she was questioned about these premises and she was able to recollect seeing corporate records of the subject company and a fax from Mitchell. At the second meeting, Robinson had copies of vending machine brochures that she saw him retrieve from a filing cabinet on the premises.

Covered in paragraphs 9–11 are the details of interviews with three other victimized individuals. Each of these individuals reported transactions similar to those experienced by the first victim contacted. They responded to classified ads for a vending machine business; were then contacted by Vendor's World and promised machines in good operating order that would be placed in good income producing locations. Based on these representations, they invested with Vendor's World only to receive machines that were not as represented, did not work, and/or were not provided with the promised locations. Note that in paragraph 9, specific mention is made of receiving literature from Vendor's World via the mail, necessary evidence to charge mail fraud. The importance of relating the details of these interviews in the affidavit is to help establish *probable cause* that a crime has been committed. Whereas one unsatisfactory business transaction might not be evidence of a scheme to defraud, a pattern of unsatisfactory transactions together with Mitchell's history of similar conduct, as reflected in this affidavit, established probable cause to believe otherwise.

Paragraph 12 relates the experiences of another victim, thus helping to solidify the pattern of misconduct already established. Additional uses of the mails were also identified. This victim came forward on August 5 as a result of becoming aware of Mitchell's activities from a television news story, but he had already scheduled a meeting with Robinson at the Main St. office in an effort to obtain a refund of his money. This scenario presented excellent opportunities for the investigation, especially with regard to finalizing probable cause for a search warrant. The victim agreed to what was considered the best alternative, that is, to be accompanied to the meeting with an undercover female investigator wearing a recording device and who would be introduced as his sister. The meeting occurred the following day. Among the statements made by Robinson and recorded by the undercover investigator was that he was now the owner and operator of Vendor's World pending resolution of Mitchell's legal problems. Thus, he clearly established his control over any Vendor's World records at the Main St. location. He also stated he would be closing their other office and consolidating their operation at this location. He also acknowledged three other customers having "problems" and said, "I got their files right here . . ."—statements which not only add to probable cause that a crime has occurred, but that evidence of the crime in the form of records were located at the Main St. office. Finally at this meeting, Robinson promised the victim he would get back to him about this refund on August 10, a contact that never subsequently occurred.

While at the Main St. office, the undercover investigator carefully observed the premises where the meeting took place and immediately after the meeting sketched these premises. This sketch was attached to the affidavit as an exhibit. As can be observed, she indicated in this sketch the office where the meeting took place and the contents of this office to include two desks and a file cabinet. This was the second of the two offices that were located on these premises.

The final investigative steps in establishing probable cause are reflected in paragraphs 15 and 16. Contact was made with the newspaper that ran the classified ads that the victims had responded to. The manager of this function confirmed that they had been placed by Vendor's World. She provided a copy of a recent advertisement placed by this company that was attached to the affidavit as an exhibit. She also confirmed the newspaper is mailed daily to thousands of mail subscribers. This use of the mails could be (although seldom is) used against the defendant as mail fraud violations because he caused the mails to further a scheme to defraud. However, because this case did not have extensive use of the mails, citing the mailing of the newspapers containing the advertisements that caused victimization helped to remove any doubt of probable cause that this particular crime had been committed.

The investigative steps reported in paragraph 16 were taken in an attempt to sort out the occupants at the 123 Main St. location. It had earlier been established that the telephone number Robinson was using was held in the name of Credit Counselors/Finance Leasing Group as opposed to Vendor's World. The post office was contacted and reported delivering mail to the address in this business name and to an individual believed to be affiliated with this business. The local utility company indicated that power service for this location was held in this individual's name. However, on file with the local municipal government were no occupational licenses in the names Vendor's World or Credit Counselors/Finance

Leasing Group. State corporate records reflected only Vendor's World with Robinson as the principal, but the corporate address was listed at another location. State corporate records reflected no listing for Credit Counselors/Finance Leasing Group. Moreover, a visual inspection of these premises (see paragraph 18) disclosed that while it was clearly marked with the number 123, it contained no other exterior signage identifying whether it was the business location of Vendor's World, Credit Counselors/Finance Leasing Group, or both. Thus, there was uncertainty as to the relationship between Vendor's World and Credit Counselors/Finance Leasing Group, especially in light of the latter entity having no established business licensure or corporate filings. Accordingly, the warrant was drafted to search the entire premises, but only for items relating to Vendor's World (the limiting phrase in this case). (*Note*: When the warrant was executed, investigators interviewed the owner of Credit Counselors/Finance Leasing Group and he satisfied them that he simply was renting space to Robinson/Vendor's World. He stated that any property belonging to Vendor's World would be found only in that part of the premises occupied by Robinson and his company, an explanation that was echoed by Robinson who also was present at the time the warrant was executed. A cursory search of other areas of the premises confirmed these statements.)

Paragraph 18 contains two important features. First, the affiant related his experience to the Court that normally businesses maintain books and records of their activities at their business locations and that these items are normally stored in desks and file cabinets. Thus, in addition to the observations made by the victim and the undercover investigator, he presented an additional reason to believe that these items would be located on these premises. Citing his experience also provided a basis to search for books and records, generally. Second, this paragraph contained a physical description of the exterior of the premises to be searched. The street address, type of structure and its color, and the specific location of the search premises within this structure are identified. The structure contained multiple units, but the search premises was clearly identified with the number 123 on the exterior door.

The final two paragraphs summarized the information presented and identified the types of items that were believed to be on hand that constituted evidence of the crimes under investigation. Witnesses observed brochures on the premises. Robinson acknowledged customer complaints and therefore would likely possess information about these customers. A witness observed corporate records on the premises as well as business correspondence. The affiant's experience suggested that business books and records, generally, would likely be on the premises where the business conducts its activities. Thus, there was a probable cause basis to seek all of these items.

Submitted to the reviewing judge along with the affidavit are the standardized forms *Application for a Search Warrant* and the *Search Warrant* itself. While custom may dictate otherwise, investigators should be prepared to complete these forms along with their affidavit. Needless to say, investigators should be fully conversant with the contents of the affidavit and the investigation in general, upon appearing before the magistrate.

Appendix D provides supplemental examples and information with regard to limiting phrases, items typically sought in white collar crime searches, and agent experience summaries.

EXECUTING THE SEARCH WARRANT

Planning and Organization

Again, to reiterate, in most white collar crimes cases the decision to acquire evidence via a search warrant is usually a step in the right direction in terms of a successful resolution. However, two potential obstacles must be dealt with in order to take this important step. The first was discussed above—developing and presenting the probable cause in affidavit form. The second potential obstacle is to execute the warrant in an organized manner so that all pertinent evidence is not only acquired, but is collected in a manner that will be useful in proving whatever ultimate charges are brought in the case. In order to achieve this latter objective, the evidence has to be collected in an orderly manner that allows for (1) an inventory to be left at the search site; (2) the identification of the investigator who seized each item and (3) who, in turn, can testify where each item was seized. Moreover, the seized evidence must be reviewed and analyzed so that relevant items can be culled and utilized in any subsequent proceedings with appropriate testimony. This process requires careful preplanning and organization. Without it, the execution of the warrant will likely be chaotic. Just imagine a group of investigators descending upon a search premises, grabbing anything they think is relevant and just throwing these items in boxes, and then handing the boxes over to the lead investigator as they walk away. This nightmare can become a reality if preplanning and organization is not undertaken.

Personnel Needs

Make a realistic assessment of your personnel needs based on the physical size of the search site (e.g., number of rooms), whether there are multiple sites to be searched simultaneously, the amount of evidence that is anticipated will be seized, and security concerns (i.e., the presence of investigation targets, employees at the premises, controlling the public, etc). As a *best practice*, err on the side of having too many law enforcement officers on hand. Additionally, arrange for the availability of standby officers who can be called to the scene in the event they are needed. In both instances, if it is determined that personnel are not needed they can be released. This is a much better situation to be in than finding yourself unexpectedly overwhelmed and needing to round up officers after the search has commenced. Such a situation can be especially problematic if the search site is distant from your agency offices, a scenario not uncommon for federal officers. Also, keep in mind that people get tired and they get hungry. One good reason to plan on using a greater number of personnel than might be thought necessary is that individual workload will be diffused, thus minimizing fatigue which in turn will hopefully speed the completion of the warrant execution. Also, if it is anticipated the warrant will be a daylong event or especially, if out of necessity, it begins at the end of the day or in the evening, make plans in advance to have food and beverages available for the investigators. Chances are the search and seizure will get done more quickly and with proper attention paid to necessary details if the investigators are not hungry and thirsty.

Setting the Date and Time

Many white collar crime cases do not present emergent situations where a warrant has to be acquired and executed as quickly as possible due to the destruction or removal of evidence. When nonemergent circumstances are present, make use of this luxury in terms of setting an optimal date and time for warrant execution (while not allowing your probable cause to grow stale or risking removal or destruction of evidence). Although case circumstances may dictate otherwise, selecting a Tuesday, Wednesday, or Thursday for the warrant execution offers some advantages to consider. First, having at least Monday or perhaps Tuesday, as well, available for appearing before the magistrate, securing needed supplies and equipment for evidence-gathering purposes, and making final plans will help to ensure a smooth execution. Conversely, avoiding Fridays for executing a search warrant when possible also offers a logistic advantage to the investigators. In the event unexpected developments occur which require the acquisition and execution of additional search warrants (e.g., evidence is uncovered at the original search site which leads to potentially valuable evidence at another location and there is urgency to secure it), gaining access to prosecutors and most importantly magistrates/judges for additional warrants as Friday winds down into the weekend can sometimes be dicey (but certainly not in all cases; and if this possibility is recognized in advance, giving such notice to prosecutors and judges/magistrates will normally eliminate any problems regarding their availability).

The other scheduling consideration is time of day. In most cases, getting an early start is advantageous as the execution can take place over the course of what for many is the normal workday. Also, an early start provides more time to deal with unexpected developments such as the need for additional warrants. Again, as suggested above, gaining access to prosecutors and judges/magistrates is often easier during normal working hours. Sometimes, however, the nature of the premises to be searched might dictate the time of execution. For example, both employees and customers can be present at business locations. In some cases, it might be beneficial to *not* have any employees or customers on the premises at the outset of execution because of potential difficulty in securing the premises. In this situation, the execution should occur before employees and customers normally arrive and they can be turned away before entering the premises. In other cases, having employees on site might be advantageous for the investigation because it provides an opportunity to identify and interview them. As will be discussed later, gaining the cooperation of individuals at the site in terms of the location of certain records and information concerning computer systems is often very helpful in completing the warrant execution in the most efficient manner possible. Thus, when setting the time of the warrant execution (assuming nonemergent circumstances are present) these various factors should be considered.

Organizational/Planning Meeting

Bringing together all those who will participate in the search prior to its execution is a *best practice* to ensure that this operation is accomplished in the most professional and efficient manner possible. The personnel involved should be briefed on the nature of the crime under investigation, the location(s) where the search will take place, and the items that are authorized for seizure under the warrant. Specific work assignments for each participant should be made during this meeting. While there are specialized assignments which will be detailed further later, in most situations the majority of the participants will be involved in the actual search and seizure of items specified in the warrant. Thus, it is important to emphasize the evidence collection, tagging, and custodial procedures that will be used. If possible, actual search locations within the premises should be assigned in advance to particular individuals. It is also important for everyone to understand the entry protocol that will be employed, that is, steps that will be taken before any evidence collection is undertaken.

A meeting of this type is especially important when the search team is an interagency effort so that personnel from the different organizations will all follow one prescribed methodology. However, holding a presearch meeting is recommended even when it involves a group of investigators who routinely work together. Whenever possible, the presearch meeting should be held the day before the search. The information presented will still be fresh in the minds of the attendees while valuable time on the day of search can be devoted to its execution. However, if this is not possible, the time spent on the day of the search holding a search team meeting will be well worth the relatively short delay in terms of ensuring an organized effort that will result in the seizure of not only identifiable evidence, but also identifiable to the seizing agent.

Staging Location

A location for the search team to assemble just prior to executing the warrant needs to be identified. This location should be in the immediate vicinity of the search site, but obviously out of view of anyone on these premises. Moreover, it should not be a location that will attract the attention of neighbors or passers-by, as a further safeguard against the occupants of the premises being alerted prior to the execution. The plan to assemble at this location should be communicated at the presearch meeting and normally the time set for assembly should be shortly before the scheduled warrant execution. The purpose of the staging location is to ensure that all personnel are present and then convoy to the search site en masse.

Securing the Premises

At the designated execution time, an investigator responsible for actually serving the warrant approaches the premises and attempts to gain entry. He or she should be accompanied by other members of the search team. Simultaneously, some search team members should also be assigned to perimeter security around the premises to prevent the flight of individuals and/or destruction/removal of evidence. The numbers of investigators assigned to these initial entry duties will be dictated by the size of the premises, number of individuals believed to be on the premises, and the level of resistance which could be encountered.

Normally, a residential search requires agents to knock and announce their intention before entering. Gaining voluntary entrance to a residence through the cooperation of an occupant is the preferred practice. If such cooperation is not extended or no one is at home, entry may be gained by force and tools, and equipment and/or a locksmith should be on hand to do so. Keep in mind that any delay in permitting entry might be the result of efforts to destroy evidence. Most importantly, if a forceful entry onto occupied premises is necessary, officer safety should be a paramount concern.

Commercial locations that are accessible to the public can be entered in normal business fashion. Commercial locations that do not do business directly with the public will still have an employee access that will permit entrance onto the premises. In either case, the investigator serving the warrant should ask to see whoever is in charge at the location, provide that person with a copy of the warrant, and explain what will transpire. In the event a search needs to commence prior to normal business operating hours, presearch investigation should determine if there are any early arriving employees, custodians, or security personnel on site. Preferably, access to the premises should be gained through these individuals. However, since these types of individuals might not feel they have any authority to permit access, being able to contact a responsible person in the firm by telephone to explain what is happening and seek their cooperation often resolves any entrance problems. Therefore, having a telephone contact number for such an individual can come in handy in such situations. However, delaying entry until a responsible person arrives should be avoided in the interest of officer safety, securing the premises, and preserving evidence. If this phone call does not provide immediate access, if no responsible official can be reached, or if no one is on the premises, entry by force should be pursued. Again, the appropriate equipment and/or a locksmith should be on hand for this eventuality. In fact, having a locksmith on hand or on standby for the search of a commercial premises may be helpful when attempting to open locked closets, file cabinets, safes, desks, rooms, and so on.

In general, the prevailing philosophy being presented here with regard to executing a search warrant is one where professionalism and courtesy is extended to those on the search premises. An important part of this philosophy is for the initial entry to be conducted in this manner in an effort to set a tone that will elicit the most cooperation possible and reduce any hostilities. Whether at a residence or at a commercial location, it is often helpful to explain that the search will be completed more quickly and be less disruptive if cooperation is extended. In many, if not most, situations this approach will likely be successful; when it is not, the search will simply proceed, but in a more hostile environment.

Once entry is made and service of the warrant is announced, the remaining members of the search team should proceed onto the premises and conduct a "protective sweep." This simply means that all occupants, employees, and/or visitors on the premises should be accounted for and a cursory search of all rooms for weapons or any other dangerous materials/items should be made. Unless certain individuals are to be taken into custody incident to the search warrant execution, non–law enforcement personnel on the premises are *not* under arrest. However, in the interest of officer safety and evidence preservation, they should not be allowed to move freely about the premises while the warrant is being executed. If there is articulable suspicion that any of these individuals may be armed with a weapon, patdowns would be in order. Otherwise, these individuals should be identified and inquiry should be made whether they have any weapons in their possession or in their vehicles that are on the premises. The members of the search team should secure any such weapons. One or more members of the search team should be assigned to oversee these individuals while the search is underway to ensure they remain in a defined area. In the case of business premises, owners and/or their attorneys may view the search activities under escort, again to ensure the safety and security of the site and its contents.

Investigators may want to attempt to interview these individuals concerning activities at the search site and/or serve grand jury subpoenas on them. Obviously, if the intent is to interview employees, those assigned to this task should have a good understanding of the overall investigation and/or be provided an interview format to guide discussions with these individuals. At the very least, employees may be able to assist in identifying the location of certain evidence, in gaining access to locked areas, files, safes, and so on and, as will be discussed later, by providing information concerning any computer systems on the premises.

As discussed earlier, in nonemergent situations one of the criteria to consider is whether to conduct the search at a commercial location at a time when there would be a normal complement of employees on hand. When there is a value in identifying and/or interviewing these employees, a search can certainly commence when they are present. However, the more employees on hand, the larger control problem becomes. If identifying and interviewing as many employees as possible is important to the investigation, one option is to dismiss them from the premises once these tasks are completed.

Of course, if the search is commenced prior to the arrival time of the normal employee complement, these individuals can simply be denied entrance to the premises until the search is completed. This scenario also highlights another security need. Entrances onto the premises should be limited while the search is underway to ensure no unauthorized individuals gain access to the site. Entrances (preferably one) that remain open should be staffed with one or more search team members to ensure the safety of the other search team members and security of the premises.

Labeling and Sketching the Search Site

Once the protective sweep has been completed and the premises has been secured, the search site should be labeled or tagged. This means that a small number of team members (one or two in small to medium size premises; perhaps more in larger premises such as large business locations) tag or label each separate area within the premises with a unique identifier (usually an alpha designator) and then any item within this area that might contain evidence (e.g., desk, file cabinet) is tagged with a unique subidentifier. Figure 5-1 provides a simple example of this process. As can be observed, this premises was divided into four areas labeled A, B, C, and D. The desk in Room A, reception area, is labeled A-1 while the file cabinet is designated A-2. This same process is repeated in each of the other areas. The walkway/common area is labeled C and the table in this area is designated C-1. The front office is labeled B and the desk and file cabinet bear the designations B-1 and B-2, respectively. The rear office is labeled D, and D-1 and D-2 are the two desks, and the file cabinet is D-3. When evidence is seized in any of these areas the location of each seized item reflects these designations. Thus, the computer on the table

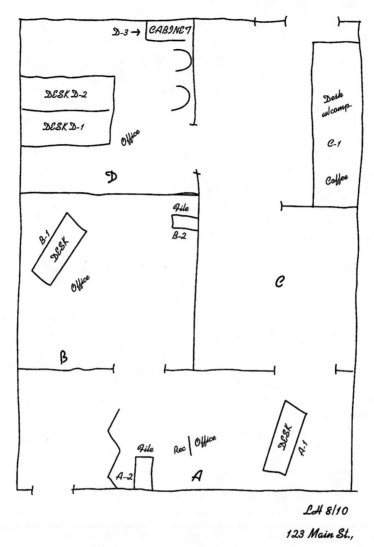

Figure 5-1   Sketch of search premises.

in the hallway is labeled as seized from C-1. This process will be discussed further later. However, it should be apparent that it provides a methodical approach to providing locations to where evidence was seized—information that may very well be necessary if this evidence is to be introduced in a judicial proceeding. Thus, this process is a crucial first step in providing for evidence authentication and it must be undertaken before any evidence is seized (unless to prevent destruction or removal). Entrusting this step to trained and detail-oriented personnel ensures that it will be carried out in the proper manner. Self-adhering paper notes can be used for labeling although tie-on tags might also be appropriate for certain types of containers. In either case, they should be boldly marked and conspicuously placed to ensure ease of observation.

Following immediately behind those labeling the rooms should be a designated sketch person and a videographer. This section will discuss sketching the search premises while the videotaping will be addressed in the next section along with photography. A sketch of the premises provides a record of the floor plan as it existed at the time of the search warrant execution (again, see Figure 5-1). Having a sketch record further helps to authenticate items seized because their location on the search premises can be pinpointed on the sketch. The person having responsibility for sketching should identify rooms not only by their obvious function (e.g., office, supply room, etc.) but also by the alpha designator assigned. Likewise, desks, file cabinets, and any other items provided an alpha/numeric designator should be included in the sketch and identified by both the alpha/numeric designator and item type (e.g., A-1, desk). Thus, the sketch provides a graphic depiction of where items were seized that may very well be helpful in presenting evidence in judicial proceedings. Additionally, as a great deal of time can pass between a search and such proceedings, sketches can also assist investigators in recalling their seizure of particular items that will be entered into evidence.

Again, selecting the search member to perform sketching duty should be done with careful consideration. The ideal situation, of course, is to have on hand a person with training and/or professional experience as an artist or draftsperson. In the alternative, select someone who, at least informally, has demonstrated some talent in these respects and who can produce a neat and detailed drawing. Depending on the size of the premises, sketching can be a time-consuming process and the person assigned should not be called upon to perform any other search related duties until the sketch is completed. However, the actual collection of evidence can commence once the site is labeled, and sketching can be performed simultaneously. Thus, while time consuming, this process will not delay the overall completion of the warrant execution. The sketch person should date and initial the completed drawing and turn it over to the investigator who has overall responsibility for the case.

It is best that only one person be assigned sketching duty to ensure continuity in the approach that is taken. However, in major search warrant executions involving multiple floors in an office building, it might be necessary to have more than one person involved in the process. In this event, each person assigned should have full responsibility for sketching an entire floor.

The Role of Video and Still Photography

Immediately following the labeling of the search site and before any actual searching and seizing begins, the entire search premises should be videotaped, room-by-room. Ideally, the video camera will also have audio capability, thus permitting the videographer to narrate his/her visual depiction of the search site as it proceeds. In this event, insure that the videographer introduces himself/herself by name and title, the date, time, location, and event (search warrant execution) at the outset of the videotaping (otherwise, the videographer should memorialize his/her duties in this regard by way of notes). Affixed labels identifying room alpha designators and furniture/fixture alpha/numeric designators should appear in the videotape. The videotape will provide a graphic portrayal of the overall search site in terms of its appearance and physical condition at the outset of warrant execution as well as specific areas where items of evidence were found.

A second videotape of the search premises is to be made at the conclusion of the warrant execution. The same person who made the first tape should make this exit tape and it should follow the same route through the premises as the first tape. The same introduction should be dictated into this exit videotape with special care to include the time it is being made. The purpose of the exit tape is to record the physical condition of the premises after the search was completed. Thus, any false allegations of ransacking or damage to the premises caused by the search team can be refuted. While ransacking the premises should not be tolerated, accidental damage can occur even though search team members should be cautioned at the presearch meeting to exercise care when performing their duties. In the event damage does occur, at least there will be a "before and after" portrayal of the property, which might help to minimize any misconduct and/or monetary claims.

The videographer should record his/her name, title, date, time, place, and event (search warrant entrance video/search warrant exit video) on a label affixed to each tape cassette and these along with any notes made by the videographer should be given to the principal investigator. As with the room labeling and sketching, selecting a videographer should be done with care. This should be a person familiar with and experienced in using the video equipment and who also exercises care and attention to detail in his/her work. Moreover, this person as well as the principal investigator should ensure as part of presearch planning that the video camera is functioning properly, its batteries are fully charged, and a supply of tapes are on hand and will be at the search site.

The use of still photography at a search site is a valuable way to document the seizure of evidence, particularly items of significance. Even in white collar crime searches where the focus is often on documentary items, photographing the location of significant items of this nature provides a graphic record of their seizure. Depending upon the case, there may be other types of highly significant evidence that should be photographed before removal. Additionally, photographing unexpected items such as money, weapons, drugs, or other valuables is also recommended. At least one search team member should be assigned still photography duty, and more if the scope of the execution is large. This person should be called upon to take photographs throughout the premises on an as-needed basis, as the search proceeds. An ideal person for this assignment is the videographer (if he/she is also skilled in still photography) because normally any still photography will not be needed until entrance videotaping is completed. The still photographer(s) should maintain a log which notes a description and location where each photo was taken along with the date, time, and type of camera used.

Evidence-Collection Procedures

Once the premises are tagged and the entrance video is made, the task of collecting evidence can begin. Depending upon the size of the premises, teams consisting of one or more individuals should be assigned specific areas to search and seize evidence specified in the warrant. If certain parts of the premises are believed to contain more crucial evidence than others, it is wise to assign individuals with the most knowledge of the investigation to these areas. This criterion for individual assignment would also apply if the circumstances require a careful discrimination between records that are subject to seizure and those that are not.

The evidence-gathering teams should be supplied with various types of evidence containers, including boxes, large envelopes, and clear plastic documentary evidence holders. This latter container is especially useful for highly significant pieces of evidence where fingerprint and/or handwriting examinations might ensue. Non-documentary evidence may require other types of containers and these should be on hand, as anticipated. In cases where the seizure of latent fingerprint evidence is anticipated and/or there is concern over contact with unknown or unhealthful substances, wearing latex gloves during the evidence-collection process should be considered a *best practice*.

As evidence is collected and placed in containers, the containers should be endorsed to describe the nature of the evidence, location including the alpha/numeric designator, name of seizing investigator and date. Through the alpha/numeric designator, the location of each item can be pinpointed on the sketch of the premises. Depending upon procedures being followed, these endorsements may be made directly on the container or on an evidence tag that is affixed to the container. Items of the same general category that are seized en masse can be placed in boxes that are endorsed as above. As suggested above, items that are highly significant to the investigation, contraband, items of high value such as cash and/or weapons should be photographed in the location where they are found before placing them in an evidence container.

Seizing Computers

In white collar crime cases, it would be the exceptional situation where computers and/or electronically stored information would not be of evidentiary value. This section will cover the acquisition of such evidence via a search warrant, although perhaps in a more superficial than in an in-depth manner. The reason for this approach is twofold: (1) unique legal considerations; and (2) technical considerations of a highly sophisticated nature. However, the discussion that is presented on this subject should provide sufficient guidance for many white collar crime search warrant scenarios. Nevertheless, it is wise to fully explore the seizure of computers and/or electronically stored evidence with legal counsel on a case-by-case basis to identify any unique problems as well as to have access to the technical expertise that is often necessary for a successful seizure. An excellent, detailed treatment of this subject entitled, *Searching and Seizing Computers and Obtaining Electronic Evidence in Criminal Investigations*, is available through the U.S. Department of Justice. As will be noted later, this section relies heavily upon information from this publication (also see Appendix D).

An initial consideration is whether to seek the seizure of the computer(s) itself, or only the information stored therein. If computer hardware on the site is evidence, an instrumentality, or fruit of a crime, it should be identified as such in the affidavit (along with a full description) and its seizure should be sought in the application for the search warrant.[16]

When investigative interest centers on data stored in a computer, the general notion of a reasonable expectation of privacy serves to guide whether a search warrant is needed to seize computer hardware and/or information stored therein. To determine whether an individual has a reasonable expectation of privacy in information stored in a computer, it helps to treat the computer like a closed container such as a briefcase or file cabinet. The Fourth Amendment generally prohibits law enforcement from accessing and viewing information stored in a computer without a warrant if it would be prohibited from opening a closed container and examining its contents in the same situation. In seeking a search warrant under these circumstances, the affidavit should focus on establishing probable cause that evidence, instrumentalities and/or fruits of a crime are stored electronically in a computer(s) (or in other electronic data storage devices) and this data should be fully described.[17]

It is the steps necessary to actually seize the electronically stored data that usually require the presence of technical experts as part of the search team and often adds an element of uncertainty to the search planning. Specifically, the issue is whether the electronically stored data can actually be seized on site or whether the hardware needs to be seized for the purpose of acquiring the data in a more controlled situation, such as a forensic crime laboratory. Learning as much as possible about the computer system at the search site and consulting with technical experts while developing probable cause and planning the search will help to reduce these uncertainties. In general, the U.S. Department of Justice (DOJ) recommendation in these situations is to pursue the quickest, least intrusive, and most direct search strategy that is consistent with securing the evidence described in the warrant. This strategy will permit agents to search on-site in some cases, and will permit them to seize the computers for off-site review in others. Flexibility is the key. However, DOJ cautions that the planned strategy and alternative approaches in the event of unexpected problems should be explained fully in the affidavit supporting the warrant application. In addition, the affidavit should provide at the outset, definitions for any pertinent technical terms relative to seizing computers or information contained therein. When a computer(s) itself is evidence, an instrumentality, or fruit of a crime, it is necessary to explain the role of the computer when providing a summary of the offense in the affidavit. Similarly, when it is believed that a computer(s)' role is that of a storage device for evidence in electronic format, justification for this belief must also be provided in the affidavit.[18]

As a general organizational plan for the execution of a search warrant involving the seizure of computers and/or electronically stored evidence, implementing the following four-step process will go a long way to ensure this effort meets with success:

1. Assemble a team consisting of the case agent, the prosecutor, and a technical expert as far in advance of the search as possible.

2. Learn as much as possible about the computer system that will be searched before devising a search strategy or drafting the warrant.

3. Formulate a strategy for conducting the search (including a backup plan) based on the known information about the targeted computer system.

4. Draft the warrant, taking special care to describe the object of the search and the property to be seized accurately and particularly, and explain the possible search strategies (as well as the practical and legal issues that helped shape it) in the supporting affidavit.[19]

The Electronic Communications Privacy Act (ECPA)

The ECPA regulates how the government can obtain stored account information from network service providers. Whenever agents or prosecutors seek stored e-mail, account records, or subscriber information from a network service provider, they must comply with the ECPA, a statute that has been described as "unusually complicated." Service of a search warrant on a network service provider is one of the legal mechanisms permitted by the ECPA for obtaining this type of information, and considering the limitations the ECPA places on the available legal processes for obtaining stored account information, it is arguably the preferred method. In essence, a search warrant served upon a network service provider can result in the production of all records and the contents of wire or electronic communication that is in electronic storage in an electronic communications system. Moreover, this method does not require any notification to be provided to the customer or subscriber. Service of a search warrant upon a network service provider, however, is more akin to serving a subpoena on a business entity for the production of records. Investigators normally play no role in this search and seizure process due to the highly technical environment in which the "search" is conducted.[20] The DOJ's *Searching and Seizing Computers and Obtaining Electronic Evidence in Criminal Investigations* presents a more detailed discussion of the ECPA for those who require further information on this topic. (See Appendix D for sample language.)

The Role of Evidence Custodian

A member of the search team must be designated as the evidence custodian. All seized items are brought to this person, who in turn logs them in for the purpose of creating an inventory of items seized. A copy of this inventory must be left on the premises (preferably in the care of the owner or some other responsible person) and, of course, this inventory also assists those who will peruse and evaluate the seized items at whatever location they are stored. Again, the selection of the evidence custodian should be carefully considered and a meticulous, detail-oriented person would be a prime candidate. Ideally, the inventory will be computer generated, thus requiring the evidence custodian to be skilled in using such a computer program. Otherwise, a manually created inventory must be neat and legible, again skills to consider if this will be the process utilized. In this case, using preprinted, multicopy inventory forms would facilitate the completion of this process. In either case, the inventory list should identify the items seized, the seizing agent, date, and location of seizure (using the alpha/numeric designators).

Storage and Analysis of the Seized Items

At the conclusion of the search warrant execution, all seized items must be transported to a location under the control of the lead investigator(s). When planning the warrant execution, consider these transportation requirements. A relatively small quantity of material might not pose any unique problems in this regard (i.e., automobiles might be adequate), but when a large quantity of seized material is anticipated or is unique in terms of size, weight, and so on, arranging for trucks and/or professional movers might be necessary.

In many instances, the storage location will be the investigative agency offices; although in cases involving a large amount of seized items or items not suitable for storage in an office environment, other storage facilities will need to be procured. Wherever the seized material is stored, it should be a location that has adequate security and is environmentally appropriate for storing these items. Normally, this means the storage area should have temperature and humidity levels comparable to a normal office environment, and be clean and dry with adequate lighting. In addition, the storage area should be large enough to permit easy access to the seized materials. Although this might seem obvious, the purpose of executing the search warrant is to seize evidence, instrumentalities, and/or fruits of a crime, and not simply to conduct a "raid" of a suspect premises. In the course of executing the warrant, the evidentiary value of some items seized might be immediately recognized. However, many cases reach a successful resolution only after investigators sift through and analyze seized items in an effort to piece together the necessary evidence of wrongdoing. This can be a daunting task when large volumes of material are involved, but one which must be undertaken. Executing the warrant and letting the seized items sit in a storage area without review and analysis is often a recipe for a case that will go nowhere. One way to facilitate, or at the very least not discourage, the review and analysis of seized material is to provide an adequate and equipped work space (i.e., tables, chairs, lighting, etc.) in *close proximity* to the stored material. This recommendation is especially pertinent if storage is off-site from the investigators' offices. In any event, whether at the agency offices or off-site, at a minimum there should be suitable working conditions to permit a cursory review of items so that potentially important material can be identified and segregated for future integration into the final investigative package. However, care should be taken to ensure that any such items retain their seizure information, that is, item description, seizure location, date, and seizing agent. Furthermore, with regard to important documentary items that might ultimately be entered into evidence, it is recommended that copies of these items be made for any interim investigative/prosecutive purposes until an actual judicial proceeding occurs that requires the original document.

CHAPTER HIGHLIGHTS

- Executing a search warrant can permit access to documents not subject to subpoena authority; it ensures the acquisition of evidence that might not be turned over incident to the issuance of a subpoena; unknown incriminating evidence might be discovered; it can facilitate witness cooperation; and it can be disruptive to ongoing criminal activity. It cannot be emphasized too strongly that white collar crime investigators should consider employing search warrants whenever possible.

- The Fourth Amendment establishes that the government can undertake reasonable searches and it lays out the methodology for obtaining such a warrant, including the requirement that the warrant be specific in terms of what is to be seized as opposed to a general warrant. While this governmental power was established in the nation's infancy, courts have examined the unique circumstances present in many white collar crime cases only in relatively recent times. These circumstances have included expectation of privacy issues; the type of evidence that can be seized (i.e., of a crime); and compliance with the particularity requirement as specified in the Fourth Amendment (i.e., with regard to the seizure of documentary material).

- Search warrants are issued by judges or magistrates based on the submission of an affidavit that establishes probable cause (1) that a crime has been committed; (2) that specific items constitute evidence of that crime; and (3) that such evidence is at the place specified in the affidavit.

- A decision to utilize a search warrant entails a twofold undertaking: (1) developing probable cause through investigation which, in turn, is incorporated into an affidavit; and (2) executing the warrant in an organized, effective manner.

- In general, the prevailing philosophy being presented here with regard to executing a search warrant is one where professionalism and courtesy is extended to those on the search premises. An important part of this philosophy is for the initial entry to be conducted in this manner in an effort to set a tone that will elicit the most cooperation possible and reduce any hostilities.

- Labeling and sketching the search site is an essential first step in ensuring that items will be useful as evidence in any subsequent legal proceeding.

- The search premises should be videotaped before any actual search and seizure activities commence (but after areas have been labeled/tagged) and at the conclusion of the search.

- Seizing computers and/or data contained therein will be encountered frequently when executing search warrants in white collar crime cases. Seizures of either type can present (1) unique legal considerations and (2) technical considerations of a highly sophisticated nature; and require advance planning.

- The appropriate follow-up to a search warrant execution is the review and analysis of the items that were seized for use as evidence in a criminal prosecution.

CHAPTER BEST PRACTICES

- A *best practice* is for investigators to identify as early as possible in the case whether the execution of a search warrant would be appropriate and if so, the initial investigative steps should be geared towards the development of probable cause for the acquisition of the warrant. (See page 96.)

- As a *best practice*, err on the side of having too many law enforcement officers on hand. (See page 109.)

- Bringing together all those who will participate in the search prior to its execution is a *best practice* to ensure that this operation is accomplished in the most professional and efficient manner possible. (See page 110.)

- In cases where the seizure of latent fingerprint evidence is anticipated and/or there is concern over contact with unknown or unhealthful substances, wearing latex gloves during the evidence-collection process should be considered a *best practice*. (See page 117.)

Notes

1. L. E. Rissler, *Documentary Search Warrants: A Problem of Particularity* (Washington, DC: Federal Bureau of Investigation, U.S. Department of Justice, 1984), p. 2.
2. M. Zalman and L. Siegel, *Criminal Procedure: Constitution and Society* (St. Paul, MN: West, 1991), p. 98.
3. D. A. McWhirter, *Search, Seizure and Privacy* (Phoenix, AZ: Oryx, 1994), p. 38.
4. M. Zalman, *Criminal Procedure: Constitution and Society*, 4th ed. (Upper Saddle River, NJ: Prentice Hall, 2004), p. 94.
5. Ibid., p. 89.
6. R. S. Stolker, *Asset Forfeiture: Financial Search Warrants* (Washington, DC: U.S. Department of Justice, Bureau of Justice Assistance, 1989), p. 12.
7. Rissler, *op. cit.*, p. 2.
8. Ibid., pp. 2–3.
9. Ibid., p. 4.
10. McWhirter, *op. cit.*, pp. 37–39.
11. Zalman and Siegel, *op. cit.*, p. 166.
12. H. E. Williams, *Investigating White-Collar Crime: Embezzlement and Financial Fraud* (Springfield, IL: Charles C. Thomas, Publisher, 1997), p. 140.
13. Zalman, *op. cit.*, pp. 96–97.
14. Stolker, *op. cit.*, p. 14, 28.
15. Computer Crime and Intellectual Property Section, Criminal Division, U.S. Department of Justice, *Searching and Seizing Computers and Obtaining Electronic Evidence in Criminal Investigations* (July, 2002). Retrieved March 7, 2005 from U.S. Department of Justice website: http://www.usdoj.gov/criminal/cybercrime/searching.html#A.
16. Ibid.
17. Ibid.
18. Ibid.
19. Ibid.
20. Ibid.

CHAPTER 6

Injunctions and Forfeitures: Halting the Crime and Taking Away the Profits

Key Terms and Concepts

- Asset Forfeiture
- Civil Injunctions
- Discovery
- Money Laundering

- Preliminary Injunction
- Preponderance of Evidence
- Temporary Restraining Order

This chapter discusses steps that can be taken to bring a quick end to fraudulent conduct and deny any ill-gotten gains to those who were involved in such conduct. Criminal investigations and any charges that subsequently arise from them can often span a lengthy time period. The execution of a search warrant can send a strong message to those responsible for suspect activity to discontinue and/or result in a cessation of activities due to disruption caused by this action. However, the intent of a search warrant is only to permit the seizure of evidence at a location where there is normally an expectation of privacy and not to force the suspect activity to cease. Thus, other legal means must be taken to ensure that the objectionable activity ceases, usually in the form of civil injunctions. Such actions can be taken incident to criminal investigations or can be stand-alone actions, depending upon the fact scenario and/or powers of the enforcement agency involved.

Most white collar crimes have as their objective the enrichment of those involved. For those tasked with white collar crime enforcement and prosecution, taking illegally obtained profits away from white collar criminals would seem to be an important goal. Successful criminal prosecutions can result in this outcome when substantial fines are levied and victim restitution is ordered. Unfortunately, the federal government has established a poor record when it comes to actually collecting such monies from defendants because assets can often be hidden or dissipated before these penalties are imposed.[1] Successful civil injunctive actions can also result in the return of illegally obtained money or property. These actions have the advantage that illegal funds can be impounded or "frozen" before the case is fully resolved, thus preserving the funds for proper distribution.

Asset forfeiture actions offer another means to take away ill-gotten gains from those involved in illegal activity; and when pursued civilly, they often provide an opportunity to do so before any other type of formal adjudication is rendered, thus preventing dissipation and/or concealment.

The material presented here on both types of actions will be at the familiarization level as opposed to dealing with any in-depth legal issues. Unique bodies of law have evolved with respect to both civil injunctive and forfeiture actions which are beyond the scope of this volume. The goal here is to help the investigator understand the role and value of these actions and the investigative steps that need to be taken to bring these actions to fruition.

CIVIL INJUNCTIONS

Bringing a white collar crime to a halt through legal mandate is often achieved through a civil injunction. Typically this process involves the issuance of a temporary restraining order on an *ex parte* basis by a court that directs the offending party to cease the objectionable activity. This restraining order is, in fact, temporary, and the issuing judge subsequently holds a hearing to consider the issuance of a preliminary injunction during which both sides can be heard. If the government prevails, the judge issues a preliminary injunction that halts the objectionable activity pending a final judicial resolution to the case. This section will introduce two types of injunctive actions, one which is applicable to a variety of federal criminal fraud violations under Title 18 of the United States Code, while the other involves unique authority that lies within the domains of various federal regulatory and enforcement agencies.

Injunctions against Fraud

A federal statute entitled "Injunctions against Fraud," 18 U.S.C. 1345 (see Box 6–1), permits the government to seek a temporary restraining order and preliminary and permanent injunctions against those violating or about to violate the federal mail and wire fraud statutes or conspiracy to defraud the United States (18 U.S.C. 371); 18 U.S.C. 287, False Claims; 18 U.S.C. 1001, False Statements; and banking and health care statutes. In addition, with regard to banking and health care offenses, the statute can be used to prevent the dissipation of assets and other property associated with the subject offense. Given the wide applicability of the mail and wire fraud statutes in white collar crime generally, along with frequent federal involvement in banking and health care violations, 18 U.S.C. 1345 provides a viable means to bring to a halt many white collar criminal activities.

It should be noted, however, that this statute specifies that when injunctive relief is sought prior to a criminal indictment, the Federal Rules of Civil Procedure apply for any ensuing litigation, which means that defendants are entitled to a broader discovery process (i.e., statutorily mandated disclosure of evidence in the hands of the government) than permitted under the Federal Rules of Criminal Procedure. Conversely, when an injunction under 18 U.S.C. 1345 is obtained after an indictment has been brought against the defendant, the discovery process follows the more restrictive criminal procedures rules. If no related criminal prosecution is anticipated, the investigator must simply be prepared to comply with the civil discovery process. However, this statute does pose a dilemma for the investigator who is pursuing a criminal prosecution arising from the same activity. On the one hand, the investigator can seek to quickly halt victimization arising from the criminal activity through an injunction under 18 U.S.C. 1345, but in doing so this will expose the investigation to a more probing discovery process. On the other hand, injunctive action under this statute can be delayed pending the completion of the investigation and obtaining an indictment that would limit discovery to the defendant. However, the cost related to this alternative, of course, is greater victimization. Often the path taken is usually dictated by what would be in the best interests of the criminal case. When it would not be in the best interest of the criminal prosecution to prematurely divulge witnesses, informants, and/or investigative strategies and techniques prior to bringing an indictment, seeking an injunction under 18 U.S.C. 1345 is often delayed until that event occurs. It has been this author's experience that the civil discovery process not only entitles defendants to the review of documentary materials in the possession of the government, but can also result in depositions being taken from investigators and government witnesses by defense attorneys about their knowledge and/or involvement in the case. Not only can such depositions prematurely expose witnesses, informants, and investigative strategies/techniques, but they also establish a testimonial record taken under oath that could become problematic for the government in a subsequent criminal proceeding. Investigators and government witnesses can be subjected to a broader scope of questioning by defense attorneys than what might be permitted in a criminal proceeding; inconsistencies in statements given under oath can arise; and defenses to government prosecution strategies can be developed. However, when no companion criminal proceeding is anticipated or it is felt that the civil discovery process will not harm any subsequent criminal case, injunctive relief under 18 U.S.C. 1345 can certainly halt victimization, and in the case of bank and health care crime, can serve to prevent assets from disappearing.

Obtaining an Iinjunction under 18 U.S.C. 1345

The government initiates a civil fraud injunction by filing a complaint. The complaint is accompanied by a declaration, the civil procedures version of an affidavit. Unlike the well-established probable cause standard associated with the issuance of a search warrant, there has been some division among the courts regarding the proper burden of proof standard necessary for the issuance of an injunction under 18 U.S.C. 1345. While a number of courts have held that probable cause is the proper standard, others have required the more onerous standard of a preponderance of the evidence.[2] Zalman and Siegel define preponderance of evidence as evidence reasonably tending to prove the essential facts in a case or the greater weight of the

---

Box 6–1　Injunctions against fraud: 18 U.S.C. 1345

(a) (1) If a person is—

    (A) violating or about to violate this chapter or section 287, 371 (insofar as such violation involves a conspiracy to defraud the United States or any agency thereof), or 1001 of this title;

    (B) committing or about to commit a banking law violation (as defined in section 3322(d) of this title), or

    (C) committing or about to commit a Federal health care offense—

the Attorney General may commence a civil action in any Federal court to enjoin such violation.

    (2) If a person is alienating or disposing of property, or intends to alienate or dispose of property, obtained as a result of a banking law violation (as defined in section 3322(d) of this title) or a Federal health care offense or property which is traceable to such violation, the Attorney General may commence a civil action in any Federal court—

        (A) to enjoin such alienation or disposition of property; or

        (B) for a restraining order to—

            (i) prohibit any person from withdrawing, transferring, removing, dissipating, or disposing of any such property or property of equivalent value; and

            (ii) appoint a temporary receiver to administer such restraining order.

    (3) A permanent or temporary injunction or restraining order shall be granted without bond.

(b) The court shall proceed as soon as practicable to the hearing and determination of such an action, and may, at any time before final determination, enter such a restraining order or prohibition, or take such other action, as is warranted to prevent a continuing and substantial injury to the United States or to any person or class of persons for whose protection the action is brought. A proceeding under this section is governed by the Federal Rules of Civil Procedure, except that, if an indictment has been returned against the respondent, discovery is governed by the Federal Rules of Criminal Procedure.

---

evidence.[3] However, the legislative history of this statute was to provide a means to a speedy end to fraudulent schemes, thus justifying the probable cause standard.[4] Nevertheless, as a *best practice*, investigators should consult with their prosecuting attorneys as to the required standard of proof necessary for an injunction under 18 U.S.C 1345 in the judicial district where this type of action will be sought. A requirement to meet the more burdensome preponderance of the evidence standard might be another reason to reconsider a preindictment injunctive action in light of the civil discovery process. Any anticipated criminal prosecution might be compromised as a result of disclosing greater details about the investigation in order to meet a preponderance of the evidence standard.

When it is determined that seeking an injunction under 18 U.S.C. 1345 is appropriate, the investigator will be called upon to prepare a declaration. In many cases, this task is akin to preparing a search warrant affidavit; although, as just suggested, if the required standard of proof is the preponderance of the evidence, a more detailed factual basis on which to believe a crime is occurring might have to be provided. The preparer of the declaration needs to be mindful that the goal of this undertaking is to establish probable cause (or perhaps a preponderance of the evidence in some districts) that a crime(s) within the purview of 18 U.S.C. 1345 (e.g., mail fraud, wire fraud, false statements, banking violations, and health care violations) is occurring. In doing so, the declaration should provide evidence of criminal intent. It should also outline the methodology employed to perpetrate the crime(s), such as using the mails, telephones, or the Internet, so that the illegal use of these communication mediums can be specifically enjoined by court order if necessary.

Due to its length, a declaration that formed the basis for an injunctive action under 18 U.S.C. 1345 is presented as Appendix E. The referenced attachments have been eliminated as well, in the interest of space. Also, individual and business names and locations have been changed and dates have been redacted. In this case, it was essential to establish intent to defraud, at least at a probable cause level. The defendants had engaged in the sale of worthless (and in some cases unhealthful) diet products under various trade styles over a several-year period. A series of prior civil enforcement actions had been taken against these defendants and their companies. These actions simply required establishing that they were misrepresenting their products, and no proof of intent to misrepresent was required. Unfortunately, the impact of these actions was limited because they resulted in only the return of mail containing orders for the worthless products along with a difficult to enforce cease and desist order. The defendants in these cases were the classic recidivist offenders who would repeatedly change trade styles and product names whenever one of their promotions was challenged in this manner. An injunction under 18 U.S.C. 1345 was sought to enjoin them from using the mails and telephones to solicit business for their diet products, thus essentially bringing to a halt what was viewed as a scheme to defraud (18 U.S.C. 1341 and 1343). The underlying theory of this case was that intent to defraud on the part of the defendants could be inferred by their continuing to market worthless diet products after having been repeatedly warned through prior enforcement actions about product misrepresentation. As the standard of proof required in this action was probable cause, intent to defraud did not have to be proven beyond a reasonable doubt. Conversely, no federal criminal indictment was planned in this case because of concerns over proving intent to defraud beyond a reasonable doubt, and therefore no civil discovery concerns were present. It was conjectured that the defendants could allege they truly believed in the efficacy of their products and, thus, had no intent to defraud. It was further conjectured that they could possibly bring in witnesses to testify that they were satisfied customers. (*Note*: A prospect that federal prosecutors did not relish was having to respond to such testimony by finding obese persons who would be willing to testify about their failure to achieve weight loss on these products and then having these individuals face further embarrassment through cross-examination.) Thus, halting this scheme through injunctive action under 18 U.S.C. 1345 was viewed as an appropriate enforcement strategy. Based on this declaration, a federal judge did issue an injunction that barred the defendants' use of the mails and telephones in marketing their worthless products.

Agency Injunctive Powers

Many state and federal regulatory agencies are empowered with injunctive authority as a primary means for dealing with violative conduct within their area of jurisdiction. While regulatory violations sometimes have criminal statute counterparts, whether a regulatory agency has authority to pursue criminal as well as civil investigations varies greatly from agency to agency, and from jurisdiction to jurisdiction. Obviously, those readers who are affiliated with regulatory agencies will be well aware of the limits of their authority and the procedures for utilizing their enforcement powers. Consequently, this section might be of greatest benefit to white collar crime investigators within law enforcement agencies who at times deal with activities that also fall under regulatory jurisdiction.

As a general proposition, regulators without criminal investigative authority but who do encounter criminal activity within their area of jurisdiction would be wise to cultivate appropriate law enforcement contacts, so that when there is a need for criminal investigative support it can be readily obtained. Such cultivation could include familiarization and training for the criminal investigators so that they can acquire an understanding of the often-unique environment and laws that exist within the regulator's area of jurisdiction. While such training and familiarization efforts have the obvious benefit of facilitating a criminal investigation, it is also possible that liaison with the criminal investigators will assist the regulators in pursuing their injunctive action. When not otherwise prohibited by law, information can sometimes be developed during the criminal investigation that might be useful in the regulatory investigation and, thus, it would be helpful for criminal investigators to know the evidentiary needs of their regulatory counterparts. At the very least, coordinating the filing of the regulatory injunctive action with the criminal process can be achieved.

Many regulatory actions begin with filing for a restraining order with an appropriate court of jurisdiction for the purpose of seeking an immediate halt to the illegal conduct. Then, the final resolution of the case is litigated through the regulatory agency's administrative law process. In many situations, filing for a restraining order will again require the submission of a declaration by an investigator. It must be emphasized that investigators should consult with regulatory agency legal counsel as to the required evidentiary standard necessary for obtaining a restraining order action and a successful ultimate litigation outcome.

Box 6–2 contains a declaration (with altered individual/business names and dates and addresses simply referred to as XXXX; attachments are referenced, but not displayed here) that was submitted in support of an application for a temporary restraining order under 39 U.S.C. 3007, which is the companion injunctive action to the Postal False Representation Statute, 39 U.S.C. 3005. The Postal False Representative Statute is an administrative response to those who solicit monies through the mails based on false representations. This statute simply requires that the U.S. Postal Service provide evidence that material misrepresentations are being made in connection with the solicitation of monies through the mail by the respondent, and intent to defraud need not be established. The proper evidentiary standard for the issuance of a temporary restraining order under 39 U.S.C. 3007 by a federal district court is probable cause, and this declaration was developed accordingly.

While the fact scenarios addressed by other agencies will vary, as will the laws that are being enforced, this declaration might provide a model that can be applied in many agency injunctive enforcement actions where intent is not an issue and probable cause is the required standard of proof.

Box 6–2   Declaration for injunctive action under 39 U.S.C. 3007

State of Florida

County of Smith   SS

Declaration of Rose Gold

I, Rose Gold, declare as follows:

1. I am a United States Postal Inspector assigned to the Florida Division of the United States Postal Inspection. I have been employed as Postal Inspector for approximately 17 years.

2. For 11 of these 17 years, I have been assigned to the investigation of mail fraud cases. I am presently assigned to a Fraud Team, which investigates possible violations of Title 39, United States Code, Section 3005, and Title 18, United States Code, Section 1341.

3. In February 19XX, the Postal Inspection Service began receiving complaints from businesses about OfficeHelpers, Ltd., P.O. Box 1475, XXXX, FL. I have examined these complaints to determine the experience the businesses have had with this company. OfficeHelpers, Ltd. employs telemarketers who telephone businesses throughout the United States requesting approval for shipment of computer printer ink cartridges that had been purportedly ordered by the business. The telemarketer asks for the name of the person to whom he or she is speaking, and OfficeHelpers, Ltd. ships the cartridges and mails an invoice to that person's attention. One of the entry fields on the invoice is "Purchase Order Number" and in all cases the word, "Verbal," is entered. An example of OfficeHelpers's invoice is included as Exhibit I. Because the person who the telemarketer speaks with is led to believe that his/her company has already placed an order, this employee usually gives approval to ship. Upon receipt of the invoice, the business usually discovers that no order had previously been placed with OfficeHelpers, Ltd. nor is OfficeHelpers, Ltd. its regular supplier of cartridges and other office supplies. They also realize that OfficeHelpers's prices for these products are three to five times higher than the amount charged by their regular vendor. Representative of the complaints I have reviewed are those filed by North East Aluminum and the Suites Hotel.

4. On October 4, XXXX, Mr. Harold Norman of North East Aluminum, XXXX, NJ, advised me that the controller of this company, Ms. Angel, received a telephone call from OfficeHelpers, Ltd., about 11 months earlier, (November, XXXX). He said that

Continued

in the beginning of December, XXXX, a shipment of cartridges and an invoice arrived. He said the invoice sought a payment of $496.02 by return mail. Mr. Norman stated he telephoned OfficeHelpers, Ltd. and spoke with a Bill Richards of this firm. He said he told Mr. Richards that his firm misled Ms. Angel and Mr. Richards agreed to drop the price of the cartridges to $56.00. Mr. Norman said he agreed to pay this price and he mailed a check to OfficeHelpers at P.O. Box 1475, XXXX, FL. Mr. Norman also said that since that time OfficeHelpers, Ltd. has telephoned his company on numerous occasions attempting to make further sales. A copy of North East Aluminum's complaint is attached as Exhibit 2.

5. On October 4, XXXX, I spoke with Mr. Larry Thomas, the manager of Suites Hotel, XXXX, CA, He advised he was contacted by OfficeHelpers, Ltd. in August, XXXX and was told the remainder of an order of cartridges which had not been shipped previously was now ready to be sent. Mr. Thomas said that since he was led to believe the hotel had already received a partial shipment, he gave approval to ship the remainder of the order. He said that within a few days he received an invoice from OfficeHelpers and at that time found that the hotel had never done business with this firm. He said that within a few days of receiving the invoice, the shipment of cartridges arrived. Mr. Thomas said the hotel normally deals with a local vendor for this type of supply, and prices charged by their local vendor were less than charged by OfficeHelpers. A copy of the complaint from the Suites Hotel is attached as Exhibit 3.

6. Several complainants have indicated that OfficeHelpers ships cartridges and mails invoices without obtaining approval. On October 1, XXXX, I spoke with Ms. Maggie May Charles, an employee at Roy's Insurance, Walnut, CA, who dealt with Office-Helpers, Ltd. Ms. Charles told me she is the employee responsible for ordering supplies for her office. She stated that in August, XXXX she received a telephone call from an individual representing OfficeHelpers, Ltd., who advised that ink cartridges which her company had ordered were about to be shipped. Ms. Charles states she did not recall ordering any cartridges from OfficeHelpers, Ltd. and told the caller she had to check with another employee who had previously been involved in ordering supplies. Ms. Charles said she checked with this other employee and found that no order had been placed with OfficeHelpers, Ltd. She said she then contacted Office-Helpers via telephone and advised this firm that Roy's Insurance did not order any supplies from them. Ms. Charles stated that notwithstanding her notice to Office-Helpers to this effect, a shipment of cartridges was received by her company along with an invoice. The invoice sought payment to be sent by mail to P.O. Box 1475, XXXX, FL. I also spoke to another employee at Roy's Insurance, Ms. Ruth Barber, who pointed out that the cost per cartridge charged by OfficeHelpers was $59.05 while this same product could be obtained from their local vendor for $11.65 each. Ms. Barber said that her review of her company's telephone records disclosed no prior dealings with OfficeHelpers. A copy of the complaint from Roy's Insurance is attached as Exhibit 4.

7. Mr. William Schwartz, Security Department of Electric Utilities, Inc., XXXX, GA, advised on October 4, XXXX that various offices within his company have been contacted by OfficeHelpers, Ltd. He stated that in some instances ink cartridges were

shipped by OfficeHelpers without any authorization while in other instances Utilities' employees were misled by OfficeHelpers into thinking that OfficeHelpers was their company's vendor for this product and these employees mistakenly gave approval for shipment. He also cited an instance in which an OfficeHelpers' caller misrepresented himself as being from the Utilities' main supply center and advised a Utilities' employee that they were due for a shipment of cartridges. As a result of this misrepresentation the real Utilities' employee provided authorization to ship. Mr. Schwartz' complaint is attached as Exhibit 5. It should be noted that in his complaint he points out that OfficeHelpers was charging $496.02 for products that are normally purchased by Utilities for $95.85.

8. Contact with the XXXX, FL Post Office disclosed that P.O. Box 1475 is rented to OfficeHelpers, Ltd. and the applicant for this box was Mr. Thomas Jayson, who described himself on the application as the president of OfficeHelpers, Ltd.

9. A check with Florida Department of State corporate records disclosed no listing for OfficeHelpers, Ltd. However, Thomas Jayson was listed a president and registered agent of CartridgeCorp of Delaware with an address of XXXX Rd., XXXX, FL. This is the street location of OfficeHelpers, Ltd.

I declare under Title 28, United States Code, Section 1748 and under the penalties of perjury that the foregoing is true and correct. Executed in XXXX, FL, on December 3, XXXX.

Rose Gold

United States Postal Inspector

ASSET FORFEITURE

While the first part of this chapter addressed ways to prevent victimization from occurring in the first place, the second section will discuss the means available to retrieve ill-gotten gains that have actually reached the hands of white collar offenders. Since 1970, federal laws have enabled investigators and prosecutors to seek asset forfeiture in white collar crime cases. Forfeiture is the taking by the government of property used and acquired with illegal proceeds without compensating the owner.[5] Typically the types of property subject to forfeiture are those that were used in the commission of a crime or facilitated the commission of a crime; or were acquired directly or indirectly with illegal proceeds.[6]

The application of forfeiture to white collar crime actually arose from efforts to stem organized crime. Congress passed the Racketeer Influenced and Corrupt Organizations statute (RICO) as part of the Organized Crime Control Act of 1970 in order to fashion an effective new weapon in the nation's fight against large-scale economic crime and organized crime.[7] However, RICO has been used far more frequently in white collar crime cases than in organized crime cases, and notable forfeitures have been achieved in such high-profile cases as those involving Charles Keating and Michael Milken.[8]

Subsequently, Congress broadened the reach of forfeiture in white collar crime cases by identifying specific types of white collar crimes that are subject to forfeiture. In addition, Congress enacted legislation (The Money Laundering Control Act of 1986) that criminalized the laundering of money derived from various types of white collar crimes and made these laundered funds and/or property derived therefrom subject to forfeiture. As Levy correctly concludes, this legislation, as a practical matter, made forfeiture available for almost every federal crime, including most white collar crimes, since the deposit in a financial institution of money derived from criminal activity renders the money forfeitable.[9]

As forfeiture authority is available in most federal white collar crime situations, it should be considered at the outset of an investigation, as opposed to an afterthought.[10] The following discussion of forfeiture as it applies to white collar crime investigations is introductory in nature. However, it should serve as a starting point for investigators who not only wish to see white collar criminals brought to justice, but who also want to ensure that they do not enjoy the fruits of their unlawful conduct. As forfeiture law is highly specialized and may vary within state jurisdictions, investigators are encouraged to seek legal counsel for specific applications.

Civil versus Criminal Forfeiture

There are two types of forfeiture: criminal and civil. Criminal forfeiture is "ad personam." It can be invoked only after the property owner has been convicted of certain types of crimes. Civil forfeiture is "in rem," that is, against the thing; it is directed at property that has been used illegally. Civil forfeiture is based on the guilt of an item of property. It is independent of any criminal proceeding against the property owner. Therefore, the acquittal or conviction of the property owner is not a factor.[11]

The two types of forfeiture proceed quite differently. In criminal forfeiture, a prosecution seeking forfeiture is initiated by filing an indictment or information identifying the property subject to forfeiture and the defendant's alleged interest therein. The indictment places the defendant on notice that the government seeks the forfeiture and it must identify the assets subject to forfeiture with sufficient specificity to permit the defendant to defend it.[12] If the case proceeds to trial, a jury is then asked to return a special verdict with regard to forfeiture of the items specified in the indictment; and upon doing so the judge will issue an order for the seizure of these items.[13]

Criminal forfeiture provides for the forfeiture of substitute assets, which means that a defendant's legitimate assets can be forfeited when the ill-gotten gains have been commingled or cannot be located. A restraining order against dissipation of assets can be issued by the court upon the defendant being charged, thus reducing the likelihood of the property targeted for forfeiture disappearing. Also, including a forfeiture count in an indictment might enhance the likelihood of a plea and because the case is in the criminal forum, it will move more quickly to resolution than a civil case. However, it should be noted that if the defendant dies or becomes a fugitive, no forfeiture action can be taken when it is sought within a criminal proceeding.[14]

In civil forfeiture, "offending" property is typically seized during the course of the investigation. Such seizures can rise incident to the execution of a search or arrest warrant, or as a result of obtaining and executing a seizure warrant. For instance, while executing a search warrant on the premises where a fraudulent scheme was being operated, cash believed to be the proceeds from this scheme can be seized as the fruits of the crime and subsequently become the subject of a civil forfeiture action, providing the agency initiating this action has statutory power to do so (many federal agencies have this authority). Conversely, an investigator must obtain a seizure warrant issued by a judge to seize fraudulently obtained proceeds that have been deposited in a bank account if the forfeiture of these funds is to be sought. Again, however, if the forfeiture action is to be initiated at the agency level, the agency must be vested with authority to do so.

Whether the seizing agency can proceed toward the forfeiture of the property is dependent upon a number of factors. In the federal system, if the seizure is being contested by the property owners, if the seized property is realty, or if it exceeds $500,000 in value, the U.S. Department of Justice, usually through the U.S. Attorney in the district where the seizure was made, becomes involved in the forfeiture litigation. When these factors are not present (and after appropriate notice is given to all those who have a potential ownership interest in property), the seizing agency can proceed with the forfeiture.

Civil forfeiture procedures would seem to offer some distinct advantages over the criminal counterpart. There is no requirement that a criminal case or criminal conviction exists prior to the forfeiture, and the property can be seized immediately. In addition, there is a lower burden of proof involved at the time of seizure, probable cause as opposed to proof beyond a reasonable doubt. If there are fugitives in the investigation, civil forfeiture allows for a quick default judgment. If the property owner challenges the forfeiture action, civil discovery rules will apply which has pros and cons for the government. On the one hand, these rules will permit the government to make further inquiry into the property owner (who might very well be the target of the case) to include financial information, but on the other hand, it might expose the government investigation to unwanted probing by such individuals. Also, under civil forfeiture there is no provision to seek substitute assets as there is in criminal forfeiture proceedings.[15]

Statutory Authority

Within the federal system, the most commonly used statutes which authorize forfeiture include 18 U.S.C. 1963(a), RICO; 18 U.S.C. 981 and 982, civil and criminal forfeiture, respectively; 18 U.S.C. 1956 and 1957, money laundering statutes.[16]

Forfeiture authority under the RICO Statute, 18 U.S.C. 1963(a), is *ad personam* only, that is, criminal forfeiture. This statute and its forfeiture provisions are powerful prosecutive tools and, as noted earlier, have been used successfully in many high-profile white collar crime cases. However, obtaining a conviction under this statute requires that the government prove a pattern of racketeering activity on the part of the defendant(s), which means that they must be proven to have committed certain identified crimes on at least two occasions. Fortunately for the white collar crime investigator, racketeering activity has been defined under this statute to include such traditional white collar crimes as bribery, mail fraud, wire fraud, bankruptcy, and securities fraud.[17]

Sections 981 and 982 of the U.S. Code authorize forfeiture in an even wider array of white collar crime offenses, and such actions can be taken in either the civil or criminal forums. The broader scope of these statutes is accomplished in two ways. First, both statutes provide for forfeiture of real and personal property involved in a transaction or attempted transaction in violation of federal money laundering statutes (18 U.S.C. 1956 and 1957). When seeking forfeiture through money laundering violations, the illegally obtained proceeds and property must be derived from statutorily defined "specified unlawful activities." These "activities" include many white collar offenses such as mail fraud, wire fraud, bribery, bankruptcy fraud, securities fraud, various banking violations, Food Stamp fraud, and environmental crimes. In addition, Sections 981 and 982 also provide for forfeiture in a host of crimes, without the need to first prove money laundering. Many of these crimes are white collar offenses, and include the "specified unlawful activities" under the money laundering statutes as discussed earlier—bank fraud, and bribery, among others.

Money Laundering

Since forfeiture for most white collar offenses can be achieved without first proving money laundering, why bother even considering these offenses at all? For the purposes of civil forfeiture, as long as there is direct statutory authority under 18 U.S.C. 981/982, there may be no need to first prove money laundering. However, as will discussed later, money laundering as proscribed under 18 U.S.C. 1956 (and sometimes under 18 U.S.C. 1957) frequently accompanies underlying white collar activities and can often be proven incident to the main focus of the investigation. It should be noted that Sections1956 and 1957 of Title 18 are both felony violations which provide for lengthy prison terms (20 and 10 years, respectively) that would be in addition to whatever prison exposure that emanates from the substantive white collar offense. For this latter reason alone, including money laundering charges in a white collar crime indictment would often be advantageous to the prosecution. Successfully proving violations of 18 U.S.C. 1956 or 1957 at trial would also permit criminal forfeiture in those cases that require money laundering as a predicate offense.

Although investigating money laundering can some times become complex, the definitions of this activity under 18 U.S.C. 1956/1957 are such that it is frequently a simpler task than might be envisioned. For instance, Section 1956 prohibits financial transactions involving proceeds from specified unlawful activity with the intent to promote the carrying on of such activity; violate federal tax laws; or knowing that the transaction is designed to conceal or disguise the nature, location, source, ownership or control of proceeds from specified unlawful activity or avoid a reporting requirement under state or federal law. The terms *transaction* and *financial transaction* are statutorily defined and are very broad in scope:

> (3) the term "transaction" includes a purchase, sale, loan, pledge, gift, transfer, delivery, or other disposition, and with respect to a financial institution includes a deposit, withdrawal, transfer between accounts, exchange of currency, loan, extension of credit,

purchase or sale of any stock, bond, certificate of deposit, or other monetary instrument, use of a safe deposit box, or any other payment, transfer, or delivery by, through, or to a financial institution, by whatever means effected;[18]

(4) the term "financial transaction" means (A) a transaction which in any way or degree affects interstate or foreign commerce (i) involving the movement of funds by wire or other means or (ii) involving one or more monetary instruments, or (iii) involving the transfer of title to any real property, vehicle, vessel, or aircraft, or (B) a transaction involving the use of a financial institution which is engaged in, or the activities of which affect, interstate or foreign commerce in any way or degree;[19]

An example of money laundering under 18 U.S.C. 1956 and subsequent forfeiture is furnished in the U.S. Department of Justice's *Asset Forfeiture Law and Practice Manual*: a person launders proceeds from a mail fraud scheme by wiring money to an account in a false name. This act constitutes a financial transaction because it involved a deposit into a financial institution, and it was done with intent to conceal or disguise proceeds from a specified unlawful activity (mail fraud) because it was deposited into an account held in a false name. Thus, these funds are subject to either civil or criminal forfeiture under 18 U.S.C. 981 or 982, respectively.[20]

Section 1957 of Title 18 of the United States Code prohibits knowingly engaging in a monetary transaction in criminally derived property of a value greater than $10,000 and which is derived from specified unlawful activity. The statute provides definitions for several key terms. For instance, a monetary transaction is defined to include the deposit, withdrawal, transfer or exchange, in or affecting interstate or foreign commerce of funds or a monetary instrument by, through, or to a financial institution. The terms *monetary instrument* and *financial institution* are also statutorily (and broadly) defined. Monetary instruments include currency, travelers' checks, personal checks, bank checks, money orders, and investment securities or negotiable instruments. Criminally derived property means any property constituting, or derived from, proceeds obtained from a criminal offense while specified unlawful activity has the same meaning as in 18 U.S.C. 1956. Violating this statute does not require any efforts to disguise or conceal the illegal funds, such as opening accounts in fictitious names. It only requires that the criminally derived property have a value greater than $10,000 and be involved in a monetary transaction. In turn, this property then becomes subject to forfeiture under 18 U.S.C. 981 and 982. For instance, consider the case of a health care provider who was engaged in a mail/wire fraud scheme that involved the submission of false billings for services to a health care insurer, which resulted in the issuance of a reimbursement check in excess of $10,000. The negotiation of this check at a bank by the provider would violate this statute and the funds involved could be forfeited.

Forfeiture Considerations and Planning

Deciding whether to seek the forfeiture of a piece of property first involves developing the requisite proof that the asset was used in the commission of a crime, facilitated the commission of a crime, or was acquired directly or indirectly with illegal proceeds.[21] Other important information an investigator needs to gather early on includes:

- What is the value and condition of the property?

- What type of custodial arrangements must be made to care for the seized property?

- Who owns the property?

- Are there existing liens?[22]

The reality is that in many instances, a cost–benefit analysis should be conducted to determine if the resale value of the asset or its usefulness to an agency sufficiently exceeds the expenses incurred for the management of the property during the pendency of the forfeiture proceedings and the property's ultimate disposal. To be clear, however, economic considerations are not always paramount as in the case when seizing a property solely to remove some type of hazardous or objectionable activity from an area. Also, the punitive value of forfeiture alone might justify taking this action in some cases, even when not cost effective.[23]

In any event, experience has shown that preseizure planning is a *best practice* to ensure a successful forfeiture action. Falcon emphasizes that preseizure planning is neither an end in itself nor a bureaucratic impediment to action. To the contrary, such planning is a means to enhance the chances of timely and successful seizure and forfeiture by carefully evaluating what should be seized and why; who should seize it, when, and how; and where problems are likely to arise along the way.[24]

Particularly in those instances where criminal forfeiture is deemed the better alternative or where the civil process is anticipated, but the nature of the property mandates judicial intervention (e.g., real property or property valued at over $500,000 in federal cases), advance discussions with the appropriate prosecutor(s) is highly recommended. Not surprisingly, the likely questions that a prosecutor will ask incident to such a meeting are similar to those an investigator should consider when first thinking about forfeiture possibilities:

- What is the crime committed?

- Is there a forfeiture provision?

- What property is forfeitable?

- What evidence makes this property forfeitable?

- How should the property be seized or how was the property seized?

- What is the value of the property and where is it now?

- Who are the owners and lien holders of the property?[25]

The answers to the questions that will likely be posed by a prosecutor as well as questions investigators should ask themselves when first considering a forfeiture action can identify potentially complicated issues, such as difficulties in establishing ownership, ownership by potentially innocent parties, costly and elaborate storage/maintenance requirements, handling occupants in seized residences, and the disposition of seized businesses. While further discussion of these issues is beyond the scope of this volume, the best path to a successful resolution of these and other thorny problems that can be encountered when seeking asset forfeiture is through preseizure planning and consultation with appropriate legal advisors/prosecutors.

Developing a Seizure Warrant Affidavit

As suggested earlier, in some instances property is seized incident to arrest or in the course of executing a search warrant, and subsequently civil forfeiture proceedings are filed against it. In other instances, such as when seizing real property, obtaining a seizure warrant from a judge is required.[26] Also, a seizure warrant must be obtained to reach potentially forfeitable funds that are being held in a bank account. The steps taken to obtain a seizure warrant are similar to those necessary for obtaining a search warrant. Most importantly from an investigator's perspective is the need to develop an affidavit in support of an application for a seizure warrant. As in the case of a search warrant affidavit, the standard of proof is at the probable cause level, although investigators should be mindful that if the property owner challenges the action the government must be able to prove at the higher preponderance of the evidence standard that the property is subject to forfeiture.[27] A sample of such an affidavit is presented in Box 6–3 and its development will be discussed in the following paragraphs. Again, names and addresses of individuals and business entities have been changed. It relates to a set of events introduced in the preceding chapter, that is, the mail fraud scheme involving Vendor's World.

Box 6–3 Seizure warrant affidavit

Affidavit

State of Florida

County of Smith

I, S.L. Lincoln, first being duly sworn, depose and say:

This affidavit is made in support of a Seizure Warrant. The Seizure Warrant is being sought for the bank account of Vendor's World, Inc., Account No. 000-111-XXXX, located at the XYZ Bank, 456 Elm St., Any Town, Florida (note: *true account number and bank name and location are not provided in this example*).

1. I am a United States Investigator assigned to the Florida Division of the U.S. Investigation Service. I have been an Investigator for over 18 years. As an Investigator, it is

Continued

part of my duties to investigate violations of the mail fraud statute, Title 18, United States Code, Section 1341 and money laundering, Title 18, United States Code, Section 1956.

2. I am submitting this affidavit to support an application for a seizure warrant to seize the bank account of Vendor's World, Inc. The signer on this account is Joseph Mitchell. It is your affiant's contention that this account was opened for the purpose of conducting a scheme in violation of the Mail Fraud Statute, Title 18 United States Code, Section 1341 and the Money Laundering Statute, Title 18 United States Code, Section 1956. Checks made payable to Vendor's World, Inc. from individuals victimized in this scheme were deposited into this account, permitting Mitchell access to funds obtained through fraudulent conduct.

3. Investigator Wood of the New Jersey Division of the United States Investigation Service advised your affiant he conducted an investigation of Joseph Mitchell that subsequently led to his indictment and conviction in federal court in New Jersey. Wood advised that Mitchell along with his wife and brother-in-law conducted a scheme to defraud in which they sold pay telephones, vending machines, and cigarette machines, to persons who responded to advertisements which these defendants placed in newspapers (*the original affidavit contained a sample advertisement as an exhibit*). These advertisements invited those interested in purchasing these machines to call a toll free number for further information. Mitchell and his codefendants would then correspond and/or meet personally with prospective buyers, and made numerous fraudulent representations concerning the physical condition of the machines that were available for sale, and the services that Mitchell and his codefendants would provide in establishing these purchasers in a vending machine business. Wood has told me that his investigation disclosed that Mitchell and his codefendants either failed to deliver any equipment, delivered equipment that was faulty or inoperable, and/or failed to install equipment at locations which would generate income. Wood told me that the indictment charged Mitchell and his codefendants with conspiracy to commit mail fraud, mail fraud, interstate transportation of property obtained by fraud and interstate threatening communications. (*A copy of this indictment was attached as an exhibit to the original affidavit*). He further advised that Mitchell was sentenced on July 28, ___ (*year purposely omitted here*) to two years imprisonment and is scheduled to begin his incarceration on August 17, ___ (*year purposely omitted here*).

4. Wood has advised me that he has received information suggesting Mitchell has conducted a similar scheme to defraud while his case was pending resolution in New Jersey. He told me he bases this belief on the fact that he has been contacted by several Florida residents claiming that they have had unsatisfactory dealings with Mitchell. Wood told me that these dealings involve the sale of vending machines, and the experiences these purchasers have had are similar to the problems experienced by the victims in the case which resulted in Mitchell's conviction in New Jersey. He suggested that I contact one of these Florida residents, Complainant #1 (*the complainant's real name was included in the original affidavit*), for further details.

5. Complainant #1 was contacted on August 3, ____ (*year purposely omitted here*). She provided me the following information.

She stated she saw a classified advertisement in the local newspaper (*which was fully identified in the original affidavit*) under the Business Opportunity Section. She said the advertisement read as follows: "Vending routes operate your own machines—snack, soda, etc., location and service provided, 1-800-XXX-XXXX" (*actual number was provided in the original affidavit*). Complainant #1 stated she saw this ad in April[year purposely omitted here] and called the number to obtain further information. In response to her telephone call, she said Robert Anderson representing Vendor's World visited her at her residence. Complainant #1 told me Anderson showed her a brochure depicting a video game machine known as Bar Brain, and told her Vendor's World would sell her two video vending machines for $5000, and provide her locations for these machines. She told me she was also guaranteed $400–$450 net profit per month per machine. She said Anderson showed her a brochure that had photographs of the machines she would be purchasing and she was assured these were, in fact, the machines she would be acquiring. Complainant #1 said that based on these representations, she provided Anderson $1000 and signed a contract for the purchase of the machines and services to be provided by Vendor's World. Complainant #1 then told me she had subsequent telephone conversations with Joseph Mitchell concerning possible locations for her machines. She said that Mitchell told her she could place her machines in one of four establishments he had made arrangements with and she selected the City Lounge (*not the actual name*). Complainant #1 said that Mitchell came to her residence on April 29, ____ (*year purposely omitted here*) to receive an additional $2000 payment due as a result of identifying the location for her machines. She said she wrote the check out for $2000, but refused to give it to Mitchell because he failed to produce a contract with the establishment that would house her machines, City Lounge. Complainant #1 stated that Mitchell told her he did not have the contract with him to which she replied that she would not give him a check without it. Complainant #1 claims that Mitchell nevertheless absconded with her $2000 check without her knowledge, upon leaving her residence on this occasion.

6. Complainant #1 further advised that David Robinson, another representative of Vendor's World called on May 20 ____ (*year purposely omitted here*) to tell her that her machines were now available and the final $2000 was due. Complainant #1 said she gave Robinson a cashier's check for $2000 and he delivered the two machines to her home. She said instead of finding the machines to be similar to those depicted in the brochure, she found them to be older models. She also found them to be in disrepair. She stated one machine would not accept quarters and the picture screen appeared to be fading. She said the picture on the other machine was blurry. She also stated that upon examining one of the machines, she noted it was manufactured in 1983. She said Anderson advised her during their April meeting that these machines would not be over four months old. Complainant #1 then contacted the manager of the City

Continued

Lounge and found that Vendor's World had not made arrangements for the placement of her machines at this location. Complainant #1 then contacted other establishments mentioned to her by Mitchell as locations he had identified for her machines. Of these four establishments, she found only one that had had any contact whatsoever with Vendor's World. On May 26, ___ (*year purposely omitted here*) Complainant #1 said she telephoned Mitchell and told him she wanted the machines she had ordered as identified in the brochure shown to her at her initial meeting with Vendor's World. The next day she said she received a call from Robinson who advised that her machines had been ordered and should be in by May 29, ___ (*year purposely omitted here*). However, Complainant #1 said her machines, in fact, never arrived on this date. On June 4, ___ (*year purposely omitted here*) she said she demanded from Robinson the return of her $5000 and he responded that he would only give her back 60% of her investment since there would be a cost of 40% to break the contract. She said she had additional settlement discussions with both Robinson and Mitchell but none of their offers involved a total refund of her $5,000. In summary, Complainant #1 feels she was promised two nearly new video vending machines, in good operating order, to be placed in an agreed upon location which would generate $900 per month in income. Instead, she said she received two inoperable, old machines, and the location promised to her had not been procured. Complainant #1 also stated her final payment check of $2000 was deposited into an account at the XYZ Bank, 456 Elm St., Any Town, Florida, Account No. 000-111-XXXX.

7. On August 5, ___ (*year purposely omitted here*) I interviewed Complainant #2, an individual identified by Complainant #1 as having had a transaction with Vendor's World. Complainant #2 confirmed that he had such a transaction. He stated he responded to an advertisement in the local newspaper in mid-February concerning a vending machine route. He said that upon telephoning the number provided in the advertisement he was advised he was dealing with Vendor's World. He stated that he asked for information concerning their vending machine opportunity be mailed to him and literature arrived via U.S. Mail shortly thereafter. Complainant #2 said his initial dealings with Vendor's World were with Alex Marx, who met with him on March 6. He said during this meeting he was provided, in writing that he would receive reconditioned vending machines in good operating condition; was guaranteed $350 per month in income; and locations for these machines would be arranged. Complainant #2 said he then began dealing with Joseph Mitchell, and next with David Robinson. He said he made subsequent payments of $4500, $800, and $4421 to Vendor's World between March 25 and April 11. He said it was not until the end of July that his machines, two soda machines and a snack machine finally arrived at the prearranged location. However, unlike the machines described in the initial literature he received from Vendor's World, the machines provided to him were old and the snack machine did not function properly.

8. On August 5, I interviewed Complainant #3, another individual identified by Complainant #1 as having had transactions with Vendor's Word. Complainant #3 stated she responded to an advertisement in a local newspaper in January. This advertisement offered a vending route opportunity. She said she telephoned the

number contained in the advertisement and spoke to Joseph Mitchell. She said Mitchell advised she could purchase new or used vending machines which would provide her an income of $300–$350 per month, per machine. He also said he would procure the locations for these machines. She said these representations were also subsequently made to her in writing, on a contract Mitchell provided her. She said that Mitchell and Robert Anderson visited her following her telephone call, to further describe this opportunity. On January 21 Complainant #3 gave Mitchell a check for $4500 to participate in this program. She said she and her husband agreed to purchase five machines. She stated that Mitchell next visited her in early March at which time she provided another check for $2500 for his service in identifying locations for the machines. A final payment of $5500 was made to Mitchell on May 21. Shortly after this payment four of the ordered machines were placed in business establishments. However, these were not the establishments agreed upon at the outset and only one of these locations agreed to keep a machine. Complainant #3 said that another Vendor's World representative, David Robinson, was responsible for removing three machines that were unwanted at the locations where they were placed. She said she received no refunds for the machines that were removed and furthermore her fifth machine was never placed at all. Complainant #3 concluded that instead of receiving $300–$350 per month from the one machine that was in operation, she has earned only about $60 in six weeks.

9.   Two other individuals filed complaints directly with the U.S. Investigation Service concerning their dealings with Vendor's World. Complainant #4 was interviewed on August 5 and he stated he responded to an advertisement in the local newspaper which appeared in late May or early June. He said he called the telephone number in the advertisement and received a return call back from Joseph Mitchell, who subsequently met with him personally. He said that Mitchell guaranteed him that he would realize income of $350 per month, service and support, and locations for placing the machines. Complainant #4 said these representations were also reflected on the contract he signed on June 10. At this time he gave Mitchell $4000 in cash for the purchase of two machines. Thereafter, he received only one machine and it was not the machine he contracted to purchase. He described this machine as a cold drink machine which does not operate properly. He said the machine is dented and leaks and has no dollar bill changer as was initially promised.

10.   Complainant #5 was also interviewed on August 5 and he too responded to an advertisement in a local newspaper, which appeared in late June. He said this advertisement invited those interested in a vending machine business to call a telephone number for further information. He said on July 1 he called this number and spoke to an individual who identified himself as David Robinson. He said Robinson told him he would make $350 per month through this program and that he subsequently received in the mail brochures and information about this vending machine opportunity. Complainant #5 stated that on July 15 Joseph Mitchell came to his residence and told him he would provide him with vending machines in prearranged locations.

Continued

He was again guaranteed an income of $350 per month, both verbally and in a contract. On July 17 Complainant #5 gave Mitchell a check for $7000 that was subsequently deposited into the XYZ Bank, 456 Elm St., Any Town, Florida, Account No. 000-111-XXXX. Complainant #5 said his purchase was for six reconditioned machines, three snack machines and three soda machines. However, he said that Mitchell asked him to change his order to two snack machines, two game machines, and two soda machines because he had found a "hot bar" where the game machines would do well. When these machines became available, Mitchell asked for a final payment of $3500 that Complainant #5 sent to him via U.S. Mail. However, shortly after mailing the check, Complainant #5 stopped payment on this check because he became aware of a television news story that reported Mitchell's prior involvement in a fraudulent vending machine operation in New Jersey.

11. On August 4, I spoke with Evelyn Jones, the classified customer service manager at the newspaper that ran Vendor's World advertising (*which was fully identified in the original affidavit*). Jones confirmed that Vendor's World did place classified advertising with the newspaper on several occasions and paid for this advertising using checks drawn on Account No. 000-111-XXXX at the XYZ Bank, 456 Elm St., Any Town, Florida bearing the name, Vendor's World, Inc. She provided me a copy of a recent advertisement (*which was attached as an exhibit in the original affidavit*). She further advised that the newspaper has thousands of mail subscription customers, and thousands of copies of each edition are mailed daily.

12. Investigation has revealed that Joseph Mitchell does have a business checking account at the XYZ Bank, 456 Elm St., Any Town, Florida, under the name Vendor's World, Inc., Account No. 000-111-XXXX and he is the only signer on this account. Investigation has further revealed that a balance of $15,600 is on hand in this account. The account has been open approximately three months. The account has been frozen because the bank learned that Mitchell was a convicted felon and it became aware of victim complaints alleging that he was involved in similar criminal activities. The bank advised it plans to mail the balance of the funds in the account to Vendor's World, Inc. last known address on Ocean Blvd., ___ (*fully identified in the original affidavit*) on August 10.

13. Your affiant submits there is probable cause to believe that Joseph Mitchell and possibly other individuals affiliated with Vendor's World have been and are currently conducting a scheme to defraud individuals interested in entering into the vending machine business. Mitchell and other Vendor's World representatives have misrepresented the condition and operating ability of the machines they are selling; they have misrepresented the amount of income potential from these machines and have misrepresented their services in providing acceptable locations for these machines. These misrepresentations are identical to those that Mitchell was responsible for in the investigation that resulted in his indictment and conviction in New Jersey. He continued the same course of conduct while he was awaiting the resolution of these other charges and the commencement of his prison term.

14. Wherefore, your affiant submits there is probable cause to believe that Account No. 000-111-XXXX held in the name of Vendor's World, Inc., at the XYZ Bank, 456 Elm

St., Any Town, Florida (*with Mitchell as the only signer*) was used to promote the carrying on of a specified unlawful activity to wit: Title 18, United States Code, Section 1341 (Mail Fraud), and the same constitutes property involved in a transaction or attempted transaction in violation of Title 18, United States Code Section 1956 (a) (1) (A) (i). Therefore, this bank account is forfeitable to the United States pursuant to Title 18, United States Code, Section 981 (a) (1) (A).

S.L. Lincoln

U.S. Investigator

Sworn and Subscribed to before me on this ___ day of August, ___

_____
United States Magistrate

As is apparent, this affidavit mirrors the affidavit for a search warrant in this case, to a large extent. The introductory paragraph and Paragraph No. 2, however, differentiate the purpose of this affidavit from an affidavit being filed in support of a search warrant. Here the purpose of the affidavit is to support an application for a seizure warrant, and the property to be seized is funds contained in a bank account held by Vendor's World, Inc. The account number and location of the bank are fully described. It was noted that Joseph Mitchell was the only signer on this account. Establishing who had access to this account was important in at least two respects. First, it helped to establish individual ownership control and eliminated the possibility of an innocent owner who may have deposited funds that were not tainted by criminal activity in the account. Second, evidence of culpability on the part of the other Vendor's World representatives, Robinson, Marx, and/or Anderson, was further defined. Access to this account by any of these individuals would have strengthened a case against them. As it turned out, only Robinson was prosecuted along with Mitchell and obviously that decision was based on evidence other than access to this account.

Beginning with paragraph 3 and continuing through paragraph 11, a chronological presentation of the investigation that had been conducted thus far is provided, in an effort to demonstrate that there was probable cause to believe that Mitchell and possibly others associated with him through Vendor's World were conducting a mail fraud scheme in the sale of vending machine business opportunities. As may be observed, much of the information received from Investigator Wood, the victims (Complainants #1–#5), and the newspaper that carried the advertising, as reflected in the search warrant affidavit, was incorporated directly into this affidavit in an effort to establish probable cause that a crime had been committed that is, mail fraud. It may be recalled that Chapter 5 details the development and presentation of this material and readers are encouraged to review this discussion for the rationale that was applied. Additionally, however, information supplied by Complainants #1 and #5 that their checks were deposited into Account No. 000-111-XXXX at the XYZ Bank, 456 Elm St., Any Town, FL, was reported in order to establish probable cause of a violation of 18 U.S.C. 1956, Money Laundering. Likewise, the use of this account to pay for advertising that promoted the carrying on of this scheme was established through information provided by the newspaper's classified customer service manager.

Paragraph 12 provided information obtained from the bank concerning the Vendor's World, Inc. account. Investigators should be prepared to issue a subpoena for this type of information, although in some instances bank officials may be able to voluntarily provide the necessary data if they believe their institution is being used to further criminal activity. The essential information provided by the bank included the address of the branch maintaining the account; the subject account number; Mitchell as the only signer; and the approximate balance. This last piece of data not only permits an evaluation by the investigating agency and prosecutor's office of the cost effectiveness of taking a forfeiture action, but it also informs the reviewing magistrate of the value of the criminal proceeds in the account. Moreover, reporting that the bank planned on closing the account and disbursing these funds to Vendor's World, Inc. on August 10 emphasized the need for prompt attention on the part of all reviewing parties. (*Note:* A seizure warrant was, in fact, issued by the reviewing magistrate on August 7 and the funds were subsequently seized.)

The final two paragraphs summarized the probable cause that was established in the preceding paragraphs and concluded that Account No. 000-111-XXXX held in the name of Vendor's World, Inc., at the XYZ Bank, 456 Elm St., Any Town, Florida, was involved in promoting and carrying on the specified unlawful activity of mail fraud and therefore was forfeitable.

As in the preparation of a search warrant affidavit, investigators should be prepared to complete the Application for a Seizure Warrant form and the Seizure Warrant form, prior to appearing before the reviewing magistrate. Likewise, it is equally important for the affiant to be fully prepared when appearing before this judicial official in terms of the facts contained in the affidavit and the investigation, in general.

Service of a seizure warrant for a bank account (or investment account, etc.) is usually accomplished by serving the warrant upon an officer of the institution. Whether the proceeds from the seized account are immediately turned over to the investigator serving the warrant may vary as some institutions might request the involvement of higher management and/or legal counsel before taking any action. At the very least, the warrant should serve notice to the institution to freeze the account immediately and agencies should expect the funds to be turned over in a reasonable amount of time.

CHAPTER HIGHLIGHTS

- Bringing a white collar crime to a halt through legal mandate is often achieved through a civil injunction. Typically this process involves the issuance of a temporary restraining order on an *ex parte* basis by a court that directs the offending party to cease the objectionable activity. This restraining order is, in fact, temporary, and the issuing judge subsequently holds a hearing to consider the issuance of a preliminary injunction during which both sides can be heard. If the government prevails, the judge issues a preliminary injunction that halts the objectionable activity pending a final judicial resolution to the case.

• Many state and federal regulatory agencies are empowered with injunctive authority as a primary means for dealing with violative conduct within their area of jurisdiction. While regulatory violations sometimes have criminal statute counterparts, whether a regulatory agency has authority to pursue criminal as well as civil investigations varies greatly from agency to agency, and from jurisdiction to jurisdiction. As a general proposition, regulators without criminal investigative authority but who do encounter criminal activity within their area of jurisdiction would be wise to cultivate appropriate law enforcement contacts, so that when there is a need for criminal investigative support it can be readily obtained.

• Forfeiture is the taking by the government of property used and acquired with illegal proceeds without compensating the owner.[28]

• As forfeiture authority is available in most federal white collar crime situations, it should be considered at the outset of an investigation, as opposed to an afterthought.[29]

CHAPTER BEST PRACTICES

• Nevertheless as a *best practice*, investigators should consult with their prosecuting attorneys as to the required standard of proof necessary for an injunction under 18 U.S.C 1345 in the judicial district where this type of action will be sought. (See page 126.)

• In any event, experience has shown that preseizure planning is a *best practice* to ensure a successful forfeiture action. (See page 136.)

Notes

1. "Study: Many criminals escape fines, restitution," *St. Petersburg* (FL) *Times*, March 6, 2005, p. 24A.
2. U.S. Department of Justice, Criminal Division, Asset Forfeiture and Money Laundering Section, *Asset forfeiture Law and Practice Manual* (Washington, DC: Author. 1998 [June]), pp. 6–31.
3. M. Zalman, *Criminal Procedure: Constitution and Society*, 4th ed. (Upper Saddle River, NJ: Prentice Hall, 2004), p. 97.
4. U.S. Department of Justice, Criminal Division, Asset Forfeiture and Money Laundering Section, *op. cit.*, pp. 6–31.
5. G. A. Kurisky, "Civil forfeiture of assets: A final solution to international drug trafficking," *Houston Journal of International Law*, Vol. 10, No. 2 (1988), p. 249.
6. W. Falcon, *Asset Forfeiture: Guide to Preseizure Planning* (Washington, DC: U.S. Department of Justice, Bureau of Justice Assistance, 1993), p. 6.
7. E. C. Weiner, "Crime must not pay: RICO criminal forfeiture perspective," *Northern Illinois Law Review*, Vol. 1 (1981), p. 234.

8. L. W. Levy, *A License to Steal: The Forfeiture of Property* (Chapel Hill, NC: The University of North Carolina Press, 1996), p. 208

9. Ibid., p. 120.

10. C. W. Larson, M. J. McLaughlin, and S. M. Badger, *Federal Asset Forfeiture: Law Enforcement's Guide to Preparing a Case for Judicial Forfeiture* (Washington, DC: U.S. Dept. of Justice, 1989), p. 2.

11. G. N. Aylesworth, *Asset Forfeiture: Forfeiture of Real Property: An Overview* (Washington, DC: U.S. Department of Justice, Bureau of Justice Assistance, 1991), p. 7.

12. Larson, McLaughlin, and Badger, *op. cit.*, pp. 9–10.

13. Weiner, *op. cit.*, p. 251.

14. G. M. Vecchi and R. T. Sigler, *Assets Forfeiture: A Study of Policy and Its Practice* (Durham, NC: Carolina Academic Press. 2001), pp. 53–54.

15. Ibid., p. 53.

16. Larson, McLaughlin, and Badger, *op. cit.*, p. 4.

17. Weiner, *op. cit.*, pp. 226–227.

18. *United States Code (2000 Edition)* retrieved September 4, 2006 from http://www.gpoaccess.gov/U.S.C.ode/.

19. Ibid.

20. U.S. Department of Justice, Criminal Division, Asset Forfeiture and Money Laundering Section, *op. cit.*, pp. 1–24.

21. Falcon, *op. cit.*, p. 6.

22. Larson, McLaughlin, and Badger, *op. cit.*, p. 5.

23. Falcon, *op. cit.*, p. 6, 25.

24. Ibid, p. 5.

25. L. E. Fann, G. G. Gordon, and A. W. Leach, *Asset forfeiture: How to Present the Forfeiture Case to the Prosecutor* (Washington, DC: U.S. Department of Justice, Bureau of Justice Assistance, 1993), p. 3.

26. Larson, McLaughlin, and Badger, *op. cit.*, p. 6.

27. J. L. Worrall, "The Civil Asset Forfeiture Reform Act of 2000: A sheep in wolf's clothing?" *Policing: An International Journal of Police Strategies and Management*, Vol. 27, No. 2, 2004, p. 229.

28. Kurisky, *op. cit.*, p. 249.

29. Larson, McLaughlin, and Badger, *op. cit.*, p. 2.

Evidence Analysis: Using the Experts

Key Terms and Concepts

- Automated Fingerprint Identification System (AFIS)
- Computer Forensics
- DNA
- Fingerprints
- Forensic Accounting
- Ninhydrin
- Questioned Documents
- Polygraph

Given the popularity of television shows and movies that have highlighted the role of forensic science in criminal investigation, it is understandable that many would overlook the applications of science and technology to white collar crime cases. Typically, the types of crimes the television and movie industries have linked to forensic science have been acts of violence such as homicides, rapes, bombings, and the occasional elaborate robbery or burglary. Perhaps because of the often complicated scenarios and what many would perceive as a lack of entertainment value, forensic science's application to white collar crime has been largely ignored by the mass media. However, for the white collar crime investigator such ignorance is not "bliss" because the application of forensic science and/or other types of technical expertise can often be crucial to successfully resolving a case. Admittedly, in a great many instances these types of examinations do focus on documents and records (increasingly in computer format), as opposed to human bodies and/or a crime scene. Nevertheless, some of the same types of examinations are employed in both scenarios. For instance, while crime scene technicians might search for and lift latent fingerprints from a home invasion and rape incident in hopes of identifying the intruder, latent fingerprints can also be left on paper documents that might help to establish physical possession and/or knowledge of the contents (when relevant to the investigation). More recent, however, is the application of DNA analysis to white collar crime. Again, if possession of a document and/or knowledge of its contents by a particular person are in question, it is possible that

DNA can be removed from the document for analysis. For example, saliva used to moisten the glue on a postage stamp or envelope can contain DNA for comparison to a known sample. And of course, as has been suggested already, the volume of paper documents is diminishing in favor of electronically stored data. Investigators often find it necessary to rely on forensic computer experts to recover and analyze this data.

However, the day of paper documents has not yet ended and accordingly their forensic analysis is often important in white collar crime cases. For instance, authenticating signatures or establishing authorship of handwriting is often helpful in linking a suspect to an offense. Probably less surprising when considering white collar crime investigation is the role forensic accounting expertise can play in these cases. Being able to track down hidden funds and the ability to identify accounting practices that are inconsistent with legitimate business operations (and conversely more likely to be associated with illegal enterprises) can be crucial to the successful resolution of a case.

Finally, and perhaps returning to the less frequently considered forensic and technical applications in white collar crime, are (1) analysis of voice for the purposes of identifying a speaker and (2) the use of the polygraph for detecting truthfulness/deception.

Thus, a white collar crime investigator who views forensic science and other technologies as applying only to the crimes featured on TV and in the movies is "missing the boat." The goal of this chapter is to help remedy any such misperceptions. However, consistent with approaches taken elsewhere in this volume when dealing with topics that have investigative applications beyond white collar crime, this goal will be addressed at the familiarization, as opposed to the "how-to," level. Moreover, the types of forensic examinations that are addressed here are those that have a broad application to the vast array of misconduct that falls under the white collar crime umbrella. Nevertheless, certain types of white collar crime or certain fact scenarios, generally, might require forensic examinations that are less frequently encountered in this context. For instance, some environmental and/or food and drug investigations might require the assistance of a chemistry analysis. While this chapter will not specifically consider the more infrequent forensic applications to white collar crime, it does hope to serve as a reminder to investigators to always fully explore the possibility of crime laboratory assistance in any case.

Obtaining Known Samples

While part of the work of forensic science is to recover and examine items of evidentiary value, the final step in this process usually involves linking these items to their origin. For example, it is one thing to develop latent fingerprints on an item, but without a known set of prints to compare them to, these latent prints might be of little value. In the case of fingerprints, state and federal indices have on file millions of sets of known fingerprints, taken incident to criminal justice system involvement or perhaps as a result of various types of employment. Nevertheless, it should be considered fortuitous when an individual of interest has a known set of prints on file. Moreover, the existence of known samples of other personal characteristic identifiers such as handwriting and DNA (although there is growing file of this type of data) is even more unlikely. Thus, the task faced by investigators is often not only to locate and obtain evidentiary items that are a product of the offense at hand, but also to acquire known samples of personal characteristic identifiers to assist in the laboratory analysis. One way of accomplishing this task is to simply request that an individual provide the needed samples. As will be discussed later with regard to handwriting, it is often desirable to obtain nonrequest handwriting specimens (i.e., documents containing the known handwriting of the individual of interest which were produced in a normal course of daily activities) from third-party sources. Finally, known samples of personal identifying characteristics can be obtained by court order when necessary. In fact, in the federal system the issuance of a grand jury subpoena (a topic that will be discussed more generally in Chapter 8) requesting the production of specified physical identifying characteristics is a common practice when seeking this type of evidentiary material from suspects, based on Supreme Court decisions in *U.S. v. Mara* (1967) and *U.S. v. Antonio Dionisio* (1973).[1]

Limitations

Notwithstanding this plea, so to speak, to consider the use of forensic and expert services in the white collar crime investigations, there are two realities that need to be voiced at the outset. First, to borrow the words of Swanson, Chamelin, Territo, and Taylor in their leading investigative text, "Crime laboratories are not intended to replace field investigations."[2]

This advice segues into a second reality. Carefully consider a possible "downside" to submitting evidence for forensic examination. Under Rule 16 of the Federal Rules of Criminal Procedure, the government must turn over, upon defendant's request, copies of any reports of examinations and tests and summaries of any expert witness statements. While not always "fatal" to the prosecution's case, it is obviously not helpful to receive lab or expert reports that fail to link a target to the alleged wrongdoing, especially since these reports are discoverable by the defense and could be used to counter the government's allegations. Clearly, avoiding negative lab or expert outcomes is not always possible. However as a *best practice*, following the advice offered earlier that emphasizes the need for a complete field investigation would be one way to minimize these occurrences.[3] The point to be made here is, don't submit evidence to crime labs or experts for analysis simply to demonstrate that something is being done on the case, or perhaps as a result of feeling frustration or bewilderment about what step to take next. Review the facts on hand and investigate further, if necessary, and use this analysis to determine whether forensic or other expert assistance will help bring the case to a resolution.

FORENSIC SCIENCE AND THE CRIME LABORATORY

Definitions

For the record, so to speak, a definition of forensic science is in order as a starting point for this discussion. One prominent authority on this subject, Richard Saferstein, calls forensic science the application of science to those criminal and civil laws that are enforced by police agencies in a criminal justice system, and he further acknowledges using this term and the term *criminalistics* interchangeably.[4] Alternatively, the American Academy of Forensic Sciences defines forensic science as the study and practice of the application of science to the purposes of the law.[5] Criminalistics is described by Nickell and Fischer as a division of forensic science and its practitioner is known as a criminalist. This position has been defined as the profession and scientific discipline directed to the recognition, identification, individualization and evaluation of physical evidence by the application of the natural sciences to law-science matters.[6] For purposes here in a discussion to enlighten the user of these services, these minor variations in definitions and terms have little significance.

A Brief History

Efforts to apply science to the law have a long history, although most advances in these endeavors can be traced to eighteenth-century Europe, beginning with the study of deaths and the effects of poisons. Photography first began to be used in the 1840s by the Belgians for the identification of criminals, while modern fingerprint identification can be credited to the Englishman Francis Galton, largely as a result of his book on this subject printed in 1892. In this book, he provided the first statistical evidence of the uniqueness of fingerprints. Within this same period, the Austrian Hans Gross wrote the first comprehensive forensic manual (1893).[7]

The turn of the twentieth century saw the emergence of the exchange principle as set forth by French criminologist Edmond Locard, a principle that continues to guide investigators and criminalists in searches for, and of, physical evidence. This principle states that whenever two objects come in contact with each other (e.g., a criminal and an object or objects at a crime scene), there is always a transfer of information, however minute, between them, that is, a criminal always removes something from the crime scene and leaves behind incriminating evidence.[8] Also occurring early in the twentieth century was the initial publication of one of the enduring texts on questioned document examination by Albert S. Osborn of New York City. The most important relatively recent development in forensic science occurred in 1985 when Alex Jeffrey of England discovered that certain portions of genes' DNA structure are unique to each person, thus setting the stage for the use of DNA for individual identification.[9]

Crime Laboratories

Typically, within the law enforcement community, investigative agencies utilize government-operated crime laboratories, although there are occasions when private sector services are utilized. Several federal agencies have their own laboratory capabilities, while state and local investigative agencies depend upon a variety of arrangements for these services. At the very least, most states operate a crime laboratory (s) to serve the needs of both the state-wide and local agencies within their jurisdictions. Some large city police departments have their own crime labs while regional or countywide labs operate in some locations.

Most crime laboratories offer a standard variety of forensic services that accommodate a wide range of criminal investigations. A full-service crime lab typically includes all or many of the following areas of specialization: chemistry and physical-evidence examination; serology and DNA analysis; firearms and tool-mark comparison; questioned documents; fingerprints; photography; and increasingly computer forensics. As suggested earlier, since the focus here is on white collar crime, forensic concern will lie with those examinations most frequently sought in these types of investigations. Thus, it would not be uncommon for white collar crime investigators to be on a first-name basis with the fingerprint examiners and document examiners and hopefully gaining similar familiarity with the forensic computer experts, in whatever lab they utilize. Nevertheless, having access to the full range of forensic services is always a plus. That said, it is important for agencies investigating white collar crime to ensure that the labs they utilize are adequately staffed with qualified experts in the fields they will request examinations in most frequently.

Expert Testimony

While advances in knowledge and technology have contributed significantly to the value and high-profile role that forensic science has attained in recent years vis-à-vis the criminal justice system, be forewarned that this is not "sacred ground." Both the science/technology upon which forensic examinations and findings are based and the experts who conduct the examinations and present the findings have, from time to time, been challenged in court proceedings. However, the *Federal Rules of Criminal Procedure* (R. 702), supported and clarified by a 1993 Supreme Court decision (*Daubert v. Merrell Dow Pharmaceuticals*), provide a flexible as opposed to a dogmatic basis for evaluating expert testimony. Rule 702 states:

> If scientific, technical, or other specialized knowledge will assist the trier of fact to understand the evidence or to determine a fact in issue, a witness qualified as an expert by knowledge, skill, experience, training, or education, may testify thereto in the form of an opinion or otherwise.

The *Daubert* ruling placed the responsibility on the trial judge to assure that expert testimony was reliable and relevant. While some legal practitioners have expressed concern over abandoning an earlier court-imposed standard of "general acceptance with the field" (*Frye* v. *U.S.*, 1923) for fear of allowing pseudo science into the courtrooms, the *Daubert* court addressed this issue by stating the adversary system should adequately challenge any shaky but admissible evidence. Experts express an opinion and judges and juries are free to assign, at their discretion, the weight this testimony should have in deliberations.[10]

Investigators must also be mindful that experts cannot render an opinion with absolute certainty. At best, their opinion is based on reasonable scientific certainty derived from training and experience. While experts should be able to vigorously defend a conclusion reached, he/she must also be able to impartially discuss findings that could minimize the significance of that analysis. Forensic scientists cannot act as advocates for a certain position, but rather as an advocate for the truth.[11]

FINGERPRINTS

The identification of an offender through fingerprint comparison is one of the most well-known and established applications in forensic science. Because fingerprints can provide positive individual identification, they are of great evidentiary value.[12] Without placing any limitations on how fingerprint identification might be helpful in white collar crime investigations, there tend to be differences in these cases compared to fingerprint applications in conventional crimes. In the latter, fingerprints often play a vital role in determining who was physically present at the crime scene (i.e., to confirm the presence of a subject or to identify an unknown individual). In white collar crime cases, a search for and comparison of fingerprints is often undertaken to establish possession or contact with items that would tend to prove involvement and/or knowledge of the offense. Very often these "items" are documentary in nature, that is, paper. Cases involving identity theft, bank and credit card fraud, insurance fraud, and some types of government program fraud frequently involve completing applications or claim forms using fictitious information, including false names and other personal identifiers. Latent fingerprints left on these forms can help establish the true identity of the individual(s) completing them. Likewise, fingerprints on stolen and forged checks or money orders can be invaluable in the investigation of possession and fraudulent negotiation of these instruments. Fraudulent operations sometimes require the acquisition of office space, utilities, mail receiving services, and so on, all of which might require the completion of applications. When the identity of individuals involved in the fraudulent activities is in question, these applications might contain fingerprints that could resolve this issue. Even in situations where the identity of the investigative target(s) is well established, there could be issues of knowledge and intent that might be clarified through a fingerprint examination and comparison. For instance, correspondence, written instructions/policies, and other documents might condone or encourage offending conduct by employees, yet the owner(s) and/or managers might deny knowledge and approval of both the document and its contents. Conceivably, the discovery of fingerprints on this type of document could be used to challenge such an assertion.

Just to reemphasize, there could be any number of other scenarios where fingerprint analysis might be valuable in a white collar crime investigation. For instance, this author, in pursuit of an individual using a credit card stolen from the mail, once found himself in a diner in the New Jersey Meadowlands (if you ever watched the TV series *The Sopranos*— the opening scenes as well as the cast of characters—you have the picture!) where he obtained the check for a food purchase made with the stolen credit card. It turned out that this check contained a latent thumb print that was identified as belonging to a local organized crime figure. This compelling evidence played a convincing role in the final disposition of this case, a felony conviction.

Fingerprints Generally

Fingerprints can be left on paper items when fingers contaminated with a foreign substance such as dirt, grease, and so on come into contact with the paper surface. Often in these cases, the prints are visible and can be used for comparison purposes. However, even seemingly clean fingers can leave behind fingerprints. The perspiration on hands and fingers *can* leave latent fingerprints on porous surfaces such as paper. In turn, laboratory processes have been developed to visualize these latent prints. To be clear, however, it is not a certainty that prints can be developed even if there was contact between the surface in question and a person's fingers or palms. Unlike the techniques that are used on nonporous surfaces such as the application of various dusting powders, latent prints on porous surfaces are usually developed through the application of certain chemicals that react with the perspiration residue, thus resulting in visualization of fingerprint ridge detail.

The most prominent of these processes is the application of the chemical ninhydrin to the porous surface. This chemical reacts with the amino acids contained in the perspiration in a way that fingerprints can become sufficiently visible for identification and comparison. Furthermore, these amino acids on paper surfaces tend to be stable over time, thus permitting the development of prints long after the contact was made (e.g., several years). One initial disadvantage to ninhydrin processing was that it took hours or days for the development of the prints. However, it was found that heat and moisture will hasten the development and most labs have specially designed cabinets that control temperature and humidity for this purpose.[13]

Alternative chemical processes for paper/porous surface evidence include DFO (1, 8-Diazafluren-9-One), which visualizes latent prints when they are exposed to a forensic light source, causing them to luminesce. In addition, an application of a solution of silver nitrate on porous surfaces such as paper will react with sodium chloride in perspiration residue, thus resulting in fingerprint visualization. Another silver-based solution called physical developer reacts with oils and fats in the fingerprint residue.[14] This reagent has been credited with developing prints on porous surfaces that amino acid reagents (such as ninhydrin) failed to recover. Additionally, physical developer has been able to develop prints that can be traced back 30 years and can be applied to water-soaked evidence. The U.S. Secret Service Laboratory has reported that use of this process in conjunction with ninhydrin has resulted in finding more prints, which in turn has led to more convictions.[15]

A final chemical process that will be described here has applications for other types of evidence that white collar crime investigators might encounter in an office setting. Super Glue fumes were found to interact with and visualize latent prints on nonporous surfaces.[16] Since 1982, Super Glue fuming has proven useful in developing latent prints on items such as garbage bags, Styrofoam, carbon paper, and rubber bands; all of which are frequently found in business offices and from time to time might be of evidentiary value.[17]

Automated Fingerprint Identification System (AFIS)

The AFIS technology has added another important dimension to fingerprint identification. These computer systems digitize prints by reading the spacing and ridge patterns and then coding them. Thus, AFIS does not compare images; rather it searches for a similar mathematical sequencing. The computer is able to make very fine distinctions among prints that further lends to the accuracy and reliability of the system. It is able to map 90 or more minutia points (ridges, endings, bifurcations, directions, and contours) for each finger. This number is high enough to individualize the print and distinguish it from all others. Although latent prints do not normally have 90 minutia points, matches can usually be made with as few as 15 to 20 minutia points. When AFIS finds a similar digitized print in its database, a fingerprint expert must actually compare the known inked prints with the questioned print to make a formal identification.[18]

As an illustration of how AFIS can assist in a white collar crime case, consider the case of an enterprising mail-order businessman, Robert Wild, who advertised numismatic quality coins for sale in periodicals, accepted money orders from purchasers that were mailed to his P.O. Box, but then never delivered the merchandise and disappeared. An ensuing investigation determined that the name, Robert Wild, was fictitious, but other than photographs of this individual (a white male in his early twenties) taken by a hold-up camera in a post office as he cashed the money orders he received, little else was known about him. These cashed money orders were processed for latent prints and several identifiable prints were developed and photographed. Given the blatant nature of the offense, a federal grand jury indicted Robert Wild, aka, John Doe, thus "freezing" the statute of limitations, in the event he was ever identified and apprehended.

So, what's missing here? Would not a similarly enterprising investigator have run the prints from the money orders through an AFIS database in an effort to identify Robert Wild? Hopefully, the answer would be yes, except the scenario described above occurred about ten years before AFIS technology was operational. But ten years after Robert Wild, aka John Doe, was indicted, this author did take advantage of the new AFIS technology and a hit was made that led to the arrest and conviction of the coin scammer, an individual whose name was not Robert Wild.

Needless to say, without the advent of AFIS technology, the above case was one that would probably have never been solved. The obvious applications of AFIS arise when unknown individuals are involved in illegal activities, in which they are leaving a path of latent fingerprints behind. The continuing contribution of known fingerprints by law enforcement agencies (e.g. as a result of arrests, convictions, and incarcerations) to AFIS databases will serve to increase the likelihood of identifications, thus making this technology an even more useful forensic tool for investigators. However, it is equally important to understand that in cases where there are known suspects, federal grand jury subpoenas can be used to compel the production of a set of fingerprints for forensic examination, if there is none on file.

QUESTIONED DOCUMENTS EXAMINATION

As white collar crime cases are often referred to as *paper cases*, the frequent need for questioned document examination should not be surprising. What may be surprising, however, are the myriad examinations that fall under this forensic umbrella, especially with the advent of computer technology in the home and business workplace. For instance, the FBI Laboratory provides the following types of questioned document examinations:

- Handwriting and pandprinting—in an attempt to identify the origin or authenticity of writing.

- Altered or obliterated writing—in an attempt to determine the presence of, and decipher, altered or obliterated writing.

- Typewriting—in an attempt to identify the typewriter that produced it and/or the make and model of typewriter involved.

- Photocopies—in an attempt to identify the photocopier that produced the documents and/or the make and model of the photocopier involved.

- Graphic arts (Printing)—in an attempt to associate printed documents with a common source or known printing paraphernalia such as artwork, negatives, and plates.

- Paper—torn edges can be examined to determine if they match; indented writings can be recovered/deciphered; and manufacturer can be identified.

- Burned or charred paper— information on burned or charred documents can sometimes be deciphered.

- Age of a document—the earliest date a document existed can sometimes be determined by examining watermarks, indented writing, printing, and typewriting.

- Carbon paper or carbon film ribbon—in an attempt to disclose the content of the text.

- Checkwriters—a checkwriter impression can sometimes be associated with the machine that produced it.

- Embossings and seals—an impression can sometimes be associated with the instrument that produced it.

- Rubber stamps—an impression can sometimes be associated with the stamp that produced it.

- Ink examinations—usually in connection with identifying the type of writing instrument involved.[19]

Not surprisingly, document examiners are now frequently called upon to examine documents produced by fax machines and computer printers and determine make and model of the machine involved. Computer printer model determination requires an extensive analysis of the specific printer technology and type of ink used.[20] It should be noted that there is general agreement that fax copies do not have sufficient quality to provide a meaningful basis of examining handwriting, typewriting, and so on.[21]

Notwithstanding modern technology, however, determining the authorship of handwriting and handprinting is frequently an issue encountered by white collar crime investigators. Check forgeries, credit card frauds, bank and loan frauds, identity thefts, and insurance frauds, to name just a few common varieties of cases, typically involve documents with questioned handwriting. While it was successfully argued in at least one case (see *U.S. v. Starzepyzel*, S.D.N.Y., 1995) that handwriting identification testimony should not be viewed as scientific in nature, this type of forensic analysis and testimony are still admissible under Rule 702 of the Federal Rules of Evidence as technical or specialized knowledge.[22] In fact, Saferstein states that the uniqueness of handwriting makes this type of evidence, like fingerprints, one of the few definitive individual characteristics available to the investigator. Document experts continually testify that no two individuals write exactly alike. He goes on to state that the unconscious handwriting of two different individuals can never be identical. Individual variations associated with mechanical, physical, and mental functions make it extremely unlikely that all these factors can be exactly reproduced by any two people. Thus, variations are expected in angularity, slope, speed, pressure, letter and word spacings, and finger dexterity. Margins, spacings, crowding, insertions, and alignment are also results of personal habits, as can spelling, punctuation, phraseology, and grammar, all which can combine to individualize a writer. The final conclusion must be based on a sufficient number of common characteristics between the known and questioned writings to effectively preclude the chance of having originated from two different sources.[23]

Obtaining Known Handwriting

A successful handwriting examination will necessitate ample known specimens (or standards) to be compared with the questioned writing. Both collected and requested specimens can be used together in an examination. It is important for the standards to be as similar as possible to the questioned writing, including the use of the same type of writing instrument, for example, ballpoint pen, fountain pen, and so on. They should be contemporaneous with the questioned writing and contain similar words and letter combinations. Standards can be two types: requested and collected. Requested standards have the advantage that they can reflect desired words and letter combinations, but might not possess the natural handwriting flow or attempts to disguise might be made. These problems can be overcome by dictating the material and having the person write the material multiple times.[24]

The FBI Laboratory recommends the following steps be followed when obtaining requested handwriting standards:

- The text, size of paper, space available for writing, writing instrument, and writing style (handwriting or handprinting) must be as close to the original writing as possible.

- Give verbal or typewritten instructions concerning the text to be written. Do not give instructions in spelling, punctuation, or arrangement of writing.

- All exemplars must be on separate pieces of paper.

- The writer and witness must initial and date each page of writing.

- Do not allow the writer to see the previous exemplars or the questioned writing. Remove exemplars from the writer's sight as soon as completed.

- Obtain exemplars from dictation until normal writing has been produced. Normal handwriting is assessed by determining whether the writing is too quickly or slowly executed and whether the handwriting is consistent.

- Obtain exemplars from the right and left hands.

- Obtain handprinting exemplars in upper- and lower-case letters.

- Obtain exemplars written rapidly, slowly, and at varied slants.

- Obtain a sufficient quantity of exemplars to account for natural variation in the writing.[25]

While a conclusive handwriting identification is powerful evidence, unlike fingerprint or DNA examinations that usually provide a definitive "Yes" or "No," it is not uncommon for questioned document examiners to provide an inconclusive report. Some of the common reasons put forth for inconclusive results include limited questioned and/or known writing; lack of contemporaneous writing; distortion or disguise in the questioned and/or known writing; lack of sufficient identifying characteristics; and/or submission of photocopied evidence instead of original evidence.[26]

DNA IDENTIFICATION

While fingerprints and handwriting have long histories of use as individual identifiers, in a little more than 20 years DNA typing and comparison has gained widespread acceptance as the genetic equivalent. Its increased use has paralleled the popularity of crime scene– and forensic-oriented popular entertainment, which in turn has tended to focus on solving sexual assaults, murders, and other crimes of violence through high technology. Nevertheless, white collar crime investigators should not dismiss this type of forensic evaluation as a tool unique to their counterparts in Homicide and Sex Crimes. Again, without presenting or suggesting any limitations, the need to establish possession or knowledge of documentary material in white collar crime cases is often an issue. While latent fingerprint examination and/or document examination usually come first to mind, DNA typing might offer identification opportunities, especially when these other methods fail. DNA is found everywhere white blood cells are found including blood, semen, skin tissue, hair root follicles, and saliva.[27] Saliva, of course, is often used to moisten mucilage on envelopes in preparation for sealing and mailing as well as for affixing postage stamps to mailing envelopes.[28] Thus, depending upon the circumstances of the case, this *might* be one way to tie a particular individual to possession of certain material and/or knowledge of the events in question. For instance, in identity theft cases, envelopes containing fraudulent applications for credit cards and loans and perhaps orders for merchandise might contain DNA from saliva used to seal them or affix postage on them. Of course, the myriad of variations that cases present could make any of the other DNA sources appropriate for examination, as well.

DNA is an acronym for deoxyribonucleic acid. English researchers led by Alec Jeffreys in 1985 discovered that portions of the DNA structure of a human gene are unique to each individual.[29] A year later this discovery was first used in a criminal trial in England.[30] Since the mid-1980s there has been a rapid development of methods and technologies that have facilitated the use and acceptance of this form of individual identifier. The current state of the art permits analysis of small and even degraded samples of biological material.[31] Notwithstanding the science behind DNA typing, there have been successful court challenges to identifications arising from this process. Usually, however, these successful challenges have focused not on the science of DNA uniqueness, but rather on the integrity of evidence that was examined and thus raising questions about the results. Specifically, faulty methods of evidence collection and storage of material containing DNA have led to these unfavorable results.[32] White collar crime investigators might not normally have experience or training in the crime scene processing techniques that have evolved in recent years to preserve the integrity of DNA evidence. Accordingly, if they should come into possession of evidence requiring DNA examination as a *best practice*, they are strongly encouraged to immediately contact appropriate forensic experts for guidance in handling, storing, and referring this material to the crime lab.

In 1990 the FBI started a DNA database known as CODIS (Combined DNA Index System). This database is organized into two indexes: one of which contains DNA profiles from unknown offenders while the other index contains known DNA profiles of convicted sex offenders and other violent criminals. Samples of DNA from crime scenes can be submitted to CODIS for comparison with the known offender profiles.[33] While such a database would seem to have limited application to white collar crime cases, it is again pointed out that like other forms of personal identifying characteristics, DNA samples can be compelled from a known suspect through legal process.

COMPUTER FORENSICS

As suggested in previous chapters, not to encounter evidence stored in a computer in a white collar crime case will likely be the exception in today's environment where electronic technology pervades both the home and office. While issues surrounding the acquisition of computer hardware have been discussed earlier, perhaps the greatest challenge involves the actual recovery and analysis of evidence contained therein. Data can be stored on a computer's hard drive and/or on portable storage devices (e.g., CDs, diskettes, tapes).[34] Addressing this challenge is the field of forensic computer science, which has been defined as the science of acquiring, preserving, retrieving, and presenting data that has been processed electronically and stored on computer media. This forensic discipline has been compared to the advent of DNA technology in terms of having a large potential effect on specific types of investigations and prosecutions.[35]

Data recovery from a computer requires computer expertise and knowledge of the prevailing laws of evidence and search and seizure. Further complicating this task can be the application of sophisticated methods to encrypt data and/or "booby traps" and destructive programs to prevent access to secret information.[36] This type of evidence, by its very nature, is fragile and can be altered, damaged, or destroyed by improper handling or examination.[37] In fact, Noblett, Pollitt, and Presley refer to it as latent evidence and as existing only in a metaphysical electronic form. The result that is reported from a forensic computer examination is the recovery of this latent information. To support the results of this examination, procedures are employed to ensure that the information exists on the computer storage media, unaltered by the examination process. Normally under the Federal Rules of Evidence, the "best evidence" principle applies, which means original as opposed to copies of documents are required. Fortunately, these rules have been updated to indicate that if data is stored in a computer or similar device, any printout or other output readable by sight, shown to reflect the data accurately, is an "original."[38] Thus, the challenge that confronts computer forensic experts is to extract information from a computer and/or peripheral storage device in a manner that preserves and accurately reflects the electronically stored data.

With regard to specific types of computer forensic examinations, by way of example the FBI Laboratory offers the following services:

- Content Examinations determine what type of data files are in a computer.

- Comparison Examinations compare data files to known documents and data files.

- Transaction Examinations determine the time and sequence that data files were created.

- Extraction—data files can be extracted from the computer or computer storage media.

- Deleted Data Files can be recovered from the computer or computer storage media.

- Format Conversion—data files can be converted from one format to another.

- Keyword Searching—data files can be searched for a word or phrase and all occurrences recorded.

- Passwords can be recovered and used to decrypt encoded files.

- Limited Source Codes can be analyzed and compared.[39]

While the techniques and procedures used to pursue such examinations will lie beyond the sophistication of many "tech-savvy" investigators, the success of these efforts will often hinge on a dialog between field and lab personnel. Dropping off or shipping pieces of computer hardware to a lab with a "Here it is, take a look at it" note attached is inadequate. As computers and storage devices can contain huge volumes of information, a *best practice* is for the lab personnel to be fully informed as to what they are looking for. Moreover, while it is important for lab personnel to understand what they are looking for specifically (e.g., spreadsheets, documents, databases, financial records), it is equally important for them to be given a general overview of the case, as well. This type of understanding and/or background information might permit the lab personnel to suggest other avenues to pursue in terms of recovering relevant electronically stored data (e.g., through Information Service Providers or from noncomputer equipment such as printers and scanners).[40] Finally, a well-briefed forensic examiner will also be prepared to identify potentially valuable data that was unknown or unanticipated by the investigators.

FORENSIC ACCOUNTING

In their general investigative text, Swanson, Chamelin, and Territo make the observation that investigators traditionally underuse forensic accountants in cases of white collar crime, an assessment they refer to as an unfortunate and potentially damaging oversight. They note that in other types of major crime cases, investigators employ such specialists as pathologists, serologists, psychiatrists, fingerprint and document examiners, and criminalists to aid in analyzing evidence. Accordingly, they make the recommendation that in many major cases of white collar fraud, forensic accountants should be called on to apply their training and expertise to legal matters and to testify in court as expert witnesses.[41]

To be clear, the purpose of this section is to tout the use of forensic accountants in white collar crime cases when unraveling and interpreting financial records that are either beyond the case investigator's abilities, too cumbersome and time consuming for the case investigator, and/or there is an anticipated need for expert accounting testimony. In fact, it is addressing the need for *expert* accounting testimony that is often the most compelling reason that white collar crime investigators will seek the assistance of a forensic accountant. If there is any perception that white collar crime investigators underuse forensic accountants, perhaps it is related to many of these investigators possessing reasonably good skills in reviewing and analyzing financial records (skills that have been acquired either through education, training, and/or experience), thus eliminating the need for this type of assistance in all cases. However, most (although not all) white collar crime investigators do not possess the educational and professional training/experience to provide *expert* testimony in enforcement proceedings on financial records analysis, testimony that can be essential in some cases. Moreover, as Manning points out, accountants and lawyers are often hired by offenders to handle their ill-gotten gains (wittingly or unwittingly) using sophisticated, if not complicated, accounting techniques to conceal the origin and/or disposition of these funds.[42] Often the best investigative response to such situations is to fight "fire with fire," that is, utilize the services of a similarly qualified professional, a forensic accountant, to follow the money. Not only is a forensic accountant trained to undertake such analyses, but as suggested earlier, he/she will be able to provide expert testimony.

Additionally, it might also be necessary to evaluate a subject's net worth and compare it to his/her lifestyle in an effort to determine if the subject is living beyond their means, a common indicator of being the beneficiary of ill-gotten gains. Again, this is analysis appropriately undertaken by a forensic accountant.[43]

Agencies that routinely encounter highly complex financial scenarios (e.g., tax enforcement, antitrust enforcement) often (and should) have on hand qualified staff to take on forensic accounting analyses. Otherwise, agencies with white collar crime investigative responsibilities should make appropriate alternate arrangements to cover this need as necessary. In this regard, agencies/investigators should be mindful that the attributes of a forensic accountant include not only accounting and auditing expertise, but also being knowledgeable in investigative techniques and evidence, and effective in report writing and testifying as an expert witnesses. They must be excellent communicators and professional in demeanor.[44]

Forensic accountants can assist in developing evidence of motive, opportunity, and benefit.[45] For example, in arson for profit cases, forensic accountants can examine the present business condition of the company and its owners to assist in establishing a motive for the arson.[46] Another example would be in commercial bribery cases where forensic accountants may be able to (1) disclose relationships between the payer of the bribe, recipient of the bribe, and a principal in the business; (2) determine if the recipient, in turn could influence the principal; and (3) identify the form and purpose of the alleged secret commission.[47]

Similar to forensic computer experts, forensic accountants cannot work in a vacuum if they are to be of assistance in a case. Ideally, the forensic accountant should be looked upon as part of the investigative team. Thus, investigator(s) must spend sufficient time together with the forensic accountant to familiarize him/her with the case at the outset and investigators should anticipate an ongoing relationship with this expert. Bear in mind, however, that as with other forensic experts, forensic accountants will provide an objective analysis, the results of which could be favorable or unfavorable to the government's case.[48] For example, some suspect transactions could be given the benefit of the doubt to ensure a proper interpretation.[49]

THE POLYGRAPH

The use of the polygraph as an aid to detect deception through untruthful statements is well known, if not well established, within investigative circles. In fact, many investigators are ardent supporters of these examinations as a means of determining truthfulness and/or obtaining confessions. With regard to the latter, while the results of polygraph examinations are not admissible in court because of reliability concerns (see *U.S.* v. *Scheffer*, 1998) any confessions obtained incident to them may be admitted. Nevertheless, even within these ranks of supporters there tends to be differing opinions as to its accuracy, which depends upon the subject, equipment, and operator training and experience.[50]

The polygraph instrument measures several physiological processes (i.e., respiration rate, heart rate, blood pressure, and skin conductance) and changes in those processes.

These measurements are believed to be stronger during acts of deception than at other times. The theory is that a deceptive response to a question causes a reaction that changes respiration rate, heart rate, blood pressure, or skin conductance compared to what they were before and after a question to which the subject was deceptive. A pattern of stronger responses to questions relevant to the issue being investigated when compared to other questions indicates the person may be deceptive.[51]

However, research in scientific psychology and physiology provides little basis for the expectation that a polygraph test could have extremely high accuracy. Although psychological states often associated with deception (e.g., fear of being judged deceptive) do tend to affect the physiological responses that the polygraph measures, these same states can arise in the absence of deception. Moreover, many other psychological and physiological factors (e.g., anxiety about being tested) also affect those responses. Such phenomena make polygraph testing intrinsically susceptible, producing erroneous results.[52] Polygraph research conducted by the National Research Council concluded that specific incident polygraph tests (e.g., probing a particular criminal act as opposed to use in connection with employment screening) could discriminate lying from truth telling at rates well above chance, though well below perfection.[53] This same study went on to state that as a tool in criminal investigations, the polygraph could be used to help focus and direct the investigations.[54] For similar reasons, this latter assessment is shared by Virj who sees a use for polygraphs in investigations for eliminating potential suspects, checking the truthfulness of informants, or examining contradictory statements of witnesses and suspects in the same case.[55]

What does all this mean for the white collar crime investigator? Aside from the reliability and accuracy concerns just discussed, the complexity and breadth of many white collar crime cases could pose problems in formulating suitable polygraph examination questions. Often the issues involved are not as straightforward as "Did you take the money?" or "Did you fire the gun?" However, as Virj indicates, polygraph examinations could play an important role in white collar crime cases in a supporting or tangential manner, for example, sorting out conflicting witness statements and verifying informant information.[56] Also, occasionally the terms of plea agreements require full cooperation and truthfulness to include verification through polygraph examinations. The bottom line is that the polygraph is a tool that white collar crime investigators should consider and have access to, in perhaps the limited circumstances where it could play an important role.

VOICE AND LINGUISTIC ANALYSES

Whether in written or spoken form, forensic efforts have been made to identify individuals by way of their voice and linguistic characteristics. Such efforts could conceivably have application in white collar crime cases, but neither approach has been fully embraced as a positive individual identifier by the courts. With regard to voice analysis, the FBI describes this procedure as a spectrographic examination to compare an unknown recorded voice sample to a known verbatim voice exemplar produced on a similar transmission and recording device such as the telephone. However, the FBI clearly acknowledges that decisions regarding spectrographic voice comparisons are not conclusive and any results of voice comparisons are provided for investigative guidance only.[57]

Forensic linguistic analyses, that is, an examination of a person's written or spoken communication, could also have conceivable applications to white collar crime cases, especially when attempting to link written or verbal messages of unknown origin to a particular individual. Again, however, these types of examinations should be viewed more as tools for providing investigative leads than as basis for positive identification in a legal proceeding. Nevertheless, proponents of linguistic analysis point out that an individual's communication, whether written or spoken, may provide clues as to his or her gender, age, race or ethnicity, or what part of the country or world the person grew up in or spent recent time. Language analysis may also provide insight into a person's educational level, political views, and religious orientation, which may provide further evidence regarding criminal motive.[58] Another approach to forensic linguistics as a personal identifier is based on the observation that linguistic production, especially syntactic structures, would appear very difficult to control. Accordingly, the more automatic a behavior, the more reliably it indicates personal identity.[59]

While voice and linguistic examinations *might* not be viewed as conclusive in the courtroom, they could very possibly point investigators in the right direction where more accepted forensic procedures could then be pursued, if necessary.

CHAPTER HIGHLIGHTS

- The task faced by investigators is often not only to locate and obtain evidentiary items that are a product of the offense at hand, but also to acquire known samples of personal characteristic identifiers to assist in the laboratory analysis. One way of accomplishing this task is to simply request that an individual provide the needed samples or in the case of handwriting, seek samples in the custody of third parties. Known samples of personal identifying characteristics can also be obtained by court order when necessary. In fact, in the federal system the issuance of a grand jury sub-poena requesting the production of specified physical identifying characteristics is a common practice when seeking this type of evidentiary material from suspects.

- In white collar crime cases, a search for and comparison of fingerprints is often undertaken to establish possession or contact with items that would tend to prove involvement and/or knowledge of the offense. Very often these "items" are documentary in nature, that is, paper. Cases involving identity theft, bank and credit card fraud, insurance fraud, and some types of government program fraud frequently involve completing applications or claim forms using fictitious information, which include false names and other personal identifiers. Latent fingerprints left on these forms can help establish the true identity of the individual(s) completing them. Likewise, fingerprints on stolen and forged checks or money orders can be invaluable in the investigation of possession and fraudulent negotiation of these instruments. Even in situations where the identity of the investigative target(s) is well established, there could be issues of knowledge and intent that might be clarified through a fingerprint examination and comparison. For instance, correspondence, written instructions/policies and other documents might condone or encourage offending conduct by employees, yet the owner(s) and/or managers might deny knowledge and approval of both the document and its contents. Conceivably, the discovery of fingerprints on this type of document could be used to challenge such an assertion.

- AFIS technology has added another important dimension to fingerprint identification. These computer systems digitize prints by reading the spacing and ridge patterns and then coding them. Thus, AFIS does not compare images; rather it searches for a similar mathematical sequencing. When AFIS finds a similar digitized print in its database, a fingerprint expert must actually compare the known inked prints with the questioned print to make a formal identification.[60]

- As white collar crime cases are often referred to as *paper cases*, the frequent need for questioned document examination should not be surprising. What may be surprising, however, are the myriad examinations that fall under this forensic umbrella, especially with the advent of computer technology in the home and business workplace.

- While issues surrounding the acquisition of computer hardware have been discussed earlier, perhaps the greatest challenge involves the actual recovery and analysis of evidence contained therein. Data can be stored on a computer's hard drive and/or on portable storage devices (e.g., CDs, diskettes, tapes).[61] Addressing this challenge is the field of forensic computer science, which has been defined as the science of acquiring, preserving, retrieving, and presenting data that has been processed electronically and stored on computer media. This forensic discipline has been compared to the advent of DNA technology in terms of having a large potential effect on specific types of investigations and prosecutions.[62] Data recovery from a computer requires computer expertise and knowledge of the prevailing laws of evidence and search and seizure.

- The use of forensic accountants in white collar crime cases should be considered when unraveling and interpreting financial records that are either beyond the case investigator's abilities, too cumbersome and time consuming for the case investigator, and/or there is an anticipated need for expert accounting testimony. In fact, it is addressing the need for *expert* accounting testimony that is often the most compelling reason that white collar crime investigators should seek the assistance of a forensic accountant.

CHAPTER BEST PRACTICES

- While not always "fatal" to the prosecution's case, it is obviously not helpful to receive lab or expert reports that fail to link a target to the alleged wrongdoing, especially since these reports are discoverable by the defense and could be used to counter the government's allegations. Clearly, avoiding negative lab or expert outcomes is not always possible. However as a *best practice*, following the advice offered earlier that emphasizes the need for a complete field investigation would be one way to minimize these occurrences.[63] (See page 149.)

- White collar crime investigators might not normally have experience or training in the crime scene processing techniques that have evolved in recent years to preserve the integrity of DNA evidence. Accordingly, if they should come into possession of evidence requiring DNA examination as a *best practice*, they are strongly encouraged to immediately contact appropriate forensic experts for guidance in handling, storing, and referring this material to the crime lab. (See page 158.)

- Dropping off or shipping pieces of computer hardware to a lab with a "Here it is, take a look at it" note attached is inadequate. As computers and storage devices can contain huge volumes of information, a *best practice* is for the lab personnel to be fully informed as to what they are looking for. Moreover, while it is important for lab personnel to understand what they are looking for specifically (e.g., spreadsheets, documents, databases, financial records), it is equally important for them to be given a general overview of the case, as well. This type of understanding and/or background information might permit the lab personnel to suggest other avenues to pursue in terms of recovering relevant electronically stored data (e.g., through Information Service Providers or from noncomputer equipment such as printers and scanners).[64] Finally, a well-briefed forensic examiner will also be prepared to identify potentially valuable data that was unknown or unanticipated by the investigators. (See page 159.)

Notes

1. R. N. Morris, *Forensic Handwriting Identification: Fundamental Concepts and Principles* (San Diego, CA: Academic Press, 2000), pp. 187–188.
2. C. R. Swanson, N. C. Chamelin, L. Territo, and R. W. Taylor, *Criminal investigation*, 9th ed. (New York: McGraw-Hill, 2006), p. 244.
3. Ibid., p. 244.
4. R. Saferstein, *Criminalistics: An introduction to Forensic Science*, 8th ed. (Upper Saddle River, NJ: Prentice Hall, 2004), p. 2.
5. J. Nickell and J. F. Fischer, *Crime Scene: Method for Forensic Detection* (Lexington, KY: University of Kentucky Press, 1998), p. 1.
6. Ibid., p. 2.
7. Ibid., pp. 6–9.
8. W. W. Bennett and K. M. Hess, *Criminal Investigation*, 8th ed. (Belmont, CA: Thomson/Wadsworth, 2007), pp. 113–114.
9. Nickell and Fischer, *op. cit.*, pp. 10–11.
10. Saferstein, *op. cit.*, pp. 14–17.
11. Ibid., p. 17.
12. Bennett and Hess, *op. cit.*, p. 131.
13. J. Almog, "Fingerprint development by ninhydrin and its analogues," in H. C. Lee and R. E. Gaensslen, eds., *Advances in Fingerprint Technology*, 2nd ed. (Boca Raton, FL: CRC Press, 2001), pp. 177–178.
14. Nickell and Fischer, *op. cit.*, pp. 134–135.
15. A. A. Cantu and J. L. Johnson, "Silver physical development of latent prints," in H. C. Lee and R. E. Gaensslen, eds., *Advances in Fingerprint Technology*, 2nd ed. (Boca Raton, FL: CRC Press, 2001), pp. 241–274.

16. Saferstein, *op. cit.*, p. 420.

17. H. C. Lee and R. E. Gaensslen, "Methods of latent fingerprint development," in H. C. Lee and R. E. Gaensslen, eds., *Advances in Fingerprint Technology*, 2nd ed. (Boca Raton, FL: CRC Press, 2001) (pp. 105–175).

18. Swanson, Chamelin, Territo, and Taylor, *op. cit.*, p. 255.

19. Federal Bureau of Investigation, *Handbook of Forensic Services* (Washington, DC: U.S. Government Printing Office, 2003), Retrieved from http://www. fbi. gov/ hq/ lab/ handbook/ intro12. htm# (accessed June 25, 2006).

20. Saferstein, *op. cit.*, pp. 472–473.

21. J. Levinson, *Questioned Documents: A Lawyer's Handbook* (London: Academic Press, 2001), p. 90.

22. C. E. Chaski, "Who wrote it?" *National Institute of Justice Journal* (September 1997), p. 17.

23. Saferstein, *op. cit.*, pp. 466–467.

24. Nickell and Fischer, *op. cit.*, pp. 170–171.

25. Federal Bureau of Investigation, *op. cit.*

26. Ibid.

27. Nickell and Fischer, *op. cit.*, p. 202.

28. Saferstein, *op. cit.*, p. 376.

29. Ibid., p. 361.

30. National Commission on the Future of DNA Evidence, *What Every Law Enforcement Officer Should Know About DNA Evidence* (DVD) (Washington, DC: National Institute of Justice, 1997).

31. Saferstein, *op. cit.*, pp. 376–377.

32. Bennett and Hess, *op. cit.*, p. 137.

33. Ibid., pp. 134–137.

34. Bennett and Hess, *op. cit.*, p. 498.

35. M. G. Noblett, M. M. Pollitt, and L. A. Presley, "Recovery and examining computer forensic evidence," *Forensic Science Communications*, Vol. 2, No. 4, October, 2000. Retrieved July 5, 2006 from http://www. fbi. gov/ hq/ lab/ fsc/ backissu/ oct2000/ computer. htm.

36. Bennett and Hess, *op. cit.*, p. 498.

37. U.S. Department of Justice, Office of Justice Programs, National Institute of Justice, *Forensic Examination of Digital Evidence: A Guide for law Enforcement*, 2004. Retrieved June 28, 2006 from http://www. ojp. usdoj. gov/ nij.

38. Computer Crime and Intellectual Property Section, Criminal Division, United States Department of Justice, *Searching and Seizing Computers and Obtaining Electronic Evidence in Criminal Investigations*, July, 2002. Retrieved July 7, 2006 from http://www. cybercrime.gov/s&smanual2002.htm.

39. Federal Bureau of Investigation, *op. cit.*

40. U.S. Department of Justice, Office of Justice Programs, National Institute of Justice, *op. cit.*

41. C. R. Swanson, N. C. Chamelin, and L. Territo, *Criminal Investigation*, 6th ed. (New York: McGraw-Hill, 1996), p. 525.

42. G. A. Manning, *Financial Investigation and Forensic Accounting* (Boca Raton, FL: CRC Press, 1999), p. 195.

43. Ibid., p. 195.

44. G. J. Bologna and R. J. Lindquist, *Fraud Auditing and Forensic Accounting: New Tools and Techniques*, 2nd ed. (New York: John Wiley & Sons, 1995), pp. 6, 44–45.

45. Ibid., p. 45.

46. Ibid., pp. 120–121.

47. Ibid., p. 124.

48. Ibid., p. 121.

49. Ibid., p. 45.

50. Bennett and Hess, *op. cit.*, pp. 183–184.

51. National Research Council, *The Polygraph and Lie detection* (Washington, DC: The National Academies Press, 2003), p. 13.

52. Ibid., p. 2.

53. Ibid., p. 4.

54. Ibid., p. 12.

55. A. Vrij, *Detecting Lies and Deceit: The Psychology of Lying and the Implications for Professional Practice* (West Sussex, UK: John Wiley & Sons, 2000), pp. 205–206.

56. Ibid., pp. 205–206.

57. Federal Bureau of Investigation, *op. cit.*

58. Bennett and Hess, *op. cit.*, pp. 132–133.

59. Chaski, *op. cit.*, pp. 15–22.

60. Swanson, Chamelin, Territo, and Taylor, *op. cit.*, p. 255.

61. Bennett and Hess, *op. cit.*, p. 498.

62. Noblett, Pollitt, and Presley, *op. cit.*

63. Swanson, Chamelin, Territo, and Taylor, *op. cit.*, p. 244.

64. U.S. Department of Justice, Office of Justice Programs, National Institute of Justice, *op. cit.*

CHAPTER 8

The Grand Jury and Criminal Charges

Key Terms and Concepts

- Agent of the Grand Jury
- Criminal Complaint and Warrant
- Grand Jury Subject
- Grand Jury Target
- Hearsay Testimony

- Immunity: Transactional and Use
- Indictment
- Information
- Proffer Agreement
- Rule 6(e)

Grand juries play a major role in the investigation and prosecution of federal crimes. On the state level, the role of the grand jury varies from one jurisdiction to another with some states emulating the federal system while in others they are employed on a more limited basis. As used in the federal system, the grand jury is a powerful tool for investigators and prosecutors, and it is a tool of great value and importance when applied to white collar crime scenarios. Not only is the grand jury a forum to formally charge individuals and/or corporate entities with a crime(s), it also provides investigators and prosecutors broad powers to acquire evidence necessary to bring such charges and for use in subsequent prosecutive proceedings. A similar assessment of the role of the grand jury in white collar crime investigations is found in the work of Beale, Bryson, Felman, and Elston:

> It is possible, of course, to have a system of criminal investigation that does not have access to compulsory process. Indeed, most criminal investigations are conducted without any resort to subpoenaed witnesses or evidence. In most jurisdictions, police investigations are conducted without the benefit of the subpoena power, and in many kinds of cases, the absence of that authority does not significantly impair the effectiveness of the investigation. Ordinarily, investigations of so-called "street crimes" such as murder, rape, robbery, and assault can be conducted effectively without resort to the subpoena power. The victims in such cases are often eager to help the investigators, witnesses are generally willing to

volunteer their statements, and physical evidence can usually be obtained on the scene of the crime or in the course of the subsequent police investigation.

The situation is otherwise with more complex offenses and particularly the so-called "white collar" crimes. In many of those cases, such as bribery or financial fraud, there is either no identifiable "victim," or the "victims" are unable to give much useful information about the offense. The "witnesses" to the offense are often the participants in the crime and will not willingly come forward to tell what they know. Instead, the only way to obtain the cooperation of those witnesses may be by compelling them to testify through the issuance of a subpoena and perhaps a grant of immunity from prosecution. In addition, the physical evidence that is needed for prosecution, such as documents revealing the details of unlawful transactions, is often in the possession of the suspects themselves. The prosecution may not be able to obtain a warrant to search for and seize that evidence because of a lack of sufficient probable cause or an inability to describe the evidence with sufficient specificity. In that event, the only way to obtain the needed evidence may be by compelling its production through a subpoena duces tecum.[1]

The goal of this chapter is to introduce these powers and their application from the investigative perspective. To be clear, the grand jury is the domain of the prosecutor, a person who has the legal education, licensure, training, and authority by virtue of his/her position to conduct proceedings in this forum. Nevertheless, because of the investigative role grand juries can play, investigators need to be familiar with their operation and powers so they can develop their strategy in a given case keeping in mind the tools the grand jury can provide. Moreover, as emphasized earlier, success in white collar crime cases is most often dependent upon a true team approach consisting of both investigators and prosecutors. Under this approach, just as investigators handle what goes on in field situations such as interviews and executing search warrants and arrest warrants with input from prosecutors, investigators must also be able to provide meaningful input to assist prosecutors in their grand jury proceedings.

THE GRAND JURY: WHAT IS IT AND WHERE DID IT COME FROM?

The grand jury is a forum through which prosecutors present evidence of alleged criminal wrongdoing to a group of citizen jurors whose sole purpose is to determine whether there is probable cause to believe that (1) a crime was, in fact, committed and (2) the subject(s) of the government's investigation committed this crime. If the grand jury believes that the prosecutor has provided them sufficient evidence to establish probable cause in both respects, it returns an indictment, a formal set of criminal charges that the accused must now answer before a trial court. Thus, grand juries unlike trial juries do not address guilt or innocence per se.[2]

The grand jury is a common law institution with historical roots traceable to at least twelfth-century England. As the English colonized North America, they brought with them their legal institutions, including the grand jury.[3] In fact, the first grand jury to be convened in the New World can be traced to 1635. However, it was not until after the American Revolution that it became a well-entrenched institution within what was now the American legal system.[4] This entrenchment can be attributed to its inclusion in the Bill of Rights. Although best known for other clauses, the Fifth Amendment also states, "No person shall be held to answer for a capital or otherwise infamous crime, unless on a presentment or indictment of a Grand Jury, except in cases arising in the land or naval forces or in the Militia, when in actual service in time of war or public danger." This means, at least on the federal level, that a person may not be brought to trial for a serious crime (generally a felony) unless a grand jury has heard enough evidence to return an indictment.[5] (It should be noted, however, that a person could waive grand jury proceedings and agree to be prosecuted by a written charge of crime called an information.[6])

At the risk of belaboring this brief historical introduction of the grand jury, importantly for our purposes here, Felkenes noted that prior to the end of the nineteenth century grand juries in America had been largely used to ferret out corruption in government. Thereafter (and certainly continuing on to the present), the use of grand juries to investigate corrupt business practices that caused bank failures, securities and insurance frauds, antitrust violations, union corruption, and illegal political contributions became widespread and commonplace prosecutorial practice.[7] Thus, well before Sutherland popularized the term *white collar crime*, grand juries were returning indictments against these kinds of offenses.

Federal versus State Grand Juries

As suggested at the outset of this chapter, among the states there is a good deal of variation in how the grand jury is used. Some states follow the federal model and require a grand jury indictment for any felony prosecution while in other states it is used at the option of the prosecutors in lieu of simply filing an information. Needless to say, in these latter states the use of the grand jury is not common. The remaining few states only require a grand jury presentment in capital cases or those with exposure to life imprisonment.[8]

Federal grand juries consist of 23 individuals, 16 of whom must be present to establish a quorum. Without a quorum present, grand juries cannot hear testimony and/or consider an indictment. Twelve members must vote in favor of an indictment for a grand jury to return a *true bill*, another term for the approval of a formal set of charges by the grand jury. Just as the roles of grand juries on the state level vary, so do their compositions in terms of numbers of jurors.[9]

Grand Jury Procedures

Unlike other court proceedings, grand juries meet in secret (an issue that will be discussed further later) and those who are being considered for indictment have no right to be represented by counsel before these proceedings, nor even present for that matter.[10] Grand jurors do have an opportunity to question witnesses who appear before them, usually after the government attorney has done so.[11] Magnuson categorized individuals who are of concern to grand juries into three groups:

1. Witness—This is someone who is called to produce evidence related to someone else's wrongdoing.
2. Subject—This is a person the prosecutor suspects may have been involved in some wrongdoing although no firm decision has been made about this person's culpability. By Department of Justice definition this is a person within the scope of the grand jury's investigation.
3. Target—This is a person who is likely to be indicted. The Department of Justice defines the term *target* as a person the prosecutor or the grand jury has substantial evidence linking him/her to the commission of the crime and who, in turn, in the judgment of the prosecutor is a putative defendant.[12]

Witnesses can also include law enforcement officers who are working on the investigation the grand jury is considering. In fact, these particular law enforcement officers are officially designated and sworn in by the grand jury as "agents of the grand jury". This designation empowers these officers to serve subpoenas issued by the grand jury and to review testimony and records gathered through this process under the recognition that this material is protected by grand jury secrecy, a topic that will be covered in more detail later.

In carrying out their responsibilities, grand juries are able to compel testimony of witnesses and the production of physical or documentary evidence without observing all evidentiary and exclusionary rules that would apply at trial. For instance, grand juries may consider hearsay testimony. Frankel and Naftalis note that although individuals who appear before the grand jury can exercise their Fifth Amendment privilege against self-incrimination and consult with legal counsel outside the grand jury room regarding questions that are being posed to them, there are few defenses available for individuals who simply fall into the witness category to not comply with a subpoena to testify. Likewise, grand jury subpoenas for records are no less difficult to fight, whether the grounds are on relevance of the records sought or burden it would cause to produce them.[13]

GRAND JURY SECRECY

As indicated earlier, grand jury proceedings are not open to the public. To the contrary, grand juries work in secrecy. Grand jury secrecy is important for several reasons: (1) to prevent the escape of persons whose indictments may be contemplated; (2) to ensure freedom of the grand jury in its deliberations; (3) to prevent subornation or perjury or tampering with grand jury witnesses; (4) to encourage free disclosure of information by those who have knowledge of the commission of a crime(s); and (5) to protect from unfavorable publicity innocent persons who are accused and ultimately exonerated.[14]

Rule 6(e)

Under the Federal Rules of Criminal Procedure, the secrecy requirements associated with the grand jury are detailed in Rule 6(e). Generally, this rule prohibits grand jurors, government attorneys, those providing ancillary services to the grand jury such as court reporters and interpreters from disclosing any matter occurring before the grand jury. Matters occurring before the grand jury include materials that would reveal the nature of the grand jury proceedings, their scope, or their direction. The rule does not apply to information gathered or prepared independently of the grand jury so long as this information was developed for its own sake and not for the purpose of discovering what occurred before the grand jury. The rule encompasses not only direct revelation of grand jury transcripts but also the disclosure of information that would reveal the direction of the investigation, the deliberations, or questions of the grand jurors. Included under matters occurring before the grand jury are grand jury transcripts, identity of witnesses and the substance of their testimony, documents subpoenaed by the grand jury, and summaries and analyses prepared by government agents which can include investigators and experts needed to analyze and interpret data/records and otherwise assist in the investigation and preparation of charges.[15]

   Determining whether information falls within the secrecy provisions of Rule 6(e) calls for the application of a two-step analysis. The first step is to determine whether the material considered for disclosure constitutes matters occurring before the grand jury. If the material does not, then Rule 6(e) does not apply. However, if the material consists of matters occurring before the grand jury, then the next step is to determine if any exceptions to the secrecy provisions apply.[16] As suggested earlier, among the limited exceptions available are government personnel who are assisting the government attorney and the grand jury in an investigation. The term *government personnel* includes not only federal employees, but state and local government employees as well. Thus, federal as well as state and local law enforcement officers can assist in a federal grand jury investigation, and thereby gain access/share information developed through the grand jury process. Moreover, disclosures of violations of state criminal law can be made to appropriate state and local officials when revealed through a federal grand jury investigation.[17]

Accounting for Disclosures

All investigators, regardless of their affiliation, are put on notice that the information disclosed to them can be used only for the purpose of assisting the federal attorney in enforcing federal criminal law. Moreover, the government attorney must provide to the federal district court judge that has oversight responsibility for the grand jury the names of those government employees (e.g., law enforcement personnel) to whom grand jury information is disclosed, and the government attorney must also certify that he/she has advised these employees of their secrecy obligation with regard to matters occurring before the grand jury (See Box 8–1).

   In meeting this requirement, government attorneys normally send letters to each government employee that puts them on notice that grand jury disclosures will be made to them

---

Box 8–1   Sample letter to judge: grand jury disclosure record and certification

Judge, United States District Court:

In accordance with Rule 6(e)(3)(B) of the Federal Rules of Criminal Procedure, this memorandum will serve to report to the Court that pursuant to Rule 6(e)(3)(A)(ii), disclosure of Grand Jury information has been and will be made to the following Government personnel, as necessary, for the purpose of assisting this office and the Grand Jury in the performance of our duty to enforce Federal criminal law:

    Internal Revenue Service: Special Agent Scott George; Revenue Agent L. W. Tell
    Federal Bureau of Investigation: Special Agent S. Z. Lewis
    United States Postal Service: Postal Inspector A. L. Hinson
    Defense Criminal Investigative Service: Special Agent R. C. Colbert

Consistent with the requirements of Rule 6(e)(3)(B), and the previous practice of this office, we will advise all personnel to whom disclosure is made that any Grand Jury material disclosed to them may not be utilized for any purpose other than assisting this office and the Grand Jury in the performance of our duty to enforce Federal criminal law.

In accordance with Rule 6(e), we request that this report be sealed.

Respectfully submitted,
Luther B. Wilson
United States Attorney
By: Annette T. Thomas, Assistant United States Attorney

Source: Adapted from S. S. Beale, W. C. Bryson, J. E. Felman, and M. J. Elston, *Grand Jury Law and Practice,* Vol. 1, 2nd ed. (Eagan, MN: West, 2004), p. 5–96. Reprinted with permission.

---

incident to their assistance in the matter being investigated by the grand jury and warns them that they cannot disclose any information obtained through their work with the grand jury. These letters typically further advise that the information they obtain through these disclosures can only be used in connection with the enforcement of federal criminal law. (See Box 8–2.)

Notably, disclosures can also be made to other government attorneys that may assist in the grand jury proceedings without going through the above-described process, providing such attorneys are responsible for the investigation of criminal matters (including supervising attorneys) as opposed to those having purely civil law responsibility. This limitation also applies to attorneys of other federal agencies and those employed by state and local governments. As will be discussed further in the next chapter, a court order can be sought for the release of grand jury material for use in a civil proceeding when a particularized need is demonstrated.[18]

Don't Violate Rule 6(e)!

Unauthorized disclosures of grand jury material can result in harsh sanctions levied by the federal district court judge with oversight responsibility for the grand jury's operation. The most

Box 8-2 Letter to government employees. re: grand jury disclosures

Dear Agent,

Your name has been disclosed to the United States District Court for the District of _____ as a person who has been and will be given access to material, including documentary and testimonial evidence, obtained through the powers of a Federal Grand Jury inquiring into possible Federal criminal violations by (*insert name of individuals or entities being investigated*).

In accordance with Rule 6(e)(3)(A)(ii), you are being given access to those materials for the sole purpose of assisting the Government attorneys involved in the grand jury investigation in the performance of their duties to enforce Federal criminal law.

The grand jury investigation is criminal in nature, and grand jury proceedings are secret. The unauthorized disclosure of grand jury matters is punishable by contempt proceedings. Grand jury matters include the identities of witnesses, their testimony and the nature and content of documents and physical evidence obtained through the grand jury investigation.

No grand jury materials may be disclosed or used for any civil or administrative purpose or for any other than for the grand jury investigation, except by order of the Court.

You are further informed that no subpoenas may be issued or served which have not been approved by a Government attorney participating in this investigation. All grand jury materials and all transcripts of testimony will be maintained in the office space provided by the United States Attorney and will be under his control and are available to you for the sole purpose of assisting the assigned Government attorneys.

Very truly yours,
Luther B. Wilson
United States Attorney
By: Annette T. Thomas, Assistant United States Attorney

Source: Adapted from S. S. Beale, W. C. Bryson, J. E. Felman, and M. J. Elston, *Grand Jury Law and Practice*, Vol. 1, 2nd ed. (Eagan, MN: West, 2004), p. 5–96. Reprinted with permission.

common sanction is a contempt citation, and when issued against a government attorney, such a citation could also include a recommendation for disbarment, suspension, or censure. Subpoenas could be quashed, indictments could be dismissed, and convictions could be reversed as a result of improper disclosures. If grand jury material is inappropriately used in a civil proceeding, a judge may order compensating disclosure to all private parties and can also forbid any further government request for disclosure. Additionally, government attorneys could be removed from the case to avoid any taint of their improperly obtained knowledge.[19]

Investigators who improperly disclose grand jury information can also face a judge's wrath. This author recalls an instance in which an investigator disclosed to a news reporter the existence of an indictment after the grand jury voted a true bill, but before they went through the formality of presenting it to a district court judge. The investigator spent several days worrying about a threatened contempt proceeding that could have resulted in a jail sentence, and was eventually happy to have the matter resolved through an agency disciplinary action.

The point to come away with here is that while the grand jury system is a valuable ally in white crime investigations, its secrecy rules must be explicitly followed and adhered to by government attorneys and designated government employees who are involved in grand jury investigations. Many investigative agencies have established procedures to safeguard the secrecy of grand material, including storage of such material in locked containers when not being used and requiring reports containing grand jury information to bear a warning endorsement to this effect as a means to limit dissemination only to authorized reviewers. Ironically, individuals who are called before the grand jury as witnesses are free to disclose their testimony and government attorneys cannot admonish witnesses to maintain secrecy over their testimony. In fact, it is common practice for counsel for defendants to debrief grand jury witnesses.[20]

GATHERING TESTIMONY AND RECORDS THROUGH THE GRAND JURY: INVESTIGATIVE CONSIDERATIONS

The function of the grand jury is largely carried out by hearing testimony from witnesses. These witnesses are usually brought before the grand jury at the discretion of the prosecutor who is presenting the case to them for their consideration. Occasionally, a grand jury will request the appearance of an individual not brought in by the prosecutor. In those instances, the prosecutor will need to evaluate that request in terms of whether it will be in the best interest of the case to do so and offer rationale for not doing so, if that is his/her decision.

Serving Grand Jury Subpoenas

A subpoena issued under the authority of the grand jury is often the means through which a witness is notified to appear. Grand jury subpoenas require *personal* delivery to the intended recipient if proper service is to be effected. Service of grand jury subpoenas to witnesses is an important role for investigators assigned to the case. It is necessary to ensure proper service so that the witness is put on notice of his/her appearance and to effect enforcement proceedings if the witness fails to comply with the subpoena.

Proper service is defined as personal delivery on a face-to-face basis, that is, the investigator physically presents a copy of the subpoena (although the served copy should bear a raised seal as evidence of authenticity) to the intended individual, and advises this person that he/she has been served. Ideally, the served individual accepts the subpoena in his/her hand and the investigator has the opportunity to provide information about complying with it, such as the date, time, and place of appearance. Federal grand jury subpoenas do not require that the recipient sign for them. The investigator who effects service completes an affidavit on the reverse side of the original subpoena that attests to the service. When the intended recipient is considered to be an uncooperative, hostile, or otherwise reluctant witness, having a second investigator on hand as a witness is a *best practice* to offset any allegations that service was not effected.

On occasion, investigators serving a grand jury subpoena on an uncooperative individual might find that this person will not accept the subpoena in their hand. In these cases, one option is for the investigator to advise the individual they are served and to drop it in front of them. Then either further advise the person about complying with the subpoena or walk away if the recipient does likewise. The investigator, along with completing the service affidavit, should make notes detailing these exceptional circumstances. Great care should be taken to avoid any action that could be alleged by the intended recipient as an assault. For instance, do not attempt to physically insert the subpoena in the uncooperative person's pocket or clothing. And consider this as a worst-case scenario to avoid: a male investigator taking this type of action when attempting to serve an uncooperative female recipient. Again, having another investigator on hand as a witness in potentially difficult service scenarios cannot be overemphasized.

Neither leaving a grand jury subpoena with another person for referral to the person named on the subpoena, leaving it at a known residence of the intended recipient, nor mailing it to the person named on the subpoena constitutes proper service. Thus, if anything less than personal, face-to-face service of the subpoena is made and the intended recipient fails to appear, enforcement of the subpoena in the form of contempt proceedings will unlikely be undertaken. One possible exception to personal service is for an attorney representing the person named on the subpoena to agree to accept it on their behalf. Subpoenas directed to corporate entities are often addressed to the registered agent for the corporation or custodian of records. It is important to ensure that service is effected on the person officially designated in these capacities or a responsible employee acting on their behalf. Particularly in this latter scenario, obtain the name and title of the person who is accepting service. Also, it is not uncommon for attorneys representing a corporate entity to agree to accept the subpoena, as well.

In the majority of instances, recipients of subpoenas will cooperate in accepting service and when cooperation is anticipated it is often beneficial for the investigator to make prior arrangements with the intended recipient to effect service so that unnecessary time and effort are not expended on this task. However, on occasion this normally routine, if not at times mundane duty, can test the skills of even the most seasoned investigator. This latter scenario can occur when attempting to serve individuals who are reluctant to appear before the grand jury. The service of a grand jury subpoena does not provide authority to forcefully enter any premises. Thus, the intended recipient simply need not respond to an investigator knocking at their door with subpoena in hand. Sooner or later such individuals usually venture into the public domain where they become fair game for service. However, more than one investigator will, either freely or reluctantly, divulge cases where serving a subpoena-shy individual took up days, if not weeks, of their time.

A *best practice* when there is a realistic chance that service of a grand jury subpoena will be difficult because the intended recipient is viewed as a reluctant or hostile witness is to not approach this task casually. Rather, gathering information about the intended recipient's whereabouts and daily activities/routines in advance may very well save time in the long run.

Whatever element of surprise is available will be lost after the first attempt, so a strategically planned first attempt will provide the best chance for success. Among the basic investigative inquiries that should be made prior to attempting service on a potentially reluctant or hostile witness are residence address verifications, motor vehicle records checks, criminal history record checks (to identify any history of violence and probation/parole status), and work locations. If it can be established where the person lives or works, and the make and license plate number of their vehicle identified, determining their daily routine becomes easier. Rather than simply knocking on the residence door to no avail or being told he/she is not there (along with the usual, "I don't know where they are or when they will return"), establishing their daily routines will permit a greater opportunity to serve them outside of their home, which might also help to reduce any potential violent reaction on the part of the recipient (in those instances where that is a concern). A *best practice* for dealing with potentially troublesome subpoena recipients is to serve them as they depart from their home, as they are about to enter their workplace, or in other public locations they are known to frequent. Whether they will make themselves available or be made available once inside their workplace are questions investigators must consider if they plan to show up at such a location asking to see the individual. Note that these recommended service scenarios might often necessitate that investigators be on location in the early morning hours. There is an old saying about the "early bird catching the worm." Many experienced investigators have found this to be true when searching for difficult-to-locate people as well. One final thought with regard to serving the reluctant witness is that if he/she is on probation/parole, contact with the supervising probation/parole officer might provide another avenue to establish the subject's whereabouts and routines and possibly to effect service incident to a scheduled probation/parole appointment.

Types of Grand Jury Witnesses

Serving on a grand jury can surely be an eye-opening experience. Grand jurors are privy to details of a wide variety of crimes and they hear from (or at least see in person) the wide range of individuals who are in one way or another involved in or affected by these crimes. These witnesses include victims, legitimate business people and professionals, experts offering opinions about matters under investigation, people associated with or sympathetic to the subjects/targets of the investigations, and sometimes the subjects or targets themselves. But who do grand jurors hear from most frequently? Not surprisingly, law enforcement officers. If they gain anything from serving on a grand jury, these jurors are provided an extensive exposure to the world of law enforcement, both its personnel in its many variations, as well as the techniques and strategies that are employed to bring wrong doers to justice.

Investigators

Law enforcement witnesses normally do not require a subpoena to produce their appearance although the issuance of subpoenas to these personnel is not without precedent, and such scenarios typically have a bureaucratic origin. For instance, an agency might request a subpoena be issued to an investigator being called as a grand jury witness in order to have a record on hand that accounts for the investigator's whereabouts and activities, especially when traveling outside of a normal jurisdiction. Typically, federal agencies will cover any travel expenses incurred by their agents to appear at distant grand juries. It might be necessary, however, in the case of needed testimony from a distant state or local investigator, for the U.S. Attorney's Office handling the prosecution to issue a grand jury subpoena to this individual if only for the administrative purpose of being able to pay for travel expenses. In any event, when a subpoena is required in these circumstances, it is seldom necessary for "proper" service to be effected and often the subpoena can be mailed or faxed to a law enforcement officer.

Of course, the most common scenario involving law enforcement witnesses is for the investigator(s) involved in the case to provide summary testimony of their investigation. In fact, some indictments are sought based solely on investigator testimony. Pursuing an indictment in this manner when possible is not only less burdensome on the prosecution, but also provides a strategic advantage, as well. Keeping in mind that presenting hearsay evidence in the grand jury is permissible and that the grand jurors can return a true bill based on hearsay evidence alone, a prosecutor could have an investigator-witness summarize an entire investigation replete with hearsay evidence, without providing any sworn testimony from other witnesses that might be called in a subsequent trial. Any grand jury testimony of trial witnesses is available to defendants, and if variations between their grand jury and trial testimony arise, the witnesses' credibility can be attacked. While investigator testimony before the grand jury *must* be truthful and accurate to the best of his/her knowledge, any discrepancies between hearsay evidence offered by an investigator in the grand jury and testimony offered at trial by the actual source of that hearsay testimony can often be more easily resolved by the prosecution. Moreover, when more than one investigator is working on a case, it might be good strategy early in the grand jury proceedings to identify which investigator(s) would be a likely trial witness(es) based on case knowledge, involvement in certain key events, and so on, and then utilize other investigators as grand jury witnesses to avoid establishing any preexisting under-oath testimony that could be the basis for raising discrepancies at trial. It is again emphasized that investigators *must* always testify truthfully and accurately, to the best of their knowledge, whenever they are put under oath. However, over the course of an investigation, especially when lengthy and complex, a statement made under oath before a grand jury in good faith could later prove to be inaccurate, either through mistake, misperception, faulty or newly developed information, and so on. Especially when such statements could be construed as of material importance to the grand jury in returning an indictment, defense counsel can attempt to discredit a trial witness, who previously under oath provided different testimony. To some extent, these types of problems can be minimized by limiting the volume and/or scope of grand jury testimony by potential trial witnesses (including investigator witnesses) and relying on hearsay testimony in the grand jury whenever possible.

In any event, not only is it an absolute necessity for the investigator-witness to provide truthful testimony, it is also essential that he or she be thoroughly prepared to testify. This means two things: (1) the investigator-witness must have an excellent grasp of the facts of the case, even if only on hearsay basis; and (2) the prosecuting attorney must review the expected testimony with the investigator-witness prior to the grand jury appearance. Particularly when the basis for an indictment is largely investigator-witness testimony, the positive impact of an investigator who clearly knows the case and whose testimony was cleanly elicited by the prosecutor cannot be overestimated. Just as serving grand jury subpoenas can become a routine task, likewise so can appearing as a grand jury witness. There is no cross-examination to anticipate and grand jurors tend to be a friendly audience. However, these seemingly comfortable surroundings should not be taken for granted by investigator-witnesses. Only professional-level demeanor and conduct should be exhibited while appearing before the grand jury. Also, be mindful that grand jurors can ask questions themselves, and the investigator-witness must be prepared to provide a responsive and informed answer.

Other Government Witnesses

Government employees other than investigators might be called upon to testify at the grand jury. Often, these types of witnesses are experts (including forensic examiners and accountants), or possess some other specialized knowledge. A prosecutor may feel that because of the highly technical nature of the subject matter, this type of witness would be a more conversant and/or credible source than an investigator-witness providing similar testimony on hearsay basis. However, again, caveats apply. Defendants can often challenge government expert opinions by providing conflicting testimony from other well-qualified experts. Therefore, prosecutors might find a tactical advantage of not having their expert's opinion reflected in a grand jury transcript in an effort to minimize opportunities for defense attorneys' analysis of and response to this witness's testimony, including the preparation of their own expert witness.

Whether these types of government witnesses will require a subpoena for their appearance will vary and this variation usually hinges on administrative concerns as described earlier, that is, as an accounting mechanism for the employee's whereabouts and/or to generate travel expenses for this person. Likewise, if a subpoena is necessary for practical purposes it is often wise to seek acceptance by way of mail or fax.

Victims

When white collar crime victimizes individuals or business entities, one of the considerations for a prosecutor is whether to have these victims appear before the grand jury to testify about their experiences. In a case that involves multiple victims, it is unlikely that all of the victims will be subpoenaed to appear. However, there are arguments for bringing in a limited number of representative victims in some instances. First, doing so provides prosecutors with a firsthand encounter with the individuals victimized by the crime under investigation. Especially when there is uncertainty whether the prosecutor is "sold" on the case, the opportunity to meet face to face with potential trial witnesses and listen to the details of their victimization can be a deciding factor in whether to go forward with the investigation. Second, and somewhat related to this first consideration, is that the grand jury is able to hear firsthand about the crime through a victim and the prosecutor can evaluate the victim as a witness and the impact this person has on the jury. Other reasons to bring a victim witness before the grand jury include circumstances involving especially compelling testimony (i.e., a complicated or aggravated set of events) or testimony that might not be available in the future, for example, due to anticipated health failure. Finally, it might be wise to obtain grand jury testimony from a victim witness when there is concern about how cooperative this person is with the investigation and/or to "lock in" statements from cooperating individuals whose status in this regard is viewed as subject to change.

Arguments against taking victim testimony at the grand jury once again revolve around establishing an under-oath record that could be subject to change. Many victimizations involve a complex set of interactions that, especially with the passage of time, can either be recalled after the grand jury appearance or cannot be recalled during trial testimony. This potential problem, which might possibly limit the effectiveness of the witness, might be avoided to some extent by not establishing a prior under-oath statement in the grand jury. In any event, when victim witnesses are to be brought before the grand jury, plan to effect proper service of grand jury subpoenas to these individuals, which might involve coordinating and arranging for this to be accomplished in other geographic areas.

General Witnesses

Another class of grand jury witnesses can be best categorized as "general witnesses." Individuals who fall into this category are typically "third parties," that is they are neither the subjects/targets of the investigation (or otherwise related or sympathetic to the subjects/targets) nor victims. They are often custodians of records from business entities that have been subpoenaed. Although frequently such records are turned over to investigators or prosecutors without the need for a personal appearance, occasionally a prosecutor will want the records described or interpreted by a person who is familiar with them. More infrequently are situations where businesses that receive a grand jury subpoena for records will surrender them only at the grand jury, a circumstance that must be accommodated if insisted upon.

General or third-party witnesses can also include individuals who observed certain pertinent events or had contact with individuals of interest to the grand jury, but are not believed to have any personal or business connection with the subjects/targets beyond the observation or contact in question. Such individuals simply might have been in the right place at the right time or the wrong place at the wrong time, depending upon their perspective. Particularly if the witness holds the latter opinion and the information he/she has to offer is material, locking in this testimony at the grand jury might be a wise step. Even when such witnesses are initially cooperative and helpful, keep in mind that with the passage of time memories can fade and enthusiasm for assisting the government in an investigation can wane. Therefore, depending on the importance of the testimony it might be valuable to bring "friendly" third-party witnesses before the grand jury, as well.

Regardless of the above third-party witness variations, investigators should be prepared to effect proper service of grand jury subpoenas to secure whatever records and/or testimony that are needed. Admittedly, business entities that receive many subpoenas for records (e.g., banks) will often accept them by mail or fax. While such procedures provide a timesaving advantage to investigators, it is important to keep careful mailing and/or fax records and follow up inquiries to ensure receipt and compliance.

Those Close to the Suspects

In addition to the power to secure documentary evidence that might not be available through other means, compelling testimony from individuals who are uncooperative or otherwise reluctant is a major asset the grand jury provides to prosecutors and investigators. Friends, relatives, coworkers, and business associates of those believed to have been involved in white collar criminal conduct are often found to be unwilling to cooperate in such investigations or they may feign cooperation by providing untruthful information. As discussed earlier, individuals falling into the uncooperative/reluctant category might do so out of loyalty to or fear of the person(s) under investigation, or perhaps in some instances a more generalized hostility to government intervention. While investigators should attempt to interview these individuals as necessary for the investigation, it might be wise to be armed with a grand jury subpoena that can be served at the conclusion of the interview. Even when a person falling into this category of witnesses appears to be cooperative and truthful, if their potential testimony is material to the case, it might be best to "lock" it in while they are still cooperating. Once an indictment is brought and a trial draws near, this same person out of remorse or fear might become reluctant to testify to information provided to investigators in an interview. However, if this testimony was provided under oath at the grand jury, the witness will have much more difficulty changing his/her story at trial. Of course, another variation of the reluctant but cooperative witness includes those who provide untruthful information during an interview with investigators. Whether the untruthfulness is identified immediately or at some later date, assuming it is material to the case, this individual should be subpoenaed to appear before the grand jury. Again the value of anticipating a problematic interview and being armed with a subpoena might avoid the necessity of investigators making a second trip to serve a person who they readily identified as lying to them.

Finally, there will be those individuals who will flatly refuse to be interviewed or otherwise cooperate in the investigation and yet it is believed they have information pertinent to the case. Obviously, in these instances they must be brought to the grand jury and compelled to provide their information under oath. While it is usually best to try to establish a working relationship with such recalcitrant individuals and gain their truthful cooperation, the possibility that this type of witness will commit perjury in their grand jury testimony should not be ignored.

The Suspects

As you may recall , the terms *subject* and *target* were introduced relative to a witness status before the grand jury. In short, a subject is an individual the prosecutor feels may have some culpability for the crime(s) under investigation while a target is an individual who is viewed by the prosecutor as likely to be indicted. Persons falling in either of these categories have no right to appear before a grand jury to "tell their side" of the story. In the event a prosecutor decides to subpoena individuals considered to be a subject or a target of the grand jury, they can exercise their Fifth Amendment right against self-incrimination when they are asked questions that could elicit incriminating statements. In fact, in those instances where they do appear (whether voluntarily or compelled by a subpoena), the prosecutor normally advises them of their *Miranda* rights at the outset of their appearance/testimony. Counsel can represent these individuals, but he/she cannot appear with the witness in the grand jury room. Rather, the witness must be afforded the opportunity upon request to consult with their counsel outside of the grand jury room whenever they feel necessary to do so prior to answering the prosecutor's question. Frequently, attorneys representing targets or subjects who receive grand jury subpoenas to testify will advise the prosecutor that their client will exercise their Fifth Amendment right against self-incrimination on all questions relevant to the investigation and the prosecutor will forego the formality of bringing the target witness before the grand jury to simply have this witness repeatedly "take the Fifth," often after delaying that response to first consult with counsel. Thus, many prosecutors will refrain from even issuing subpoenas for testimony to targets and subjects because of the small likelihood that any meaningful testimony will be elicited. In those rare instances where a target or subject indicates a desire to testify before the grand jury, the same caveats apply here as they do when simply interviewing such individuals. The prosecutor, often through the assistance of the investigator(s), must be fully prepared to deal with a sometimes glib, articulate witness who might be able to provide convincing rationalizations for wrongdoing, absent some very probing questions. Not only should a well-prepared prosecutor be able to cast doubt on the credibility of this type of witness who testifies before the grand jury, but he/she should also take this opportunity to set the stage for perjury charges, as well.

Of course, it is conceivable that a target/subject witness could successfully raise doubts in the minds of the grand jurors as to guilt. Some high-profile (and big ego) white collar criminals have adopted an offensive-oriented defense strategy whereby they attack the prosecution both in public and in court. Seeking to voluntarily appear before a grand jury to state their case and then reporting their testimony (at least their version) to the press would fall into this type of strategy. A somewhat favorable impact on the grand jury by a target/subject witness might not affect the eventual return of a true bill since only 12 votes are needed. However, it is wise to consider the effect of similar persuasive testimony on a trial jury where a unanimous vote for guilt is required when deciding whether to proceed against a target/suspect who performed so well before the grand jury.

Immunity and Proffers

Occasionally, an individual with criminal liability is viewed as more valuable to an investigation as a cooperating witness than as a defendant or a person otherwise exercising his/her Fifth Amendment right against self-incrimination. This individual might possess key knowledge that cannot be developed independently, but his/her role in the offense is minimal compared to others. In these instances, a grant of immunity from prosecution might be in order.

Like grand jury proceedings, issues involving immunity lie in the domain of the prosecutor. It is entirely inappropriate for investigators to suggest or in any way discuss the possibility of immunity with any potential witness or defendant in an investigation without the knowledge and concurrence of the prosecuting attorney. Although the term *investigator* is more frequently used in this book because it is more all-inclusive of state and local officials, at the federal level, investigators are generally referred to as *agents*, which carries the connotation that they are agents of the government, that is, they are representatives of the government. Consequently, if an investigator unilaterally represents to a potential defendant or witness that they will receive immunity from prosecution in return for their cooperation, the government may be "stuck" with this position even though the prosecuting attorney did not authorize such protection. Thus, for investigators to take it upon themselves to offer or imply immunity without the knowledge and concurrence of the prosecuting attorney involved in the case is a major "no-no" within the investigation profession. In practice, investigators can and do make representations of immunity, but only after having discussed taking this action with the prosecutor. For instance, prior to interviewing low-level employees in an offending organization, it might be useful for an investigator to know whether he/she can represent to a reluctant person who falls into this category that they will be a witness and not a defendant in the case if they truthfully cooperate. Obviously, it would be best for the investigator to be confident that a person has, in fact, limited culpability before making such a statement.

However, the granting of immunity to individuals with greater degrees of culpability is usually a more involved process, both in terms of establishing justification not to prosecute an offender and because of the likelihood of defense counsel intervention. In these instances not only must the question be asked, "Do we want to extend immunity to this person;" but also there is an issue of what kind of immunity is appropriate. The government formally can extend either transactional or use immunity to a person with criminal liability in order to obtain their cooperation. Transactional immunity protects the person from prosecution for the offenses under investigation while use immunity simply limits the government from using the immunized testimony against the person in any prosecution of this person.[21]

Not surprisingly, most individuals with criminal liability would seek transactional immunity prior to cooperating with the government investigation. One way to evaluate the type of immunity to extend, if any at all, is to interview the person with criminal liability under the terms of a proffer agreement. A proffer agreement provides for a person with such exposure to be interviewed by the government and any statements made cannot be used against him/her. These agreements are usually in writing from the government attorney to the defense counsel.

The value of a proffer to the government is that the testimony and knowledge of the witness can be determined before granting any type of formal immunity. Normally it is unwise to grant formal immunity from prosecution to anyone unless his or her knowledge and conduct in the offense under investigation is fully understood. Moreover, proffer agreements sometimes permit the government to make derivative use of the information provided, that is, that while statements themselves cannot be used against the interviewee, investigators can follow up on information provided to determine the truthfulness of the information and/or expand the investigation.[22] For the potential defendant, cooperating under terms of a proffer agreement offers an opportunity with limited liability to convince the government that he/she can be of more value to the government's case as a cooperating witness than as another indicted person at the defense table.

Not all defense attorneys will advise clients to enter into proffer agreements and obviously the power to make derivative use of information is a stumbling block in some proffer agreement negotiations. Another obstacle is that while a potential defendant is protected from the use of any incriminating statements in a federal prosecution, this might not be the case with regard to state jurisdiction, a prospect that might be even more troubling in joint federal/state investigations.[23] These issues, however, extend beyond the scope of an investigative guide and are more properly a subject for law books and lawyers.

AN INDICTMENT

At this point, it would be instructive to read through an indictment, not only to become familiar with its format, but more importantly to identify exactly what must be proven and what evidence would need to be on hand if the prosecution is to be successful. Appendix F contains a multiple-defendant federal grand jury indictment that charged conspiracy, mail fraud, wire fraud, and money laundering. This indictment also sought the criminal forfeiture of the laundered funds. The case involved a telemarketing operation that solicited monies based on false representations they made to members of the public who wished to sell memberships they had previously purchased to various vacation campground properties across the country in amounts ranging from $1,000 to $10,000. Typically these were individuals who no longer had use for the memberships, but as long as they were the owners they were responsible for paying yearly maintenance fees of $250 to $495. Thus, by selling a membership that was no longer being used, these owners believed they would not only recoup some of their initial outlay of funds, but also avoid payment of the annual maintenance fees. American Campground Resales (ACR) (not the true name of the company) charged an upfront fee ranging from $250 to $495 to such individuals to find buyers for their memberships. In its efforts to obtain these upfront fees, ACR made false representations to interested sellers with regard to its success in finding buyers. The fact was the investigation failed to identify any successful transactions and no refunds were made contrary to ACR's promises. Readers at this point are encouraged to become familiar with this indictment in Appendix F and then return here to a discussion of its various sections.

Count 1: Introduction

This indictment contains a conspiracy charge and it is the common practice for a conspiracy violation to be outlined in Count 1 when it is included in an indictment. Paragraphs 1, 2, and 3 provide a general or basic introduction to the victims, the defendants, and the business entity the defendants were affiliated with along with this entity's purported purpose. Note in this case the business entity was a sole proprietorship and not a corporation. Thus, the business entity was not a named defendant here. Had ACR been a corporation and had it had assets, there may have been a compelling reason to charge the corporation, especially since this indictment sought criminal forfeiture. Conversely, if ACR had been a corporation without any assets (as was the case in its status as a sole proprietorship), this indictment most likely would have still charged only the individual defendants since the investigation was able to tie illegal conduct directly to these specific individuals.

In cases where conspiracy is not charged, Count 1 will typically outline the details of the case and conclude with the specific act that constitutes a violation of a substantive offense. Here, however, as is the common practice when conspiracy is charged, the details of the entire case are provided in the context of the conspiracy violation.

The Agreement

Section 371 in Title 18 of the United States Code reads in part: "If two or more persons conspire either to commit any offense against the United States or any agency thereof in any manner or for any purpose and one or more such persons do any act to effect the object of this conspiracy, each will be fined under this title or imprisoned not less than five years, or both." Paragraph 4 identifies the offenses against the United States that this indictment alleges the defendants conspired to commit: 18 U.S.C. 1341 (mail fraud); 18 U.S.C. 1343 (wire fraud); and 18 U.S.C. 1956(a)(1) (money laundering); and 18 U.S.C. 1957 (money laundering).

The Manner and Means

Paragraphs 5 through 14 describe the conspiracy the defendants entered into to violate these offenses against the United States. These paragraphs allege that the defendants, after contacting owners of campground memberships and offering to resell these memberships, solicited fees for this service ranging from $250 to $495. Paragraph 7 specifically states that the defendants knowingly made false and fraudulent pretenses, representations, and promises to prospective sellers in order to induce them to pay the upfront fee. These false and fraudulent pretenses, representations, and promises were identified as:

- That ACR was highly experienced and successful in the field of campground resales;

- That the seller would receive a full refund if ACR failed to sell their campground membership;

- That ACR had already located a buyer for the seller's membership;

- That the buyer had already tendered a specified sum of money as deposit toward the purchase;

- They identified by name a purportedly satisfied customer whose campground membership was sold through ACR;

- That ACR had more than 15 years' experience in advertising and marketing campground resales;

- That ACR representatives visit RV shows across the country to meet potential buyers;

- That buyers were available to purchase campground memberships.

When sellers, after submitting their upfront fees, inquired about why their membership had not been sold, the defendants then engaged in further fraudulent pretenses, representations, and promises as follows:

- That the buyer's financing had fallen through and that additional time was needed for the buyer to secure other financing;

- That the buyer could not secure financing and a substitute buyer must be requalified to close the deal;

- That the delay in selling the membership was caused by processing problems with campground organizations; and

- That the seller should be patient and everything would work out.

Investigators must recognize that these specific allegations must be proven and most often this proof will come through testimony of victims. These are not simply allegations a prosecutor can make to a jury and then the jury will decide if the conduct was unlawful. Just as outlined previously in the development of a search warrant, interviews of victim witnesses must cover the very specific details of any conversations or other contacts they had with the suspects in order to identify false promises and representations that resulted in their victimization. Thus, again it is reiterated that when interviewing victim witnesses in the beginning of an investigation, keep in mind these individuals might be needed to provide crucial testimony at trial and their stories must be very accurately recorded and carefully maintained for future use.

Paragraph 11 specifically addresses a monetary transaction that forms the basis for charging conspiracy with regard to money laundering. The concluding Manner and Means paragraphs allege that defendants also conspired to obstruct efforts by the victims to obtain refunds and that the defendants assumed false names when conducting business with customers.

Overt Acts

Paragraph 15 identifies specific acts taken by specific defendants that satisfy the statutory requirement that "one or more persons do any act to effect the object of the conspiracy." Again, it must be emphasized that the burden falls on the government to prove these allegations at trial, which in turn means that evidence of these acts must be developed during the investigation. This evidence can consist of testimony and/or documentary/physical evidence (although it must be remembered that the latter evidence requires testimonial introduction). Interestingly, note that many of the overt acts can be proven through information developed in interviews and from public records. Subparagraph (1) can be proven from information obtained on a public record, an occupational license that was maintained by the local municipality. In subparagraph (3) the landlord of the property where ACR was located was identified through public records and agents then interviewed this person. Testimonial evidence in support of subparagraphs (4)–(5), (7)–(9), and (12) was developed through interviews with victims. Grand jury subpoenas were needed to acquire bank records in support of the allegations made in subparagraphs (2), (10)–(11), (13), and (15). Finally, forensic examinations of the "John E. Jennings" signatures provided evidence in support of the allegations made in subparagraphs (6) and (14). Observe that responsibility for at least one overt act was identified for each defendant, thus limiting the defense from any one defendant that they were not part of the conspiracy.

The Mail and Wire Fraud Counts

This indictment follows a normal format wherein after the conspiracy is outlined in Count 1, the substantive offense counts then follow. These counts relate to a scheme to defraud that has essentially been described in the conspiracy charge. Accordingly, the reader is referred back to Count 1 for the details of the scheme and the remaining paragraphs under this section simply identify individual uses of the mails or wires (i.e., telephone calls), each of which constitutes a separate violation of the mail and wire fraud statutes. Observe that each count assigns responsibility for the violation to specifically identified defendants and that unlike the conspiracy count, none of these counts includes all the defendants. Only Betty Frank was named in every one of these counts. Although she may not have had personal contact with each victim(s) named in the mail and wire fraud counts, she was brought into these violations under Title 18, United States Code, Section 2, Aiding and Abetting, because of her role as a principal in ACR. However, with the exception of Frederick Frank who was charged only with money laundering violations, all of the remaining defendants were accused in two or more counts of mail or wire fraud.

In this indictment the mail fraud counts reflect the versatility of how this statute can be applied. In Count 2, the use of the mails is described as an envelope sent via the U.S. Postal Service by a specifically identified victim located in Seattle, WA, to ACR's address in Florida, a location that was within the judicial district where the indictment was brought. Here defendants Frank and Halo are charged with causing the use of the mails. A violation of the Mail Fraud statute only requires that the mails further the scheme to defraud, that is, in some foreseeable way a use of the mails aided the defendants in their efforts to conduct a scheme to defraud. In this count, the defendants caused a victim to mail a check that represented her upfront fee to ACR, thus a very clear use of the mails in furtherance of a scheme to defraud.

Conversely, Count 3 charged these same defendants with the actual use of the mails since they are alleged to have mailed an envelope from their location within the judicial district where the indictment was brought to another victim in the state of Washington. In this count the defendants mailed a refund guarantee to a victim, a document that contained false promises of a refund from ACR in the event a sale could not be consummated. The receipt of this document by the victim helped allay any concerns about ACR and delayed reporting fraud allegations. By providing such documents to victims, ACR was able to avoid detection and continue its victimization over a longer time period. Again, this type of use of the mails falls clearly within the meaning of the term *in furtherance of a scheme to defraud.*

As with most federal crimes, the statute of limitations is five years for mail and wire fraud. The five-year statute of limitations date relates to the date of use of the mails or wires (i.e., the telephone call). The postmark on a mailing envelope often provides the best evidence of date of mailing (hence, do not discard envelopes or fail to obtain them, either voluntarily or through a search warrant or subpoena). However, when envelopes are not available the person responsible for the mailing (or receipt of a mailing) can provide testimony as to the date and ideally some type of documentary evidence to bolster this testimony. For instance, a witness may be able to recall a mailing date based on the date on the check he/she wrote and sent to the fraudulent company. In any event, the standard language used in an indictment is "On or about" a certain date in an effort to avoid the necessity for absolute precision. Only in cases where there is a question about whether the statute of limitations has expired will the issue of dating precision become more pressing.

Counts 7, 12, 13, and 15 charged wire fraud. Similar to mail fraud, the use of the wires (which here refer to telephone calls) must only further the scheme to defraud, that is, this communication in some way assisted the fraud to reach fruition. The wire fraud counts charged here name Betty Frank (because she was the principal in ACR) and the particular telemarketer with whom the victim dealt. In each count, the named defendant is alleged to have had a telephone conversation on or about a certain date with a specifically identified person. Developing information to support a wire fraud charge often starts with the victim interview. Again, determining how a victim communicated with the subjects cannot be over-looked in these interviews. Establishing the date of these conversations can rely on victim testimony, preferably supported by telephone records or caller-ID data. However, the "on or about" criterion for establishing the date of the call provides some leeway if there is doubt about the exact date. Unlike mail fraud counts where documents and written communications can assist witnesses in their testimony with regard to their victimization, proving wire fraud counts in this and many types of white collar crime cases rely on victim recollections of telephone calls. Once again, the victim interview becomes crucial to obtain a detailed account of these conversations. Often it is necessary to "walk" the victim through the call from its inception to its conclusion in order to re-create its sequence, and from there its contents. These witnesses should be encouraged to recall exact terms and phrases used as well the impressions and implications they came away with along with reasons they felt this way. As discussed earlier, multiple interviews, perhaps with different investigators, might be necessary to obtain the full details of any victim witness's contact with the case subjects.

The Money Laundering Counts

As discussed in Chapter 6, money laundering under federal statutes constitutes a broad spectrum of financial transactions involving monies that were acquired through criminal activity. In this indictment, Count 17 charged Betty Frank and her husband, Frederick Frank, with money laundering [18 U.S.C. 1956(a)(1)(A)(i)] incident to their involvement in a wire transfer of $15,000 that was identified as proceeds from the fraudulent telemarketing scheme. The count further charges that the purpose of this transfer was to promote and carry on the fraudulent activity. Thus, it was not sufficient to simply identify the wire transfer of the funds from the ACR bank account to another bank account, but the purpose of this transfer had to be established as well. In this case, Frederick Frank had plans to open another ACR telemarketing operation in Las Vegas and these monies were wired to his Las Vegas bank account to fund his efforts in this regard, thus promoting and carrying on the mail and wire fraud scheme. Again, note that the indictment contains an "on or about date" when this particular money laundering violation occurred and at least part of this activity must have occurred within the judicial district where the indictment was brought.

Counts 18 and 19 charged two more money laundering violations, but through a different statute, 18 U.S.C. 1957. Under this statute, it must only be proven that a person engaged in a financial transaction with criminally derived funds in excess of $10,000. The broad application of this statute is very clear when one considers that among the permitted definitions for the term *monetary transaction* are deposits and withdrawals. In these counts, the Franks deposited $25,000 of funds from the fraud scheme on one occasion and then withdrew $11,003 of their criminally derived proceeds on another.

Aiding and Abetting, Title 18, United States Code, Section 2, was also charged in each money laundering violation to account for the contributions of each named defendant in the described illegal activity.

Forfeitures

The indictment concludes with a forfeiture count. As you may recall from Chapter 6, asset forfeiture can be accomplished through civil and criminal processes. In Chapter 6 we reviewed an example of a civil forfeiture of criminally derived proceeds that were located in a bank account. In this case, while the required predicate money laundering violations as laid out in Counts 17, 18, and 19 could be established, the whereabouts of the identified funds at the time of the indictment were unknown. A criminal forfeiture action, if successful, entitles the government to the forfeiture of substitute assets in the possession of the defendants in lieu of those specifically identified in the money laundering counts. Thus, seeking criminal forfeiture in this case was the only alternative available to possibly recover monies that were fraudulently obtained. Unfortunately, the Franks were fugitives for about two years and by the time they were apprehended they dissipated whatever assets they acquired during their telemarketing days. However, the inclusion of the forfeiture count in the indictment also contributed to the government's leverage in subsequent plea negotiations that followed their arrests, and a costly and lengthy trial was averted.

ALTERNATE CHARGING APPROACHES

This chapter has emphasized and focused on the use of the grand jury in white collar crime cases because of its prominent role in investigating and bringing charges in these cases, at least on the federal level. However, there are two other criminal charging vehicles that warrant discussion: the information and the criminal complaint and warrant.

Information

Zalman and Siegel define an information as a formal written criminal accusation drawn up by a prosecutor setting out the charges against a defendant.[24] In states that do not utilize grand juries, the filing of charges by prosecutors in this manner is the norm. In the federal system, cases are frequently disposed of through the filing of information, but the circumstances giving rise to these filings are usually the result of negotiated plea agreements. A target in an investigation can agree to plea guilty to an information prior to being indicted or a named defendant can do so after being indicted, thus avoiding a trial. As a result of the plea negotiations, the charges outlined in an information that a person agrees to plea guilty to are often (although not always) more limited in scope than what could have been charged, or has actually been charged in a preceding indictment, in recognition of a willingness to plea guilty. Negotiated settlements in cases are discussed in more detail in Chapter 10.

Criminal Complaint and Arrest Warrant

White collar criminal offenders can also be arrested through filing a criminal complaint (with an accompanying investigator affidavit establishing probable cause) with a judge and requesting the issuance of an arrest warrant. In fact, perhaps through media influence, for most laypersons this is the more familiar process in levying criminal charges against an offender. Again, in many state jurisdictions where use of the grand jury system is limited, the complaint and warrant process is a primary mechanism for initiating criminal proceedings against all types of offenders including those accused of white collar crimes. Even in the federal system where all felony charges must be brought via grand jury indictment, there are situations where proceeding initially by a criminal complaint and warrant is necessary. Usually these situations arise incident to exigent circumstances such as the imminent flight of the defendant, an aggravated fact scenario that mandates an immediate intervention, or the culmination of an undercover operation.

Nevertheless, most federal prosecutors are often reluctant to proceed via complaint and warrant in many types of white collar offenses and investigators should share these reasons for their reluctance, as well. First and foremost, causing an arrest starts the "speedy trial" clock ticking, that is, the defendant must be indicted within 30 days of the arrest (18 U.S.C. 3161). While obtaining and presenting sufficient evidence to secure an indictment *might* not be problematic within such a time frame, once it is brought the ability to use grand jury powers to further develop the case is lost. Specifically, grand jury subpoenas can no longer be used to compel witness testimony and acquire records, which can result in a strategic disadvantage to the prosecution. As discussed earlier, prosecutors often use the grand jury to "lock-in" testimony from important witnesses, especially those who might be reluctant or recalcitrant. That advantage is no longer available once an indictment is brought in a case, notwithstanding the fact that trial subpoenas can compel such individuals to appear at trial. Likewise, while trial subpoenas can be used to secure records necessary for presentation at trial proceedings, the ability to obtain these items in advance for careful review and analysis is lost. Both situations can result in the government not being as fully prepared for trial as desired. Conversely, when all pertinent evidence is on hand at the time of indictment, a defendant *might* be more inclined to seek a plea agreement, thus averting a trial.

A second argument against initiating a case through a complaint and warrant is that the defendant is entitled to a preliminary hearing within ten days of the arrest. At this hearing, the government must present probable cause evidence to sustain the arrest. This evidence is usually put forth via investigator testimony and the investigator can be cross-examined by defense counsel. This hearing has the potential to expose aspects of the investigation that would not be advantageous to the prosecution (e.g., existence of informants, cooperating individuals), at least at that point in the formal proceedings.

CHAPTER HIGHLIGHTS

- The grand jury is a forum through which prosecutors present evidence of alleged criminal wrongdoing to a group of citizen jurors whose sole purpose is to determine whether there is probable cause to believe that (1) a crime was, in fact, committed and (2) the subject(s) of the government's investigation committed this crime. If the grand jury believes that the prosecutor has provided them sufficient evidence to establish probable cause in both respects, it returns an indictment, a formal set of criminal charges that the accused must now answer before a trial court. Thus, grand juries unlike trial juries, do not address guilt or innocence per se.[25]

- Federal grand juries consist of 23 individuals, 16 of whom must be present to establish a quorum. Without a quorum present, grand juries cannot hear testimony and/or consider an indictment. Twelve members must vote in favor of an indictment for a grand jury to return a *true bill*, another term for the approval of a formal set of charges by the grand jury. Just as the roles of grand juries on the state level vary, so do their compositions in terms of numbers of jurors.[26] Unlike other court proceedings, grand juries meet in secret and those who are being considered for indictment have no right to be represented by counsel before these proceedings, nor even present for that matter.[27] Grand jurors do have an opportunity to question witnesses who appear before them, usually after the government attorney has done so.[28]

- Grand jury proceedings are not open to the public. To the contrary, grand juries work in secrecy. Grand jury secrecy is important for several reasons: (1) to prevent the escape of persons whose indictments may be contemplated; (2) to ensure freedom of the grand jury in its deliberations; (3) to prevent subornation or perjury or tampering with grand jury witnesses; (4) to encourage free disclosure of information by those who have knowledge of the commission of a crime; and (5) to protect from unfavorable publicity innocent persons who are accused and ultimately exonerated.[29] Under the Federal Rules of Criminal Procedure, the secrecy requirements associated with the grand jury are detailed in Rule 6(e). Generally, this rule prohibits grand jurors, government attorneys, those providing ancillary services to the grand jury such as court reporters and interpreters from disclosing any matter occurring before the grand jury.[30]

- Grand jury subpoenas require *personal* delivery to the intended recipient if proper service is to be effected. Service of grand jury subpoenas to witnesses is an important role for investigators assigned to the case. It is necessary to ensure proper service so that the witness is put on notice of his/her appearance and to effect enforcement proceedings if the witness fails to comply with the subpoena.

- Not to be forgotten amidst this discussion of the use of the grand jury as a charging forum is the fact that other criminal charging vehicles can be utilized in white collar crime cases. Charges can be lodged through the filing of an information (usually incident to a plea agreement) or through filing a criminal complaint with a judge and requesting the issuance of an arrest warrant. It should be noted however that the complaint and warrant alternative is often pursued only in exigent circumstances because of "speedy trial" (18 U.S.C. 3161) and/or preliminary hearing considerations.

CHAPTER BEST PRACTICES

- When the intended recipient is considered to be an uncooperative, hostile, or otherwise reluctant witness, having a second investigator on hand as a witness is a *best practice* to offset any allegations that service was not effected. (See page 175.)

- A *best practice* when there is a realistic chance that service of a grand jury subpoena will be difficult because the intended recipient is viewed as a reluctant or hostile witness is to not approach this task casually. Rather, gathering information about the intended recipient's whereabouts and daily activities/routines in advance may very well save time in the long run. (See page 176.)

- A *best practice* for dealing with potentially troublesome subpoena recipients is to serve them as they depart from their home, as they are about to enter their workplace, or in other public locations they are known to frequent. (See page 177.)

Notes

1. S. S. Beale, W. C. Bryson, J. E. Felman, and M. J. Elston, *Grand Jury Law and Practice*, Vol. 1, 2nd ed. (Eagan, MN: West, 2004), pp. 6–3, 6–4; Reprinted with permission.
2. Administrative Office of the United States District Courts, *Handbook for Federal Grand Jurors*. (Washington, DC: Author, [n.d]), p. 4.
3. J. L. LeGrande, *The Basic Processes of Criminal Justice* (New York: Glencoe Press, 1973), p. 98.
4. G. T. Felkenes, *The Criminal Justice System: Its Functions and Personnel* (Englewood Cliffs, NJ: Prentice Hall, 1973), pp. 230–231
5. M. E. Frankel and G. P. Naftalis, *The Grand Jury: An Institution on Trial* (New York: Hill and Wang, 1977), p. 3.
6. Administrative Office of the United States District Courts, *op. cit.*, p. 4.
7. Felkenes, *op. cit.*, p. 233.
8. Frankel and Naftalis, *op. cit.*, p. 16.

9. Ibid., p. 16.

10. Le Grande, *op. cit.*, p. 100.

11. Administrative Office of the United States District Courts, *op. cit.*, p. 8.

12. R. J. Magnuson, *The White Collar Crime Explosion: How to Protect Yourself and Your Company from Prosecution* (New York: McGraw-Hill, 1992), pp. 131–132.

13. Frankel and Naftalis, *op. cit.*, pp. 20–21.

14. American Bar Association [A project of the Criminal Practice and Procedure Committee of the Antitrust Section; R. V. Hartwell, III and C. J. Mugel, eds], *Handbook on Antitrust Grand Jury Investigations*, 2nd ed. (Chicago: Author, 1988), p. 55.

15. Ibid., p. 57

16. Ibid., p. 54

17. Ibid., p. 71

18. American Bar Association [A project of the Criminal Practice and Procedure Committee of the Antitrust Section; R. V. Hartwell, III and C. J. Mugel, eds], *op. cit.*, p. 62.

19. Ibid., p. 75.

20. Ibid., p. 55.

21. U.S. Department of Justice, *U.S. Attorney's Manual, Criminal Resource Manual, Section 717* (Washington, DC: Author, 1997).

22. Ibid., Section 719.

23. Ibid., Section 719.

24. M. Zalman and L. Siegel, *Criminal Procedure: Constitution and Society* (St. Paul: West, 1991), p. 592.

25. Administrative Office of the United States District Courts, *op. cit.*, p. 4.

26. Frankel and Naftalis, *op. cit.*, p. 16.

27. Le Grande, *op. cit.*, p. 100.

28. Administrative Office of the United States District Courts, *op. cit.*, p. 8.

29. American Bar Association [A project of the Criminal Practice and Procedure Committee of the Antitrust Section; R. V. Hartwell, III and C. J. Mugel, eds], *op. cit.*, p. 55.

30. Ibid., p. 57

Civil and Administrative Investigations

In Chapter 1 we discussed the unresolved controversy about whether white collar crime should include acts that are technically not crimes under any criminal code, but rather violations of civil law or administrative regulations. As you may recall, this book sides with the position taken by American criminologist Edwin Sutherland, who argued for inclusion under the white collar crime umbrella conduct that was illegal but not necessarily criminal. Sutherland observed that much of the conduct he considered white collar crime was not investigated by traditional law enforcement agencies nor adjudicated in the criminal courts. Rather, these offenses were usually handled civilly or administratively, often by regulatory type agencies. However, he felt that most of these types of actions arose because the offenders did engage in the type of conduct that would also constitute a criminal violation, usually in the form of criminal fraud.[1]

More importantly for the purposes here, however, are two realities about white collar crime enforcement generally:

1. Legal proceedings that address civil or regulatory violations are usually dependent upon first gathering the facts and evidence of alleged wrongdoing, meaning that it is necessary to undertake an investigation.

2. In practice, white collar crime enforcement efforts are frequently carried out using a two-pronged attack, that is, employing both civil/administrative and criminal sanctions, when available, in a single case. The advantage gained by employing such a two-pronged approach is that civil/administrative sanctions, when applicable, can often provide a means to halt the offending activity (thereby minimizing

victimization while a possibly time-consuming criminal investigation takes place) and to impose conditions on future conduct upon the individuals and/or organization(s) involved. This latter type of sanction is sometimes an attractive alternative to criminal proceedings against individuals when the case against them is weak, and it also provides oversight and guidance to offending organizations that will continue to operate even after a criminal prosecution.

CIVIL VERSUS ADMINISTRATIVE

For our purposes here, the term *"civil* law or violation" applies to noncriminal enforcement statutes, sanctions, authority, proceedings, and so on that are contained in the federal or state codes, and an appropriate federal or state court has oversight in their application and litigation. An example of civil law enforcement authority has already been introduced in Chapter 6 in the form of 18 U.S.C. 1345, the Injunctions Against Fraud. Recall as well that asset forfeiture has a civil law aspect.

Another civil enforcement statute with potential federal government-wide application is the False Claims Act (31 U.S.C. 3729, et seq.). This act permits the government to seek a civil penalty ranging from $5,000 to $10,000 per violation in addition to three times the amount of damages incurred incident to any person submitting a false or fraudulent claim for payment. A unique feature of this act is that it provides for private citizens, in addition to the government itself, to be plaintiffs if they have evidence of a false or fraudulent claim having been submitted to the government for payment. Such litigation is known as a *qui tam* action and a prevailing private citizen plaintiff can share in the monetary award.[2]

In addition, many other agencies, both state and federal (e.g., the Securities and Exchange Commission, the Postal Service, Federal Trade Commission, and state consumer protection agencies), have civil authority to enjoin offending conduct within their unique jurisdictions and this authority requires them to seek relief through the federal or state court systems.

Conversely, the term *administrative* applies to regulations that (1) govern agency or department operations, including its administration of contracts, grants, and entitlement programs; and (2) provide operational oversight of certain industries and those who work within these industries. Enforcement and sanction provisions are often incorporated into such regulations as a way to deal with misconduct. These regulations and their enforcement and sanctioning provisions are essentially civil laws. Regulatory violators are not exposed to the possibility of incarceration and in fact are usually referred to in administrative enforcement proceedings as respondents, not defendants. The enforcement and sanctioning provisions include fines (sometimes called monetary or civil penalties) and the authority to impose oversight conditions to ensure lawful conduct to prevent any future violations.

In addition to agency-specific administrative authority, the Program Fraud Civil Remedies Act of 1986 (31 U.S.C. 3801, et seq.) can be applied by any federal agency when victimized by false claims relating to any of its programs, including contracts, grants, and entitlements. This act applies only when the amount of the false claim or group of claims when submitted at the same time does not exceed $150,000, thus enabling agencies to use their administrative powers to recoup losses that might not be large enough to warrant intervention by the Justice Department. Penalties can be a fine of up to $5,000 plus twice the amount of the false claim.[3]

Another powerful administrative weapon is the authority to suspend and debar a company from doing business with the government. This type of action, because it can bring about a company's demise, can be as feared and aggressively defended as a criminal proceeding.[4] Unlike laws that are enacted by a legislative body, regulations are usually promulgated by an agency to establish for the public record its operating procedures and, where applicable, to establish rules governing an industry or activity that it has jurisdiction over (e.g., the securities industry, hazardous waste disposal, pharmaceutical manufacturing). Typically, legislative bodies (on the federal level, Congress) will pass laws that provide general guidelines for a particular industry or activity and then authorize/direct the agency with oversight jurisdiction to develop, apply, and enforce regulations that reflect the intent of these laws. This latter process is referred to as "rule making" and is often a collaborative effort between the agency and "interested" members of the public, which usually means the affected industry and sometimes public interest "watchdog" organizations. Upon completion of this process, the regulations are adopted and in the case of federal agencies, they are incorporated into the Code of Federal Regulations (CFR), as opposed to the United States Code.

Unlike criminal and civil laws that are incorporated into the federal or state codes and are litigated in the court system, regulatory litigation and enforcement takes place at the agency level in what are known as administrative law proceedings. These proceedings in many respects mirror procedures that are employed in civil court cases, but the forum involved here is an "administrative court" presided over by an administrative law judge or hearing officer. Moreover, in-house counsel usually represents the agency in these proceedings as opposed to a Department of Justice attorney (or the state equivalent). Thus, agencies with regulatory oversight and enforcement authority maintain their own "court" system, as well.

Although it is important to be mindful of the distinctions being drawn here between the terms *civil* and *administrative*, from a purely investigative perspective they are more similar than different and will be treated somewhat synonymously in this chapter. This assessment is based on the fact that because they are not criminal violations, certain powerful criminal investigative tools cannot be applied in either forum. Another important similarity is that the burden of proof required in the civil and administrative arenas is a preponderance of the evidence (i.e., evidence reasonably tending to prove the essential facts in a case; the greater weight of the evidence)[5] as opposed to the proof beyond a reasonable doubt burden in criminal cases—a difference, however, that does not mean that investigators can do their job less well in pursuing these cases.

CIVIL/ADMINISTRATIVE INVESTIGATIONS—WHAT INVESTIGATIVE TOOLS ARE NOT AVAILABLE?

Investigators whose scope of responsibility lies within the civil/administrative arena do not have at their disposal certain important investigative powers available to those who conduct criminal investigations. To be clear, many agencies responsible for regulatory enforcement possess statutory authority only to conduct civil/administrative investigations, and likewise the investigative personnel employed by such agencies, by virtue of their defined scope of employment, are only permitted to pursue this type of investigation. On the other hand, a number of enforcement agencies are responsible for both criminal and civil/administrative enforcement. While in some situations there may be a bureaucratic separation between the criminal investigative and civil/administrative activities, it would not be uncommon to find criminal investigators, at times, involved in civil/administrative enforcement actions. In fact, criminal investigators who wish to pursue an Injunction Against Fraud under 18 U.S.C. 1345 will quickly find themselves dealing outside of their normal confines and in the civil arena.

In any event, whether investigative authority is limited to civil/administrative or not, one thing that is for certain is that processes and tools commonly used in criminal cases are not available. Most notable in this regard of course is that the powers of the grand jury can only be used in criminal investigations. Thus, the grand jury cannot be used to take testimony from witnesses or to gather evidence in connection with violations that are solely civil or administrative in nature. Search warrants as authorized under Rule 41 of the Federal Rules of Criminal Procedures also cannot be used when investigating solely civil or administrative violations. Nevertheless, it should be noted that some agencies are empowered by law or regulation to conduct on-site compliance inspections, an authority which provides in a civil/administrative context the ability to search for regulatory violations.

Finally, forfeiture authority as defined in Title 18 of the U.S. Code (see Chapter 6) applies only to select criminal statutes and not to civil/administrative violations, even though forfeiture action, itself, can be taken through civil means. However, final resolutions in civil/administrative cases can sometimes include disgorgement of ill-gotten gains, a result not unlike a forfeiture action.

However, as suggested at the outset of this chapter, it is not unusual for white collar crime to be addressed through a two-pronged attack that incorporates both criminal and civil/administrative actions and taking this approach should be considered a *best practice* when circumstances permit. Thus, it would be incorrect to view criminal and civil/administrative investigators operating as totally separate entities with no interaction. On the contrary, many regulatory agencies are in routine contact and/or work with criminal agencies with whom they share mutual interests. For instance, the Securities and Exchange Commission (SEC), although it pursues its own regulatory investigations and takes enforcement actions under this authority, regularly makes referrals to criminal investigative agencies when it believes criminal fraud and securities laws have been violated. Moreover, it is not uncommon for SEC personnel, because of their expertise, to assist in any subsequent criminal investigation. These kinds of criminal–regulatory relationships, while generally beneficial from an enforcement perspective, have posed both legal and operational problems vis-à-vis the sharing of information gathered under differing authorities (especially with regard to grand jury information). On the other hand, the two-pronged attack that often emanates from these relationships can create "thorny" issues for defendants and their attorneys. Arising from this milieu is the concept of parallel proceedings, a topic that will be discussed at the conclusion of this chapter. Suffice it to say for now, however, that sharing of information between criminal and civil/administrative investigators can be lawfully accomplished within certain boundaries, thus to some extent minimizing the investigative limitations that are encountered within the civil/administrative forum.

WHAT INVESTIGATIVE TOOLS ARE AVAILABLE IN CIVIL/ADMINISTRATIVE CASES?

Although the grand jury and search warrants issued in criminal cases are powerful tools, as discussed at length in earlier chapters, there are other viable and important ways to gather documentary and testimonial evidence in white collar crime cases, whether criminal or civil/administrative. In addition, techniques commonly associated with criminal investigations can often be employed in civil/administrative cases. For instance, the use of forensic science, undercover techniques, and even consensual electronic surveillance are possibilities to consider, barring limitations imposed by agency policies and statutory prohibitions. Finally, many regulatory agencies possess authority, although often limited to within the scope of their jurisdiction, to acquire records, conduct inspections, and/or take testimony from witnesses. Let's consider each of these tools a little further.

Information from the Public

As may be recalled, a good deal of discussion was devoted at the outset of this volume to establishing a well-publicized, accessible complaint and information gathering system. Although such a system is recommended for all white collar crime investigative organizations, when grand jury and search warrant powers are not available as information gathering tools, the acquisition of needed testimony and records from the public on a voluntary basis is especially important. Moreover, for those agencies whose jurisdiction involves general public victimization (as opposed to victimization of select industry groups or government programs, etc.) the value of receiving complaints and information in this manner is even more pronounced. As covered earlier, it is often necessary to take affirmative steps in identifying white collar crime victims, that is, not simply relying on voluntarily submitted complaints. Unfortunately, when conducting civil/administrative investigations, identifying victims through records seized with a search warrant or obtained via a grand jury subpoena will not be options. Thus, voluntary submission of complaints and information by victims can become a primary source of witness identification and testimony and documentary evidence, both of which will have a great bearing on the success or failure of the investigation.

Documentary Evidence

In Chapter 3 we discussed the availability and collection of documentary evidence at length. Without reiterating this discussion in its entirety, it may be helpful to review some important points along these lines. First, a wealth of information lies in the public domain and it is often important to fully exploit *all* possibilities within this domain when other means of gathering documentary evidence are not available. Certainly, court records and government mandated financial and licensure filings are well-known sources to investigators. It is worthwhile to become familiar with state public disclosure laws. These vary from state to state, and in some states are so liberal that most information maintained by that state and the municipal agencies lying within its boundaries is subject to public disclosure. While it is *essential* for an investigator to develop expertise in accessing routinely used public records, it is the mark of an experienced, skilled investigator to identify useful and needed records held in government files that lie outside of his/her normal information network.

Also, do not dismiss the value of media reports. At the very least, media reports can provide a summary and sometimes details of the wrongdoing, the identities of the alleged wrongdoers and possibly statements made by them, as well as the identities of victims and other witnesses. While the facts in these reports may or may not be confirmed through subsequent investigation, these reports should not be ignored. Just as it is easy to rely on routinely accessed government records, this could become the case with exposure to media sources as well. Thus, it is recommended that investigators expand their media exposure to include highly specialized and perhaps obscure sources, whether in print or electronic formats (e.g., websites, television, radio).

Finally, there are two old standbys that are frequently overlooked in our high tech era. First, investigators can always simply ask for the records they are interested in, or information from those records. Even when you expect the answer to be "no," sometimes you may be pleasantly surprised. Second, do not forget to check the phonebook or online phone directories for addresses and phone numbers!

Nonpublic Documentary Evidence

In addition to publicly available documents, keep in mind that many government agencies are able to disclose nonpublic information to other government organizations that are carrying out lawful enforcement functions, whether criminal or civil/administrative. Again, the key issue here is to become familiar with what is available and how to go about obtaining it. Sometimes it might be a matter of a phone call or e-mail while at other times a written request on agency letterhead will be required.

While much documentary information can be gathered through public and government sources, those conducting civil/administrative investigations are, nevertheless, likely to encounter limitations that are routinely overcome in criminal investigations through the issuance of grand jury subpoenas. However, many agencies have been granted administrative summons or subpoena power as an alternative. For instance, Inspector General agencies possess administrative subpoena authority to compel production of all information, reports, answers, records, accounts, papers, and other documentary evidence necessary to perform their investigative functions. They can be used to obtain both personal records and corporate records, those of contractors and subcontractors, and those in the hands of third parties. However, these subpoenas, unlike grand jury subpoenas, cannot be used to compel testimony. There is no probable cause or other standard to determine under what circumstances a subpoena maybe issued. Challenging these subpoenas and/or enforcing compliance with them must be pursued through the appropriate federal district court.[6] However, be aware that such challenges can require agent testimony that could reveal details about the nature and full scope of the investigation.[7]

Service of Civil and Administrative Summons or Subpoenas

The Federal Rules of Civil Procedure (Rules 4 and 5) allow for civil process including subpoenas to be served on the intended recipient, his or her attorney, or left with a person described as being of suitable age and discretion, who resides in the dwelling known to be the residence or place of abode of the intended recipient.

Guidance in the proper service of administrative summons and subpoenas should be sought through the legal counsel of the issuing agency due to possible variations in policies and procedures. For example, administrative subpoenas issued in connection with health care fraud investigations under Title 18 of the United States Code, Section 3486, require that personal service must be effected upon individuals while service to corporations, partnerships, and other unincorporated business associations is to be made upon an officer, managing or general agent, or any other agent authorized by appointment or law to receive service of process. On the other hand, administrative subpoenas issued under Section 3016 of Title 39, United States Code, in connection with Postal Service false representation investigations provide for service by registered or certified mail to both individuals and business entities, in addition to personal service. In the case of business entities too, these subpoenas can also be left at the principal office or place of business of that entity.

Although civil/administrative investigations in most cases might not arouse the level of avoidance and/or hostility sometimes associated with criminal investigations and grand jury subpoenas, investigators should nevertheless evaluate this potential and take any steps necessary (as described in the prior chapter) to ensure timely and proper service.

Testimonial Evidence

The primary information gathering tool available in civil/administrative investigations, at least at the outset, is interviewing individuals who are believed to have knowledge that would be useful to the investigation. Again, there will be no complete reiteration at this point of the material covered earlier concerning interviewing in white collar crime cases. Rather, mention will be made only of certain unique features that are present in the civil/administrative context as well as important considerations relative to reducing verbal statements to writing.

Fifth Amendment issues that often have to be considered when conducting interviews incident to criminal investigations will probably be less of a concern in civil/administrative cases if the inquiries being made relate solely to noncriminal, as opposed to criminal, matters. Of course, this statement assumes that there is, in fact, no related or companion criminal investigation (a topic that will be discussed in more detail at the conclusion of this chapter). Also, it must be recalled that the Fifth Amendment privilege against self-incrimination is personal in nature and applies only to custodial situations (see Chapter 4). Thus, within a purely civil or administrative context, culpable individuals cannot "hide" behind the Fifth Amendment, although they can still simply refuse to cooperate and be interviewed. Importantly, however, individuals and business entities who participate in many government programs or regulated industries are required by law to cooperate with investigators from the agency with oversight responsibility, or face sanctions.[8] Thus, investigators must be fully conversant with their agency policies and procedures so that they can take full advantage of their lawful powers, especially when criminal investigative tools are not available. Normally, agency training programs delve into these specifics.

As discussed earlier when considering interviews generally, whether to take a written statement incident to an interview will vary with the circumstances. Although agency policy might dictate otherwise, it is often best for investigators to obtain written statements only if there is some reason to believe that important information being provided might not be repeated in the future due to lack of cooperation, anticipated memory failure due to the passage of time, and/or possible unavailability of the witness. Even in these circumstances, caution must be exercised with regard to obtaining a complete and accurate written statement. Often, especially early in the investigative process and/or in complex fact scenarios, evaluating whether a statement is complete and accurate can be difficult. Finally, since a statement that is personally authored and written will carry greater credibility, care must be taken to ensure that it clearly communicates the information that the person has verbally provided so that it is not open to alternate interpretations.

There are provisions within the Federal Rules of Civil Procedure and the Administrative Procedures Act (see 5 U.S.C. 556) that permit taking depositions incident to civil and administrative litigation, respectively. A subpoena to submit to a deposition can be issued by the appropriate presiding judicial official (i.e., a district court judge or administrative law judge) upon application by counsel for a party to the litigation and sworn testimony is then taken from the witness. Unlike a grand jury proceeding, counsel can represent the witness during the questioning, which can involve interceding on the witness's behalf to some extent during the questioning. The Federal Rules of Civil Procedure also provide for interrogatories, which are written responses to questions submitted by an opposing party in a civil litigation.

Obviously, depositions and interrogatories are a means to gather testimonial evidence in civil and administrative cases and their application should be discussed with appropriate government counsel. Again, one word of caution when dealing in the civil/administrative arena: investigators can be deposed by the opposing party during which they can be questioned under oath about the case, a line of inquiry that could be problematic for any parallel criminal investigation. In these circumstances, this potential should be fully discussed by all those involved on the government side. One possible remedy is to purposely separate the two investigative efforts and restrict the flow of information about the criminal case to those on the civil/administrative side, thus limiting any statements they can make about this aspect of the case. As will be discussed at the conclusion of this chapter, this strategy may also be necessary to address other problems that can arise in parallel proceedings.

Forensic Science

In Chapter 7 we discussed the application of forensic science to white collar crime investigations. Although this discussion was generally framed within the context of criminal investigations, evidence developed through forensic examination could also be very useful in civil/administrative cases as well. However, three caveats apply. First, evidentiary items that are to undergo forensic examination must be lawfully obtained. While investigators conducting civil/administrative investigations are not without means to accomplish this, we often think of recovering or acquiring evidence for forensic examination through search warrants and grand jury subpoenas. For instance, obtaining known handwriting exemplars or fingerprints through the grand jury process will not be available here. Nevertheless, items for forensic examination in civil/administrative cases can be surrendered voluntarily or might be obtained through an administrative subpoena or summons. Moreover, as suggested above and to be discussed before we conclude this chapter, there are lawful ways to use evidence collected through the grand jury process in civil/administrative investigations. Finally, one of the hallmarks of the skilled investigator is to find legal ways to acquire needed evidence. Known handwriting can sometimes be obtained from secondary sources such as documents authored/completed by the person of interest. Fingerprints may be on file and available through a government agency.

Second, agencies with only civil/administrative authority might not have ready access to a law enforcement or other government-sponsored forensic laboratory and there could be prohibitions within some forensic laboratories against becoming involved in noncriminal matters, if only because of resource limitations. When agencies do not have their own forensic capability, efforts should be made to establish a relationship with a competent lab. Although most forensic labs have ample workloads, sometimes through personal networking and liaison, an ad hoc or limited working relationship can be crafted. While it would seem that undertaking such efforts would lie within the realm of agency supervisors and managers, a *good* investigator with excellent interpersonal skills can often be an outstanding agency ambassador, a role that is sometimes able to secure arrangements that elude upper echelon bureaucrats. In any event, the time to establish a relationship with a forensic laboratory is not when a pressing need arises. Rather, these needs should be anticipated and planned for in advance, as any other required and/or anticipated investigative resource.

Of course, another option with regard to acquiring forensic services is to hire qualified private experts, with an emphasis placed on the descriptor *qualified*. While government forensic labs in recent years have come under scrutiny, there continues to be an accepted level of confidence in the services provided. If private forensic services are retained, the bona fides of such experts should undergo thorough verification. Thus, under this scenario as well, it is best to anticipate a need for forensic services and make these arrangements in advance.

The third and final caveat is to determine whether by statute or agency policy the use of forensic examination generally or particular types is prohibited. Some agencies might find the use of forensic examinations a "foreign" concept and be quick to rule, "We don't do that!" Absent some type of statutory prohibition, that type of response might warrant a diplomatic educational effort by investigators who simply want to do their jobs well and have the latest tools to work with.

Undercover Techniques

Before anyone gets too agitated about linking the term "undercover" with civil/administrative investigations, limitations and definitions will be put forth. First, agency policy and perhaps statutory prohibitions might make this discussion moot in some contexts. However, even when such approaches are permissible, the training and scope of employment of investigators with solely civil/administrative authority might also be limiting factors in adopting these approaches. However, the term *undercover techniques* can be defined as simply a government agent assuming a fictitious private citizen identity and acquiring information that is being made available to members of the public. Thus, an investigator can establish a fictitious name and an address he or she controls (e.g., post office box or mail receiving agency address). Information about suspect promotions that are being publicly advertised can be requested to be sent to this name at the address set up for this purpose. Moreover, orders for the suspect product or service can also be submitted using this name and address. Thus, investigators can personally acquire evidentiary material that can be used in subsequent proceedings.

Likewise, some suspect promotions might be offered at public gatherings, through personal telephone contact or one-on-one meetings. Attending a public gathering–type meeting might require a fictitious name and address for registration purposes. In any event, investigators would need to pay careful attention to the proceedings, making mental notes of the representations being made. Unless others in the crowd are taking notes as well, it would be unwise for an investigator to do so. Rather, notes reflecting the date, time, location, content, and identities of those hosting the meeting should be made immediately after its conclusion once privacy can be acquired. In fact, dictating these notes into a tape recorder might provide the best immediate method to memorialize these proceedings. In this type of scenario it would be wise to be cognizant of the impact the proceedings are having on other participants. For example, if other participants seem to be swayed by the misrepresentations being made by virtue of their statements or gestures, these observations should be reflected in the notes of the meeting.

Telephone conversations with promoters of suspect products or services can also provide valuable evidence, but again how to capture the content must be considered and planned for. First, a telephone and number must be established for this purpose. Whether using a stationary phone or a cell phone, ensure that the telephone number is not identified as belonging to any government entity nor to any government employee. The alternatives available usually are to establish phone service in a fictitious name or simply program the phone/number to so that outgoing calls are shown as "private caller" (although be mindful that some recipients of phone calls will block such numbers). In any event, it is again imperative that notes of phone conversations including dates, times, names of parties involved, and content of the conversations need to be immediately memorialized at the conclusion so that no details are omitted due to the passage of time.

Meeting one-on-one in an undercover capacity with the subjects of an investigation could be problematic for non–criminal enforcement personnel, even if this approach is not barred by statute. The primary issues of concern here would be questions about training and safety. Although the more nefarious aspects of undercover work might not be present given the nature of the circumstances and individuals involved in many civil/administrative cases, investigators should be trained in this technique before undertaking any such operation. It would be especially important for such meetings to be observed and monitored by other investigators and to have a plan for intervening if the safety of the undercover investigator is compromised. The problem this latter concern raises is that civil/administrative investigators usually are not armed nor do they possess other police-type powers (e.g., power of arrest) in the event physical intervention becomes necessary. Even in the context of a one-on-one routine sales call, proper planning for undercover meetings requires that investigator safety be a primary consideration.

Electronic Surveillance

Again, for some agencies, employing this technique might be out of the question due to legal or policy constraints. Moreover, any comments expressed here apply only to the federal sector.

Section 2511 in Title 18 of the United States Code permits "a person acting under color of law to intercept a wire, oral, or electronic communication, where such person is a party to the communication or one of the parties to the communication has given prior consent to such interception" (paragraph 2c). Thus, under this statute an investigator conducting a civil/administrative investigation can lawfully record a conversation he or she has with an investigative subject. For many agencies whose authority is limited to the civil/administrative arena, it might be realistic to operate within this statute only for the purpose of recording telephone conversations. The equipment necessary to do so is commonly available and inexpensive, unlike the more sophisticated and expensive equipment typically employed in face-to-face undercover meetings. Moreover, the warnings about engaging in one-on-one undercover meetings as discussed earlier are reiterated here. Successfully employing this approach requires investigator training and a viable plan to ensure safety for all investigators involved, which considers how physical intervention, if necessary, will be carried out.

Covertly recording the proceedings of public meetings could be undertaken although effectively accomplishing this can be problematic. Background noise in a large-room setting or out of doors can make the recording of pertinent speakers' voices inaudible, even when using sophisticated surveillance equipment. When attempting to record a public meeting, it is wise to also prepare notes that reflect the statements made because the quality of the recording might not be immediately known.

Whenever electronic surveillance techniques are employed it is important to treat the recordings obtained as evidentiary material. A duplicate of the tape recording should be made for "working" purposes, which includes the preparation of a transcript. The original tape recording should be stored consistent with agency evidence procedures so that its authenticity can be attested to at any type of litigation proceeding. Written notes should be made regarding the time, place, location, identities of persons involved, and recording equipment used.

Two final words of caution about electronic surveillance or the fruits thereof, which were echoed in Chapter 4, will be reiterated here. First, paragraph 2(d) in Section 2511 of Title 18 permits private citizens to record conversations with others, either with all parties consenting or just one party consenting (i.e., the party recording conversation, unbeknownst to the other party). Unlike federal law, many states prohibit private citizens from recording conversations without both parties consenting. An enterprising citizen who takes it upon himself or herself to record a conversation with someone suspected of wrongdoing (or so they believe) without their knowledge and then turns it over to authorities could be creating two types of problems: (1) depending upon the state where this act occurred, he or she might have committed a criminal act; and (2) government use of such evidence thereafter *might* be challenged.

Second, an investigator could request a cooperating private citizen to record a telephone conversation without the investigator being present, a scenario that might be attractive if a call is anticipated, but at an unknown time; and it also protects the citizen from any allegation of illegal conduct since he/she would be acting on behalf of the government. However, the investigator must ensure the cooperating citizen can properly operate the recording equipment and does not use the equipment for any other purpose. Also, it should be impressed on the cooperating citizen to make written notes of the time and date of the call.

In summary, while 18 U.S.C. 2511 would seemingly permit electronic surveillance techniques in civil/administrative cases, investigations must be guided by agency policies and/or any overriding statutory prohibitions. When no such obstacles exist, these techniques can afford valuable evidence-gathering opportunities.

PARALLEL PROCEEDINGS

> A grand jury investigation seldom takes place in a vacuum. Particularly when a regulatory or white collar offense is under investigation, the grand jury's efforts are often accompanied by a parallel civil or administrative proceeding.[9]

This observation supports the argument put forth at the beginning of this chapter that white collar crime investigations are often a two-pronged attack. Very often in white collar crime cases, two or more investigative organizations become involved in examining essentially the same misconduct. In a typical scenario, an agency with regulatory oversight authority either through complaints or its own compliance apparatus becomes aware of civil/administrative violations. Under its authority, the regulatory agency would pursue its own investigation with a view toward imposing sanctions it has available, usually at the outset an injunctive action to halt the offending activity. During the course of this civil/administrative investigation, evidence of criminal misconduct that is an outgrowth of the activity already being examined may be revealed and is turned over to an appropriate criminal investigative agency. Alternatively, a criminal investigative agency might receive complaints or other information through its own sources that causes it to open a criminal case and then seeks to coordinate with a regulatory agency that has authority and expertise in that area of the investigation.

Either scenario gives rise to potential problems that have been alluded to, both in our discussion of the grand jury and in this present chapter. These problems largely stem from grand jury considerations, especially Rule 6(e). Thus, it is appropriate to conclude our focus on civil/administrative investigations with a more detailed discussion of how and to what extent these types of cases can merge with criminal investigations.

The overriding consideration is that grand juries can only be used for criminal investigations and thus cannot be used to pursue violations that are purely civil/administrative in nature.[10] Conversely, information developed through the grand jury incident to a criminal investigation is generally subject to the secrecy provisions of Rule 6(e), thus establishing at least an initial obstacle in its application to civil/administrative cases.

Let's consider what is permissible when civil/administrative and criminal investigations are focusing on the same misconduct/subjects. First and foremost, there is no prohibition against different government agencies cooperating in parallel investigations even if one is handling the civil end and the other the criminal. In fact, prior to any grand jury proceeding, the civil agency may be purposely assigned to develop evidence for the ultimate use in criminal investigation as long as it is doing so within the scope of its investigative authority. After a grand jury investigation begins, this flow of information usually is restricted to the extent that the civil agency can still provide information to the criminal investigators, but not vice versa because then the grand jury could be construed as being used for civil purposes. Part of the rationale for not limiting what the criminal investigation can receive from the civil investigation is that the grand jury's powers can usually reach anything that can be obtained civilly anyway.[11] A second bit of good news is that information developed through the grand jury can be authorized for use in civil proceedings through an application to the court that has oversight of the particular grand jury.[12]

So what is the "bad" news? For starters, parallel proceedings have been challenged on the grounds that a defendant's Fifth Amendment privilege against self-incrimination has been violated. This issue can arise when a defendant wants to assert the Fifth Amendment in defense of a criminal violation, but by doing so cannot defend himself/herself in the civil case. In another Fifth Amendment scenario, confusion over the dual nature of an investigation arises when the government approaches an individual and makes inquiries incident to a civil investigation when in fact there is also a criminal investigation underway as well that she/he doesn't know about. This can result in the individual providing statements/information that might not have been made if the existence of a criminal inquiry had been known. Here, however, courts have ruled that the government does not have to disclose during a civil inquiry the existence of a criminal prosecution as long as they do not make affirmative misrepresentations about the scope of the investigation, that is, state their inquiries are only civil in nature and there is no criminal probe, when they know this not to be the case.[13]

Defendants can also raise a discovery issue when the government uses the civil proceeding to obtain evidence for criminal use that they would not otherwise be able to acquire. Courts can order stays of civil discovery proceedings to remedy this situation.[14]

THE NEED FOR THE TWO-PRONGED ATTACK

Under the broad concept of white collar crime supported here, it is clear that agencies with solely civil/administrative authority play a major enforcement role in this realm. Moreover, civil/administrative white collar crime enforcement takes place not only on the federal level, but on the state level as well. While successful enforcement actions taken in these forums are generally at the preponderance of evidence level (as opposed to the more burdensome criminal standard of proof beyond a reasonable doubt), investigators also have fewer investigative tools at their disposal. Hopefully, our discussion in this chapter has dispelled any notion that civil/administrative investigators have their "hands tied behind their backs." Making aggressive use of standard investigative techniques together with frequently available specialized statutory authority offers opportunities for effective enforcement. Moreover, when these civil/administrative investigations and the enforcement actions that can be taken through them are teamed with criminal prosecutions, the end result can be a halt and remedy to public harm as well as punishment to the offenders.

CHAPTER HIGHLIGHTS

- For our purposes here, the term "*civil* law or violation" applies to non–criminal enforcement statutes, sanctions, authority, proceedings, and so on that are contained in the federal or state codes, and an appropriate federal or state court has oversight in their application and litigation. Conversely, the term *administrative* applies to regulations that (1) govern agency or department operations, including its administration of contracts, grants, and entitlement programs; and (2) provide operational oversight of certain industries and those who work within these industries. Enforcement and sanction provisions are often incorporated into such regulations as a way to deal with misconduct. These regulations and their enforcement and sanctioning provisions are essentially civil laws. Regulatory violators are not exposed to the possibility of incarceration and in fact are usually referred to in administrative enforcement proceedings as respondents, not defendants. The enforcement and sanctioning provisions include fines (sometimes called monetary or civil penalties), debarment, and the authority to impose oversight conditions to ensure lawful conduct to prevent any future violations.

- "A grand jury investigation seldom takes place in a vacuum. Particularly when a regulatory or white collar offense is under investigation, the grand jury's efforts are often accompanied by a parallel civil or administrative proceeding."[15] An overriding consideration is that grand juries can only be used for criminal investigations and thus cannot be used to pursue violations that are purely civil/administrative in nature.[16] Conversely, information developed through the grand jury incident to a criminal investigation is generally subject to the secrecy provisions of Rule 6(e), thus establishing at least an initial obstacle in its application to civil/administrative cases.

- Let's consider what is permissible when civil/administrative and criminal investigations are focusing on the same misconduct/subjects. First and foremost, there is no prohibition against different government agencies cooperating in parallel investigations even if one is handling the civil end and the other the criminal.[17] A second bit of good news is that information developed through the grand jury can be authorized for use in civil proceedings through an application to the court that has oversight of the particular grand jury.[18]

- Hopefully, our discussion in this chapter has dispelled any notion that civil/administrative investigators have their "hands tied behind their backs." Making aggressive use of standard investigative techniques together with frequently available specialized statutory authority offers opportunities for effective enforcement.

CHAPTER BEST PRACTICE

- However, as suggested at the outset of this chapter, it is not unusual for white collar crime to be addressed through a two-pronged attack that incorporates both criminal and civil/administrative actions and taking this approach should be considered a *best practice* when circumstances permit. (See page 197.)

Notes

1. E. Sutherland, "White collar criminality," *American Sociological Review*, Vol. 5, No. 1, 1940, pp. 1–12.
2. S. A. Warnke and C. D. Kirby, "Health care fraud and abuse," in O. G. Obermaier and R. G. Morvillo, eds., *White Collar Crime: Business and Regulatory Offenses*, Vol. 2 (New York: Law Journal Press, 2005), pp. 19–29.
3. P. B. Galvani and G. M. Coburn, "Government contract fraud: Detecting it and controlling the damage," in O. G. Obermaier and R. G. Morvillo, eds., *White Collar Crime: Business and Regulatory Offenses*, Vol. 1 (New York: Law Journal Press, 2005), pp. 7–28, 29.
4. R. J. Magnuson, *The White Collar Crime Explosion: How to Protect Yourself and Your Company From Prosecution* (New York: McGraw-Hill, 1992), p. 140.
5. M. Zalman, *Criminal Procedure: Constitution and Society*, 4th ed. (Upper Saddle River, NJ: Prentice Hall, 2005), p. 97.
6. N. A. Kaplan, P. L. Friedman, R. S. Bennett, and H. C. Trainor, eds., *Parallel Grand Jury and Administrative Agency Investigations* (Chicago: American Bar Association, 1981), pp. 283–284.
7. Magnuson, *op. cit.*, p. 147.
8. Kaplan, Friedman, Bennett, and Trainor, eds., *op. cit.*, p. 283.
9. S. S. Beale, W. C. Bryson, J. E. Felman, and M. J. Elston, *Grand Jury Law and Practice*, Vol. 2, 2nd ed. (Eagan, MN: West, 2004), p. 10–1.
10. Ibid., p. 10–2
11. Ibid., pp. 10–6,7
12. Ibid., pp. 10–2,3
13. Ibid., pp. 10–3,4
14. Ibid., pp. 10–3,4
15. Ibid., p. 10–1.
16. Ibid., p. 10–2.
17. Ibid., pp. 10–6,7.
18. Ibid., pp. 10–2,3.

Reaching a Disposition

Appropriately, this final chapter covers the concluding investigative steps in bringing a white collar crime case to a resolution. It will begin with a discussion on preparing a comprehensive investigative report that is submitted to a prosecutor and is a basis upon which a prosecutive decision is made. An overview of possible outcomes that can arise incident to the completion of the investigation will then be provided, followed by a discussion of the roles investigators play in the concluding phases of most cases.

The preparation of such a report should not be an unanticipated step in any investigation, but the necessary content items in a white collar crime case are somewhat unique. What may be unanticipated is that submitting this report is not the end of the investigator's role in the case, but rather marks a transition point whereby the prosecutor's role becomes primary and the investigator's role becomes supportive. As discussed early in this volume, a *best practice* in white collar crime cases is to seek prosecutor involvement early in an investigation and to work as a joint team from the outset. During the investigative phase, prosecutors learn the case and its cast of characters as they develop, and provide legal guidance and support as needed. However, once the investigation is complete, prosecutors make charging decisions and handle any ensuing litigation. While the investigator may no longer be at center stage at this point, his/her work on the case is far from complete and continues to be crucial to the case's outcome. These responsibilities will be discussed later.

Before addressing these topics, however, be forewarned that for the sake of simplicity some liberties were taken with regard to applying certain terms to the entire spectrum of the white collar crime enforcement and litigation process. For instance, the term *prosecutor* as used here applies to all types of government attorneys who are responsible for litigating enforcement actions, even though enforcement attorneys in some regulatory agencies might bear other titles. The term *defendant* as used here will be the label for any individual/business entity against whom an enforcement action is being sought, notwithstanding the fact that in regulatory actions, respondent is most often the appropriate term used to identify the alleged offending party. Finally, the term *trial* will be the universal label for the judicial proceeding where the charges in the case are ultimately and fully litigated. Again, in regulatory actions, the title of this type of proceeding might vary.

REPORTING THE RESULTS

Investigative agencies usually have mandated reporting requirements and formats that obviously must be observed. These reporting requirements may entail both periodic progress reports as well as a comprehensive investigative report that is submitted to the prosecutor. The suggestions put forth here focus on the latter-type report only, and could serve as a guide in developing an appropriate format for white collar crime cases or perhaps to supplement existing procedures. To be clear, however, the format being recommended and discussed here for a final comprehensive investigative report is narrative in style as opposed to a data entry or fill-in-the blanks format. These latter formats are simply inadequate to report the details and intricacies of a white collar crime.

Why a Comprehensive Report?

Many agency managers would cringe at such a question since investigative reports seem to be part of the standard bureaucratic requirements of most law enforcement organizations. To be sure, it is the responsibility of law enforcement managers to provide oversight and quality control to agency cases and to stay informed about investigators' activities. Investigative reports help managers meet their responsibility in this regard. A final comprehensive investigative report is an important quality control mechanism to evaluate the work of investigators, especially since these reports are submitted outside the agency and are a basis upon which a prosecutive decision will be made. As agencies typically expend considerable resources in investigating a white collar crime, it is in their interest and the public's interest that the cases be fully and competently investigated and the reports of these investigations that are submitted to prosecutors be well written and contain all the pertinent information. So for starters, the comprehensive investigative report is important for "in-house" agency purposes.

Second, the comprehensive investigative report is important for its intended purpose, that is, to provide details of an investigation to a prosecutor so that a determination can be made about taking an enforcement action. Granted, in many instances prosecutors are involved in white collar crime cases early in the investigations and thus are not unfamiliar with many of the facts contained in the report. However, having all the evidence gathered and pertinent facts presented in one report is often helpful for prosecutors in evaluating the merits of the case in terms of prosecution, especially in investigations that extend over lengthy periods of time. And while early prosecutor involvement is the encouraged *best practice* put forth here, it may in fact, not be a custom followed by all investigative and prosecutive agencies. Alternatively, in some locales or jurisdictions it might not be a practice employed·for all types of white collar crime cases, for example, prosecutor involvement might not be sought in cases of lesser victim loss and/or complexity until the investigation is complete. In these latter scenarios, the final comprehensive investigative report might very well be a prosecutor's first introduction to the case, a situation that accentuates the need for these reports to be complete and well written.

A final answer to the "Why a comprehensive report?" question is that the preparation of these reports serves as an excellent evaluation tool or "checklist" for the investigator. Preparing this report will require the investigator to bring together a great deal of information, sometimes gathered over months (or even years!), in an effort to tell a story about a white collar crime offense and to provide the evidence available to prove it. This process forces the investigator to review information and evidence gathered, evaluate it, and organize it in a manner that will accomplish these tasks. Equally important is that this process will help to highlight any deficiencies, questions, and/or "holes" in the case, that is, areas that need to be "shored-up" through further investigation before the case is actually presented to the prosecutor. Finally, preparing this report should force the investigator to consider defenses that will be encountered and to identify information/evidence that is available or needs to be developed to overcome them.

Thus, a final comprehensive investigative report serves three purposes: (1) It informs agency management about the case, monitors investigative work and performance, and it is a necessary quality-control tool; (2) it provides the prosecuting agency with a complete report of the investigation which can be used to make a prosecutive decision and as a guide in preparing charges and litigating the case; and (3) preparing the report is a helpful exercise for the investigator because she/he must bring together and organize all the evidence, areas requiring further investigation will become apparent, and defenses can be identified.

A COMPREHENSIVE INVESTIGATIVE REPORT: ESSENTIAL COMPONENTS

While exact formats and section headings can vary, the following paragraphs discuss topics pertinent for inclusion in a comprehensive investigative report of a white collar crime. The rationale for the sequencing of these topics will be presented although there may be alternatives to this sequencing depending upon the nature of the case and/or agency desires. Again, however, the only format-related requirement envisioned here is that it be in narrative style.

A Quick Introduction

A brief opening paragraph should quickly introduce the investigation, the nature of the offense, name(s) of offender(s) (both individual and business entities), the time period over which the offense occurred, number of victims (including type of victims, if appropriate), and amount of losses. The purpose of this paragraph is to inform the reader, in summary fashion, of the nature of the case that is outlined in the remainder of the report. Especially where this report serves as a prosecutor's first introduction to a case, where there has been a change in prosecutors during the course of the investigation or prosecutor involvement has been intermittent, and/or when dealing with a prosecutor's office with a heavy workload, the information contained in these few sentences often determines whether a case is placed on the "front burner" or on the far corner of the desk. This reality often has little to do with the quality of the investigation and whether the case can be prosecuted successfully. More likely, such decisions are based on prevailing prosecutive priorities (which are often driven by "political winds"), unique fact scenarios, and/or aggravating features such as a recidivist offender(s), sympathetic (e.g., elderly) or high-profile victims (e.g., celebrities), and large dollar losses. Obviously, the facts of a case are what they are and cannot be altered to enhance prosecutor interest. When cases do possess features that enhance prosecutive merit, they should be highlighted and this can be appropriately accomplished in the introductory paragraph. To be clear, however, many white collar crimes are prosecuted that are not high-profile cases. Having said that, some prosecutor's offices have imposed minimum dollar loss thresholds to be used as a guide for accepting or declining a case for prosecution. Thus, to revisit an earlier area of emphasis, it becomes very important to identify all victims and thereby capture all available dollar losses. Box 10–1 below provides a sample introductory paragraph for a fictitious case.

In the three sentences below, the reader is quickly informed of

1. The nature of the case, thus readily identifying any prosecutive priorities or unique crimes;
2. The identity of the alleged offender, in the event this person is a recidivist or otherwise noteworthy;
3. Where the alleged crime took place to establish jurisdiction and the period over which it occurred to determine when the statute of limitations will expire;
4. Who the victim is and how much was lost.

Box 10–1   Introductory paragraph in a comprehensive investigative report

Introduction

Outlined in this report are the details of a false billing and kickback scheme that victimized the federal Medicare program, perpetrated by Ken E. Walk, d/b/a Mobility for All, Inc., located in Chicago, IL. Incident to providing durable medical equipment including wheelchairs and motorized scooters to Medicare beneficiaries (most of whom were elderly and disabled) between January 2004 and June 2006, Walk submitted bills for reimbursement for equipment that was neither requested nor furnished to Medicare beneficiaries, resulting in payments to him totaling $520,000. Over this period, Walk also paid kickbacks to physicians totally $60,000 for the referral of patients for whom he provided wheel chairs and motorized scooters at Medicare expense.

Identifying the Offender(s)

This section of the report provides necessary personal/corporate data about the offender(s) and should bear an appropriate label such as "Alleged Offenders," "Proposed Defendants," "Proposed Respondent," and so on. It is placed immediately following the Introduction because it fully identifies the subject(s) of the investigation that will be discussed in the following section. The information furnished should include (but is not limited to):

1. Full Name (include officers/directors for corporate offenders);
2. Known Aliases (for corporate offenders include all names under which the corporation does business);
3. Residential and/or Business Addresses;
4. Occupation/Nature of Business Activity;
5. Date of Birth (individual defendants);
6. Social Security Number/Taxpayer Identification Number; Provider Number, or applicable licensure number, and so on;
7. Marital Status and Number of Children (individual offenders);
8. FBI Number (if applicable) (individual offenders);
9. Alleged Violations (in this case);
10. Summary of Prior Litigation Record (criminal and/or civil actions);
11. History of Violence, Alcohol/Drug Abuse, and Flight Risk (individual offenders).

Detailing the Case

The next section of the report is the investigator's opportunity to fully describe the offense, that is, what happened, where and when did the illegalities occur, who was victimized and how much was lost, who was responsible for the offending, and what evidence is available to prove these allegations. This section should be labeled with an appropriate heading such as "Details of the Offense."

Depending upon the scope and complexity of the case, this could be the lengthiest portion of the report and might be the most difficult to organize and write. Perhaps the most standard approach to writing this section is to do so in a chronological manner, that is, start telling the story at the beginning of the offending activity and conclude it at the point this activity ended or indicate it is continuing. Before this story can be presented effectively in writing, however, the investigator must bring together all that has been learned over the course of the investigation, identify the salient material, and organize it in a manner to produce a coherent chronology of the events. This undertaking might very well first require a review of all evidence, interviews, and other investigative steps taken before any meaningful narrative can be created. Undertaking such a review will be particularly helpful in task-force cases (because of multiple investigator involvement) and/or those that spanned over lengthy periods of time (because we all just forget things over time!). The good news is that there are two important by-products to undertaking a complete review of the investigation and then attempting to reduce it to writing. First, this is an opportunity for the investigator to fully acquaint or reacquaint herself/himself with the case. While the preparation of this report is in anticipation of relinquishing the leading role over to the prosecutor, in preparing for and pursuing any litigation, the prosecutor will invariably have questions and he/she will look to the case investigator for the answers. Thus, investigators must know their case, inside and out.

Second, as suggested earlier, undertaking this review and writing this portion of the report affords an opportunity for the investigator to identify missed steps, deficiencies or "holes" in the case that need to be addressed before the case can be presented for prosecution. Moreover, an objective assessment of the facts of the case might suggest defenses to expect should an enforcement action be undertaken. Any such concerns should be verbally discussed with the prosecutor either before submitting the report or thereafter.

Identifying the Evidence

Just as the case must be laid out in an organized, coherent manner, making very clear the evidence available to prove the case is essential. This can be accomplished in the following three sections of the report. The first of these sections should identify and detail each misrepresentation, act of fraud, and/or other illegal conduct committed in the course of the case and should be labeled accordingly. While the overall description of the case as discussed in the preceding section may deal with these topics more generally, this section should very specifically frame them in terms of specific falsehoods presented or specific acts of other unlawful conduct, by whom, how, when, and why (i.e., what impact was intended). A review of Chapter 8 and the Indictment Appendix (F) will serve as quick reminders as to why it is important and helpful to break out this type of information in a comprehensive investigative report. The manner and means section, (and overt acts section when conspiracy is charged) of an indictment can be more readily completed when this type of information is provided as suggested here and should be done so in chronological order.

Again for illustration purposes, Box 10–2 contains an abbreviated example of how this information can be presented.

Box 10–2   Misrepresentations, acts of fraud, and/or other illegal conduct

1. On or about March 31, 2004, Ken E. Walk submitted a claim for reimbursement to the Medicare program totaling $25,660 in connection with purportedly furnishing motorized mobility devices and wheel chairs to the following 12 Medicare beneficiaries: Allen Klein, Mary Decker, Florence Davis, Alvin Franklin, Curtis George, Leah Langley, Helen Thomas, Louis Fink, Cary Kirkland, Hector Ortiz, Manuel Perez, and Jorge Ramos. On April 16, 2004, he received reimbursement from the Medicare program in the amount of $25,660.

2. On or about May 1, 2006, Ken E. Walk met with physician Frank Lamper, at Dr. Lamper's offices in Chicago, IL, at which time Walk gave Lamper a check for $1,000 in return for referring ten patients in need of wheel chairs or motorized mobility devices.

Following the presentation of the acts of misrepresentation, fraud, and/or other illegal conduct, the next section should lay out the evidence, at least in summary fashion, that is available to prove each of these allegations. This section should be separately labeled (e.g., "Evidence of Offending," "Proof of Allegations," etc.) and bear a corresponding number to the allegations put forth above. An example of how this type of information can be presented is depicted in Box 10–3.

The final step in outlining the evidence in the case is identifying the witnesses and a brief summary of their testimony. This section can be labeled "Relevant Testimony," "Witness Testimony," or the like. The witnesses can be introduced alphabetically or in the sequence their testimony relates to events in the case. Include the full name of the proposed witness, postal and e-mail addresses, and telephone numbers to facilitate contact. See Box 10–4 for an abbreviated example.

Similar to providing the detailed narrative of the case, bringing together the information required in these three sections is an undertaking that will assure the investigator is thoroughly familiar with the evidence needed to undertake a prosecution or other enforcement litigation and/or alternatively will highlight any "missing pieces" that need to be pursued.

Box 10–3   Evidence of offending

Investigation has developed evidence to prove the violations of law outlined in this report. This evidence, in summary fashion, is identified in the following paragraphs that bear numbers corresponding to the allegations made above.

1. Medicare records reflect a claim for reimbursement in the amount of $25,660 submitted by Ken E. Walk, d/b/a Mobility for All, Inc., on March 31, 2004, and payment in this amount dated April 16, 2004. Interviews with the 12 Medicare beneficiaries identified in this claim determined that while they had each previously done business with Ken E. Walk, d/b/a Mobility for All, Inc., none had ordered the items reflected in the claim dated March 31, 2004. Moreover, Walk could not provide any records to substantiate the orders reflected in this claim in response to the issuance of a grand jury subpoena that requested the production of such documents. An interview with the former officer manager at Mobility for All, Inc., Evelyn Sue Rogers, disclosed that on several occasions she developed lists of former customers and their Medicare beneficiary numbers which Walk then used in preparing claims to Medicare for equipment that was neither ordered nor furnished.

2. A check dated May 1, 2006, in the amount of $1,000 drawn on an account in the name of Mobility for All, Inc., at the First U.S.A. Bank was identified incident to a review of subpoenaed records form this account. The check was made payable to "Cash," signed by Ken E. Walk, and was annotated "Services." The check was deposited into a money market account held in the name of Frank Lamper at Equity Investment Services. Lamper has stated that this check was in payment for referring 10 of his patients who needed durable equipment to Walk.

Box 10–4 Witness testimony

Hernandez, Jennifer K., Custodian of Records, Medicare Program, Department of Health and Human Services, Washington, DC; J.Hernandez@HHS.gov; telephone 202-222-2200—will testify relative to the details of the receipt of claims from Ken E. Walk, d/b/a Mobility for All, Inc., and payments in response to these claims.

Decker, Mary, The Serene Manor Nursing Home, 2242 E. 123rd Ave. Chicago, IL; telephone 312-899-0077—will testify that she does receive Medicare benefits and that in 1999, prior to residing at the Serene Manor Nursing Home, she acquired a motorized mobility scooter through Mobility for All, Inc. However, she has not purchased any type of equipment from this company nor has she had any contact with them since then.

Rogers, Evelyn Sue, 8620 Euola St. #902, Chicago, IL. 312-666-1212 (w); 312-586-0232 (h)—will testify that she was previously employed as the manager at Mobility for All, Inc., and worked directly for Ken E. Walk. She will testify that she was directed by Walk to prepare lists of former customers along with Medicare beneficiary numbers and that while she was not advised of the reason for doing this, she became aware that Medicare reimbursements were being received in these names, but there were no corresponding orders on file. She will testify that she became concerned about the possibility that these billings were false and left the employ of Mobility for All, Inc., because of that reason.

Robertson, Harold, Custodian of Records, First USA Bank, P.O. Box 4868, Chicago, IL; telephone 312-440-4800 ex 812; e-mail records@firstusabank.com—will introduce records from the checking account held in the name, Mobility for All, Inc.

Losses and Victims

This section should present a total number of victims and dollar loss, at least to the extent these totals can be accurately calculated at the time of the report's submission. Given limited prosecutive resources and the time and effort involved in prosecuting most white collar crimes, cases with larger dollar losses are more likely to go forward than those with small losses, even when sufficient evidence might be on hand in such cases to prevail. In fact, to reiterate a point made earlier, many prosecutors' offices have established dollar loss thresholds that must be reached in order for a case to be prosecuted. Aside from the concern over limited prosecutive resources, cases with a large dollar loss tend to be more aggravated from the public's perspective, which in turn might manifest itself in a sympathetic jury appeal. Also, large dollar losses combined with a large number of victims tend to argue against unintended or accidental outcomes and in favor of the prosecution's version of the events. Finally, in many, if not most, white collar crimes, the dollar loss will have a direct impact on sentencing in criminal prosecutions. The federal courts and those in many states sentence criminal offenders pursuant to statutorily defined guidelines in an effort to provide uniformity and proportionality in the punishments that are imposed. Federal sentencing guidelines for white collar crimes are largely driven by dollar loss, that is, the larger the dollar loss to victims, the more severe the sentence will be. Sentencing guidelines that reflect the dollar loss impact for selected white collar crimes are contained in Appendix G.[1]

This section should also describe the nature or class of individuals or business entities that were victimized. Whether there is a defined class of victims may vary with the case. In the case of individuals, victims could simply be consumers generally, investors generally, and so on. In the case of business entities, some schemes might target a particular type of industry while other schemes might be nonpreferential in this regard. And of course, government agencies are also considered victims when they are defrauded. In particular, however, investigators should be cognizant of schemes that target groups of individuals who could be viewed as vulnerable victims. Recall in Chapter 2 that capturing information about a victim's age at the complaint stage was recommended because of enhanced sentencing penalties in many jurisdictions for targeting the elderly. Whether from these efforts or through subsequent investigation, when elderly victims are found to have been targeted, this information should be highlighted in this section along with an explanation about why they were targeted as victims. Additionally, recognize that other vulnerable groups (e.g., racial/ethnic minorities, non-English speakers, specific religions, the disabled) could be targeted by white collar criminals and when such targeting becomes apparent, it should likewise be discussed here, even if no enhanced penalties apply. Specific efforts to victimize vulnerable people are usually looked upon as an aggravated feature in the case by prosecutors and would be portrayed as such to juries.

Summary

A brief concluding paragraph should summarize the nature of the case, identify again those responsible, and indicate the provable violations of law. While this information appears elsewhere, highlighting the crux of the case may be helpful, especially when the report is lengthy. As a matter of formality and courtesy (but as will be discussed later, a reality as well), the investigator should offer to be of further assistance and provide his/her contact information.

Presenting the Report

As discussed, even in cases where early prosecutor involvement is established, the extent of this involvement can vary considerably, ranging from daily contacts to a more "hands-off" approach. Especially in these latter instances, it is a *best practice* that a meeting with the prosecutor be arranged and the comprehensive investigative report be personally presented and discussed at that time. Obviously, in cases where the prosecutor has been more closely involved and may know the case as well as the investigators, the report can be presented with less formality (although its value as a continuing reference and guide to the case is no less diminished). In either scenario, however, the submission of the comprehensive investigative report is an appropriate point to advise the prosecutor of any potential weaknesses in the case due to witness or evidence problems or perhaps anticipated legal challenges such as motions to suppress evidence. Moreover, discuss any possible defenses that could be put forth. Importantly, be ready to address how any problems or anticipated defenses can be dealt with. While it is ultimately the role of prosecutors to evaluate case weaknesses and anticipate and counter defenses, investigator insights and opinions on these matters are often welcome and may result in quickly answering questions or resolving concerns. In any event, taking such an affirmative step will avoid the worst-case scenario where a prosecutor is "blindsided" at an inopportune time such as in a trial or when negotiating with defense counsel regarding a problem that should have been brought up earlier by the investigator.

Along these lines, bring to the attention of the prosecutor any evidence that is favorable to the proposed defendant. Obviously, this type of material might be "a problem" issue discussed earlier anyway, but it must also be turned over to the defense in the event charges are brought, as required under *Brady* v. *Maryland* (373 U.S. 83 [1963]). Also be sure to bring to the prosecutor's attention any oral or written statements made by the proposed defendant to government agents and the results of any expert or scientific examinations that bear on the case/proposed defendant. These materials are required under discovery mandates, a topic that will be detailed later.

Final Considerations

As a matter of professional practice and compliance with the law, it is absolutely essential and required that investigators pursue their work objectively, honestly, fairly, and accurately. Preparing and presenting a comprehensive investigative report is a highly important and significant part of the overall investigative process and this report must reflect the values of objectivity, honesty, fairness, and accuracy. The facts in the case should "speak for themselves." Editorializing and using inflammatory, prejudicial remarks are entirely inappropriate. Use clear, simple language and *no misspellings* or *grammar errors*.[2]

THE POSSIBLE OUTCOMES

Once an investigation is complete and the facts gathered appear to support an enforcement action, this information must be conveyed to the prosecuting body. At this point, prosecutors have several options: (1) the case can be referred back to the investigator for further work; (2) the case can be declined; (3) the case can be accepted for prosecution; and (4) either before or after filing charges a negotiated plea or settlement can be sought. When charges are filed (and not subsequently dropped or dismissed), a trial or other formal litigation hearing will occur if a negotiated plea or settlement is not reached by the trial or hearing date. Each of these options will be commented upon further in the following paragraphs.

Referred Back to Investigator

This option is more likely to occur in situations where prosecutor involvement had been nonexistent or minimal over the course of the investigation, and perhaps compounded by investigator inexperience. The good news in this type of outcome is that a prosecutor reviewing the case sees sufficient merit to warrant further development and offers specific guidance and suggestions to make the case suitable for prosecution. This feedback should be taken in a positive manner and viewed as a learning experience. Moreover, as will be discussed later, investigators are continually called upon to perform case-related tasks up to the day the final prosecutive event takes place (e.g., sentencing) and even sometimes thereafter. Thus, continuing to investigate a case is likely to occur in most scenarios anyway.

Case Declined

There have been hints and suggestions made earlier in this volume that not all investigations are accepted for prosecution. Recall discussions about the need to fully document losses and number/type of victims and how some prosecutor's offices have established loss thresholds as a guide to accepting cases for prosecution. The reality is that most prosecutors have the discretion not to prosecute a case presented to them by an investigative agency. There are at least three criteria that are applied in evaluating a case's prosecutive merit. First, unlike burglaries, robberies, homicides, and so on, it is not uncommon to encounter white collar crime scenarios where there is uncertainty whether an offense has actually occurred. For instance, was a product or service really misrepresented or did complaints arise from customers who failed to fully inform themselves of the applicable terms and conditions. Similarly, was a product defective, resulting in poor performance or even injury, or was operator error involved. Without dismissing the possibility of individuals undertaking their own civil actions, whether these situations and many others as well constitute a basis for a government enforcement action can be a dilemma. This quandary is perhaps most often encountered when criminal violations are being considered, but civil and regulatory enforcers may also confront it, as well, depending upon their authority. Thus, cases can be declined because there is not sufficient evidence that a violation occurred.

A somewhat related basis for declining a case is insufficient evidence generally, that is, an offense may have occurred, but evidence to establish responsibility is not at hand. A straightforward example of this type of scenario might be in credit card fraud, check fraud, or insurance fraud cases where it is clear a crime has occurred, but those responsible either cannot be identified or evidence developed is not sufficient to sustain a conviction. However, insufficient evidence is also a frequent basis for declination in other types of white collar crime where intent to commit the offense is a required element of proof. Even in cases with otherwise strong indicators of fraud (e.g., multiple complaints, large losses, identifiable misrepresentations, and inferior quality product or service), evidence that this was the intended outcome/plan and did not occur due to mistakes or poor business practices must be developed.

Finally, just as investigating white collar crimes are often time-consuming, resource-intensive efforts, so are they from a prosecutive perspective as well. Thus, prosecutors' offices often seek ways to apply their resources in the most efficient manner possible, which usually means limiting their attention to cases they feel affect the public most adversely. As suggested earlier, most often this type of resource management approach manifests itself in the form of monetary loss thresholds, sometimes combined with victim criteria as well (e.g., number of victims, vulnerable victims). At the risk of being redundant, identifying all available losses and victims can be the difference between a case being declined or accepted for prosecution.

Admittedly, this type of resource management approach can eliminate otherwise perfectly viable cases from being prosecuted. Check and credit card frauds of limited scope are frequent causalities at some U.S. Attorney's Offices, although many of these declined federal cases are subsequently prosecuted in state courts, assuming sufficient evidence is available. To be fair, however, this arguably bureaucratic approach to deciding who gets prosecuted and who does not has a practical side. In many cases where the losses are small and the victims are few, whether a violation actually occurred can be murky and/or the issue of proving intent, at least through establishing a pattern of misconduct, can be difficult. Thus, the possibilities of successful outcomes in such cases would be in doubt.

Case Accepted for Prosecution

The goal of any investigation is to bring together sufficient evidence to support the desired enforcement action, that is, criminal prosecution, regulatory sanction, and so on. Thus, a decision by a prosecutor to move forward on an investigation in terms of filing charges and litigating the case is the ideal outcome that investigators strive to achieve. Again, while accepting a case for prosecution is by no means the end of the investigator's role, it is nevertheless a satisfying point because it is a direct reflection of thorough investigative work. When a decision is made to file charges, be aware that one of the outcomes can be a trial or other formal litigation proceeding to determine guilt or innocence. However, many cases are resolved before such proceedings as will be discussed next.

THE NEGOTIATED SETTLEMENT

Whether a case involves potentially criminal, civil, or administrative charges, it can be resolved without going to trial or other formal proceedings. In fact, more cases are resolved through a negotiated settlement (which for purposes here includes plea bargaining in criminal cases) than undergo a formal litigation process. Moreover, in many cases settlement negotiations occur even without formal charges being filed. The mere existence of an investigation causes many targets to seek legal counsel and taking this step sometimes starts a negotiation process. Entering into settlement negotiations prior to filing charges is often advantageous for both the government and the target (if only in terms of making the best out of a bad situation). For the government, not only can a costly and lengthy litigation process be avoided, further investigation might be averted as well. Having said that, however, it is not wise to enter into such discussions too prematurely. One of the motivations a target might have to rush to the negotiation table is a hope that investigators won't discover more victimization or other crimes than they are already aware of. Another motivation might be an attempt to falsely shift responsibility/culpability to others, thus gaining a more favorable sentence or other sanction. Thus, it cannot be overemphasized that an investigation must reach a point where investigators and prosecutors have developed a detailed understanding of the scope and magnitude of the case, including respective levels of culpability in multidefendant cases. Another potential "pitfall" in negotiating a settlement prior to filing charges is that deliberate stalling by the defense can take place. Without a trial date pending, and especially if the offending activity is continuing, there can be little incentive to finalize a resolution.

Nevertheless, negotiating settlements in cases prior to filing charges is routinely undertaken because it saves investigator/prosecutor time and effort, and ensures the government a "win" (i.e., a conviction or other finding of responsibility on the part of the defendant), a consideration that is particularly appealing when there might be some uncertainty about achieving this outcome if the case were to be fully litigated (an argument the government will invariably take notwithstanding occasional criticism about entering into settlements some may consider too lenient). For the target of the investigation, there is usually some hope of favorable treatment in terms of sanction.

Perhaps with greater frequency, however, negotiating settlements in cases occurs after charges have been filed. For the government, taking this approach reduces some of the concerns outlined earlier. By this point, investigators and prosecutors should have developed a solid understanding of the case and thus should be able to fully assess its impact and the culpability of the defendant(s). Also, the imposition of a trial date creates a deadline for reaching any negotiated settlement, thus reducing delaying opportunities, if the defendant wishes to seek favorable treatment as a result of acknowledging responsibility. Of course, if charges are filed, prosecutors and investigators should be prepared and anticipate going to trial. Having said that, the same motivations to reach a negotiated settlement tend to apply as they did prior to filing charges. Again, the issues of the efficient and effective use of limited investigative and prosecutive resources combined with the sure "win" often make pursuing this option attractive when a defendant wishes to dispose of the case in this manner, as well.

As discussed in Chapter 8, in federal criminal cases, negotiated settlements prior to the return of an indictment usually result in the filing of an information, a charging document to which the defendant enters a guilty plea before a judge. The violation(s) outlined in an information are usually more limited than what would have been charged in an indictment.

With regard to the sure "win" consideration, for the government to obtain a guilty verdict at trial is never a certainty. The complexity of many white collar crime cases often makes them difficult and confusing for juries to understand. Proving the element of intent must often be accomplished through inferences, a concept that has proved unappealing to some jurors in this day of scientific evidence. And whether before a jury or just a judge (or other hearing officer), skillful defense attorneys are adept at presenting persuasive arguments of innocence. In fact, the complexity of many white collar crimes sometimes offers opportunities to put forth seemingly viable explanations of the events in question in a manner that attributes no culpability to the defendant(s).

Regardless of when negotiations take place, expect to encounter certain approaches and be prepared to evaluate and deal with them. First, in criminal cases negotiations frequently begin with defense counsel inquiring, "Isn't there civil statute that can be applied here?" or "My client will plea to a misdemeanor." Such overtures are usually *pro forma* and quickly dismissed. However, occasionally these types of overtures will include representations about how the defendant can assist the government with the case at hand or other matters. Alternatively, investigators might be aware of information a defendant has that if provided, might justify lenient treatment. Either scenario requires a careful assessment that, in turn, probably means further investigative work before making a decision to extend such favorable treatment.

Absent the above exceptional circumstances, in many white collar crime cases negotiating the amount of loss becomes the focal point in reaching a settlement agreement. The loss figure in a case plays a determinative role in the final sanction in many types of white collar crimes and its calculation can become a contentious issue. Thus, investigators must be prepared to demonstrate and prove how the losses alleged were arrived at. Also, in many cases the culpability of the defendant will be disputed. Even when defendants agree to enter into a negotiated settlement, they are frequently adverse to acknowledging and accepting responsibility. And in multidefendant cases, expect defendants to point at each other in terms of who was most culpable. Thus, again, investigators must come to these negotiations armed with facts that correctly portray individual culpability.

Negotiating a settlement is an artful process that primarily lies in the domain of the prosecutor. However, as suggested, investigators do play an important role in this process in terms of providing facts from their investigation and evaluating information put forth in the negotiation process. Ideally they should have input into the final agreement. Depending upon whether the case is prosecuted criminally or within the administrative civil arena, sanctions such as imprisonment, house arrest, probation, fines and civil penalties, forfeitures, restitution, and the conditions under which future business/occupational activities may be pursued can be on the table. As most cases are ultimately disposed of through negotiated settlements, this process plays the predominant role in meting out justice to white collar offenders.

Nevertheless, negotiated settlements are not always reached and some cases are fully litigated through trials and other formal proceedings. In these instances, investigators will have a continuing role in the case, as will be discussed in the next section. Before leaving the subject of negotiated settlements, however, two parting thoughts are offered. First and perhaps not necessary to point out, seeking a negotiated settlement is seldom a negative reflection on the quality of the investigation. Second, bear in mind the concept of negotiation implies that both parties come away with some benefit in hand. For the defendant/respondent, this usually means some type of lenient treatment (or possibility thereof) in return for an acknowledgment of wrongdoing. As indicated at the outset of this chapter, sometimes this process results in agreements where questions arise about the propriety of the penalties or terms imposed, usually because they are viewed as too lenient. Most likely, a few investigators fall into the ranks of those who have raised such questions on occasion, and maybe have even expressed feelings of frustration in this regard. Such questions and feelings are understandable, considering these are individuals who have put their "hearts and souls" into bringing justice to white collar offenders. However, these same questions and possibly feelings of frustration can arise over sentences or other sanctions imposed unilaterally by judges at the conclusion of a trial or other formal hearing. At least in the negotiated settlement process, investigators usually play a role and ideally have input into the final agreement. Further, they can usually obtain an explanation from the prosecutor why particular terms were agreed upon. Similar opportunities are usually not available when a judge renders a sentence or other sanction. Many investigators have made peace with the reality that sentencing/sanctioning responsibilities lay in the domains of prosecutors, defense attorneys, and judges; and rather, derive their satisfaction from knowing that this phase in the litigation process would never occur without their efforts in the first place.

REACHING A DISPOSITION: TRIALS AND BEYOND

As suggested earlier, not all cases are brought to a conclusion through the negotiated settlement process and a trial will be necessary. However, when negotiated settlements are reached, is it time for the investigator to move on to the next case? The answer is "no, not yet" in many instances, particularly in criminal prosecutions. Plea agreements typically contain a provision for defendants to be fully debriefed and to cooperate in the investigation and usually investigators are called upon to conduct the debriefing and follow-up on any information provided. This involvement will be the first of the final steps discussed in this section.

The second of the final steps is the investigator's role in the event of a trial. This role can be twofold in nature. First, even in the most thoroughly investigated cases, a great deal of preparation is required to go to trial, an undertaking that is commonly shared between the prosecutor and the investigator. Second, investigators will often be witnesses at trials. These responsibilities will be examined in more detail below.

Debriefing Defendants

Many plea agreements in criminal prosecutions contain provisions requiring the defendant to cooperate with the government in the investigation, including being fully debriefed. In practice, this requirement is often fulfilled to a large extent before a guilty plea is entered under the terms of a proffer agreement. As may be recalled from Chapter 8, a proffer agreement constitutes terms under which a person with potential criminal liability can be interviewed by the government for purposes of evaluating his/her information, and any incriminating statements made cannot be used against the person. In the context of Chapter 8, proffer agreements were discussed incident to making decisions about extending immunity to individuals in return for their information and cooperation. At this point in a case, the government is concerned about (1) ensuring that the defendant is fully acknowledging his/her role in the illegal conduct, which in part is accomplished by the defendant outlining the details of the offending activities; and (2) providing information about, and cooperating with the government against other individuals involved in the case at hand, or perhaps with regard to other illegal activity about which they have knowledge. Moreover, proffer agreements, particularly when used incident to plea-bargaining negotiations, will permit derivative use of the information provided to enable investigators to make follow-up inquiries about its truthfulness as well as to usefulness in further investigation.[3] Thus, through this process the government can become satisfied that proper culpability is being acknowledged by and assigned to the defendant. Moreover, the government may very well learn more about the illegal activity in the case and/or be made aware of other illegal activity.

As sentencing guidelines such as those in operation in the federal system provide rewards for cooperation with the government (e.g., a reduced imprisonment or permit house arrest/probation in lieu of imprisonment), benefits for cooperating in this manner accrue to defendants as well, in terms of improving their sentencing possibilities. Defendant cooperation can also include testifying at trials against codefendants or in other cases, and providing undercover/informant services. Taking on these types of roles can greatly reduce a defendant's sentencing exposure, and in some instances can result in avoiding otherwise almost certain imprisonment.

Prosecutors tend to rely heavily on investigators during the debriefing process and especially for any subsequent follow-up inquiries that are required and/or for monitoring other cooperation provided by the defendant. At initial debriefing sessions, defense attorneys usually attend along with their client and often the prosecutor will sit in as well. But investigators should be prepared: this is often their interview to conduct and as with other critical interviews that occur in any case, this one does require thorough preparation. At this point in the investigation, even in cases where a settlement is being sought prior to the filing of any formal charges, a good deal should be known about the events in question and the defendant's culpability with regard to them. Defendants will often be more truthful and provide more thorough information if the interviewers are well versed on the facts of the case. Conversely, being poorly prepared may suggest to the defendant that he/she can get away with divulging a minimum amount of information.

Three goals should be sought in this interview: (1) Known information should be confirmed/verified; (2) new and/or "missing pieces" of information should be obtained (although it may be prudent not to blatantly expose these gaps of knowledge about a case as it may invite less than fully truthful information); and (3) information about the offending activities of codefendants and/or unrelated illegal activity should also be obtained.

Depending upon the nature of the case, debriefing interviews can stretch over the course of hours and even days. In fact, when this process is expected to be extended in nature, it may be best to purposely limit the length of each session or topics to be covered to avoid fatigue and to permit an incremental review of information. Being able to review and digest information obtained in one session and then be able to revisit issues that are unclear or inconsistent at a subsequent session is often invaluable. Moreover, do not be surprised to find a somewhat "strained" atmosphere in an initial debriefing session. Defendants frequently appear to be uncomfortable in this setting, if not actually frightened. Many will still have a tendency to proclaim their innocence despite acknowledging guilt to their attorneys and recognizing that a negotiated settlement will be in their best interest (a condition referred to by one prominent federal prosecutor as "white collar disease").[4] Even though this type of interview is being held because the defendant is seeking a negotiated settlement and is there to cooperate, contentiousness might still be encountered. Investigators can expect to encounter a wide range of emotions and attitudes in debriefing sessions, from contrite and forthcoming to angry and non-cooperative. Many skilled defense attorneys, when they recognize that cooperating and seeking a negotiated settlement is in the client's best interest, will prepare the client for debriefing and will positively facilitate the interview when necessary. Another advantage of multiple debriefing sessions is that this uneasiness on the part of the defendant often subsides somewhat after the initial interview.

Along these lines, recall in Chapter 4 the admonition to not purposely create an aggravated relationship with investigative subjects, that is, be professional. This advice was offered because all too often the day arrives when the investigator sits across from the investigative subject, now defendant, and attempts to elicit this person's cooperation in a debriefing interview. Investigators now need to establish a working relationship with the defendant, an undertaking that can be hampered if personal animosities get in the way.

In any event, notes should be taken at each debriefing session and promptly incorporated into a detailed memorandum of interview. In the event more than one investigator is present, it might be wise to designate a note-taker/memorandum writer. As previously suggested, debriefing sessions can provide leads for further investigation, especially in multidefendant cases, or perhaps with regard to unrelated illegal activity. Moreover, it is possible in some cases that the cooperating defendant might be able to continue to associate with the offending activity that he/she is being prosecuted for, thus providing opportunities for informant/undercover initiatives.

Finally, do not discount using polygraph examinations incident to debriefing sessions required under negotiated settlement agreements. In cases where a cooperating defendant offers information that is inconsistent with other statements or facts developed, the information being provided is highly critical or sensitive, and/or there is concern over the "cooperating" defendant's truthfulness, polygraph examinations are frequently administered and have proven helpful, notwithstanding their limitations as discussed in Chapter 7. It would be wise to anticipate this need, when possible, and make submission to a polygraph examination a provision in the settlement agreement.

Preparing for and Assisting at Trials

Trials are the ultimate stage for prosecutors, but investigators play a critical supporting role in these productions. It is also a role that will likely consume the investigator's time and efforts once the preparation process begins in earnest until the verdict is announced and even thereafter. Although the exception, some white collar crime trials have gone on for months, but trials lasting several weeks are commonplace.

Among the first trial preparation discussions that will take place between the prosecutor and investigator will be to identify the witnesses and evidence that will be needed to prove the charges that have been filed. Granted, it would be unlikely that these topics would not have been discussed previously between the prosecutor and investigator. With a trial pending, however, not only would there be a sense of urgency at this point to finalize decisions in this regard, but also important tasks to be accomplished that are associated with these decisions. First, there is a matter of complying with statutorily mandated discovery processes that permit the defense to review/copy certain evidence in possession of the prosecution. The specific types of materials that fall under discovery provisions may vary from jurisdiction to jurisdiction and differ as well between criminal and civil/administrative proceedings. In federal criminal proceedings under Rule 16 of the Rules of the Criminal Procedure, the following materials (in summary format) are subject to discovery:

- Defendant's oral statement to a government agent;

- Defendant's written or recorded statement to a government agent;

- Defendant's grand jury testimony;

- Defendant's prior criminal history record;

- Books, papers, data, documents, photographs, tangible objects, buildings or places (or copies or portions of any of these items) in the government's possession/control if any such items are material to preparing the defense, if the government intends to use any such items in its case-in-chief at trial, and/or if the item was obtained from or belongs to the defendant;

- Results or reports of any physical or mental examination and any scientific test or experiment if this item is material for preparing the defense or the government intends to use this item in its case-in chief at trial;

- A written summary of any expert-witness testimony that includes the witness's opinions, bases, and reasons for these opinions, and the witness's qualifications.

It should be noted that discovery in federal criminal proceedings does not include reports, memoranda, or other internal documents made by government agents incident to the investigation and prosecution nor statements made by government witnesses (although 18 U.S.C. 3500 does require witness statements to be turned over to the defense after a witness has testified on direct examination).

Also, as mentioned previously, under *Brady v. Maryland* (373 U.S. 83 [1963]), evidence known to the government that is favorable to a defendant in terms of being material to either guilt or punishment must be turned over to the defense. Thus, it is imperative that any such information be identified in these initial trial preparation discussions so that it will be turned over to the defense.

A second concern to be addressed in initial trial preparation discussions are what witnesses will be needed and whether there is any documentary evidence that needs to be acquired prior to trial. Once potential witnesses are identified, subpoenas for their appearance must be obtained and served. Incident to service, arrangements should be made for a trial appearance interview to go over their expected testimony. While in most cases this will not be the first interview with the witness, having this person meet face to face with the prosecutor to go over the specific, expected trial testimony provides a comfort level for both parties. Taking this step should be considered a "must" and not just a best practice in the trial preparation process, and not doing so is akin to taking an unnecessary risk.

Although most evidence will be in hand at this point, there still may be documentary items that need to be secured. In criminal cases, grand jury subpoenas can no longer be used after an indictment is returned, but trial subpoenas can be served to obtain any needed records, and so on. Where "last minute" evidence gathering may come into play most often is in the acquisition of original items of evidence for trial purposes, as opposed to copies that may have been relied upon throughout the investigation. Another category of evidence that sometimes awaits "last minute" acquisition are items that require certification, usually by a governmental agency, attesting to authenticity.

Finally, investigators and prosecutors usually collaborate on trial strategy, organizing the presentation of the government case, and assessing expected defenses and how to deal with them.

When the trial begins, investigators can take on two roles: providing assistance in a wide range of capacities including witness coordination, organizing and furnishing evidence as needed, observing testimony, and offering suggestions (both during the proceedings and after each day's conclusion); and being a witness, as necessary.

Witness coordination means arranging for witnesses to be on hand as planned and as needed. One might think that witnesses simply receive a subpoena for a trial beginning on a certain date and they will be there. Unfortunately, the reality is a little more complicated. Particularly in jurisdictions with busy caseloads, courts sometimes find it difficult to establish fixed and certain trial dates. A date might be set for the trial and that date will appear on trial subpoenas but with the understanding that there is some flexibility involved. In these circumstances, the best advice that can be offered to witnesses is to be "on-call" beginning on that date. The other confounding factor in witness coordination, and one that will be present whenever there is a multiday proceeding, is the order in which the witnesses are to appear. Even when the trial starts, it is not wise to have all witnesses on hand. Rather, the investigator and prosecutor must work together to establish a schedule as to when each witness should be present and ready to testify.

If witness coordination is beginning to sound complicated, consider these potentials as well. There will be witnesses, even among the heretofore eager and cooperative, who will find the date of their appearance, if not the trial generally, to be inconvenient, in conflict with other plans, and/or no longer of interest. Nevertheless, if their testimony is important to the case, they must be served a subpoena, undergo a preparatory interview, and diplomatically yet firmly ensure their appearance. Finally, within the "problem witness" category are those who are elderly and infirm and yet must leave home to appear at the trial. As some white collar crimes prey on vulnerable victims, it will not be unusual to have such individuals as witnesses, and moreover, they can be very effective not only in their testimony but also in providing evidence of the type of person the defendant(s) sought to victimize. From personal experience, investigators have provided witnesses who need assistance (perhaps because of age or health limitations) round trip transportation to the court, and have even accompanied fearful first-time flyers who had to travel by air to the proceedings. All of which is to say that witness coordination is a very important task that requires organization, persistence, creativity, and congeniality.

Normally, an investigator sits with the prosecutor at the prosecution table for the purpose of organizing and handing evidence as needed and also for the purpose of listening to and observing testimony. In this latter role, the investigator is a second set of ears and eyes for the prosecutor and he/she can offer suggestions during the proceedings. Likewise, during breaks and at the end of each day's proceedings expect to meet with the prosecutor to share thoughts and observations, evaluate the day's events, and plan for the next day.

Investigators are often witnesses in trials, as well. Their testimony can include providing a summary of the investigation and records analyses, introducing evidence that they obtained (e.g., during the execution of search warrant), and relating statements that a defendant may have made. Just as other witnesses should meet with the prosecutor to go over expected testimony, this would be a *best practice* for investigator witnesses, as well. While being a witness is part of their job and many investigators are experienced in this respect, even a short interview with the prosecutor will help to avoid surprises and/or misunderstandings. The art of being an effective witness will only be summarized here, as a detailed discussion is more appropriate for a general investigative text and/or agency training. The quick summary, however, is as follows:

1. Be thoroughly knowledgeable about the topics and evidence on which testimony will be given.
2. Present a professional appearance and demeanor.
3. Always tell the truth.

Given all the responsibilities investigators can have in trial preparation and in providing trial assistance, even if there had been only one investigator assigned to the case through the investigation, it is a *best practice* to have additional assistance during this phase.

The Verdict

Prevailing at trial is a highly satisfying experience for investigators, especially after all the hard work that is required to realize such an outcome. Not surprisingly, most investigators experience emotions at the polar opposite when a jury or judge returns a verdict of not guilty or other unfavorable ruling. This latter outcome can and will occur, from time to time. While feelings of disappointment are understandable, a reanalysis of the investigation and/or how the case was prosecuted might result in learning points that will help to avoid similar outcomes in the future. Moreover, as white collar crime cases can involve multiple defendants and multiple charges, verdicts can be mixed along these lines, as well. In multidefendant cases, some defendants can be found guilty while others are exonerated; in multiple count cases defendants can be found guilty of some charges and not others. Although not nearly as disappointing as losing a case in its entirety, an objective review of mixed verdict cases may also reveal strategies and approaches that would help to avoid such outcomes in the future.

While the "guilty as charged" verdict is the outcome investigators strive for, when this result occurs in criminal proceedings (and perhaps in different ways in other proceedings, as well), expect to make contributions in the sentencing phase. Probation officers complete presentence investigations to assist judges in determining a just sentence and one that is consistent with any prevailing sentencing guidelines. As suggested earlier, in white collar crime cases, the financial loss incurred in the case is a major sentencing determinant in federal prosecutions and the investigator is usually the primary source for the government's calculation of this figure. Defendants may contest this figure and/or present their own calculations, steps that investigators may be asked to respond to in terms of explaining the government position and analyzing any alternative loss calculations. Also, the names and addresses of victims may also be requested so that any court-ordered restitution can be effected.

Other criteria that will factor into determining a sentence under the federal sentencing guidelines include prior criminal history, the role of the defendant in the offense, the planning and complexity of the offense, and any activities the defendant undertook to obstruct the investigation. Investigators may be asked to provide this type of information to the probation officer compiling the presentence investigation.

Finally, do not be surprised if a convicted defendant suddenly desires to cooperate in an effort to gain some leniency. While such requests are often honored, whether they are fruitful varies. Sometimes such debriefings can simply resolve lingering questions. More beneficial however is information that implicates previously unknown individuals in the case at hand or information about new offenses. The receipt of such information at this point can be very timely for an investigator since the present case is about to come to a close and he/she will be looking for the next challenge to pursue.

CHAPTER HIGHLIGHTS

- A comprehensive investigative report serves three purposes: (1) it informs agency management about the case, monitors investigative work and performance, and it is a necessary quality-control tool; (2) it provides the prosecuting agency with a complete report of the investigation which can be used to make a prosecutive decision and as a guide in preparing charges and litigating the case; and (3) preparing the report is a helpful exercise for the investigator because she/he must bring together and organize all the evidence, areas requiring further investigation will become apparent, and defenses can be identified.

- The recommended elements of a comprehensive investigative report include:
  - Introduction
  - Offender data
  - The details of the case
  - Outline of specific violations and supporting evidence
  - A description of losses and victims
  - A final summary statement

- As a matter of professional practice and compliance with the law, it is absolutely essential and required that investigators pursue their work objectively, honestly, fairly, and accurately. Preparing and presenting a comprehensive investigative report is a highly important and significant part of the overall investigative process and this report must reflect the values of objectivity, honesty, fairness, and accuracy. The facts in the case should "speak for themselves." Editorializing and using inflammatory, prejudicial remarks are entirely inappropriate. Use clear, simple language and *no misspellings or grammar errors.*[5]

- Cases referred for prosecution can be:
  - Returned for further investigation
  - Declined
  - Accepted for prosecution

- Cases accepted for prosecution may be resolved through a negotiated settlement (e.g., plea bargain in criminal cases) or a full litigation proceeding (e.g., trial).

- Many plea agreements in criminal prosecutions contain provisions requiring the defendant to cooperate with the government in the investigation, including being fully debriefed. Prosecutors tend to rely heavily on investigators during the debriefing process and especially for any subsequent follow-up inquiries that are required and/or monitoring other cooperation provided by the defendant.

- When cases go to trial, investigators should expect to be involved in trial preparation, provide assistance to the prosecutor during the trial, and furnish witness testimony as required.

CHAPTER BEST PRACTICES

- As discussed, even in cases where early prosecutor involvement is established, the extent of this involvement can vary considerably, ranging from daily contacts to a more "hands-off" approach. Especially in these latter instances, it is a *best practice* that a meeting with the prosecutor be arranged and the comprehensive investigative report be personally presented and discussed at that time. (See page 217.)

- Just as other witnesses should meet with the prosecutor to go over expected testimony, this would be a *best practice* for investigator-witnesses, as well. While being a witness is part of their job and many investigators are experienced in this respect, even a short interview with the prosecutor will help to avoid surprises and/or misunderstandings. (See page 227.)

- Given all the responsibilities investigators can have in trial preparation and in providing trial assistance, even if there had been only one investigator assigned to the case through the investigation, it is a *best practice* to have additional assistance during this phase. (See page 228.)

Notes

1. Note in Appendix G that prior criminal history of a defendant also plays a substantial role in determining his/her sentence. Not reflected in this appendix are other factors that both add or subtract points in the sentence calculation process. Factors that subtract points from the total include cooperation and acceptance of responsibility (i.e., entering a guilty plea), while those that add points include playing a major role in the offense and obstructing the investigation.
2. G. A. Manning, *Financial Investigation and Forensic Accounting* (Boca Raton, FL: CRC Press, 1999), pp. 350–354.
3. U.S. Department of Justice, *U.S. Attorney's Manual, Criminal Resource Manual, Section 717.* (Washington, DC: Author, 1997).
4. Gary H. Montilla, a former assistant United States attorney, Middle District of Florida, Tampa.
5. Manning, *op. cit.*, pp. 350–354.

Appendix A

Common White Collar Crimes

Antitrust Violations—These cases address collaboration/cooperation by businesses to control prices and competition within a market or industry. When businesses agree among themselves to set prices or prearrange market share (e.g., collusive bidding on contracts), they deprive consumers of the advantages that free market competition brings, that is, lower prices and better services/products.[1] These practices can also limit the ability of businesses that are not party to collaboration/cooperation to successfully compete in the particular market or industry. Federal legislation outlawing these types of practices was among the earliest attempts to address white collar crime in the U.S. The Sherman Anti Trust Act was originally passed in 1890 and provided for both criminal and civil penalties. Thereafter, other laws were enacted (e.g., the Clayton Act of 1914) to supplement efforts to curb antitrust activities, using civil/administrative processes. Although state laws also prohibit antitrust practices, the U.S. Department of Justice and Federal Trade Commission are usually the primary enforcers in this area. These cases can not only involve complex economic analyses of the impact of proposed mergers or the control a business has over an entire industry/market, but they can also require the use of standard investigative techniques such as the development/use of informants and electronic surveillance when criminal price fixing or bid rigging conspiracies are being pursued.

Bank and Loan Frauds—Banking and commercial lending institutions can be victimized by white collar crime in a variety of fashions. Discussed separately below are check fraud and forgery, credit and debit card fraud, confidence games, embezzlement, identity theft, and real estate and mortgage fraud, all scenarios where these institutions can be victimized. However, banks and commercial lenders also make other types of loans (e.g., automobile loans, boat loans, personal loans, etc.) and they can be defrauded through the submission of false information as to the identity and creditworthiness of the borrower. Sometimes this false information is actually provided by an intermediary such as an automobile dealership that seeks to ensure a sale by inflating a customer's creditworthiness. Banks can also be victimized as a result of money laundering schemes (most often unknowingly, but occasionally with the cooperation of a bank employee). On the other hand, banking and lending institutions can, themselves, engage in illegal practices that victimize their customers (e.g., undisclosed fees or terms on loans) or place customer deposits at risk. The savings and loan crisis of the 1980s and early 1990s exposed widespread corrupt management and lending practices that led to the collapse of this industry. Billions of dollars of taxpayer money have been expended to cover the losses due to the commitment of the federal government to ensure a sound banking system. Another variation where the lending industry victimizes the customer is the advance fee scheme. In these cases, individuals purporting to represent lenders/investors collect upfront fees from would-be borrowers (usually a percentage of the loan) under the false representation that funding will be forthcoming. However, the loans never materialize and the lending representative either disappears or explains the deal fell through and the upfront fees are nonrefundable. While state agencies do regulate banks within their borders, the federal government assumes the major burden of regulatory oversight in this area, largely because it does insure customer deposits. Accordingly, federal investigators play a prominent role in all types of bank and loan fraud cases. Obviously, knowledge of banking operations and analysis of bank records are usually prerequisites to the successful resolution of these cases. Title 18 of the U.S. Code, Section 1344 makes defrauding a financial institution a felony, but there are a number of other federal statutes including mail and wire fraud that are charged in these cases.

Bankruptcy Fraud—Bankruptcy laws provide for an orderly disposition of debts and assets resulting from business failures and individuals who can no longer meet their financial responsibilities. This process, however, can be manipulated to protect and hide assets from liquidation that could be used to satisfy outstanding debts, by providing false and fictitious information during the bankruptcy proceedings. However, more elaborate bankruptcy frauds, often referred to as "bust out schemes," involve planned bankruptcies of businesses. In these schemes, business owners (sometimes upon acquiring existing companies with established credit histories or establishing a new company with a name similar to a well-known, successful company) make large orders of merchandise on credit and then sell it off quickly without paying for it. They then remove all the money and assets from the company and file for bankruptcy. These investigations are typically conducted by federal agencies because bankruptcy cases are federal court proceedings. Bankruptcy fraud is a felony under federal law (18 U.S.C. Section 157) and other federal fraud statutes such as mail and wire fraud, might also apply. The FBI estimates that 10% of all bankruptcy filings involve fraud.[2]

Bribery of Public Officials—Whether elected, appointed, or career civil servants, officials/employees at all levels of government can be in a position, as a result of the authority they hold, that could make them susceptible and/or amenable to bribery by those who seek favorable as opposed to nonpreferential treatment. Approving a zoning change or a land development request, ignoring code/regulatory requirements, or awarding a contract are common scenarios where money or other things of value have been offered by those who would benefit from a favorable decision and/or sought by those who have the power to grant them. Even lower level government employees who have access to confidential and potentially valuable information or who can make procurement decisions outside of the more cumbersome government contracting processes can be bribery targets. It should be noted that bribery statutes typically make both the offering of a bribe and the acceptance of a bribe a violation (e.g., see 18 U.S.C. 201, Bribery of Public Officials). These cases are usually criminal investigations and agencies at the federal, state, and local levels exercise authority in this area. However, a related type of conduct that Coleman described as being in the "gray area" and "stopping short of criminal behavior" are conflicts of interest.[3] These are situations where government officials, particularly those who hold elected positions, make decisions or cast votes on matters in which they have a personal interest, particularly financial in nature. For instance, an elected municipal official might have the opportunity to approve a variance or zoning request from a developer that will result in an increase in the value of real estate he/she owns in the same vicinity. A state or federal lawmaker might be involved in legislation affecting an industry or company that he/she has holdings in. These types of situations have given rise to many highly publicized, if not politically motivated, ethics investigations, but as Coleman noted, seldom are criminal charges brought. On the other hand, clearer regulations govern many career and appointed civil servants who wish to take on employment in the private sector with businesses they dealt with as part of their government duties. Failure to abide by these regulations could provide a stronger basis for an enforcement action.

Business/Franchise Opportunity Fraud—Many individuals aspire to self-employment and unfortunately there are those who take advantage of these aspirations by providing fraudulent or misrepresented opportunities or plans to fulfill these dreams. In these cases, victims are solicited to pay a fee to acquire the know-how, supplies/equipment, service and rights to engage in a business or franchise. These schemes misrepresent the income potential, assistance and/or services, supplies and equipment to be provided (in some cases these are nonexistent while in other cases the quality, quantity, and so on are misrepresented). The purchase money is not returned, often the offender disappears, and whatever the victim is left with is worthless. Both civil/administrative and criminal sanctions can apply in these cases. While state/local agencies may have authority in this area, these types of cases are often pursued by federal agencies (e.g., Federal Trade Commission on a civil/administrative basis; and the FBI and Postal Inspectors for criminal violations such as mail and wire fraud) because they are frequently interstate in nature. Establishing a pattern of fraud in these cases is essential; a process that often requires victim interviews and analyses of pertinent documentary evidence.

Charity Fraud—Charity fraud takes advantage of the goodwill and beneficence of many people who are willing to donate their own funds to support what they believe to be a worthy cause. Charity frauds commonly fall into two categories. One category falsely represents that it collects funds for a particular cause when in reality no funds are turned over but rather are simply for the use of those making the solicitations. Often such schemes arise incident to a current calamity and/or adopt organization names similar to existing, well-known charities. The other variation attempts to cleverly evade such brash thievery by soliciting funds for a charitable cause, but then making only a token donation to those in need. The remainder of the funds is applied to "overhead and administrative" expenses of the solicitation organization (which is not necessarily the charity). While charitable solicitation is often regulated by states and sometimes at the municipal/county levels, whether there is any requirement for a certain percentage of funds to be applied to the charitable work or any disclosure at all in this regard, varies. Moreover, whether this latter scenario is in violation of any law will depend upon (1) truthful compliance with any disclosure requirements; and/or (2) analyses of the solicitation representations and financial records of the fund-raising organization. Both civil and criminal sanctions can apply in these cases and those approaching from a criminal prosecution perspective would benefit from joining forces with appropriate regulatory personnel. Federal, state, and local enforcement agencies address charity fraud.

Commercial Bribery/Kickbacks—Bribery occurs in private-sector business transactions as a way of influencing one company to do business with another company. Those who wish to gain an unfair advantage in acquiring a desired business relationship can offer employees with decision-making authority over selecting contractors, subcontractors, vendors and suppliers, money, and other things of value as an incentive. Rather than evaluating a proposed business relationship based on the merits and costs of the services/products involved, offering these types of incentives can result in higher costs to companies and/or inferior products/services while enriching the decision maker. While both bribes and kickbacks seek to influence business relationship decisions, kickbacks usually take place after the desired business transaction has been consummated and their value is often based on a percentage of the transaction. These types of cases are more frequently investigated by federal agencies because they often have interstate features; although specialized white collar crime units at other levels of government may also take on these types of investigations in some circumstances.

Computer Crime—Given the pervasive use of computers for both personal and business purposes, many of the white collar crimes discussed in this appendix could arguably be placed in this category because they are frequently facilitated through the use of computer technology and/or the Internet. However, for purposes here this category will be limited to vandalism through the introduction of viruses, and so on; unauthorized intrusion, for example, "hacking"; and theft of information stored on computers. Law enforcement in general and the law, itself, has had to play "catch-up" in dealing with these types crimes. Computer literacy generally has become a prerequisite for those investigating/prosecuting white collar crime and access to highly trained technical personnel is often a necessity. Agencies at the federal level and many state agencies have developed specialized units to provide this type of technical assistance. Applying the legal system to computer technology scenarios has resulted in new interpretations of existing laws, when possible, and alternatively the passage of new laws that more readily apply to this modern-day environment.

Confidence Swindles—Ironically, crimes falling into this category can be (but not always) as "low tech" as the previous category is "high tech." Included here are the efforts by individuals to gain the trust of people they target, in an effort to convince them to relinquish control of their money or property. The age-old "bank-examiner" scheme, whereby a bank customer is convinced by a con artist to turn over account information in an effort to assist in ferreting out an embezzling employee, is still alive and well. Of course, the outcome here is that the con artist uses the account information to steal the unwitting customer's funds. However, confidence games can also rely on the anonymity of the mail and more recently the Internet. The receipt of letters from overseas or e-mail messages seeking to establish a "trusted" banking relationship or to enter or claim a lottery prize has become commonplace. For those who are convinced of the sincerity and legitimacy of such opportunities, their participation can become a source of bitter disappointment and even financial loss. For instance, the banking relationships ultimately seek personal account information for unauthorized uses or the deposit/cashing of counterfeit checks. The lottery schemes falsely seek payments for lottery entries or fees to claim nonexistent lottery winnings. These schemes prey on the gullible, the trusting, and/or the unsophisticated. Local and state law enforcement is often confronted by the "low tech" varieties while federal authorities deal with those promoted through the mails and the Internet. Although criminal penalties apply in these cases, halting mail and Internet promotions have also relied upon civil/administrative remedies such as injunctive actions to prevent victimization.

Consumer Fraud—This category covers a wide range of misconduct, all of which results in consumers being cheated in transactions for goods and services. Many types of consumer fraud are detailed under other more specific categories within this appendix, including charity fraud; confidence swindles; home and automobile repair fraud; telemarketing fraud; defective or dangerous products; product misrepresentation and failure to deliver; business and franchise opportunity fraud; and vacation/travel frauds. While these latter categories do cover a great many consumer fraud scenarios, this general category is still a necessary catch-all for the seemingly endless variety of these schemes. Many face-to-face retail transactions where customers are cheated (e.g., short-changed or short-weighted transactions, purchased merchandise is switched before it is handed over; false advertising, bait and switch promotions) might be best included in this general category. Faulty and shoddy workmanship in services that do no fall clearly under the home repair category (e.g., carpet cleaning) or failure to honor warranties or product return policies are other practices which can fall under this general consumer fraud category. Automobile dealerships have also come under scrutiny due to practices that could fall under this category; for instance, attractively priced vehicles have been advertised that are not on hand; nondisclosure of known mechanical defects on used vehicles; tampering with odometers to lower mileage on used cars; adding nonrequested services such as auto club memberships to the sales contract and misrepresenting an auto leasing agreement as a purchase contract. Local, state, and federal authorities are involved in consumer fraud and both criminal and civil/administrative actions can be applied. A careful analysis of the written and verbal representations made in connection with the subject transaction is required to be successful in these cases.

Credit/Debit Card Fraud—Credit and debit card fraud can arise from the use of stolen cards or simply the unauthorized use of account numbers. Credit and debit cards can be stolen from individuals, incident to common street crimes such as robberies, burglaries, and larcenies. They can also be stolen during the manufacture/distribution process, that is, before they reach the intended cardholder. Moreover, credit/debit card account numbers can be gleaned from business or personal records, including those maintained on computer files. Once obtained, stolen cards/account numbers can be used to acquire merchandise and services as well as to obtain cash advances. The use of stolen credit/debit card account numbers can facilitate fraudulent Internet and/or telephone transactions. The issuing companies typically suffer most of the monetary losses as opposed to the true cardholders. Credit cards can also be obtained through the submission of applications that contain false information such as name, address, identifiers (e.g., date of birth, social security number), and employment/income information. This information can be totally fictitious or based on the identity of an existing person (see section "Identity Theft"). Another variation of the use of falsely obtained cards is through the counterfeiting of these cards. In either case, the issuing company/bank often suffers the monetary losses incurred. Credit/debit card fraud is a criminal offense under federal and state laws, and is investigated by local, state, and federal agencies. Typically the identities of the offenders are unknown at the outset of the investigation. Records from the credit card issuers and banks are frequently required.

Check Fraud and Forgery—The misuse of checks can take on many variations, but common scenarios involve the theft of a completed or issued check (i.e., the payee and amount has been entered by the payer) and then it is negotiated through a forged endorsement of the payee; blank checks are stolen (incident to robbery, burglary, or larceny or during the manufacturing/distribution process) and negotiated using a forged payer's signature; the use of stolen checking account numbers incident to Internet or telephone transactions; and checks from real or fictitious businesses or individuals can be counterfeited and then negotiated. The monetary losses in these cases often fall to the banks that negotiated the checks, or in some instances, commercial check cashers and other private establishments that accepted the instrument or account number might also be held liable. Check fraud and forgery are criminal offenses under federal and state laws, and are investigated by local, state, and federal agencies. Typically the identities of the offenders are unknown at the outset of the investigation. Bank records are usually necessary to pursue these cases.

Defective or Dangerous Products—These cases involve the investigation of products and services when there are complaints or questions about their safety and/or effectiveness for use or consumption. Included under this category are cases involving tainted or adulterated foods and drugs; ineffective or dangerous drugs and medical devices; and consumer products that have caused (or have the potential to cause) illness or injury. These types of investigations can be both criminal and civil/administrative in nature. The federal Food and Drug Administration and Consumer Product Safety Commission are often in the forefront in these cases although state level regulatory agencies with similar responsibilities may also become involved when the offending activity occurs within their jurisdiction. When criminal violations are being pursued, criminal enforcement agencies at the federal, and sometimes state and local levels, join forces with the regulatory agencies to pursue that aspect of the case. These types of cases often require expert forensic, medical/pharmaceutical, or engineering analysis.

Embezzlement/Employee Theft—Embezzlement of money by employees at banks and other businesses has been an age-old problem for employers. Compounding this problem in today's technological environment is the ability to embezzle using computers. Walking out the door with secreted stolen funds is no longer necessary. Computers provide employees access to company funds that can be transferred to other accounts they control. Alternatively, they can generate checks from company accounts to be mailed to addresses that they establish. Perhaps more pervasive is the theft of nonmonetary items of value that employees have access to while on the job. Purloining product or service inventory and work-place supplies, unauthorized use of services such as telephone and Internet access, work-hour falsification, sick leave abuse, and so on, all are forms of employee theft. Even in those instances where the individual value of the item stolen is small, collectively employee theft can result in large business losses. Bank embezzlements, because of federal insurance coverage, are frequently prosecuted using criminal charges. Other types of embezzlements and employee thefts, especially where the losses are large, can also result in criminal prosecutions, as well. Federal, state, and local investigators handle embezzlement investigations and these cases usually require analysis of company financial records, and with increasing frequency an analysis of computers used to commit these offenses. Employees who are caught embezzling or stealing from their employers are subject to dismissal and possibly pursued through civil action to recover the losses sustained.

Environmental Crimes—This category of white collar crimes incorporates conduct, usually related to business/industrial activities, that damages or puts at risk the safety and well-being of our environment and, in turn, the health and safety of individuals exposed to such conduct. For instance, manufacturing and industrial processes can result in harmful by-products and waste materials that can foul water, air, and/or land, if not disposed of properly as put forth in various state and federal regulations. While certainly worker health can be affected by such exposures (as will be discussed later), poisoned air, land, and water can have far-reaching and lasting consequences on human health. Environmental crimes investigations can be both criminal and civil/administrative in nature and usually are handled by environmental protection units at the federal and state levels because of their complex, often highly technical nature. However, it is not unusual for general criminal investigative agencies at the federal or state levels to assist in these cases when there are aggravated circumstances that warrant a criminal prosecution (e.g., when fatalities are involved).

False Billing Schemes—Schemes in this category involve attempts to solicit payments for merchandise or services never ordered or provided. For example, unscrupulous promoters mail out invoices to businesses for routine office supplies such as copy toner at a nominal cost, without having supplied or intending to supply the product. These promoters recognize that because of the routine nature of the product involved and the nominal cost, many businesses through oversight or lax controls, simply pay it. Alternatively, documents that appear to be invoices are sent to businesses, but are really only solic-itations (as sometimes disclosed in small, faint print) to purchase a product or service, again usually of a routine nature and a nominal cost. In this variation, the product or service is supplied if a remittance is submitted. Another scheme in this genre involves the mailing of unordered COD merchandise, which some recipients unwittingly accept and pay for, even though they never authorized the shipment (in a particularly vicious version of this scheme, promoters send COD merchandise in the names of recently deceased individuals in the hopes that their survivors will feel compelled to accept and pay for the package). These schemes are "classic" mail frauds and possibly wire frauds, as well, especially if the Internet is used in submitting the false invoices. Together with the fact they are usually interstate in scope, these features normally provide a compelling basis for federal investigation. Civil/administrative actions can also be effective in preventing victimization in these cases.

Government Program/Contract Fraud—Governments at all levels disburse money and services in connection with citizen-benefit programs and make purchases of needed goods and services. Both types of government expenditures have been victimized by fraud. Some individuals seek to acquire funds/services for which they are not eligible, but provide false qualifying information. Examples include welfare benefits, Social Security benefits, and programs that assist qualified individuals to attain desired housing, educational, and business goals (government funded health care programs will be discussed later). Other individuals/firms seek to do business with governments, but fail to adhere to their contractual obligations (to include failing to provide products or services or providing goods/services which do not meet the contract specifications in terms of quality, quantity, timeliness, or other requirements). Enforcement proceedings in these types of cases can be either criminal or civil/administrative. Normally, federal agencies address federal program and contract fraud while state/local agencies investigate offenses with activities that affect state and local benefit programs and procurement processes. Knowledge of the intricacies of the victimized programs and contracting procedures are necessary prerequisites in these investigations.

Health Care Fraud—For purposes here, health care fraud refers to efforts to victimize both government and private health care insurance providers. Insureds/beneficiaries can directly defraud their health care insurance coverage through the submission of fraudulent claims, or in the case of government health care programs, obtain benefits to which they are not entitled. Perhaps greater health care fraud victimization can be attributed to health care providers who bill for services not rendered, provide unnecessary services, and engage in kickback schemes for patient referrals. These providers can include physicians and other health care professionals, ancillary health care service companies furnishing diagnostic testing, durable medical goods and various types of therapies, and hospitals. Health care fraud is another highly complex type of white collar crime that requires a knowledge of the health care industry and the insurance programs that it is so dependent upon. Victimization of the federal Medicare program is usually addressed by federal agencies while state agencies usually address Medicaid fraud because this program is state operated (although with a large infusion of federal funds). Victimization of private health insurers can be addressed by either federal or state agencies depending upon the scope of the scheme. Section 1347 of Title 18 of the United States Code makes it a felony to defraud any type of health care benefit program.

Home and Auto Repair Fraud—Shoddy workmanship or unnecessary repairs/services are typical complaints lodged by consumers when they have an unsatisfactory home or auto repair experience. Those who require an upfront fee and then fail to perform the promised work have also marred the home repair industry. Many of these cases are localized in nature and are addressed by local/state authorities including consumer protection and code enforcement agencies using both criminal and civil/administrative statutes. However, Rosoff, Pontell, and Tillman provide the details on well-known, *nationwide* firms that defrauded auto repair customers: Goodyear, Firestone, Sears, Roebuck, and AAMCO.[4] The widespread victimization that can arise when nationwide firms are involved often mandates the involvement of federal agencies such as the Federal Trade Commission.

Identity Theft—Identity theft refers to the illegal or otherwise unauthorized acquisition of a true person's name, address, date of birth, social security number/card, driver's license, employment information, and banking/credit account numbers and cards, and so on, for the purpose of using this identifying information to commit other crimes. This type of information is acquired in a variety of manners including through robberies, burglaries, and larcenies of both individuals/residences and business locations; and mail theft. Personal data stored electronically at both home and business locations can also be illegally accessed for the purpose of engaging in identity theft. Once this information is obtained, not only can a victimized person's existing bank and credit accounts be accessed, but also new accounts using this information can be established. Particularly when the true person has a strong credit history, the purchases of goods and services and acquisition of funds through loans can quickly lead to large financial losses, usually sustained by banks/lenders, credit card issuers, and merchants. Again, using the Internet to conduct transactions with false/assumed identity information often provides further protection against apprehension to the offender. Identity theft is investigated at the local, state, and federal levels and investigations can lead to a host of charges that cover the illegal acquisition of the personal information and its subsequent fraudulent use (e.g., credit card fraud, bank fraud, forgery, mail fraud, wire fraud). Typically the identities of the offenders are unknown at the outset of the investigation. Records from the credit card issuers, banks and other lenders, and merchants are frequently required.

Insurance Fraud—In addition to health insurance (as discussed earlier), insurance companies provide coverage against many other risks we routinely assume in our daily lives, most notably our homes and our autos. Filing false claims on these coverages alleging losses that did not occur or inflating losses that did occur is all too common. Some false insurance claim scenarios become quite complex when policies are purchased in fictitious names and then false losses are reported. In other cases, physicians and attorneys have conspired together to exploit auto accidents in an effort to maximize the profits they can receive from insurance companies (in some of these cases auto accidents have actually been staged). Insurance proceeds are often the motivation behind arsons and malingering workers all too frequently abuse their workers' compensation insurance coverage. While in these latter situations insurance companies are the victims, these companies and/or their employees have a history of being offenders, as well. Misrepresentations in the sale of insurance products (e.g., life insurance) have occurred, either as a matter of company policy or as a result of rogue insurance agents. Insurance premiums have been collected from customers by unscrupulous agents and then not remitted to the company issuing the policy. Mismanagement, embezzlement, and/or fraud within insurance companies themselves can lead to business failure, a situation that could possibly place policyholders at risk. Insurance companies are under state rather than federal oversight/regulation; thus insurance company operations are monitored/investigated by state insurance regulatory departments. Many states have organized special insurance fraud units to investigate insurance frauds, particularly those involving the submission of false claims and activities of unscrupulous insurance agents. Federal agencies can also become involved in insurance fraud, whether committed by individuals or agents/companies, when the scope of the activity is large and widespread. Knowledge of the insurance industry/operations and policy provisions are usually necessary to go forward with these investigations.

Intellectual Property Piracy/Industrial Espionage/Counterfeiting—While counterfeiting currency has been a criminal activity for as long as there have been formal monetary systems, newer forms of counterfeiting involve the manufacture of and sale of goods that mimic well-known, established, and often pricey brands. Items of clothing and watches come readily to mind. Following along in this vein is the unauthorized copying and sale of items of intellectual property, for example, computer software, and music and movies on DVDs. While identifying the end-user distributors is often not difficult, discovering that the source of these phony or pirated products is out of the immediate jurisdiction and often out of the country can be frustrating. Finally, company secrets and information with respect to products, manufacturing/distribution procedures, business/financial affairs, and so on can often be of value to competitors and can be subject to theft by unscrupulous insiders as well as those who gain access from outside the firm. As computers play pervasive roles in the business world, including the storage of company secrets, they can be points of vulnerability for industrial espionage. Thus, technical expertise to unravel computer crimes to include the identification of "hackers" may very well be necessary when dealing with industrial espionage cases.

Product/Service Misrepresentation/Failure to Deliver/Failure to Pay—Our capitalist, free-market economy provides many advantages to the consumer because competition tends to bring forth better goods and services at cheaper prices. However, the competition for product/service sales has also spawned the phenomenon of advertising that touts one product/service over another in terms of qualities and characteristics. While consumers usually benefit from the information advertising imparts, at times products/service are materially misrepresented in an effort to make sales. While misrepresentations can occur in face-to-face transactions, they are particularly troublesome when the transaction occurs through the mail, telephone, and/or Internet. In these situations, purchasers usually do not have the opportunity to physically inspect the goods desired or discuss a service with a known, local provider. Instead, they must rely on written or verbal representations made by unknown individuals from afar. Not surprisingly, this type of scenario has historically lent itself to the sale of misrepresented goods and services, a situation that is continuing unabated with the growth of the Internet as a sales medium. And of course, there have been ample instances of promoters who simply take consumers' money and provide nothing at all. The "flip" side of this latter scenario is where merchandise is ordered (1) in false names; (2) using addresses where the named recipient does not reside; and/or (3) payment is remitted using fraudulent credit card account numbers, stolen and forged checks, or just as often simply not submitted at all. These scenarios are referred to as Failure to Pay cases. Due to the interstate nature of these types of activities, federal criminal enforcement agencies and the Federal Trade Commission most often are involved, although state consumer protection agencies frequently take action when the offenders reside within their borders.

Rebate and Coupon Fraud—A popular retail marketing strategy is to offer consumers discounts on merchandise if they submit a coupon, either incident to the sale or after the transaction. However, this strategy can be fraudulently exploited. Individuals who did not purchase the product, often using fictitious names/addresses along with fabricated receipts and rebate coupons, have submitted mail-in rebate forms in order to receive payments they would not ordinarily be entitled to. In fact, those who engage in this type of fraud often submit multiple rebate requests using a variety of fictitious names and addresses that they control. Retailers have engaged in fraud by submitting cents-off coupons to manufacturers for products they did not actually sell. They augment the cents-off coupons they receive from customers with those they clip themselves from newspapers. Alternatively, cents-off coupons can be clipped from newspapers and submitted for payment to manufacturers using a fictitious store name and address. These types of cases are often pursued on the federal level due to their interstate nature and are often prosecuted under the federal mail fraud statute.

Real Estate and Mortgage Fraud—The classic cases of real estate fraud have often involved the sale of unimproved parcels of land for vacation or retirement home sites. These frauds have employed high pressure sales tactics at locations far removed from the actual parcels of land (thus preventing on-site inspection) and have involved material misrepresentations about the lots themselves, as well as the plans for development and improvements. Those who purchase find they have become owners of land that is far below the value they paid for it. Although sales of primary residences are more tightly controlled through real estate and lending regulations, home purchasers have been victimized by inflated property appraisals, nondisclosed defects in the property, nondisclosed title/ownership problems on the part of the seller, mortgage lenders who falsify a borrower's creditworthiness to ensure a sale or misrepresent the terms of the mortgage, and so on. Conversely, would-be buyers have also falsified their employment, income, and financial resources in an attempt to misrepresent their creditworthiness. Wrongdoing in the real estate and mortgage industries can involve state and federal regulatory and criminal fraud/banking violations. Both federal and state agencies pursue these types of cases, with the former being more prominent when there is interstate involvement.

Securities/Investment Frauds—For purposes here, this category will cover frauds involving stocks, bonds, and commodities (although recognizing that "investments" can cover a wide range of possibilities including valuable collectibles [e.g., art, coins, stamps, etc.] as well as real estate and business/franchise opportunities as discussed above). While an ever-growing portion of the population is now investing in stocks, bonds, and perhaps to a lesser extent commodities, if only through retirement funding plans, relatively few individuals are fully conversant with the intricacies of this complex industry. Fortunately, it is a highly regulated industry on both the federal and state levels. Nevertheless, the securities industry has been plagued by those who have taken advantage of their occupational positions and specialized knowledge in this field, usually to the detriment of uninformed outsiders, that is, the investing public. From the 1990s onward, there have many high-profile "insider trading" cases, that is, situations where individuals connected to securities industry take unlawful advantage of nonpublic, confidential information they acquire to enrich themselves. Other common illegal practices include "churning," whereby brokers unnecessarily make trades on behalf of clients just to generate commissions; and manipulating the value of a stock through false and misleading information and thus creating an artificial demand.[5] Another all too common fraud in this category involves the sale of unregistered securities, that is, investment opportunities offered to the public that are by regulatory definition securities, but have not been registered as such with the Securities and Exchange Commission and perhaps state securities agencies. The failure to take this step is often an indicator that at the very least, full disclosures about the nature and risks of the investment are not being made. The Securities and Exchange Commission is the primary regulator and enforcer in this area, but because it does not possess criminal investigative powers, federal agencies with such authority assist in these cases when criminal prosecution is sought. State security regulators also become involved with offending activity within their borders.

Tax Frauds—Tax frauds encompass efforts by both individuals and business entities to either evade tax responsibility altogether by failing to file or to fraudulently minimize the amount owed. Governments collect a variety of taxes including those on income, sales of merchandise/services, real estate, and personal property, all of which can be evaded or manipulated by those inclined to do so. Enforcement actions in these cases can be both civil and criminal in nature and these investigations are normally conducted by specially designated revenue collection agencies.

Telemarketing Fraud—The use of the telephone to commit fraud could be looked upon as a facilitation/communication medium in much the same way as using the mails and the Internet, neither of which are separate categories here. However, fraudulent telemarketing activity warrants separate consideration due its unique features. It has evolved into what could be described to as a "cottage industry." Although pervasive in nature and not always interconnected, fraudulent telemarketing organizations tend to adopt a common organizational structure, which in turn requires common occupations within that structure. They rely on the use of high-pressure, fraudulent sales tactics (sometimes scripted and sometimes not, or some variation thereof) delivered by telephone, which offers the simultaneous advantages of both personal conversation and anonymity. A wide variety of merchandise, services, investments, travel, employment, and even lottery participation opportunities have been offered through fraudulent telemarketing to both individuals and business entities. Due to the interstate nature of these cases, they are usually pursued by federal agencies, although state and local agencies have made significant contributions when the offending activity lies within their jurisdiction. Both civil and criminal sanctions can be applied.

Vacation/Travel Promotions—Fraudulent promoters have put together misrepresented vacation and travel packages that take advantage of the desires of many to enjoy a break from their everyday routines at an affordable price. Purchasers of such packages find the amenities (e.g., hotel arrangements, services, travel arrangements, and tickets to desired events) and/or costs are not as promised. Additionally, fraud and misrepresentation has plagued the timeshare resort industry (which might also qualify under the real estate category in some circumstances) as to the terms of participation and amenities to be provided. Sales of phony vacation certificates via the telephone and Internet promise "pay now–travel later" opportunities that purchasers subsequently find are seldom, if ever, available due to alleged "space limitations." In those instances where purchasers can actually use the certificate they purchased, they usually find the accommodations, travel arrangements, other amenities, and add-on costs, at the very least disappointing; and then there are instances where a purchaser attempts to use a certificate and finds the promoter has disappeared. Federal authorities (both criminal enforcement agencies and the Federal Trade Commission) are often involved in these types of investigations due to their interstate nature although state agencies will become involved when offenders reside and do business within their borders.

Workplace Safety Violations—Many occupational environments expose workers to risks of injury and illness and federal and state regulations have been enacted to minimize, if not eliminate, these possibilities. Some affected employers find these regulations, however, to be burdensome in terms of the cost to implement required safety equipment and procedures, and/or the adverse impact the regulations have on productivity and profit. Many types of hazardous work environments are by federal and state regulation subject to inspection, and the responsible agencies (at the federal level, the Occupational Safety and Health Administration [OSHA]) conduct investigations when violations are suspected (all to often as a result of a death, injury, or widespread sickness among workers). Most enforcement actions are civil/administrative in nature although in rare instances criminal prosecutions have occurred.

Notes

1. S. M. Rossoff, H. N. Pontell, and R. H. Tillman, *Profit Without Honor: White-Collar Crime and the Looting of America* (Upper Saddle River, NJ: Pearson Prentice Hall, 2004), p. 66.
2. F. Adler, G. O. Mueller, and W. S. Laufer, *Criminology*, 6th ed. (New York: McGraw-Hill, 2007), p. 322.
3. J. W. Coleman, *The Criminal Elite: The Sociology of White Collar Crime* (New York: St. Martin's Press, 1985), pp. 108–112.
4. Rossoff, Pontell, and Tillman, *op. cit.*, pp. 50–52.
5. Adler, Mueller, and Laufer, *op. cit.*, p. 320.

Appendix B

Transmittal Letter and Investigative Questionnaire
(generic; modify to specific case circumstances)

AGENCY
Mailing Address
City and State

Dear _____,

Incident to an official investigation, the (Agency) is examining the business practices of (name of business entity and/or individual). We have reviewed information that suggests you may have had contact and/or conducted a transaction with this firm (or individual). It would be very helpful to us to learn more about your dealings in this regard. Accordingly, we ask that you complete the enclosed questionnaire and return it to us in the post-paid envelope provided. Any relevant documents (or copies thereof) should also be submitted.

This inquiry should not be construed as an allegation of any violation of law by the (subject business and/or individual).

Thank you for your cooperation.

Investigator
Agency

NAME _____

ADDRESS _____

TELEPHONE NUMBERS (H) _____ (W) _____

(C) _____

EMAIL ADDRESS _____

DATE OF BIRTH _____

1. Are you familiar with (business entity and/or individual; address)? YES   NO

2. If YES, please explain briefly the nature of your dealings and/or transaction you engaged in with this firm (or individual).

3. How did you become aware of this business entity (individual)?

4. Why were you interested in dealing or conducting a transaction with this firm (or individual)?

5. Describe how your contacts were conducted (in person, via phone, mail, Internet).

6. Did you engage in a transaction with this business entity (or individual)?

7. What were you told that caused you to make a decision to engage in a transaction with this business entity (individual)?

8. How much money did you pay to enter into this transaction?

9. How was this payment made (cash, check, credit card, money order) and how did you submit it to (business entity/individual) (in person, mail, telephone/Internet transaction)?

10. Did you receive the goods/services promised?

11. Are you satisfied with the transaction? YES   NO Please explain your answer.

12. Over what period of time did your dealings/transactions take place (inclusive dates)?

13. Please add any other details you feel would help us understand your dealings and/or transaction with this business entity (individual)

YOUR SIGNATURE

KINDLY ENCLOSE WITH YOUR COMPLETED QUESTIONNAIRE COPIES OF ALL CORRESPONDENCE, LITERATURE, ADVERTISING MATERIALS, PAYMENT DOCUMENTS AND ANY OTHER RECORDS THAT YOU HAVE RELATING TO THIS MATTER.

YOUR COOPERATION IS GREATLY APPRECIATED.

THANK YOU

Appendix C

Memorandum of Telephone Interview

PERSON INTERVIEWED:	Maggie May Charles Roy's Insurance Company
ADDRESS:	160 Riverview Dr. Walnut, CA
TELEPHONE NUMBER:	800-XXX-XXXX
DATE OF INTERVIEW:	October 1, XXXX
TIME OF INTERVIEW	4:45 PM–5 PM (ET)
DATE THIS MEMO PREPARED:	October 2, XXXX
INTERVIEW CONDUCTED BY:	Rose Gold U.S. Postal Inspector

Maggie May Charles was interviewed on October 1, XXXX concerning a telephone call she received from Office Helpers of XXXX, FL.

Ms. Charles stated she is the person in her office responsible for ordering supplies. She stated that some time in August, XXXX she received a phone call from an individual representing Office Helpers of XXXX, FL, advising that the ink cartridges which her company ordered were about to be shipped. Ms. Charles stated that she did not recall ordering any cartridges from Office Helpers, but she said that she had to check with Ruth Barber, another company employee who had been involved in ordering supplies. She explained further that she was taking over for Barber who was on medical leave at the time of the call. She said she checked with Ms. Barber because she thought Ms. Barber might have ordered these supplies. However, she said that she learned from Barber that she (Barber) did not order any supplies from Office Helpers. Ms. Charles said she called Office Helpers and advised them no order had been placed with their firm. She said that when she advised the Office Helpers' employee of this, he became rude to her.

Ms. Charles stated that notwithstanding her advice to Office Helpers, that Roy's Insurance Company did not order any supplies from them, a shipment of ink cartridges were received by her company along with an invoice. She said she believes the cartridges were shipped by a freight company while the invoice was mailed. She also said that her company normally buys these same supplies from another vendor.

Rose Gold
U.S. Postal Inspector

Appendix D

Supplemental Search Warrant Information

Limiting Phrases Contained in Warrants for Documents

Types of limiting phrases that have been approved by courts include:[1]

1. Documents, records, etc. which are evidence and fruits of certain specified commodities fraud statutes, sought from an operation which was permeated with fraud (*U.S.* v. *Sawyer*, 799 F.2d 1949, 1508 (11th Cir) cert. denied, 107 S. Ct. 961 (1987).

2. Representative handwriting samples. *U.S.* v. *Soto-Gomez*, 723 F.2d 649,653 (9th Cir.0. cert. denied, 466 U.S. 977 (1984).

3. Papers indicating the ownership or occupancy of premises used for a drug laboratory. *U.S.* v. *Whitten*, 706 F.2d 1000, 1008–1009 (9th Cir), cert. denied 465 U.S. 1100 (1984).

4. Documents, papers, receipts and other writings which are evidence of a conspiracy to import heroin. *U.S.* v. *Vanichromanee*, 742 F.2d 340, 347 (7th Cir. 1984).

5. All checkbooks, cancelled checks, deposit slips, bank statements, trust accounts receipts, check stubs, books and papers, etc. which would show fraudulent intent or any elements of the crime of false pretense or embezzlement. *State* v. *Kornegay*, 326 S.E. 2d 881, 894–895 (N.C. 1985).

Types of limiting phrases that have been ruled insufficient include:

1. Certain property, namely notebooks, notes, documents, address books and other records . . . which are evidence of violations of [certain statutes identified only by number]. *U.S.* v. *Spilotro*, 800 F.2d 959 (9th Cir. 1986).

2. All records pertaining to the suspect's bail bonding business for the past six years. In Re Grand Jury Proceedings, 716 F.2d 493, 496–499 (8th Cir. 1983). (The court held that this warrant was a general warrant violating the Fourth Amendment).

3. In a tax fraud investigation, "all files, bank records, employee records, precious metal records, marketing and promotional literature. Voss v. Bergsgaard, 774 F. 2d 402, 404–406 (10th Cir. 1985).

4. Documentary evidence tending to show the whereabouts of [defendant] on certain dates. (*People* v. *Frank*, 700 P.2d 415 (Cal.1985)).

Business Records Subject to Seizure[2]

- Cash receipts and disbursement journal
- Payroll journal
- Sales journal
- Purchases journal
- General journal or any other journal maintained in the regular course of business
- General ledger (all accounts and subsidiary accounts)
- Operating accounts
- Financial statements
- Invoices, bills, bills of lading, statements, and all other source documents

- Bank records, including signature cards, statements, checks, deposit tickets, debit and credit memos, check registers, and correspondence
- Contracts, including rental or lease agreements
- Insurance policies
- Federal and state tax returns
- State board of equalization tax returns
- Articles of incorporation and bylaws
- Minutes books correspondence
- Correspondence
- Title search and examination file
- Title reports
- Title policies
- Certificate of title
- Correspondence
- Escrow instructions (buyer's and seller's)
- Payoffs of existing financing
- New loan instructions and documents
- Title reports
- Identity statements
- Closing statements (buyer's and seller's)
- Demands and/or beneficiary statements

Example of Agent Experience Summary: Kickback/Tax Fraud Investigation[3]

a. Based on my experience, knowledge, and training, I have found that businesses and corporations typically maintain books and records at their location of business. I have further found that it is common practice in the business community to maintain journals, ledgers, and other records showing the receipt and disposition of funds. I have also found in my experience in dealing with business records that the flow of funds into and out of a company can be tracked by tracing the paper trail. The paper trail is created by the entries into the business records and bank accounts, and by the documents received or prepared to support a transaction.

b. I have further found that the business records of individuals businesses and companies are used as a basis for the preparation of business, corporate and individual income tax returns. I have also found business records are ordinarily kept and maintained at the place of business for extended periods of time, often several years, in order to provide for revenue and expense transactions if questioned by IRS examiners at a later date, among other reasons.

c. Based on experience as a special agent for the IRS, I have found that businesses and corporations involved keep records of illegal payments, including kickback payments disguised as legitimate expenses, in order to eliminate drawing attention to themselves and their criminal activity. I have further found that the violators will often deduct the illegal payment disguised as legitimate business expense, such as consulting fees, promotion fees, etc. in order to further profit from their illegal activity. I have found that violators employ many tactics to deduct the illegal payments, including the use of currency, the alteration and falsification of records, the use of shell companies as fronts, and the use of fictitious accounts and nominees because they know as a matter of law kickbacks and other illegal payments are not legally deductible as a business expense on federal income tax returns.

d. Therefore, based on my experience as a special agent and the facts set out in this affidavit, I have probable cause to believe and do believe that [subject individuals and companies] and others known and unknown to me were involved in a conspiracy to conceal and cover up illegal kickback payments by preparing and causing to be prepared false corporate documents, falsifying corporate books and records, and filing fraudulent income tax returns which were false as to material matter, in such a way as to defraud the United States, by impeding and impairing the IRS in its function of examination, assessment, and collection of federal income taxes, in violation of 18 USC 371.

e. Based on the above information contained herein, I have probable cause to believe and do believe that within the office premises and residence described in the attachment to this affidavit are now located records of this illegal scheme, including all records described in the description of property attachment to this affidavit for search warrant.

Sample Language Relating to Search and Seizures of Computers and/or Information Contained therein[4]

a. *Defining the terms records and information:* The terms "records" and "information" include all of the foregoing items of evidence in whatever form and by whatever means they may have been created or stored, including any electrical, electronic, or magnetic form (such as any information on an electronic or magnetic storage device, including floppy diskettes, hard disks, ZIP disks, CD-ROMs, optical discs, backup tapes, printer buffers, smart cards, USB storage devices, memory calculators, pagers, personal digital assistants such as Palm Pilot computers, as well as printouts or readouts from any magnetic storage device); any handmade form (such as writing, drawing, painting); any mechanical form (such as printing or typing); and any photographic form (such as microfilm, microfiche, prints, slides, negatives, videotapes, motion pictures, photocopies).

b. *Describing a particular document:* Any copy of the X Company's confidential May 17, 1998 report, in electronic or other form, including any recognizable portion or summary of the contents of that report.

c. *For a warrant to obtain records stored with an ISP pursuant to Electronic Communications Privacy Act:* All stored electronic mail of any kind sent to, from and through the e-mail address [JDoe@isp.com], or associated with the user name "John Doe," account holder [suspect], or IP Address [xxx.xxx.xxx.xxx]/Domain name [x.com] between Date A at Time B and Date X at Time Y. Content and connection log files of all activity from January 1, 2000, through March 31, 2000, by the user associated with the e-mail address [JDoe@isp.com], user name "John Doe," or IP Address [xxx.xxx.xxx.xxx]/Domain name [x.x.com] between Date A at Time B and Date X at Time Y, including dates, times, methods of connecting (e.g., telnet, ftp, http), type of connection (e.g., modem, cable/DSL, T1/LAN), ports used, telephone dial-up caller identification records, and any other connection information or traffic data. All business records, in any form kept, in the possession of [Internet Service Provider], that pertain to the subscriber(s) and account(s) associated with the e-mail address [JDoe@isp.com], user name "John Doe," or IP Address [xxx.xxx.xxx.xxx]/Domain name [x.x.com] between Date A at Time B and Date X at Time Y, including records showing the subscriber's full name, all screen names associated with that subscriber and account, all account names associated with that subscriber, methods of payment, phone numbers, all residential, business, mailing, and e-mail addresses, detailed billing records, types and lengths of service, and any other identifying information.

d. *Hardware description:* IBM Thinkpad Model 760ED laptop computer with a black case.

e. *Suggested affidavit language addressing possible staleness of information upon which probable cause is based:* Based on your affiant's knowledge, training, and experience, your affiant knows that computer files or remnants of such files can be recovered months or even years after they have been downloaded onto a hard drive, deleted or viewed via the Internet. Electronic files downloaded to a hard drive can be stored for years at little or no cost. Even when such files have been deleted, they can be recovered months or years later using readily available forensics tools. When a person "deletes" a file on a home computer, the data contained in the file does not actually disappear; rather, that data remains on the hard drive until it is overwritten by new data. Therefore, deleted files, or remnants of deleted files, may reside in free space or slack space— that is, in space on the hard drive that is not allocated to an active file or that is unused after a file has been allocated to a set block of storage space—for long periods of time before they are overwritten. In addition, a computer's operating system may also keep a record of deleted data in a "swap" or "recovery" file. Similarly, files that have been viewed via the Internet are automatically downloaded into a temporary Internet directory or "cache." The browser typically maintains a fixed amount of hard drive space devoted to these files, and the files are only overwritten as they are replaced with more recently viewed Internet pages. Thus, the ability to retrieve residue of an electronic file from a hard drive depends less on when the file was downloaded or viewed than on a particular user's operating system, storage capacity, and computer habits.

f. *Description of how computer is being used in the criminal activity:* Based on actual inspection of [spreadsheets, financial records, invoices], your affiant is aware that computer equipment was used to generate, store, and print documents used in [suspect's] tax evasion, money laundering, drug trafficking, etc.] scheme. There is reason to believe that the computer system currently located on [suspect's] premises is the same system used to produce and store the [spreadsheets, financial records, invoices], and that both the [spreadsheets, financial records, invoices] and other records relating to [suspect's] criminal enterprise will be stored on [suspect's computer].

g. *Sample Language to Justify Seizing Hardware and Conducting a Subsequent Off-site Search:* Based upon your affiant's knowledge, training and experience, your affiant knows that searching and seizing information from computers often requires agents to seize most or all electronic storage devices (along with related peripherals) to be searched later by a qualified computer expert in a laboratory or other controlled environment. This is true because of the following:

1. The volume of evidence. Computer storage devices (like hard disks, diskettes, tapes, laser disks) can store the equivalent of millions of pieces of information. Additionally, a suspect may try to conceal criminal evidence; he or she might store it in random order with deceptive file names. This may require searching authorities to examine all the stored data to determine which particular files are evidence or instrumentalities of crime. This sorting process can take weeks or months, depending on the volume of data stored, and it would be impractical and invasive to attempt this kind of data search on-site.

2. Technical Requirements. Searching computer systems for criminal evidence is a highly technical process requiring expert skill and a properly controlled environment. The vast array of computer hardware and software available requires even computer experts to specialize in some systems and applications, so it is difficult to know before a search which expert is qualified to analyze the system and its data. In any event, however, data search protocols are exacting scientific procedures designed to protect the integrity of the evidence and to recover even "hidden," erased, compressed, password-protected, or encrypted files. Because computer evidence is vulnerable to inadvertent or intentional modification or destruction (both from external sources and from destructive code imbedded in the system as a "booby trap"), a controlled environment may be necessary to complete an accurate analysis. Further, such searches often require the seizure of most or all of a computer system's input/output peripheral devices, related software, documentation, and data security devices (including passwords) so that a qualified computer expert can accurately retrieve the system's data in a laboratory or other controlled environment.

In light of these concerns, your affiant hereby requests the Court's permission to seize the computer hardware (and associated peripherals) that are believed to contain some or all of the evidence described in the warrant, and to conduct an off-site search of the hardware for the evidence described, if, upon arriving at the scene, the agents executing the search conclude that it would be impractical to search the computer hardware on-site for this evidence.

Notes

1. R.S. Stolker, *Asset forfeiture: Financial search warrants* (Washington, DC: U.S. Department of Justice, Bureau of Justice Assistance, 1989), p. 12.
2. Ibid., p. 38
3. Ibid., pp. 36–37.
4. Computer Crime and Intellectual Property Section, Criminal Division, U.S. Department of Justice, *Searching and Seizing Computers and Obtaining Electronic Evidence in Criminal Investigations*. July, 2002. Retrieved March 7, 2005 from U.S. Department website http://www.usdoj.gov/criminal/cybercrime/searching.html#A.

Appendix E

Sample Declaration: Injunctive Action under 18 U.S.C. 1345

(Note: the sequence of events described below spanned a period of four years. For purposes of this example, actual days and months are provided, but the specific year is identified by XXXX (-1); XXXX; XXXX (+1); and XXXX (+2); individual, agency, and business names and geographic locations have been changed. Referenced exhibits have been omitted in the interest of space)

DECLARTION OF MICHAEL LIU

I, Michael Liu, declare as follows:

1.   I am an investigator with the United States Investigation Service. I have been employed in this capacity for 6 years.

2.   For most of these 6 years, I have been assigned to the investigation of fraud cases, including violations of the federal mail and wire fraud statutes, 18 U.S.C. 1341 and 1343 respectively.

Overview

3.   I am presently investigating the sale of diet products by George Carlton, Robert Callous, and Raymond Carlton, the officers and operators of several firms currently located at 207 Calvary St., Los Angeles, CA. These individuals have been found through Postal Service administrative litigation and in one case, through the federal judicial forum, to have sought money through the mails based on false advertising. These defendants continue to make the same false representations about essentially the same products, but seek to evade existing consent agreements, cease and desist orders and false representation orders by simply changing the manner in which they receive remittances. Through advertisements in nationally circulated publications, they take orders over the telephone and obtain payments by way of credit cards or COD sales. By following this practice, their advertising has been able to remain essentially unchanged despite the various enforcement actions taken for false representations. Set forth below is an overview of these products, the outstanding orders, and the manner in which they have been marketed.

Company Name/Officer	Product	Enforcement Actions Taken	Initial Ingredients	Current Ingredients	Current Advertising/ Sales Medium	Mail Orders
Huge People, Inc. George Carlton Robert Callous	Diet-All	Administrative complaint filed 7/10/XXXX; Consent agreement signed 10/7/XXXX; Breach of consent agreement filed 1/22/XXXX (+2); Supplement to consent agreement filed 2/23/XXXX (+2)	Grapefruit extract; Konjac Gluco-mannan; Guar Gum	Grapefruit Extract; Guar Gum Cyanopsis Tetra Gonoloba; Fucus Modusus	Many of the same representa-tions; Telephone orders With credit card/COD payments; No mail orders accepted	Yes

(*continued*)

(*continued*)

Appetite Suppressors, Inc. George Carlton; Robert Callous	Fat Burners	Consent agreement signed 10/7/XXXX; Breach of consent agreement filed 1/22/XXXX (+2); Supplement to consent agreement filed 2/23/XXXX(+2)	Grapefruit Extract; Guar Gum L-Phenyla-lamine	Grapefruit Extract; Guar Gum L-Phenyla-lamine	Advertising representations have remained essentially the same for nearly 2 years; telephone orders with credit card/ COD payments; No mail orders accepted	Yes
Bodi- Firm Corp. Raymond Carlton (P.O. Box application also bears the name Huge People owned by George Carlton and Robert Callous)	Fat-Gon	Administrative complaint filed 11/22/XXXX (+2); TRO issued in USDC 11/28/XXXX (+2); Preliminary Injunction issued 12/08/XXXX (+2); False Representation Order and Cease and Desist Order issued 12/23/XXXX (+2)	Phenylpropano-lamine (PPA)	Fat-Gon is no longer sold	Fat-Gon is no longer sold	Yes
Sutton Phar-maceuticals George Carl-ton and Robert Cal-lous (Ray-mond Carlton opened the P.O. Box)	Fat-Trim	Sale of this product subject to Supple-ment to consent agreement filed 2/23/XXXX (+2)	Phenylpropano-lamine (PPA)	Phenylprop-ano-lamine (PPA)	Advertising representations have remained largely unchanged; telephone orders with credit card/ COD payments; No mail orders accepted	Yes

I. CHRONOLOGY OF EVENTS: HUGE PEOPLE, INC./DIET-ALL

Enforcement Action

4.   On July 18, XXXX, an administrative complaint alleging violations of Title 39 United States Code, Section 3005 was filed by the General Counsel of the U.S. Postal Service against Huge People, Inc.; George Carlton; Robert Callous; and Raymond Carlton. The complaint alleged that the respondents sought money through the mail based on false representations with regard to the sale of Diet-All. [*A copy of the this complaint was attached to the original declaration.*]

5.   On October 7, XXXX, respondents George Carlton, Robert Callous, and Raymond Carlton, individually, and as directors of Huge People, Inc., and Appetite Suppressors, Inc., entered into a consent agreement and also agreed to the issuance of a cease and desist order. It should be noted that respondent Appetite Suppressors, Inc., was not a named respondent in the original complaint, but was added to the Consent Agreement and Cease and Desist order as a result of settlement

negotiations. [*A copy of the consent agreement and cease and desist order was attached to the original declaration.*] The cease and desist order provides that the respondents will cease and desist from representing that:

- Ingestion of the Diet-All tablet or any product containing substantially the same ingredients will cause significant weight loss in virtually all users.

- Ingestion of the Deit-All tablet, or any product containing substantially the same ingredients, will cause significant weight loss without discipline, calorie restricted diets, or strenuous exercise.

- Ingestion of the Diet-All tablet, or any product containing substantially the same ingredients, will allow users to continue to eat high calorie foods and yet still lose a significant amount of weight.

- An obese person who takes the Diet-All tablet, or any product containing substantially the same ingredients, may reasonably expect to lose a significant amount of weight, while continuing to eat all he or she wants.

Comparison of Advertisements

6.   I have reviewed an advertisement in the August 18, XXXX(-1) edition of the *ABC* magazine (*see exhibit A [attached in original declaration]*) for Diet-All, placed by Huge People, Inc., and compared it to an advertisement for Diet-All placed by Huge People, Inc., in the *DEF* magazine about two years later (*see exhibit B*). My review disclosed that the two advertisements are virtually the same except that a mail order coupon which appeared in the earlier advertisement has been replaced in the later advertisement with instructions on how to place an order by telephoning an "800" number and submitting payment by credit card. Thus, compliance with the previous Consent Agreement against Huge People, Inc., is achieved through not soliciting money through the mails, rather than modifying the misrepresentations about the product being sold as required in the Cease and Desist Agreement this company entered into. I also noticed that the P.O. Box mailing address remained unchanged in the two advertisements.

Follow-Up Enforcement Action

7.   On October 18, XXXX(+1), U.S. Investigator McKenna of Memphis, TN, submitted a mail order to Huge People, Inc., at their P.O Box for Diet-All. This address again appeared in an advertisement for Diet-All in the October 10, XXXX(+1) edition of *ABC* magazine. On October 23, XXXX(+1), McKenna received by U.S. Mail his order of Diet-All. Based on this purchase, the General Counsel of the U.S. Postal Service filed a petition alleging a breach of the Consent Agreement [*a copy of this document was attached in the original declaration*]. An order holding all mail addressed to Huge People, Inc., at their P.O. Box address was issued on January 24, XXXX(+2) [*a copy of this document was attached in the original declaration*].On February 23, XXXX(+2) a supplemental agreement was reached with the respondents to resolve the alleged breach of the earlier Consent Agreement [*a copy of this document was attached in the original declaration*]. In part, this agreement required the respondents to place the legend , "No mail orders accepted" and omit both street and post office box addresses on their advertising for any weight loss products.

Follow-Up Comparison of Advertisements

8.   I reviewed an advertisement for Diet-All bearing the legend, "No mail orders accepted," which appeared in the April 10, XXXX(+2) edition of the *XYZ* magazine. In comparing this advertisement with Exhibit B, I noted many similarities including the following:

Exhibit B	Exhibit C
• Experts agree: this is the fastest weight loss Program ever!	Clinical studies show: fastest weight loss program ever
• I lost 71 pounds in six weeks! . . .You can too or your money back!!!	I lost 142 pounds fast. Eating five and six meals a day of all my favorite foods!!
• Absolutely safe-no hunger-no drugs-no Calorie counting-and no strenuous exercise!	This is the easiest diet that I have ever tried!
• Now you can eat all you want of these great foods while extra weight disappears: bacon, and eggs, roast chicken, roast beef and pork, shrimp, lobster, butter, salad dressings, mayonnaise.	Now you can eat all you want of these great foods while extra weight disappears: bacon, eggs, roast pork, roast beef, spare ribs, chicken, shrimp, lobster (dripping in butter) and much more. . . .
• Yes, if you are in normal health, you will be amazed at this doctor's program that helps You lose as much weight as you wish faster and more safely than anything you've ever tried. After all, whoever heard of a weight reduction programs that requires no doctor's prescription and lets you eat high calorie foods your heart's content?	You will be amazed at this doctor's program that helps you lose as much weight as you wish faster and more safely than anything you've ever tried. After all whoever heard of a weight loss program that requires no doctor's prescription and lets you eat all the high calorie foods to your heart's content?
• No self control needed as 20-30-60-100 Unwanted pounds and inches melt away.	Yes, Diet-All is the only true all-you-can-eat diet program. You don't have to count calories or starve yourself.

Both ads provide testimonials from users who experienced dramatic weight losses. Exhibit B provides testimonials from George C. of Florida and Ray C. of New York while Exhibit C provides a testimonial from Larry H., who states that he went from 327 pounds to 185 pounds. In exhibit B, George C. states he lost 37 pounds in two weeks while Ray C. of New York states he lost 71 pounds in six weeks and has never gained a pound back. Larry H. states in Exhibit C, "One morning I was putting on my shorts and got chest pains and was having trouble breathing." In Exhibit B, an unattributed testimonial states, "I used to look at least 10 years older, unattractive, but worst of all, any day I expected a heart attack, stroke or diabetes and decided this was too serious a problem to expect my family to live with. The expense and care would have wiped us all out financially, even if I didn't die from all these diseases."

II. CHRONOLOGY OF EVENTS: APPETITE SUPPRESSORS, INC./FAT BURNERS

Comparison of Advertising

9.   Attached as Exhibit D is an advertisement for Fat Burners that appeared in nationally circulated publications in XXXX. This product was sold by Appetite Suppressors, Inc., a respondent in the aforementioned consent agreement. I have compared this advertisement to Exhibit E that

appeared in XXXX (+1). The two advertisements are nearly identical with the exception of different graphics and the mail order coupon has been replaced with instructions for ordering by telephone and credit cards. This latter change is in compliance with the consent agreement. However, the representations concerning the ability of Fat Burners to cause weight loss are unaltered from the pre-consent agreement advertisement.

Enforcement Action

10.   Fat-Burners, Inc., was also included in the supplement to agreement containing consent order to cease and desist dated February 23 XXXX (+2) [*a copy of which was attached to the original declaration*]. This agreement, in part, required that respondent Appetite Suppressors, Inc., to place the legend, "No mail orders accepted" on its advertisements and omit street and/or post office box address information.

Follow-Up Comparison Advertising

11.   I compared Exhibit E with an advertisement for Fat Burners that appeared in nationally circulated publications about six months later (Exhibit F). The two advertisements are nearly identical. The major difference between them is that Exhibit F bears the legend, "No mail orders accept," and a post office box number or street address does not appear. While these latter differences are attributable to aforementioned supplemental agreement, representations concerning the ability of Fat Burners to cause weight loss are unaltered from earlier advertising.

III. CHRONOLOGY OF EVENTS: BODI-FIRM CORPORATION/FAT-GON

Advertising

12.   On or about April, XXXX, direct mail advertisements for a product labeled Fat-Gon were sent to members of the public by Bodi-Firm Corporation, P.O. Box 31108, Los Angeles, CA (See Exhibit G.). The advertisements portrayed Fat-Gon as a diet aid, which would result in substantial weight loss in short periods of time.

Investigation

13.   Investigation determined Bodi-Firm was incorporated on August 24, XXXX (-1), and the president of this corporation is Raymond Carlton of Los Angeles, CA. A review of the application for P.O. Box 31108, Los Angeles, CA disclosed that this box was rented in the names Huge People, Inc., and Bodi-Firm.

14.   Based on my experience as an investigator, I felt that the representations made about the ability of Fat-Gon to cause weight loss were false. I ordered Fat-Gon by mail from Bodi-Firm and subsequently received this product. I then submitted it along with the related advertising to an expert for analysis. This expert, Professor Phyllis Lawrence, Ph.D., of the Department of Nutrition and Food at State University [*not the true names of the expert and affiliated institution*], confirmed my suspicions. Professor Lawrence further indicated that the active ingredient in Fat-Gon is phenylpropanolamine (PPA).

15.   Based on Professor Lawrence's report, the General Counsel of the U.S. Postal Service filed an administrative complaint on November 22, XXXX against Bodi-Firm Corporation and Raymond Carlton, alleging violations of Title 39, United States Code, Section 3005 in connection with the sale of Fat-Gon.

On November 28, XXXX, a temporary restraining order pursuant to Title 39, United States Code, Section 3007 was sought in U.S. District Court, Los Angeles, CA. On that date U.S. District Court Judge Smith [*not the true name of the judge*] issued the requested order. Judge Smith scheduled a hearing on a preliminary injunction for December 9, XXXX. Raymond Carlton did not appear for this hearing and Judge Smith issued the preliminary injunction. Furthermore, Raymond Carlton failed to respond to the administrative complaint and on December 27, XXXX, a false representation order and cease and desist order were issued against Bodi-Firm and Raymond Carlton. The cease and desist order, in part, bars Bodi-Firm Corporation and Raymond Carlton from representing that:

a. Fat-Gon or any product containing phenylpropanolamine (PPA) will cause or aid in the reduction of weight and/or fat without restriction of the user's accustomed calorie intake.

b. Fat-Gon or any product containing PPA will cause most users or the average user to achieve a significant weight loss without discipline, restricting calorie intake or exercise.

c. Most users or the average user can obtain significant permanent weight loss by means of Fat-Gon or any product containing PPA alone without dieting.

d. An obese person who takes Fat-Gon or any product containing PPA may reasonably expect to lose a significant amount of weight while continuing to eat all he or she wants.

16. The cease and desist order further bars Bodi-Firm Corporation and Raymond Carlton from representing in connection with the sale of any products through the U.S. Mails that:

a. Any product or any portion of a product makes a material contribution to weight or fat loss.

b. Any product or portion of a product prevents food from being converted into stored fat.

c. Any product or portion of a product will cause significant weight loss without discipline, calorie restricted diets or exercise.

d. Any survey or other scientific or independent test supports any conclusion (i.e., any substantiation claim).

e. Any claim substantially similar to any of a–d above, unless such party possesses and relies upon reliable and competent evidence substantiating such claim, prior to dissemination of the claim to the public. "Reliable and competent evidence" means either:

   i. at least two well controlled, double blind, clinical studies that are conducted in accordance with generally accepted scientific procedures by qualified, objective persons and that yield statistically significant results;

   ii. or in the case of a nutritional equivalence, the certification or other sworn statement of a state licensed nutritionist that the product is nutritionally equivalent to a specific food in all respects, with those specifically quantified.

17. Part III of the cease and desist order against Bodi-Firm Corporation and Raymond Carlton requires that these respondents to forthwith cease and desist from representing, whether via testimonials or otherwise, that a specific amount of weight loss or a specific amount of weight loss in a specific amount of time, has been achieved by particular users, unless such representation is typical of users as substantiated by reliable and competent evidence as defined with Part II of the order.

A representation (through the use of testimonials or otherwise) of a specific rate or amount of weight loss achieved by actual users shall be deemed a representation of the rate or amount of weight loss which consumers can expect to achieve.

IV. CHRONOLOGY OF EVENTS: SUTTON PHARMACEUTICALS/FAT-TRIM

Investigation

18. On January 23, XXXX (+2) Investigator L.J. Jones of Cleveland, OH, advised that a local newspaper referred to his attention a copy of an advertisement for a weight loss product labeled as Fat-Trim. The advertisement invited customers to purchase this product, through the mail from Sutton Pharmaceuticals, P.O. Box 3401, Los Angeles, CA. The advertisement that is attached as Exhibit H indicated that Fat-Trim would cause substantial weight loss by those using it. Investigator Jones sent me this advertisement for review. Upon receiving it, based on my experience as an investigator, I felt that the representations made about the effects of this product in causing weight loss were untrue. In order to further evaluate the product, I ordered it from Sutton Pharmaceuticals on January 31, XXXX (+2), at a cost of $22.98. As of this date, I have never received a response to this order.

19. Incident to ordering Fat-Trim, I began to make inquiries as to the ownership of Sutton Pharmaceuticals. Contact with the local post office disclosed that P.O. Box 3401 was rented to Raymond Carlton of Los Angeles, CA. The California Department of State, Division of Corporate Records, advised on February 21, XXXX (+2), that Sutton Pharmaceuticals was incorporated in the State of California on December 22, XXXX (+1). The directors of this corporation are George Carlton and Robert Callous. The corporate address was listed as 207 Calvary St., Los Angeles, CA. After waiting three weeks and not receiving my order of Fat-Trim, a formal written request to purchase this product was served at the offices of Sutton Pharmaceuticals by Investigator Ross Clive on February 21, XXXX (+2). The request was served on Susan Callous at this location. Ms. Callous was furnished a money order for $22.98 to cover the cost of Fat-Trim. The formal request indicated that Fat-Trim should be furnished to me by February 28, XXXX (+2). An employee of Sutton Pharmaceuticals personally delivered a sample of Fat-Trim to me on February 28, XXXX (+2).

20. On March 6, XXXX (+2), I requested Professor Lawrence, Ph.D., of the Department of Nutrition and Food at State University to conduct an expert evaluation of Fat-Trim. I provided Professor Lawrence a label from this product and the related advertising. On March 19, XXXX (+2), Professor Lawrence furnished her expert opinion. This opinion, in pertinent part, identifies the active ingredient in Fat-Trim as phenylpropanolamine as well as several misrepresentations as to the ability of this product to cause weight loss. It should be noted that this is the same active ingredient contained in Fat-Gon.

Comparison of Advertising

21. I have reviewed several advertisements for Fat-Trim which appeared in nationally circulated publications between the period February 20 and July 3, XXXX (+2) [Exhibits H and I]. Most of the representations about the ability of Fat-Trim to cause weight loss are the same in each of these advertisements, with one notable exception. In the July 3 advertisement the title of the advertisement

reads, "Diet pill approved for sale in U.S.," followed by, "FDA Considers . . . 100% safe and effective." The earlier advertisement bears the endorsement, "FDA approves sale of weight loss pill in U.S." The other notable difference between the July 3 advertisement and the earlier advertisement is that it contains the legend, "No mail orders accepted," and any street or post office address is omitted. As indicated above, the earlier advertisement invited customers to order Fat-Trim through P.O. Box 3401, Los Angeles, CA. The July advertisement includes instructions on how to order Fat-Trim over the phone using Visa or MasterCard for payment.

Enforcement Action

22. These changes are an apparent attempt to conform to a motion to amend the agreement containing consent order to cease and desist [*exhibit attached in original*]. While Sutton Pharmaceuticals is not a named respondent in this order, respondents George Carlton and Robert Callous, as officers of Sutton Pharmaceuticals, are required to print the legend, "no mail orders accepted," on any advertising for any weight loss program as well as to omit any information concerning a street address or post office box number on such advertising.

Follow-Up Comparison of Advertisements

23. I compared the July 3 advertisement for Fat-Trim (Exhibit I) with the April, XXXX (+1) advertisement for Fat-Gon (Exhibit G). I made this comparison because these two products contain the same ingredient (PPA). While the formats of the two advertisements differ, there are many similarities in the representations made concerning the two products as outlined in the chart below:

24. With regard to item (b) below, there are safety concerns that the user of a PPA product should be aware of. In fact, purchasers of Fat-Gon and Fat-Trim are supplied with a list of health conditions which are not compatible with the use of a PPA product. However, this information is not provided at the time of sale unless the purchaser makes a telephone inquiry with a customer service representative

Fat-Gon	**Fat-Trim**
25 MG Phenylpropanolamine HCl Advertising April, XXXX (+1)	25 MG Phenylpropanolamine HCl Advertising July 3, XXXX (+2)
a. New Scientific Break Through For the Overweight Man or Woman	Diet Pill Approved for Sale in U.S.
b. Don't Deprive Yourself of That Figure You Want When You Can QUICKLY-SAFELY-AND-EASILY Lose the Weight You Desire	FDA Considers 100% Safe and Effective
c. Throw Away Calorie Counting Charts and Diet Programs	. . . makes people lose weight without changing their eating habits, without exercise and without keeping track of calories
d. After losing 105 pounds in only 60 days . . .	. . . one person losing over 100 pounds in only 2 months . . .
e. . . . Allows you to stuff yourself with the richest and most delicious foods . . . And still lose all the weight you desire	. . . people who take Fat-Trim can go on eating unlimited portions of their favorite foods and still lose weight.

(see paragraph 26). Otherwise, the purchaser relies on the statements made in item (b), paragraph 23, and discovers health warnings only after the purchase is made. Moreover, I have been advised by Professor Lawrence of side effects of PPA that are not listed on the product label, including symptoms of excessive central nervous system stimulation, seizure, and intracranial hemorrhage.

V. USE OF THE MAILS AND WIRES

25. I receive at my office in Los Angeles by U.S. Mail on a subscription basis issues of the following publications: *ABC, DEF,* and *XYZ.* Advertisements for Fat Burners, Diet-All and Fat-Trim have frequently appeared in these publications. I have placed orders for Diet-All, Fat Burners, and Fat-Trim as a result of observing advertisements for these products in these publications. I have received Fat Burners on May 4, XXXX (+2) via U.S. Mail; Fat-Trim on May 8, XXXX (+2) by U.S. Mail; and Diet-All on May 16, XXXX (+2) by U.S. Mail. Along with Fat Burners and Diet-All, I also received diet programs for these products. My order of Fat-Trim was not accompanied by a diet plan.

26. According to personnel at the Los Angeles, CA, Post Office, Huge People, Inc., Appetite Suppressors, Inc., and Sutton Pharmaceuticals, Inc., mail out on a daily basis in excess of 1000 packets similar to those I received containing Fat Burners, Fat-Trim and Diet-All. Postal records also show that between December 19, XXXX (+1) and May 1, XXXX (+2), $54,000 in postage was set on the postage meter assigned to Huge People. This is the postage meter which printed postage labels on the packages containing Fat Burners, Fat-Trim, and Diet-All which I received by U.S. Mail.

27. Investigator Julie Jeffrey of Pittsburgh, PA, placed orders for Diet-All, Fat Burners, and Fat-Trim by calling the 800 telephone numbers listed in advertisements for these products. Investigator Jeffrey placed orders by initiating telephone calls from Pittsburgh, PA, to the offices of Huge People on May 9 and 10, XXXX (+2); Appetite Suppressors on May 11, XXXX (+2); and Sutton Pharmaceuticals on May 14, XXXX (+2), all of which are located in Los Angeles, CA. While ordering these products, Investigator Jeffrey asked various questions concerning the ingredients, use and effects for each of them. In each instance she was referred to the customer service number. During the telephone conversations with the customer service representative she was provided the following information:

May 10, XXXX (+2) – Diet-All

The customer service representative stated that the average customer who has 30 pounds to lose can lose 10–21 pounds during the first two weeks. She also advised that grapefruit extract aids in burning stored fat cells in the body. She stated that this product has a 95–98% success rate for those that follow the program. Although Exhibit H states, "I lost 142 pounds fast! Eating 5 and 6 meals a day of all my favorite foods," the customer service representative stated that only non-carbohydrate foods are unrestricted.

May 11, XXXX (+2) — Fat Burners

The customer service representative stated that Fat Burners contained grapefruit extract which "aids in burning stored fat cells in your body." While Exhibit K states, "In fact, I ate all I wanted of every high-calorie food that I like," the customer service representative advised that the average customer who had 30 pounds to lose can lose 10–21 pounds in the first two weeks and three to five pounds each week thereafter.

<u>May 14, XXXX (+2) — Fat-Trim</u>

Although Exhibit P indicates Fat-Trim is a safe product, the customer service representative advised that if you have certain conditions, you should not use Fat-Trim. These conditions include high blood pressure, prostate problems, alcoholism, diabetes, pregnancy, and nursing mothers, among others. The customer service representative further advised that weight loss could be as much as 25 pounds in three months and that Fat-Trim has been a successful program with many excellent reports.

<u>CONCLUSION</u>

28. The defendants, despite numerous administrative and judicial actions taken to correct misrepresentations about their diet products, continue to utilize these falsehoods to obtain money from the public. Simply put, scientific evidence does not support the type of representations the defendants repeatedly make about their diet aids. Moreover, the previous enforcement actions have put the defendants on notice as to these misrepresentations. Therefore, I submit there is probable cause to believe that Huge People, Inc.; Appetite Suppressors, Inc.; Sutton Pharmaceuticals; Bodi-Firm Corporation, George Carlton; Robert Callous and Raymond Carlton are engaged in a scheme to defraud the public in their sale of diet products and are utilizing the U.S. Mails and the interstate telephone system to further the scheme in violation of 18 U.S.C. 1341 and 1343.

I declare under Title 28 U.S.C., Section 1747 and under the penalties of perjury that the foregoing is true and correct.

Executed in Los Angeles, CA on July 5, XXXX (+2)

Michael Liu
U.S. Investigator

Appendix F

Indictment

(Note: All names—individual and business entities—and locations have changed from the original; the events spanned over the course of more than one year and these dates are expressed as XXXX and XXXX+1)

UNITED STATES DISTRICT COURT
DISTRICT OF FLORIDA

UNITED STATES OF AMERICA

v.

BETTY FRANK
FREDERICK FRANK
CHARLES HALO
KEITH DICE
LONNIE WAYNE
REED LAWRENCE
ROBERT BISON

INDICTMENT

COUNT ONE

A. Introduction

At all times material to the charges herein:

1. Thousand Trails, American Adventures, All Seasons Resorts, and Outdoor World were legitimate camping organizations providing campground facilities to their members. The cost of memberships ranged from $1,000 to 10,000 and entitled the purchaser to stay at any of the company's campground sites with use of recreational facilities and activities. Members were also required to pay yearly maintenance fees between $200 and $400.

2. American Campground Resales (ACR) was a sole proprietorship with offices in Heart of Palm, FL, and Las Vegas, NV, which purportedly engaged in the business of reselling campground memberships. Individuals potentially interested in selling their campground memberships were solicited over the telephone, by ACR telemarketers. ACR telemarketers represented to prospective sellers that ACR for a fee could sell their memberships to existing and willing buyers.

3. BETTY FRANK, FREDERICK FRANK, and CHARLES HALO were owners or managers of ACR. KEITH DICE, LONNIE WAYNE, REED LAWRENCE, AND ROBERT BISON were employed by ACR as phone operators or telemarketers.

B. The Agreement

4. Beginning in approximately July, XXXX, and continuing thereafter until in or about July 1, XXXX+1, in the District of Florida, and elsewhere,

BETTY FRANK
FREDERICK FRANK
CHARLES HALO
KEITH DICE
LONNIE WAYNE

REED LAWRENCE

And

ROBERT BISON

Defendants herein, did knowingly and willfully combine, conspire, confederate, and agree with one another and with others both known and unknown to the grand jury, to commit the following offenses against the United States:

a. to knowingly and willfully devise and execute a scheme and artifice to defraud and for obtaining money and property by means of false and fraudulent pretenses, representations and promises, in violation of Title 18, United States Code, Section 1341;

b. to knowingly and willfully devise and execute a scheme and artifice to defraud and for obtaining money and property by means of false and fraudulent pretenses, representations and promises, in violation of Title 18, United States Code, Section 1343;

c. to knowingly conduct financial transactions affecting interstate commerce, which involved the proceeds of specified unlawful activity, i.e., mail fraud and wire fraud, with the intent to promote the carrying on of specified unlawful activity, all in violation of Title 18, United States Code, Section 1956(a)(1);

d. to knowingly engage or attempt to engage in monetary transactions in criminally derived property of a value greater than $10,000 which property was derived from a specified unlawful activity, in violation of Title 18, United States Code, Section 1957.

C. Manner and Means

5. It was part of the conspiracy that the defendants and others would and did telephonically contact the owners of campground memberships, and offer to resell their memberships.

6. It was further a part of the conspiracy that the defendants and others would and did solicit from interested sellers a purportedly "refundable deposit" of money, ranging from $250 to $495.

7. It was further a part of the conspiracy that the defendants and others would and did knowingly make false and fraudulent pretenses, representations, and promises to prospective sellers/victims in order to induce them to pay the sales fee, including but not limited to the following:

a. that ACR was highly experienced and successful in the field of campground resales;

b. that the seller/victim would receive a full refund if ACR failed to sell their campground membership;

c. that ACR had already located a buyer for the seller/victim's membership;

d. that the buyer had already tendered a specified sum of money as a deposit toward the purchase;

e. that one Loren Richard was a satisfied customer who sold his campground membership through ACR;

f. that ACR had more than fifteen years experience in advertising and marketing campground resales;

g. that ACR representatives visit RV shows across the country to meet potential buyers;

h. that the company had certain characteristics and a certain background and reputation.

8.   It was further a part of the conspiracy that the defendants and others would and did falsely represent to sellers/victims that buyers were available to purchase campground memberships.

9.   It was further a part of the conspiracy that the defendants would and did make subsequent false and fraudulent pretenses, representations, and promises to prospective sellers/victims of campground memberships as to why their campground membership had not been sold, including, but not limited to the following:

   a. that the buyer's financing had fallen through and that additional time was needed for the buyer to secure other financing;

   b. that the buyer could not secure financing and a substitute buyer must be re-qualified to close the deal;

   c. that the delay in selling the memberships was caused by processing problems with campground organizations;

   d. that the seller should be patient and everything will work out.

10.   It was further part of the conspiracy that defendants BETTY FRANK and FREDERICK FRANK would and did award commissions to salespersons based on retainers and deposits forwarded by victim/sellers to ACR.

11.   It was further a part of the conspiracy that the defendants would and did cause monies to be drawn from the ACR checking account at the XYZ Bank of Florida to be wire transferred to Las Vegas, NV, for the purposes of funding payroll expenses.

12.   It was further a part of the conspiracy that the defendants and others would and did use various devices to obstruct efforts by victims to obtain refunds or credits.

13.   It was further a part of the conspiracy that the defendants would and did assume false names in conducting business with prospective sellers/victims.

14.   It was further a part of the conspiracy that the defendants and others would and did perform acts and make statements to hide and conceal, and cause to be hidden and concealed, the purposes of and acts done in furtherance of said conspiracy.

Overt Acts

15.   In furtherance of the conspiracy and to effectuate the objectives thereof, the following overt acts, among others, were committed in the District of Florida and elsewhere:

   1. On or about July 23, XXXX, defendant BETTY FRANK obtained an occupational license to do business as American Campground Resales.

   2. On or about August 7, XXXX, defendant BETTY FRANK opened a commercial checking and account at the XYZ Bank of Florida doing business as American Campground Resales.

   3. On or about December 1, XXXX, defendant CHARLES HALO visited Mr. Randall Land for the purposes of locating office space for American Campground Resales.

   4. On or about January 10, XXXX+1, at Heart of Palm, FL defendant REED LAWRENCE had a telephone conversation with a victim in Victoria, Texas concerning ACR's sale of a Thousand Trails Campground membership.

5. On or about January 24, XXXX+1, in Heart of Palm, FL defendant LONNIE WAYNE had a telephone conversation with a victim in Mechanicsville, MD concerning ACR's sale of an Outdoor World Campground membership.

6. On or about February 1, XXXX+1, defendant CHARLES HALO signed the name "John E. Jennings" on forms sent to victims.

7. On or about February 18, XXXX+1, defendant KEITH DICE had a telephone conversation with a victim in Orange, VA regarding the sale of a campground membership.

8. In approximately March XXXX+1 defendant KEITH DICE had a telephone conversation with a victim in Castroville, TX regarding the sale of a campground membership.

9. In or about March XXXX+1 defendant ROBERT BISON had a telephone conversation with a victim in Villa Park, IL regarding the sale of a campground membership.

10. On or about March 20, XXXX+1, FREDERICK FRANK wrote check number 114 drawn on his account at the Mountain State Bank of Nevada in the amount of $1,052.72 payable to Duncan Smith.

11. On or about March 25, XXXX+1, the defendant BETTY FRANK caused a cashier's check in the amount of $5,000 to be transferred to FREDERICK FRANK'S account at the Mountain State Bank of Nevada.

12. On or about April 1, XXXX+1, in Heart of Palm, FL defendant LONNIE WAYNE had a telephone conversation with a victim in Danville, IL concerning ACR's sale of a Thousand Trails Campground membership.

13. On or about April 11, XXXX+1, defendant BETTY FRANK caused $8,000 to be wire transferred from ACR's bank account at the XYZ Bank of Florida to FREDERICK FRANK'S checking account at the Mountain State Bank of Nevada.

14. On or about April 22, XXXX+1, defendant FREDERICK FRANK signed the name "John E. Jennings" on a resale agreement for victims Harold and Lillian Tucker.

15. On or about May 2, XXXX+1, defendant BETTY FRANK caused $15,000 to be wire transferred from the XYZ Bank of Florida account of ACR to the checking account of FREDERICK FRANK at the Mountain State Bank of Nevada.

16. The Grand Jury re-alleges and incorporates by reference the allegations set forth in Counts Two through Nineteen as overt acts as though fully set forth herein.

All in violation of Title 18, United States Code, Section 371.

THE MAIL AND WIRE FRAUD COUNTS
COUNT TWO
A. The Scheme

1. Beginning in or about December XXXX and continuing thereafter until in or about July XXXX+1 at Heart of Palm in the District of Florida, and elsewhere,

BETTY FRANK
FREDERICK FRANK

CHARLES HALO
KEITH DICE
LONNIE WAYNE
REED LAWRENCE
And
ROBERT BISON

defendants herein, did knowingly devise and intend to devise a scheme and artifice to defraud and for obtaining money and property from victims by means of false and fraudulent pretenses, representations, and promises.

B. The Manner and Means of the Scheme

2.   The substance of the scheme to defraud and its manner and means are described in paragraphs contained in Sections A and C of Count One of this Indictment, and the Grand Jury re-alleges and incorporates by reference those paragraphs as though fully set forth herein.

Execution of the Scheme

3.   On or about December 4, XXXX, at Heart of Palm, in the District of Florida,

BETTY FRANK
And
CHARLES HALO

defendants herein, for the purpose of executing the aforesaid scheme to defraud, and for so obtaining money, and attempting to do so, knowingly did cause to be delivered by the United States Postal Service, according to the directions thereon, an envelope containing a check from Ruth Hammer, 200 East Meadow St., Seattle, WA, addressed to:

American Campground Resales
4488 Northern Trails Highway
Suite 303
Heart of Palm, FL

In violation of Title 18, United States Code, Sections 1341 and 2.

COUNT THREE

1.   The substance of the scheme to defraud and its manner and means are described in paragraphs contained in Sections A and C of Count One of this Indictment, and the Grand Jury realleges and incorporates by reference those paragraphs as though fully set forth herein.

Execution of the Scheme

2.   On or about January 14, XXXX+1, at Heart of Palm, in the District of Florida,

BETTY FRANK
And
CHARLES HALO

defendants herein, for the purpose of executing the aforesaid scheme to defraud, and for so obtaining money, and attempting to do so, knowingly did cause mail matter to be delivered by the United States Postal Service, according to the directions thereon, an envelope from American Campground Resales in Heart of Palm, FL, containing a refund guarantee addressed to:

Barry Walter
100 East Elm St.
Edmonds, WA

In violation of Title 18, United States Code, Sections 1341 and 2.

COUNT FOUR

1.   The substance of the scheme to defraud and its manner and means are described in paragraphs contained in Sections A and C of Count One of this Indictment, and the Grand Jury re-alleges and incorporates by reference those paragraphs as though fully set forth herein.

Execution of the Scheme

2.   On or about January 20, XXXX+1, at Heart of Palm, in the District of Florida,

BETTY FRANK
And
CHARLES HALO

defendants herein, for the purpose of executing the aforesaid scheme to defraud, and for so obtaining money, and attempting to do so, knowingly did cause to be delivered by the United States Postal Service, according to the directions thereon, an envelope containing a check from Elizabeth Vernon, 1000 Smith Blvd., Scroggins, TX, addressed to:

American Campground Resales
4488 Northern Trails Highway
Suite 303
Heart of Palm, FL

In violation of Title 18, United States Code, Sections 1341 and 2.

COUNT FIVE

1.   The substance of the scheme to defraud and its manner and means are described in paragraphs contained in Sections A and C of Count One of this Indictment, and the Grand Jury re-alleges and incorporates by reference those paragraphs as though fully set forth herein.

Execution of the Scheme

2.   In or about January XXXX+1 at Heart of Palm, in the District of Florida,

BETTY FRANK
And
REED LAWRENCE

defendants herein, for the purpose of executing the aforesaid scheme to defraud, and for so obtaining money, and attempting to do so, knowingly did cause mail matter to be delivered by the United States Postal Service, according to the directions thereon, an envelope from American Campground Resales in Heart of Palm, FL, containing a letter and refund guarantee addressed to:

Max Ray
15 East Carolina Ct.
Victoria, TX

In violation of Title 18, United States Code, Sections 1341 and 2.

COUNT SIX

1.   The substance of the scheme to defraud and its manner and means are described in paragraphs contained in Sections A and C of Count One of this Indictment, and the Grand Jury re-alleges and incorporates by reference those paragraphs as though fully set forth herein.

Execution of the Scheme

2.   In or about January XXXX+1 at Heart of Palm, in the District of Florida,

BETTY FRANK
And
LONNIE WAYNE

defendants herein, for the purpose of executing the aforesaid scheme to defraud, and for so obtaining money, and attempting to do so, knowingly did cause mail matter to be delivered by the United States Postal Service, according to the directions thereon, an envelope from American Campground Resales in Heart of Palm, FL, containing a money back guarantee addressed to:

Mr. and Mrs. Guy Allen
P.O Box 80422
Mechanicsville, MD

In violation of Title 18, United States Code, Sections 1341 and 2.

COUNT SEVEN

1.   The substance of the scheme to defraud and its manner and means are described in paragraphs contained in Sections A and C of Count One of this Indictment, and the Grand Jury re-alleges and incorporates by reference those paragraphs as though fully set forth herein.

Execution of the Scheme

2.   On or about January 29, XXXX+1, at Heart of Palm, in the District of Florida,

BETTY FRANK
And
REED LAWRENCE

defendants herein, for the purpose of executing the aforesaid scheme to defraud, knowingly caused to be transmitted and caused to be transmitted by means of wire communications in interstate commerce, certain signs, signals, pictures, and sounds, to wit: a telephone call between Howard Calvin in Gary, Indiana and a representative of American Campground Resales in Heart of Palm, FL, concerning the sale of a campground membership.

In violation of Title 18, United States Code, Sections 1343 and 2.

COUNT EIGHT

1.   The substance of the scheme to defraud and its manner and means are described in paragraphs contained in Sections A and C of Count One of this Indictment, and the Grand Jury re-alleges and incorporates by reference those paragraphs as though fully set forth herein.

Execution of the Scheme

2.   On or about February 5, XXXX+1, at Heart of Palm, in the District of Florida,

BETTY FRANK
And
ROBERT BISON

defendants herein, for the purpose of executing the aforesaid scheme to defraud, and for so obtaining money, and attempting to do so, knowingly did cause mail matter to be delivered by the United States Postal Service, according to the directions thereon, an envelope from American Campground Resales in Heart of Palm, FL, containing campground sales information addressed to:

Louis Sally
324 Bradshaw Ave
Stafford, VA

In violation of Title 18, United States Code, Sections 1341 and 2.

COUNT NINE

1.   The substance of the scheme to defraud and its manner and means are described in paragraphs contained in Sections A and C of Count One of this Indictment, and the Grand Jury re-alleges and incorporates by reference those paragraphs as though fully set forth herein.

Execution of the Scheme

2.   On or about February 20, XXXX+1, at Heart of Palm, in the District of Florida,

BETTY FRANK
And
ROBERT BISON

defendants herein, for the purpose of executing the aforesaid scheme to defraud, and for so obtaining money, and attempting to do so, knowingly did cause mail matter to be delivered by the United States

Postal Service, according to the directions thereon, an envelope from American Campground Resales in Heart of Palm, FL, containing a marketing authorization form addressed to:

Beth Chole
11 Cole St.
Ft. Washington, MD

In violation of Title 18, United States Code, Sections 1341 and 2.

COUNT TEN

1.   The substance of the scheme to defraud and its manner and means are described in paragraphs contained in Sections A and C of Count One of this Indictment, and the Grand Jury re-alleges and incorporates by reference those paragraphs as though fully set forth herein.

Execution of the Scheme

2.   On or about February 22, XXXX+1, at Heart of Palm, in the District of Florida,

BETTY FRANK
And
KEITH DICE

defendants herein, for the purpose of executing the aforesaid scheme to defraud, and for so obtaining money, and attempting to do so, knowingly did cause mail matter to be delivered by the United States Postal Service, according to the directions thereon, an envelope from American Campground Resales in Heart of Palm, FL, containing a refund guarantee addressed to:

John Roy
2233 Archer Ct.
Virginia Beach, VA

In violation of Title 18, United States Code, Sections 1341 and 2.

COUNT ELEVEN

1.   The substance of the scheme to defraud and its manner and means are described in paragraphs contained in Sections A and C of Count One of this Indictment, and the Grand Jury re-alleges and incorporates by reference those paragraphs as though fully set forth herein.

Execution of the Scheme

2.   On or about February 25, XXXX+1 at Heart of Palm, in the District of Florida,

BETTY FRANK
And
KEITH DICE

defendants herein, for the purpose of executing the aforesaid scheme to defraud, and for so obtaining money, and attempting to do so, knowingly did cause mail matter to be delivered by the United States

Postal Service, according to the directions thereon, an envelope from American Campground Resales in Heart of Palm, FL containing a marketing authorization form addressed to:

Taylor West
8521 View Point Rd.
Orange, VA

In violation of Title 18, United States Code, Sections 1341 and 2.

COUNT TWELVE

1.   The substance of the scheme to defraud and its manner and means are described in paragraphs contained in Sections A and C of Count One of this Indictment, and the Grand Jury re-alleges and incorporates by reference those paragraphs as though fully set forth herein.

Execution of the Scheme

2.   On or about March 14, XXXX+1 at Heart of Palm, in the District of Florida,

BETTY FRANK
And
LONNIE WAYNE

defendants herein, for the purpose of executing the aforesaid scheme to defraud, knowingly caused to be transmitted and caused to be transmitted by means of wire communications in interstate commerce, certain signs, signals, pictures, and sounds, to wit: a telephone call between Wallace Laurent in Muncie, Indiana and a representative of American Campground Resales in Heart of Palm, FL concerning the sale of a campground membership.

In violation of Title 18, United States Code, Sections 1343 and 2.

COUNT THIRTEEN

1.   The substance of the scheme to defraud and its manner and means are described in paragraphs contained in Sections A and C of Count One of this Indictment, and the Grand Jury re-alleges and incorporates by reference those paragraphs as though fully set forth herein.

Execution of the Scheme

2.   On or about March 28, XXXX+1, at Heart of Palm, in the District of Florida,

BETTY FRANK
And
REED LAWRENCE

defendants herein, for the purpose of executing the aforesaid scheme to defraud, knowingly caused to be transmitted and caused to be transmitted by means of wire communications in interstate commerce, certain signs, signals, pictures, and sounds, to wit: a telephone call between Viola Maney in Dos Palos, CA, and a representative of American Campground Resales in Heart of Palm, FL, concerning the sale of a campground membership.

In violation of Title 18, United States Code, Sections 1343 and 2.

COUNT FOURTEEN

1. The substance of the scheme to defraud and its manner and means are described in paragraphs contained in Sections A and C of Count One of this Indictment, and the Grand Jury re-alleges and incorporates by reference those paragraphs as though fully set forth herein.

Execution of the Scheme

2.   On or about January 20, XXXX+1 at Heart of Palm, in the District of Florida,

BETTY FRANK
And
ROBERT BISON

defendants herein, for the purpose of executing the aforesaid scheme to defraud, and for so obtaining money, and attempting to do so, knowingly did cause to be delivered by the United States Postal Service, according to the directions thereon, an envelope containing a check from Luis Hernandez, 47 Oak Lane, San Antonio, TX, addressed to:

American Campground Resales
4488 Northern Trails Highway
Suite 303
Heart of Palm, FL

In violation of Title 18, United States Code, Sections 1341 and 2.

COUNT FIFTEEN

1.   The substance of the scheme to defraud and its manner and means are described in paragraphs contained in Sections A and C of Count One of this Indictment, and the Grand Jury re-alleges and incorporates by reference those paragraphs as though fully set forth herein.

Execution of the Scheme

2.   In or about March XXXX+1 at Heart of Palm, in the District of Florida,

BETTY FRANK
And
LONNIE WAYNE

defendants herein, for the purpose of executing the aforesaid scheme to defraud, knowingly caused to be transmitted and caused to be transmitted by means of wire communications in interstate commerce, certain signs, signals, pictures, and sounds, to wit: a telephone call between Jack Beck in New Berlin, WI and a representative of American Campground Resales in Heart of Palm, FL, concerning the sale of a campground membership.

In violation of Title 18, United States Code, Sections 1343 and 2.

COUNT SIXTEEN

1.   The substance of the scheme to defraud and its manner and means are described in paragraphs contained in Sections A and C of Count One of this Indictment, and the Grand Jury re-alleges and incorporates by reference those paragraphs as though fully set forth herein.

Execution of the Scheme

2.   On or about April 4, XXXX+1, at Heart of Palm, in the District of Florida,

BETTY FRANK
And
KEITH DICE

defendants herein, for the purpose of executing the aforesaid scheme to defraud, and for so obtaining money, and attempting to do so, knowingly did cause mail matter to be delivered by the United States Postal Service, according to the directions thereon, an envelope from American Campground Resales in Heart of Palm, FL containing a sales agreement addressed to:

Raymond and Roberta Burke
RR 1
Castroville, TX

In violation of Title 18, United States Code, Sections 1341 and 2.

THE MONEY LAUNDERING COUNTS
COUNT SEVENTEEN

On or about May 2, XXXX+1, in the District of Florida,

BETTY FRANK
And
FREDERICK FRANK

the defendants, did knowingly and willfully conduct and attempt to conduct a financial transaction affecting interstate and foreign commerce, to wit, a wire transfer of $15,000 from American Campground Resales' account number 123456789, at the XYZ Bank of Florida to FREDERICK FRANK'S account number 987654321 at Mountain State Bank of Nevada, which involved the proceeds of specified unlawful activity, that is, mail fraud and wire fraud, in violation of Title 18, United States Code, Sections 1341 and 1343, with the intent to promote the carrying on of specified unlawful activity, to wit: mail fraud and wire fraud, in violation of Title 18, United States Code Sections 1341 and 1343, and that while attempting to conduct such a financial transaction, that is the funds in the amount of $15,000 represented proceeds of some form of unlawful activity.

In violation of Title 18, United States Code, Sections 1956(a)(1)(i) and 2.

COUNT EIGHTEEN

On or about May 16, XXXX+1, in the District of Florida, defendants,

BETTY FRANK
And
FREDERICK FRANK

did knowingly engage and attempt to engage in a monetary transaction, affecting interstate and foreign commerce, in criminally derived property of a value greater than $10,000, that is, deposit of a monetary instrument in the amount of $25,000, such property having been derived from specified unlawful activity, that is mail fraud and wire fraud, in violation of Title 18, United States Code, Sections 1341 and 1343.

In violation of 18 United States Code, Sections 1957 and 2.

COUNT NINETEEN

On or about May 20, XXXX+1 in the District of Florida, defendant,

BETTY FRANK

did knowingly engage and attempt to engage in a monetary transaction, affecting interstate and foreign commerce, in criminally derived property of a value greater than $10,000, that is, a withdrawal of funds in the amount of $11,003, such property having been derived from specified unlawful activity, that is mail fraud and wire fraud, in violation of Title 18, United States Code, Sections 1341 and 1343.

In violation of 18 United States Code, Sections 1957 and 2.

Forefeitures

1.   The allegations contained in Counts Seventeen through Nineteen of this indictment are hereby re-alleged and incorporated by reference for the purpose of alleged forfeitures pursuant to the provisions of Title 18, United States Code, Section 982.

2.   The defendants, BETTY FRANK, FREDERICK FRANK, and CHARLES HALO, shall forfeit to the United States of America, pursuant to Title 18, United States Code, Section 982(a)(1), any and all right, title, and interest they may have in any property, real or personal, involved in violations of Title 18, United States Code, Sections 1956 and 1957, alleged in Counts Seventeen through Nineteen of this indictment, or any property traceable to such property.

3.   If any of the property described above as being subject to forfeiture, as a result of any act or omission of the defendants:

1.   cannot be located upon the exercise of due diligence;

2.   has been transferred or sold to, or deposited with, a third person;

3.   has been placed beyond the jurisdiction of the Court;

4.   has been substantially diminished in value; or

5.   has been commingled with other property which cannot be subdivided without difficulty;

the United States of America shall be entitled to forfeiture of substitute property under the provisions of Title 21, United States Code, Section 853(p) as incorporated by Title 18, United States Code, Section 982(b)(1)(A) and (B).

A TRUE BILL,

_____

_____

UNITED STATES ATTORNEY

By: _____
ASSISTANT UNITED STATES ATTORNEY

Appendix G

Federal Sentencing Guidelines[1]

Cases Involving Fraud and Deceit

a. Base Offense Level: 6

b. Specific Offense Characteristics

    1. If the estimated, probable, or intended loss exceeded $2000, increase the offense level as follows:

Loss	Increase in Level
$2000 or Less	No Increase
$2001–$5000	add 1
$5001–$10,000	add 2
$10,001–$20,000	add 3
$20,001–$50,000	add 4
$50,001–$100,000	add 5
$100,001–$200,000	add 6
$200,001–$500,000	add 7
$500,001–$1,000,000	add 8
$100,000,001–$2,000,000	add 9
$200,000,001–$5,000,000	add 10
Over $5,000,000	add 11

    2. Imprisonment by Offense Level (in months)

Criminal History Category (Points as determined by criminal history)

Offense Level	I (0–1)	II (2–3)	III (4–6)	IV (7–9)	V (10–12)	V (13 or more)
1	0–6	0–6	0–6	0–6	0–6	0–6
2	0–6	0–6	0–6	0–6	0–6	1–7
3	0–6	0–6	0–6	0–6	2–8	3–9
4	0–6	0–6	0–6	2–8	4–10	6–12
5	0–6	0–6	1–7	4–12	6–12	9–15
6	0–6	1–7	2–8	6–12	9–15	12–18
7	0–6	2–8	4–10	8–14	12–18	14–21
8	0–6	4–10	6–12	10–16	15–21	18–24
9	4–10	6–12	8–14	12–18	18–24	21–27
10	6–12	8–14	10–16	15–21	21–27	24–30

(*contiued*)

Criminal History Category (Points as determined by criminal history)

Offense Level	I (0–1)	II (2–3)	III (4–6)	IV (7–9)	V (10–12)	V (13 or more)
11	8–14	10–16	12–18	18–24	24–30	27–33
12	10–16	12–18	15–21	21–27	27–33	30–37
13	12–18	15–21	18–24	24–30	30–37	33–41
14	15–21	18–24	21–27	27–33	33–41	37–46
15	18–24	21–27	24–30	30–37	37–46	41–51
16	21–27	24–30	27–33	33–41	41–51	46–57
17	24–30	27–33	30–37	37–46	46–57	51–63
18	27–33	30–37	33–41	41–51	51–63	57–71
19	30–37	33–41	37–46	46–57	57–71	63–78
20	33–41	37–46	41–51	51–63	63–78	70–87
21	37–46	41–51	46–57	57–71	70–87	77–96
22	41–51	46–57	51–63	63–78	77–96	84–105
23	46–57	51–63	57–71	70–87	84–105	92–115
24	51–63	57–71	63–78	77–96	92–115	100–125
25	57–71	63–78	70–87	84–105	100–125	110–137
26	63–46	70–87	78–97	92–115	110–137	120–150
27	70–87	78–97	87–108	100–125	120–150	130–162
28	78–97	87–108	97–121	110–137	130–162	140–175
29	87–108	97–121	108–135	121–151	140–175	151–188
30	97–121	108–135	121–151	135–168	151–188	168–210
31	108–135	121–151	135–168	151–188	168–210	188–235
32	121–151	135–168	151–188	168–210	188–235	210–262
33	135–168	151–188	168–210	188–235	210–262	235–293
34	151–188	168–210	188–235	210–262	235–293	262–327
35	168–210	188–235	210–262	235–293	262–327	292–365
36	188–235	210–262	235–293	262–327	292–365	324–405
37	210–262	235–293	262–327	292–365	324–405	360–Life
38	235–293	262–327	292–365	324–405	360–Life	360–Life
39	262–327	292–365	324–405	360–Life	360–Life	360–Life
40	292–365	324–405	360–Life	360–Life	360–Life	360–Life
41	324–405	360–Life	360–Life	360–Life	360–Life	360–Life
42	360–Life	360–Life	360–Life	360–Life	360–Life	360–Life
43	Life	Life	Life	Life	Life	Life

3. Fines by Offense Level

Offense Level	Fine
1	$25–$250
2–3	$100–$1000
4–5	$250–$2500
6–7	$500–$5000
8–9	$1000–$10,000
10–11	$2000–$20,000
12–13	$3000–$30,000
14–15	$4000–$40,000
16–17	$5000–$50,000
18–19	$6000–$60,000
20–22	$7500–$75,000
23–25	$10,000–$100,000
26–28	$12,500–$125,000
29–31	$15,000–$150,000
32–34	$17,500–$175,000
35–37	$20,000–$200,000
38 and above	$25,000–$250,000

Notes

1. United States Sentencing Commission, *Guidelines Manual* (Washington, DC: Author, 2005).

Index